LABOR, WRITING TECHNOLOGIES, AND THE SHAPING OF COMPOSITION IN THE ACADEMY

NEW DIMENSIONS IN COMPUTERS AND COMPOSITION

Gail E. Hawisher and Cynthia L. Selfe, editors

LABOR, WRITING TECHNOLOGIES, AND THE SHAPING OF COMPOSITION IN THE ACADEMY

Pamela Takayoshi
Kent State University

Patricia Sullivan
Purdue University

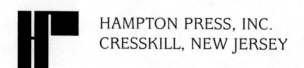

HAMPTON PRESS, INC.
CRESSKILL, NEW JERSEY

Printed in the United States of America

Library of Congress Cataloging-in-Publication Data

Labor, writing technologies, and the shaping of composition in the academy / [compiled by] Pamela Takayoshi, Patricia Sullivan.
     p. cm. -- (New dimensions in computers and composition)
    Includes bibliographical references and index.
    ISBN 1-57273-666-6 (casebound) -- ISBN 1-57273-667-4 (perfectbound)
    1. English language--Rhetoric--Study and teaching (Higher)--Technological innovations. 2. Academic writing--Study and teaching (Higher)--Data processing. 3. Report writing--Study and teaching (Higher)--Data processing. 4. Computers and literacy. 5. Work. I. Takayoshi, Pamela. II. Sullivan, Patricia, 1951-

    PE1404.L26 2006
    808'.0420711--dc22
        2006032365

Hampton Press, Inc.
23 Broadway
Cresskill, NJ 07626

This book is dedicated to the memory of Thomas R. Watson. The chapters in this collection were first presented at the 2000 Thomas R. Watson Conference on Rhetoric and Composition at the University of Louisville. In 1995, Dr. Watson gave $1.2 million to the English Department of the university of Louisville to endow a biennial International Conference in Rhetoric and Composition and a Visiting Distinguished Professor of Rhetoric and Composition. This gift is a mark not only of Dr. Watson's extraordinary generosity but also of his imaginative and far-sighted vision. It attests to his understanding of the fundamental importance of a literate citizenry and of the vital task faced by the liberal arts, particularly English Studies, in educating students to become critical, active, and engaged readers and writers.

Dr. Watson's generous spirit lives on in the Thomas R. Watson Conferences on Rhetoric and Composition and in the edited collections that have come out of those conferences:

- *History, Reflection, and Narrative: The Professionalization of Composition, 1963-1983*. Edited by Mary Rosner, Beth Boehm, and Debra Journet. Stamford, CT: Ablex, 1999.
- *Multiple Literacies for the Twenty First Century*. Edited by Brian Huot, Beth Stroble, and Charles Bazeman. Cresskill, NJ: Hampton, 2004.
- a forthcoming volume on identity and literacy, edited by Bronwyn Williams.

A Louisville physician, banker, and entrepreneur, Thomas R. Watson was born August 16, 1935, in Graves County, Kentucky; he died January 15, 1996. He was married to Sylvia Watson and had two daughters, McCall Watson Eng and Emily Watson Ragan.

CONTENTS

INTRODUCTION

LITERACY WORK IN A TECHNOLOGY-RICH CULTURE: ISSUES AT THE INTERSECTION OF LABOR, TECHNOLOGY, AND WRITING INSTRUCTION

Pamela Takayoshi
Kent State University

Patricia Sullivan
Purdue University

We begin with the most unsettling term in this volume's title, *labor*. Why does a compositionist in the 21st century need to think about labor in addition to our central focus on written literacy and its instruction? Our use of the word *labor*,[1] suggests our interest in the physical, material experience of being a compositionist. In higher education, our work (as teachers, researchers, scholars, administrators, constructors of our institutions) is increasingly mediated by what Stuart Blythe (Chapter 10) calls "mundane artifacts in our midst." Focusing our attention on these artifacts reveals a great deal about what is valued and contested in the labor of being a compositionist in the 21st century. We add the term *technology* to our consideration of academic labor in written literacy, interested in the way it shapes (and is shaped by) our understandings of college writing. How does technology figure into the identities of writers and workers involved with 21st century writing and its instruction? The authors in this volume explore the intersections between academic labor, work conditions, writing technologies, and workplace technologies in the 21st century. Our goal, ultimately, is to consider these (and other key) questions as we voice the issues faced by Composition Studies when it views itself as a site of literacy labor in the highly technologized 21st century academic culture.

Earlier versions of these chapters were presented at the third Thomas R. Watson Conference on Rhetoric and Composition: Labor, Writing Technologies, and the Shaping of Composition in the Academy (which was held at the University of Louisville, October 5–7, 2000). That conference brought together scholars interested in the professionalization of composition as a discipline and in the technologization of composition as a profession to explore the intersections between professional and technological issues. As we remember those discussions through the lenses provided in these chapters, we are struck by the fact that the Watson Conference's public linking of literacy, technology, and work surprised some people attending it, and perhaps some readers, too. The conference recognized that teachers of writing in college do work and that many of us find the work of teaching writing, studying writing, and administering writing programs inextricably woven with technology. The conference also provided a forum for speakers who assumed that increasingly our literacy work, particularly at the college level, will be conducted inside a technologically rich environment. But such a presumptive linking of technology and literacy instruction made some participants uneasy, perhaps because composition and rhetoric has normally treated technology as a tool rather than as an ideological component or as an environment. Even when technology proponents contended, as most did, that technology and writing must always be taught in ways that encourage technology critique, those not used to including technology as a major component of written literacy theory seemed silenced by the technology discussions. Furthermore, technology proponents themselves, perhaps because they are often treated as technicians in their home departments, sometimes seemed wary that themes of (and worries about) automation might dominate the conference in ways that would make technology (and by association them) the blame gatherers for literacy workers' coming problems. It is the memory of those uneasinesses that propels this introduction.

The conference's focal terms—*labor*, *technology*, and *literacy*—aimed to focus participants' attention on components of 21st-century writing studies that have not often been conjoined. We hoped that raising questions about the ways that common constructions of these terms' boundaries obscure some issues important to 21st century writing (and writing pedagogy) research would prompt new perspectives on issues shared by the three domains. By simultaneously considering work/labor, writing instruction, and technology we focused discussion in ways that allow issues shared by those domains to take new shapes. Of course, those domains can be viewed through their irritations of each other as well as through their potential overlaps. So, although we choose to embrace the overlaps, we begin by rehearsing reasons why labor and technology have been problematic in Composition Studies.

COMMON UNEASINESSES WITH LABOR AND WITH TECHNOLOGY

Labor is not often written about in Composition Studies, as it has traditionally been the province of economics and sociology where it has been treated alternatively as a politico-social movement or as a component of production. The fact that its meanings shimmer between political and machine-oriented dimensions contributes two reasons why the term has been avoided or marginalized in writing studies: Its political connections with union movements class the term as operating beneath the class of the scholar/teacher, whereas its assembly line connections to Fordism rob the term of creativity (and consequently make it mundane). Although the field could connect the term with the labor movements of the late 19th and early 20th centuries which aimed to protect children and others from inhuman conditions, and thus embrace it as a working example of social justice, we more often think of it as the focus of a government agency that collects and dispenses information about occupations and unemployment.

We do not think that these connections negate the need for organized labor to protect the working conditions of teachers. In fact, teachers at lower levels have used collective bargaining with some success to improve wages and to save health coverage. But college teachers have, for the most part, defined themselves as scholars rather than workers and have been slow to organize as workers (or protest working conditions in any way that cuts across disciplinary lines). The strong disciplinary allegiances that have been reinforced by the institutional structuring of universities into college and departmental units, the differential pay structure across disciplines, and the differing models for tenure, all have kept the professoriate from organizing to battle common problems in their working conditions. Furthermore, full-time college teachers have not often been sympathetic to the plight of part-time teachers[2] or graduate students. A disturbing example of this is related by Michael Berube in *The Employment of English* when he talks about how the Yale University faculty used the Modern Language Association (MLA) to help them subdue English graduate students who were joining others at Yale in striking for better working conditions. Both the Yale English faculty and the MLA constructed the problem as one that

required the graduate instructors to choose disciplinary loyalty over worker solidarity, and neither considered the union-busting dimensions of their
actions or the class struggle they reinforced. Students were asked to choose
between being a scholar of English and being a laborer. The view of English
Studies conveyed to those students, however, does not reflect the taxonomy of positions found in departments of English across the United States.
Stanley Aronowitz's study of jobs confirmed what most of us know, that
there are few college jobs in English that deliver a focus on scholarly work
and that increasingly the positions are focused on teaching and administration. Horner makes the point of that story clearer when he argues that "faculty cannot recognize their work as labor without putting at risk the class
cultural status they enjoy as professional academics engaged in ostensibly
non-material work. While faculty are and have always been vocal about
feeling pressured, their commitment to their own status as non-laborers
whose work is located outside the material realm both accounts for that
pressure . . . and stands in the way of offering much resistance to it" (12).
In real ways, the scholarly world those Yale students were asked to uphold
will not exist in most of their 21st-century working futures.

We have evidence that composition instructors might more easily see
themselves as workers than others in English Studies through activism on
the part of workers and through published scholarship that includes a sense
of compositionists as workers. The Wyoming Resolution, an example of
activism that seeks better working conditions for part-time writing teachers,
has often been discussed and nationally supported by CCCC as a needed
reform in the working lives of most college writing teachers. Writing
Program Administrators have led the examination of academic work in
composition as they have argued that programmatic work should be
defined as intellectual work (see Irwin Weiser and Shirley Rose's edited collection as a starting point), a term that marries academic endeavors with
work/labor. Accompanying those efforts are studies of academic labor conditions such as the survey that Theresa Enos conducted on the state of
women in Composition Studies. Others looking at workplace writing have
examined both the literacy instruction that prepares future workers for their
working lives (see the Garay and Bernhardt edited collection as a starting
point) and at the nature of writing at work. Some discussions have even tied
work, economics, and literacy, as Gee, Hull, and Lankshear do in *The New
Work Order*. Although these efforts are laudable, few highlight and none
focus on the connection between work/labor, technology, and literacy.

That technology is missing from those discussions is problematic.
Since *Workforce 2000* (Johnstone and Packer) was published, the government has promoted the education (read training) of workers, particularly in

the area of technology use. The federal government has focused on bridging the technology gap, on putting the Internet in every school, and on improving technological literacy. The approach that the government has supported assumes that technology knowledge creates (or at least sustains) a divide among workers with the more technologically proficient receiving the most (and the most interesting) employment opportunities. Given that assumption, governmental workforce education has emphasized technology. Not all have embraced technology as the answer to workplace training, however. Some labor analysts have generated gloomy predictions, such as those in Rifkin's *The End of Work,* that blame technology (and its automation and downsizing) for coming (and current) labor crises that result in no need for a large, knowledgeable, stable workforce. Although not always tied to Marxist critique, technology is usually connected with Fordist moves toward efficiency and preferring machine solutions over human ones. Even Reich's attempt to envision a post-fordist workplace divides workers into those who are laboring at the behest of technology from those who are symbolic analysts (and thus can manipulate technology).

Labor has been suspicious of technology because of its close association in the United States with automation and job loss. Although socialist countries such as Sweden (see Pelle Ehn or Suzanne Bodker) produce studies that have workers participate in the building of workplace technology, and have thus developed technology-friendly work environments, this work culture has pitted technology against human labor. Even Computers and Writing scholars are far more likely to cite Shoshana Zuboff's case studies of the death of the master printer at the hands of automation than to cite JoAnn Yates' historical documentation of the birth of the modern office through developments in writing technology. Furthermore, in Composition Studies, proponents of technology have not made strong connections between labor and technology (as Hart-Davidson and Peeples point out in Chapter 15). This may be the case because the scholars interested in labor issues see technology as a threat to an already heavily managed and deskilled workforce. It may also be that Computers and Writing scholars have focused on teaching and not turned their/our attention to the other places technologies affect our lives as academic workers. Computers and Writing scholars have distanced themselves from earlier identity positions of worker by insisting on more intellectual identity positions. As a field, we have moved from an early focus (1980s) on writing technologies as teaching tools to a self-consciously constructed notion of ourselves as interested in more theoretical and intellectual problems of identity, discourse, literacy, ethics. Brian Huot and Pam Takayoshi have argued that this move away from the mundanity of teaching with technology is the result of the natural growth of a discipline, but perhaps it was a more self-conscious move to distance ourselves from the material practices to something valued in the academy as more lofty.

Increasingly, technology is not just a practical matter that we can choose to engage or ignore. Like technologies in American culture, technologies have become an everyday presence in composition work—Internet and writing technologies have been woven into the fabric of our intellectual work, communication technologies have expanded the network of people with whom we communicate and depend on to do our jobs, and computers support and complicate writing pedagogies. Likewise, academic labor issues within composition reflect larger cultural trends of displacement and alienation within an information economy largely supported by a part-time and contingent labor force. This volume brings together perspectives on labor and technologies that speak to one another even though they have not been in direct conversation with one another before, and the chapters offer readers much to think about as we look to the future of our workplace and our identity as composition workers. In this volume, authors make explicit the sometimes seamless and invisible ways these situations have come to exist and to reflect on what these situations suggest for our future work.

LABOR, WRITING TECHNOLOGIES, AND THE SHAPING OF COMPOSITION AS A 21ST CENTURY DISCIPLINE

The changing nature of the workforce and the increasingly ubiquitous presence of technologies in composition studies promise to affect, sometimes singly but oftentimes in conjunction with one another, not only the ways we work but the very shape of the discipline. As Deborah Brandt analogously argued about technology and literacy in *Literacy in American Lives*, it has become increasingly difficult to separate work from technology because the rapid and diverse expansion of technology has interacted with what it means to labor. A growing body of scholarship is concerned with the shape of work within composition studies, and there is a strong tradition of scholarship that reflects on writing technologies. At this historical moment, then, it is dangerous to think about one to the exclusion of the other. When we think about technology in composition studies, we are neglectful if we don't think about how technologies affect our lives as researchers, scholars, and workers in the academy; likewise, when we reflect on the work of composition studies, we are neglectful if we don't consider the material situatedness of our practices. And increasingly, that material, social practice involves technologies. Technological practices such as distance education, virtual universities, and web-based teaching in higher education—which often enter university and college life with little or no resistance—carry with them the potential to radically alter the shape of faculty work, indeed of the faculty itself. For example, a recent estimate suggests that 45% of the nation's college faculty work part time and not necessarily by choice (Pratt). Consider this trend toward part-time labor in conjunction with an estimate that by 2002, 85% of 2-year colleges and 84% of 4-year colleges will be offering distance-learning courses (Cyberatlas, online). When we consider these two pieces of demographic information in tandem, we might wonder what effect each trend might have on the other, and what effect the two together will have on the future of academic work. Will such technologies of delivery exacerbate composition's reliance on part time labor? Will technologies of delivery restructure composition's workforce? Who will benefit? Who will be harmed? We might think also of this one conjunction of work and technology as a specific instance that raises larger disciplinary questions: What effect do writing technologies have on the nature of our work? What workplace complications are presented by technologies?

Technological practices complicate existing definitions of writers, writing, and publishing, which in turn affect our roles as writers, writing teachers, and writing theorists. Virtual universities and distance education complicate labor issues involving part-time and contingent labor, tenure and promotion, and intellectual property. As universities face pressure from students, business, and government to incorporate technology into the fabric of higher education, these issues present themselves as important and pressing. For a long time, technology has been treated as the domain of the subdiscipline of computers and composition—as though writing technologies are a practical matter that could be thought of separately from other disciplinary concerns. Although we have built a large body of informed research and theory on teaching writing with computers, there is much work to be done with the other types of work in which we engage as academics. In other words, although composition scholarship has considered the ways in which technology affects teaching and learning, we have failed to consider the ways in which technology changes the ways we do our work across a range of institutional identities: researchers, scholars, administrators (of writing programs, writing across the curriculum programs, assessment programs), workers held accountable to bureaucrats, workers negotiating bureaucratic mandates, and gendered and raced workers. This thinking requires that, in the words of Cynthia Selfe, we "must try to understand—*to pay attention to*—how technology is inextricably linked to litera-

cy and literacy education in this country" (24). Technologies have been nat-
uralized in our lives as composition scholars, teachers, and workers, and
paying attention to them often requires an explicit attempt to make visible
what works invisibly. Increasingly, then, technology is not just a practical
matter that we can choose to engage or ignore. As in American culture
more generally, technologies have become an everyday presence in composition work—Internet and writing technologies have been woven into
the fabric of our intellectual work, communication technologies have
expanded the network of people with whom we communicate and depend
on to do our jobs, and computers support and complicate writing pedagogies. Word processing, e-mail, web authoring and researching have woven
themselves seamlessly into our everyday lives, even those in less technologically rich settings. Whereas theorists were concerned about technological access even 5 years ago, some level of technological access is now
available at most colleges and universities, as technology has been and
continues to be of high priority (rightly or wrongly) for schools and institutions of higher learning across the country. Likewise, academic labor issues
within composition reflect larger cultural trends of displacement and alienation within an information economy largely supported by a part time and
contingent labor force.

At the heart of the conference where earlier versions of these chapters
were delivered and at the heart of this volume circulate(d) several concerns: What labor, workplace, and technology issues should composition as
a profession be concerned with as we enter the next millennium? How
does technology affect the shape of academic labor? How have working
conditions in composition affected the ways we've used technology? The
authors in this collection have turned their critical attention to these questions, arguing that composition workers (researchers, scholars, administrators, and teachers) have much to think about in the coming years as we
articulate our professional identity. Although there are as many ways to
organize these chapters into themes as there are readers of this collection,
our reading of these chapters as a collective suggested four themes: voicing our (past and future) professional identities, mediating technology-
shaped identities, exploring possibilities for agency in institutional settings,
and identifying sustainable technological practices. Along the way, the
authors move from examinations of individual workers through an exploration of composition forging a professional identity.

Part 1, "Voicing Our (Past and Future) Professional Identities," explores
the ways that technologies lead us to re-examine—and even redefine—the
work we do. These chapters all focus on the conditions of our work as compositionists and the ways that writing technologies impinge on that work—

our understandings of the work, the shape of the work, and the ways the work builds the institutions in which we work.

In "When the Cutting Edge of Technology is at Your Throat: A Report from the Front," Richard Miller counter balances the rhetoric of technology's revolutionary change with his own experiences as a Writing Program Administrator awash in the quotidian details of involving writing technologies in the life of a large university writing program. While acknowledging that there are many reasons to be cautious about technology, Miller suggests that the pressure for introducing technologies into curriculum provides a chance to reimagine what writing programs might be, who might work in them, and under what conditions. Asking how it is that institutions change, Miller argues that it is possible, under conditions not of one's making, to become agents for change, to do more than critique and resist.

In "Composition, or a Case for Experimental Critical Writing" Janet Carey Eldred begins by forcing our attention to the definition of the very word that describes our field, pointing out that the term *composition* situates our work in particular ways that both open and closes possibilities for the ways we envision our work. By re-imagining composition as a term, Eldred explores what composition might look like as we enter the 21st century. Looking at the ways composition has historically defined itself in discussions of personal versus professional academic writing, Eldred is ultimately asking us to think about how relevant those terms and concepts are now. Arguing that we can learn a great deal by juxtaposing what we have traditionally kept separate, Eldred demonstrates that compositions that combine the personal and the academic ohld enormous promise for us as individual writers and as a field.

In "Technological Labor and Tenure Decisions: Making a Virtual Case Via Electronic Portfolios," Kristine Blair begins with a common problem at many universities: Tenure and promotion procedures continue to privilege print-based evidence of teaching and research productivity or do not acknowledge the impact of technology on teaching, scholarship, and service. Despite these problems, Blair makes the case for electronic teaching portfolios as professional development tools for both faculty and graduate students and outlines a range of training and professional development initiatives. Through her own administrative work developing electronic portfolios with faculty across disciplines, Blair understands that institutional education is necessary about the potential of electronic portfolios as manifestation and measurement of the impact of technology on academic labor. Ultimately, she argues that such efforts are a way of providing incentive and reward for faculty to utilize technology in ways that genuinely enhance their teaching and overall professional development.

In "Assessment as Labor and the Labor of Assessment," Peggy O'Neill, Ellen Schendel, Michael Williamson, and Brian Huot argue that writing assessment has been foundational to composition's formation as a discipline. In place of the dominant view of classroom and programmatic writing assessment as particularly onerous and taxing labor, they argue that assessment can work for composition studies by providing a visible representation of what we value as teachers, programs, and professionals. Through explorations of the labors involved in writing assessment and the place of technology in the history and development of many writing assessment practices, these authors demonstrate that the tension between labor and technology in writing assessment accounts for the ongoing political differences between various approaches. In the end, O'Neill et al. articulate the centrality of labor and technology in writing assessment, while at the same time asserting the importance of human labor for reading and assessing student writing.

Taken together, the chapters in this section suggest numerous ways that technologies push compositionists to examine our existing disciplinary definitions of our work. They offer answers from several different locations on the institutional map to the question "How does technology promise (or threaten) to affect the very work that defines us?" In addition to offering these specific considerations, their thoughtful and careful examinations also open up space for further reflection on the continuing effects of technologies on the professional identities of composition workers. Questions and areas for further exploration suggested by these authors include the following:

- What does it mean to be a teacher of writing? A program administrator? A researcher? A scholar? Do the changing economies suggest mutations in what those roles are and/or how they are valued?
- What role should composition workers take in response to accountability movements (which are sometimes connected with the corporatization of universities)? Can we develop proactive (rather than reactive) responses that voice how we want to be assessed before someone else identifies it for us?
- How do we need to think about access now when our facilities (i.e., the actual equipment, the infrastructure, and our abilities to shape it into pedagogies that don't erase people) contribute to differing access levels? At one end of the spectrum of access, some of us will maintain a future that's much

like our present while others become much more like service workers. What can and should be done about such differential access? How much is access under our control? How
do our abilities, historical happenstance, visions of technologies, and sophistication in using it affect our success?

• How do we conceptualize literacy work with technology?
What counts as literacy work? Who should determine what
counts and how it is counted?

Part 2, "Mediating Technology-Shaped Identities," focuses on the contributions and complications of mediating identities—student, teacher, administrator, citizen—through technologies. As individuals and institutions
increasingly conduct their work through technologies, these authors ask:
"What happens to the relationships among individuals, institutions, texts,
knowledge, and identity?"

In "WAC for Cyborgs: Discursive Thought in Information-Rich
Environments," Charles Bazerman reflects on the ways that writing technologies create intellectual challenges for users. Although the acquisition
and interpretation of information has always been associated with writing
in schools and knowledge professions, the relevant knowledge universes
remained tightly circumscribed compared to the current and future richness of electronic informational environments. Arguing that the easy
accessibility of data and the attractiveness of exposing students to more
extensive data earlier in their education has made the need for students to
articulate what they have found more pressing, Bazerman asserts the
increasing importance of Writing Across Curriculum and ECAC initiatives
to help students in learning how to use and make sense of data and how
writing might help them develop the understanding they need to access,
work with, and come to conclusions from the data.

In "'Whatever Beings': The Coming (Educational) Community," Victor
Vitanza explains and develops the views of Georgio Agamben in relation to
the changes taking place in our world. Concerned specifically with changes
in terms of subjectivity, language, and community, Vitanza argues that subjectivity relations are changing to a third term—what he labels "whatever
beings" or "whatever singularities." Recognizing that if subjectivity is
changing, then language and community are changing as well, Vitanza
focuses on rethinking the relationships of thought and human beings in
terms of subjectivity, language, and community. Vitanza envisions the
problem of change as not being driven by technology in the classroom but
by "potentialities" in the class(less) room. In his paracritique, he relies on
cultural and digital studies, which are wholly informed by an economy of

thinking originated during the Industrial Revolution, as a way of speaking the new economy of "thinking whatever."

In "'Outing' the Institution: (Re)Writing Technologies With a Rhetoric of Female-to-Male Drag," Tara Pauliny turns our attention to university sites as spaces in which the rhetorical technology of female-to-male (FTM) drag collides with normative expectations about identity and institutionalized power. By expanding the term *technology* to include the rhetorical deployment of language structure, dress, behavior, and physical postures traditionally coded masculine or dominant, Pauliny argues that FTM drag articulates how women engage with and utilize these masculine codes in subversive, threatening, and/or persuasive ways. Ultimately, Pauliny argues that when positions of power and privilege are appropriated by nondominant subjects, the hegemonic boundaries of academic culture are deviated and the regulatory structures of such sites are "outed" in potentially productive ways.

In "(Cyber)Conspiracy Theories?: African-American Students in the Computerized Writing Environment," Samantha Blackmon considers the ways agency is (and can be) enacted by students in technologically mediated classrooms. Beginning with the assertion that computer technologies (such as the Internet) can exacerbate already existing inequities in education, Blackmon cautions against tendencies toward the "cyberhuman" ideal—the raceless, sexless, genderless, classless entity that is the same as any other online. Blackmon points out that African-American users, in particular, must ignore racialized selves if they are to accept and interact with technology as a "cyberhuman." Using student-based data and historical references, Blackmon argues that historical access is an issue compositionists of the 21st century must begin to understand.

The chapters in Part II suggest that if academics working through and with technologies are to be useful to the populations they work with, they must develop and adopt assertive and active relationships with technologies and, most importantly, with the people who engage them. The authors of these chapters assert anew the connections between technologies, knowledge formations, power relations, idealism, and subjectivity. By thinking hard and offering some complex speculations about the mediation of technology-shaped identities, these authors raise a number of further questions and areas for further exploration:

- What happens when the authority for information needed comes to individuals from a computer? What new role does the teacher have when the data is in the machine? What new role do the students have?

- In an information-rich environment governed by computer technologies, what options exist for students beyond the obvious data-processing clerk and/or critic?
- When the things that teachers normally teach and the things students normally learn are partially learned and known by computers, what happens to the teaching relationship and situation?
- How is computer access differential? Who gets access? Partial or full access? Who gets no access? How do these differing levels of access affect the ways individuals are shaped by technologies?
- Of the traditional outward markers of identity (race, class, ability, gender, sexual preference), which get identified in these situation-less places? How?
- In considerations of emerging technologies, too often minority perspectives are not considered, except in terms of access (and then, access is only thought of in a very material, mundane way). What can composition teachers, scholars, and researchers do to guard against this tendency? What can we do to create and contribute to more complicated understandings of access?
- What is literacy when it's heavily mediated by technology? Does it differ from our existing understandings of literacy and its attendant issues?

Part III, "Exploring Possibilities for Agency in Institutional Settings," examines questions of agency—can compositionists working with technologies in the new economy assert agency? What does it look like? What constrains and encourages possibilities for agency? By looking at theories of agency and measuring them against institutional experiences of composition teachers, scholars, administrators, and researchers, the authors in this section reveal places where agency might take place (and, as importantly, the places where it is constrained) and the shapes it might take.

In "Agencies, Ecologies, and the Mundane Artifacts in Our Midst," Stuart Blythe reflects on the possibilities for agency in institutional settings. Arguing that agency is something exercised between individuals, Blythe asserts that agency should be considered as a concept akin to power—an effect of interaction between people rather than something one possesses. From this, he explains that agency is situated, that it is an effect of organizational affiliation and that, because organizations are constructed discursively, agency is often a matter of rewriting organizational documents (such as policy or organizational charts) or changing how such documents are perceived by others.

In "Roots and Routes to Agency: Space, Access, and Standards of Participation," Annette Harris Powell explores the ways compositionists have thought about and theorized agency and social action, asking how we can help students to enact agency in technological, educational settings. She shows how agency is crucial to considerations of access and further, how agency is crucial to users shaping virtual space (including the ubiquitous Web) to their own desires, needs, and interests. Reporting on a summer technology camp in which she taught middle school students from underserved populations, Powell argues that beginning with the practices students bring with them is an important first step toward building practices that focus more on action than on critique alone.

In "(Mis)Conceptions: Pedagogical Labor and Learning-Enhancement Programs," Joseph Zeppetello argues that although education cannot be reduced to algorithms, there is a fundamental misperception among computer programmers regarding pedagogical labor. After a series of experiences with book publishers and programmers, Zeppetello comes to the conclusion that outsiders do not understand the labor of composition work, and it is our responsibility as compositionists to educate outsiders to the contours of our work. It is only when the labor of compositionists comes out of the margins of academic professionals, he asserts, that we can expect those outside the academy to understand the value and nature of our work.

In "Labor Practices and the Use Value of Technologies," Marilyn Cooper uses Karl Marx's concepts of use and exchange values to think about the value of educational technologies in academics' everyday lives. She argues that the use value of educational technologies is discovered in the everyday work of faculty, staff, students, and administrators. Cooper turns to the story of the development of Interchange (a synchronous chatting program) as an example of how the use value of educational technologies is discovered. This ongoing process of discovering a technology's use value suggests that instead of seeing technologies as discrete products, we need to understand workers, technologies, and the environment in which they work as ongoing systems of relations. Finally, Cooper asserts, if we are to reform academic labor practices, the use values of technologies and the everyday work of users must be taken into account.

In "Literacy Work in E-Learning Factories: How Stories in Popular Business Imagine Our Future," Patricia Sullivan examines popular narratives about education, training, and technology that can readily be found in popular writing in business. Through this examination, Sullivan exposes typical positions built by those narratives about authority, agency, instructional space, and pedagogy and contrasts those positions with the ones taken by e-learning stories told by educators, paying particular attention to the ways that both consumer-based and institutionally based economies are woven into these narratives about e-learning. She demonstrates that, perhaps not surprisingly, teachers lose agency and ownership over pedagogy to machines in most tales; institutions and disciplines, moreover, fare little better, a point that Sullivan argues should be taken very seriously by composition studies.

These careful and thoughtful considerations of agency and its possibilities in the contemporary university offer substantial grounds for scholars to continue building on, perhaps in response to questions that these chapters raise such as the following:

- What possibilities for agency are enhanced and shut down by new economies of knowledge and technologies?
- When the place of the institution can be relocated (and displaced from any physical location at all) through technologies, what role does the institution play in our working lives?
- How does an institution portray itself now that buildings are threatened as the institutional marker? What does the institution do to retain its authority?
- How does the displacement of the institution affect the way individuals access and work with it?
- What does composition uniquely contribute to a discussion of what will count as literacy? How do we gain entrance to those conversations outside composition circles?

The final section, "Identifying Sustainable Technological Practices," considers the ways the work of compositionists contribute to a set of practices that ultimately define the profession. These authors argue that by working to gain control over these practices, we gain control over the meanings our work might take for ourselves and outsiders. By looking at practices engaged in by compositionists (professional self-definition, assessment, teaching, and community-based work), these authors raise a larger question for the field—where does composition head next? How can we build sustainable practices that are beneficial to professionals and those with whom they interact?

In "Techniques, Technologies, and the Deskilling of Rhetoric and Composition: Managing the Knowledge-Intensive Work of Writing Instruction," Bill Hart-Davidson and Tim Peeples raise questions about the

roles program administration and networked computer technologies play
in the deskilling of writing instructors. They ask whether the professionalization of Writing Program Administrators and the spread of computer
technology into college-level writing instruction have improved the work
lives of teachers of writing, and whether these two interrelated changes
contributed to a broader recognition of the value of writing and, thereby, of
those who teach and study writing in the academy. Through an interrogation of cases that frame the issues in writing contexts, they argue for a view
of the work writing specialists do as knowledge-intensive with the understanding that true knowledge work demands that workers be able to
impact the ends and not merely the means of production in their work context.

In "Writing Assessment and the Labor of 'Reform' in the Academy,"
Margaret Willard-Traub examines a specific variety of academic labor—the
labor of writing assessment—in order to articulate how still-evolving
assessment practices nationwide respond to broader political realities
impinging on the field of composition. Pointing out that public debates
about the aims and philosophies of higher education often equate assessment's "reform" function with its ability to promote a particular kind of
"accountability," Willard-Traub argues that accountability has little to do
with encouraging positive changes in the working conditions of faculty and
graduate students, with increasing tenure stream faculty's collaborative
investment in writing instruction, or with increasing the institutional status
of writing instruction. In order to focus on how assessment can improve
the conditions under which students learn by improving the conditions
under which college and university writing teachers labor, Willard-Traub
argues for using the professional development of faculty over time as a
measure of accountability. She ultimately constructs a positive example of
how we can make bureaucratic work into intellectual work that rewards all
those involved.

In "Between Ethnographic and Virtual Worlds: Toward a Pedagogy of
Mediation," David Seitz and Julie Lindquist establish the need to design
proactive approaches to shaping our teaching (with and without technologies) and the social implications of those pedagogies. They argue that stu-
dent-conducted ethnographic research can function as a counterpractice to
the overdetermination of technology in teaching, contributing to the development of critical technological literacy. Drawing on examples from
research in computer-mediated communications, other composition teachers' projects using the Internet and the web, and their own students' work,
Seitz and Lindquist assert that students' comparative ethnographic
research of local and online groups will call into question how much of cul-

ture is material, that online research will help students develop larger social contexts for the local situations they research, and that the mediation of hypertext will help rethink the ways students represent their ethnographic research.

In "Sustaining Community-Based Work: Community-Based Research and Community Building," Jeffrey T. Grabill argues that writing teachers and researchers have yet to seriously interrogate the concept of *community* or what it means to relocate our work to community contexts. Demonstrating that our current understanding of community and community-based work is too limiting to sustain meaningful work outside the academy, Grabill argues that sustained and sustainable community work is necessary if composition workers are to be useful in our communities. As an example, he uses his own work developing a neighborhood Web site to be used for community development and activism. Along the way, Grabill develops a methodology for community-based work that offers a new way for writing researchers and teachers to work in community contexts.

These careful and thoughtful considerations of agency and its possibilities in the contemporary university offer substantial grounds for scholars to continue building on, perhaps in response to questions that these chapters raise such as the following:

- Is sustainability a value that captures some spirit of composition work generally? Can sustainability be thought of acontextually or is it always defined by its very context?
- With the rapid "development" of improved versions of technologies and of new technologies, what happens to the possibility of sustainability with the introduction of technologies into a system or setting?
- What disciplinary structures can be put into place to encourage sustainability?
- What are the boundaries for composition work? Is literacy teaching going to continue to be primarily a university-based work or is it possible that it will move into other general venues of life?

The authors in this volume put work, technology, and composition studies together directly in ways that are unprecedented. Labor and technology have cross pollinated, particularly in areas of policymaking for the future where the literature on labor is curiously compatible with the consideration of technology. Both discussions seem to swing wildly between bright pronouncements and gloomy ones on the employment and technology fronts, with the more optimistic approach seeing technology as a corrective (and the lack of technology as a problem to be solved). The authors in this volume occupy a theoretical space somewhere between the bright pronouncements and the gloomy ones—focused as they are on a specific disciplinary formation, they ground their explorations in a world bounded by the material constraints of a set of specific practices. Put directly, the authors of this collection think about the key terms of *work*, *writing technologies*, and *composition studies* productively and creatively. Why? Workers (including us) are suspicious of technological solutions to workers' problems. As compositionists themselves, the authors of this collection work to envision the kind of working culture they desire, balancing the light and the dark, yet, as a whole, sharing Cynthia Selfe's insistence that the stakes in the academy were never higher. Beginning with these chapters, others concerned with the stakes (and our participation in conversations which define, refine, dispute, and resist those stakes) might arm themselves with perspectives to enter the fray.

ENDNOTES

1. Labor, as defined by the Oxford English Dictionary, carries with it connotations of difficult, compulsive, or manual work for wages (as opposed to the work rendered by entrepreneurs for a profit). Work, on the other hand, is a more general term for an activity in which one performs or exerts effort to complete something. With labor, there is an emphasis on the physical—difficult, painful processes of exertion in the service of something else. Employment does not figure in the definition of labor—it is a "specific service rendered to production." In the definition of work, however, there is not so much emphasis on the physical—it is considered something that occupies one (occupies one's energy, thought, activity).
2. The Wyoming Resoultion in support of part-time teacher needs and the work of CCCC in support of this resolution stand out as important ethical actions and as a welcome contradiction to this generalization.

REFERENCES

Aronowitz, Stanley. "The Last Good Job in America." *Post-Work: The Wages of Cybernation*. Eds. Stanley Aronowitz and Jonathan Cutler. New York: Routledge, 1998. 203-23.

Berube, Michael. *The Employment of English: Theory, Jobs, and the Future.* New York: New York University Press, 1998.

Bodker, Suzanne. *Through the Interface: A Human Activity Approach to User Interface Design.* Mahwah, NJ: Lawrence Erlbaum, 1991.

Brandt, Deborah. *Literacy in American Lives.* Cambridge: Cambridge University Press, 2001.

Ehn, Pelle, ed. *Work-Oriented Design of Computer Artifacts.* Mahwah, NJ: Lawrence Erlbaum, 1990.

Enos, Theresa. *Gender Roles and Faculty Lives in Rhetoric and Composition.* Carbondale: Southern Illinois University Press, 1996.

Garay, Mary Sue, and Stephen Bernhardt, eds. *Expanding Literacies: English Teaching and the New Workplace.* Albany: State University of New York Press, 1998.

Gee, James Paul, Glynda Hull, and Colin Lankshear. *The New Work Order: Behind the Language of the New Capitalism.* Boulder, CO: Westview Press, 1996.

Huot, Brian, and Pamela Takayoshi. *Teaching Writing with Computers.* Boston: Houghton Mifflin, 2003.

Johnston, William B. and Arnold E. Packer. *Workforce 2000: Work and Workers for the 21st Century.* Indianapolis: Hudson Institute, 1987.

Pratt, Linda. "Disposable Faculty: Part-Time Exploitation as Management Strategy." *Will Teach for Food. Academic Labor in Crisis.* Ed. Cary Nelson. Minneapolis: University of Minnesota Press, 1997. 264–277.

Reich, Robert. *The Future of Success: Working and Living in the New Economy.* New York: Knopf, 2000

Rifkin, Jeremy. *The End of Work: The Decline of the Global Labor Force and the Dawn of the Post-Market Era.* New York: G.P. Putnam's Sons, 1995.

Selfe, Cynthia L. *Technology and Literacy in the Twenty-First Century. The Importance of Paying Attention.* Carbondale: Southern Illinois University Press, 1999.

Weiser, Irwin, and Shirley Rose. *The Writing Program Administrator as Researcher: Inquiry in Action and Reflection.* Portsmouth, NH: Boynton Cook, 1999.

www.cyberatlas.com. Site accessed October 1999.

Yates, JoAnne. *Control through Communication: The Rise of System in American Management.* Baltimore: Johns Hopkins University Press, 1989.

Zuboff, Shoshana. *In the Age of the Smart Machine: The Future of Work and Power.* New York: Basic Books, 1988.

PART ONE

Voicing our (Past and Future) Professional Identities

1

WHEN THE CUTTING EDGE OF TECHNOLOGY IS AT YOUR THROAT

A REPORT FROM THE FRONT

Richard E. Miller

Rutgers University

How do institutions change? How can we tell when they have changed? One way to tell the story of how institutions change is to consider the promises that have been made on behalf of instructional technology. Consider this example taken from my own university (Rutgers), where senior officials embarked upon an ambitious plan—and by ambitious I mean $100 million worth of ambition—to put all of Rutgers online by the beginning of the 21st century. When finished, RUNet 2000 was to have provided "fast and easy access to the Internet and to university computing resources from on and off-campus locations including residence halls," thereby enabling the entire Rutgers' learning community to take full advantage of "advanced video and multimedia communication and instructional tools" (RUNet 2000). In Fall 2000, in his annual address on the state of the university, Fran Lawrence, then president of Rutgers, provided a progress report of sorts on the RUNet 2000 plan:

> As we move toward the completion of RUNet 2000, the possibilities for links between our institution and enormous resources elsewhere are simply staggering. Our challenge will be to stay at the leading edge of this pedagogical revolution and use it to our advantage—to bring the three-dimensional art works in from Rome, or the primary school classroom in from Puerto Rico—in the interest of creating an environ-

> ment in which the potential for active, fully engaged education is virtu-
> ally endless. We must continue to explore the potential of technologi-
> cally enriched learning, and to redefine and expand the meaning of
> community engagement through continuing education, further
> advancing the seamless educational environment that will serve our
> students throughout their lives.

This dreamy talk of revolutionary change is the stuff of which vision statements are made. It is the work of such talk to forever beckon toward an
evolving world, one rich with opportunity, one where students will be
brought into direct contact with the riches of the past and all will join
together to form a global community of learners in pursuit of the highest
forms of human excellence. From the bird's eye view, high above the university, everything looks clean and clear; anything seems possible. Who
wouldn't find such a world appealing? Who wouldn't support all efforts to
bring this world into existence?

    At the ground level, however, institutional change does not tend to live
up to all the advance publicity. As the associate director of a writing program that has more than 200 teachers covering more than 500 sections a
year, I have seen what the technological revolution looks like beneath the
kind of celebratory rhetoric just cited and beneath all of the claims made
in our profession's elegant theories about cyborgs, hypertext, and the virtual community. And from my vantage point, the technological revolution
seems less a model of organization, or efficiency, or reason than the end-
less unfolding of unforeseen calamities. That is, from the viewpoint of
someone buried in the quotidian details of building labs and training teachers, one finds beneath all the rhetoric about the speed and efficiency of the
networked world a sea of mundane concerns about site licenses, IP
addresses, cross-campus connectivity conflicts, student access rates, user
incompetence, managerial incompetence, frozen machines, vandalized
machines, stolen machines, budget reports that are delayed, incomplete,
uncertain, and, of course, antiquated brick and mortar facilities that are not
prepared to house the newly networked learning environments. This, then,
is another way to tell the story of how institutions change: Take the view
from below and focus on chaos, confusion, broken promises.

    If one looks down at institutions of higher learning from above, any
manner of reform can seem possible: Just introduce enough money and
create the right incentives and the system will move off in the desired
direction. If one looks at institutions of higher learning from below, however, significant change can seem impossible: From this vantage point,
everything passed down from on high appears to be just more rhetoric and

everything one does or is required to do can never be anything other than a reaction to a situation one does not control. As writing teachers, we all know how seductive the composing process can be, how in the act of writing, in the quiet space of reflection, putting words on the page in the right order can take on an importance that is entirely out of proportion with the possible consequences those words might actually have. So, we plan on paper and, for reasons I still don't quite understand, we are perpetually surprised when things don't go according to plan—when, as in the case of RUNet 2000, the money arrives, but the networking falls far behind schedule, producing in its wake rampant frustration, ridicule, and finally despair that anything much will happen. So, all over campus one finds those who want to use the technology, but can't; those who don't want to use the technology, but feel they are being forced to; and plenty of people who wonder why all these funds are being poured into the ground, when the buildings above ground are falling down. For those who believe that planning itself has the highest significance, that the deepest meanings reside in the words we've used to articulate our desires about what the future might hold, there is always the sense that there could have been a better plan, one that would have foreseen all the problems that emerged once the actual plan was put into effect. In this world, there are those who plan and those who critique the plans of others. It is a world of boundless optimism and table-pounding exasperation, of dreamers and revolutionaries. It is a world where so much depends—or at least seems to depend—on the words we choose.

What I argue here, however, is that there is an alternative to rehearsing these familiar ways of telling the story of how institutions change; indeed, I believe that indulging in the activity of carefully scrutinizing and perhaps even ridiculing the language of vision statements distracts us from taking advantage of the opportunities that such visionary rhetoric, and the funding that follows it, presents to writing instructors and the programs that employ them. And so, although there are doubtless many reasons to embrace the view from below and cast the rush toward technology as the final phase in the ruination of the university, I suggest that we see this as a time of unparalleled opportunity, one where we have a chance to reimagine what writing programs might be, who might work in them, and under what conditions.

To learn how to tell a different kind of story about institutional change, one that breaks free from the paired rhetorics of celebration and despair, we must learn how to identify where our powers for self-determination lie and what resources we have at our disposal to initiate changes from below, changes that can improve the quality of instruction we offer *and* improve the working conditions of those who teach writing. At my institution, this has meant that those of us involved with administering and teaching in the Writing Program have had to let go of the deeply embedded disciplinary inclination to focus on the language of official documents and the presumably nefarious intentions of university officials and to concentrate our energies, instead, on defining what the function of a writing program might be in the 21st- century. And the director of the program and I have had to also let go of being frustrated and outraged by the fact that nobody consulted us to see if we approved of the university's plan to invest so heavily in technology.

Had anyone from central administration consulted me, I would have advised against committing $100 million to such a project and I would have provided what I would have thought at the time were compelling reasons to reject the latest bit of educational gimmickry. But I wasn't consulted nor was the director of the Writing Program, nor the chair of the English Department, nor the Rutgers faculty as a whole, for the simple reason that decisions about how the university's funds are to be allocated do not require consultation with university employees: These are matters that are resolved by the president, his cabinet of advisors, and the board of trustees. I might prefer a different organizational structure, but my desires and the desires of my colleagues are irrelevant in this area. These are the realities that pertain at my institution and they are the realities that pertain generally in higher education, where examples of genuine, well-functioning faculty governance are very difficult to find. Is it possible, then, under conditions not of one's making or of one's choosing, to become an agent for change? Are there any options available besides resistance and critique? For most of my professional life, I would have answered both of these questions in the negative. Now I would say that such responses are evidence of a failure to understand how and why institutions change, but I'm getting ahead of my story.

REDEFINING OUR RESOURCES:
THE LIMITS OF SAYING NO

What role do academic units actually have to play in the process of institutional reform? If we return to the RUNet 2000 documents, we can see that the administration's original plan went something like this.

Step 1: Secure sufficient funds to make the university a player in the race for technology.

Step 2: Hardwire 260 academic buildings and dormitories on three campuses spread across the state in 4 years or less.

Step 3: Concurrent with Step 2, provide incentives to get faculty and students to use the new resources.

Step 4: Watch the university community reap the rewards of being able to go online at will.

In this plan, to the degree that teachers of any kind figure at all, it is as entities who acquire grants to develop curricula using instructional technology, who can be induced to participate in reduced rate purchase plans for hardware and software, and who respond favorably to peer pressure. It's safe to say, however, that during the early stages of RUNet 2000 those of us who worked in the Writing Program were not exactly eager to play along with this plan. In fact, we were happy enough to sit in the shadows of the technological revolution: We had three computerized classrooms that were primarily used by developmental students to work on word processing, a decision that had been made years ago and that seemed a pedagogically defensible use of the limited space and the limited resources available to us. To our way of thinking, there was no way for these three classrooms to accommodate the 12,000 students who enroll in our courses annually, so dedicating the labs to developmental students allowed us to target a more manageable sector of the student population, one that clearly benefitted from acquiring basic "keyboarding" and revising skills. So, as far as we were concerned, there was no harm in letting the technological revolution pass by, because we understood the value of the Writing Program to reside in our text-based pedagogy and in our efforts to assist students in mastering print-based culture.

We were not entirely opposed to rethinking the Writing Program's curriculum, however. Indeed, in the early 1990s, when the administration requested that a portion of the first-year writing course be devoted to public speaking, Kurt Spellmeyer, director of the Writing Program, responded with a proposal for introducing a public speaking requirement that the administration accepted. On its face, the request itself is sure to be just what faculty fear most—an administrative intrusion into curricular design—and the program's decision to grant the request is bound to appear as one more example of the university's transformation into the handmaiden to the business community. The story is more complicated than that, however. When the administration made this unprecedented request, they were concerned about the university's perceived inability to attract top graduate students because of teaching assistant (TA) working conditions and they were motivated as well by threats from prominent senior faculty members who vowed to seek employment elsewhere if the administration did not find a way to address the matter. The administration was also looking for a way to make a deal to reduce TA workloads without appearing to have caved into the union. The public speaking requirement provided a way to break the stalemate: It gave the administration a rationale for reducing TA workloads (the TAs were now taking on the additional demand of teaching public speaking) and it provided the university with the kind of business-friendly publicity it was seeking. And so, in exchange for taking on the public speaking requirement, TAs in the Writing Program had their workload reduced to two courses annually: Now, instead of teaching two sections in the fall and one section in the spring, TAs teach two in the fall and take the spring off.

It is reasonable to ask what the cost of collaborating with the administration was on this matter. Currently, all teachers of Expository Writing 101, our required course, are asked to make certain that each of their students speaks publicly in class a minimum of three times during the semester. And the public speech they must engage in is the kind that *we* believe the academy is best suited to promote—speculative, deliberative, meditative speech, the kind that generates new ideas and invites discussion, as opposed to the kind that's valued on the used car lot—the hard sell, the bullet proof argument, the 10 reasons why you must agree that I'm right. That's it.

This seems like an insignificant curricular change, which is precisely why we had agreed to it initially: We felt certain that it would not adversely effect the quality of our course and we knew for a fact that it would measurably improve the quality of life for the 112 TAs employed by our program. What has since surprised and delighted us is to see that the public speaking requirement has actually improved the quality of class discussions and the quality of the writing produced in our required writing course. With the public speaking requirement, each class is now compelled to participate in the very activity that our program values most highly—engaging in a dialogue with the assigned materials. So, here's an example of uninvited change that brought about unanticipated, beneficial pedagogical consequences.

Signing on with the administration during the early phases of the RUNet 2000 project seemed a different matter, however. It was one thing to redefine the composition course so that it concentrated on reading, writing, and speaking; the requests that followed seemed designed to take the course off in entirely unwelcome directions. And so, when Kurt and I were asked by the administration to introduce a computer literacy component into the required writing course ("This is what a mouse is, Bobby"), we said no. And when we were asked to introduce a web design component into the course ("This is what a web page is, Bobby"), said no again. We weren't going to agree to anything that would compromise the pedogogical or intellectual commitments of the course and we perceived anything that smacked of computer skills or graphic design as an intrusion into the text-based world of the required course that had to be immediately rejected out of hand. What did we know? We were in the word and paper business and no amount of bullying or insults was going to get us out of it. Our strategy was simple.

Say no to everything.

Everything changed, however, when the chair of the English Department instructed me to work with the director of Undergraduate Studies to produce a proposal requesting a grant from the student computing fee committee. This was not a task that either the director of Undergraduate Studies or I was very enthusiastic about, so we reluctantly put together a request for funds to convert a classroom into a computer lab for faculty and graduate students in the English Department. The review committee did more than reject this proposal; they called us in and ridiculed us for producing a proposal that was so lacking in vision. We were sent back to the drawing board. Our revised request for funds to replace the ancient computers in the Writing Program's three writing labs was similarly rejected for lack of ambition, a failure to innovate. Think bigger, the holders of the purse strings said, think *much* bigger.

Our last shot was a proposal I drew up to revise the Writing Program's entire curricula so that it incorporated what we in the program saw as pedagogically defensible uses of instructional technology: no basic skills components, no entry-level student web page design component, but required use of the web in our research courses and a concerted effort to make online interactions a part of every course eventually. The proposal was both that big and that vague. The skies—or at least the university coffers—opened: The computer fee committee granted us $175,000 and the dean's office in the Faculty of Arts and Sciences kicked in another $40,000. All for machines, of course. (We were repeatedly told that not a cent of these funds was to be spent on machines for faculty or on labor: Since this was the students' money—it comes directly from the $100 computing fee they pay every semester, it was our fiduciary responsibility to see to it that it the funds only spent on things that directly benefitted the students.)

So, in the end, it would seem, the administration got what it wanted—access to the Writing Program's most precious resource—all the entering students. And the Writing Program? Well, initially, we got a lot of machines and an understandably chilly reception from the English Department. Under the funding program that was approved, part-time and full-time writing teachers and TAs in the Writing Program were slated to have access to the new machines. And the full-time faculty in the English Department? Under the logic of the student-centered funding fee, the faculty were left out in the cold: Because the funding committee rejected any proposals that involved giving machines to faculty, the tenured and tenure-track members of the department could expect nothing better than the 5-year old machines that were slated to be replaced in the writing labs. The faculty, in other words, were awarded the Writing Program's hand-me-downs.

Welcome to the new economy.

HOW CHANGE HAPPENS

As all of this was happening and it was becoming clear that I was going to be the one to spearhead the effort to bring instructional technology into the Writing Program's curriculum, I had only one thought: This is going to be a disaster. At the time these new responsibilities were accruing to me, my qualifications were these: I knew enough about word processing to get my essays to print and I knew enough about e-mail to keep in touch with friends. I had never taught in a computerized classroom. I had never built a web page. I had never visited a chat room.

These details are important.

Who will be the people who carry out this much celebrated, much anticipated technological revolution? This much I can say: The bulk of this work won't be carried out by qualified people, at least not by people who are qualified at the beginning of the process. This, too, is a characteristic of institutional change.

After the machines were ordered, here's what happened. When the truck driver from Dell arrived unannounced late one afternoon with his 18-wheeler packed with more than 260 boxes of CPUs, monitors, servers, printers, and speakers, he had no one to help him get the boxes into our building. He drove; he didn't unload. That was not his job nor, apparently, was it anyone else's at the university that afternoon. And so it became my job and the job of a hastily gathered crew of graduate students. As the sun set, we used every imaginable form of wheeled conveyance to get all these boxes stacked in our lab and in offices around the building, the stream of boxes going in the building and workers coming out for another load splitting around a colleague stalled in the doorway, lecturing a student—I'm not making this up—about Wordsworth's pastoral poetry.

Here's what else happened: The Writing Program made a deal with the English as a Second Language program, exchanging access to our labs for 25 additional computers they no longer had room for. We stored these machines in another office; a pipe burst, the ceiling collapsed, and I am left with the unforgettable image of picking up CPU after CPU with water pouring out the side. There were weekends spent moving dozens of units around campus in my van, slicing open boxes, putting together desktops, installing software, configuring machines for the network, crawling around on the floor. There were encounters with colleagues who, in a good natured way of course, repeatedly referred to me as a janitor—the work of providing students and teachers with access to technology being understood, in this instance, as roughly equivalent to cleaning out toilets. Necessary work, to be sure, but certainly beneath the dignity of the rank and file professoriate. And, of course, there were all those students forever lined up outside the labs, where the machines weren't ready, wouldn't work, wouldn't ever work—the same students who paid the computer fee that the administration has determined can only be spent on machines, not labor, not leadership, not expertise. These are just details, of course, but they are the details out of which we might construct a rather different theory of institutional change than the one that underwrites the ceaseless cycle of planning and critique.

SOME SURPRISES

Improved Working Conditions

That's the down side of joining the technological revolution and, at times, I wondered if there would ever be an upside. But, now that we are into the eighth year of the project, I think it's safe to say that the benefits far outweigh the momentary frustrations that have been produced by our attempts to incorporate instructional technology into our curriculum.[1] Indeed, much to our surprise, embarking on this project has served to improve the working conditions of teachers in our program and to enhance the program's pedagogical practice in measurable ways. I touch on each of the effected areas here.

Job Creation. To begin with, by making it clear to the administration that the competition for *technologically savvy* teachers is quite intense, we have been able to argue for the following new lines in the Writing Program:

- a new assistant director line for an administrator/teacher in charge of instructional technology;
- a permanent administrative position for the assistant director in charge of business and technical writing;
- our first tenure-track hire in comp in 6 years and we have been assured two more hires over the next 4 years.

Improved Salaries. We have also been able to argue for improved wages for the 25 full-time instructors and the 7 assistant directors of the program: From 1999 to 2001, we successfully pressed for a $4,000 pay increase for all our instructors, and a $2,000 raise for our administrators. These raises were in addition to contractual increases negotiated by the union.

Increased Computer Access. Although the administration was at first reluctant to expend any funds on new machines for teachers, cooler heads were soon able to see that the Writing Program could not get very far with integrating instructional technology into its curriculum if its teachers had an even harder time getting to that technology than the students.

- Now, all offices used by the Writing Program's teaching faculty are equipped with at least one computer with direct access to the web and there is a commitment from the administration to put a computer on every desk in every office. For those teachers who have been assigned a carrel rather than an office, there are ongoing discussions about acquiring laptops that would have wireless access to the web.
- Starting in Fall 1999, all newly hired full-time instructors were provided with laptops equipped with high-speed modems and ethernet cards. With the generous assistance of the dean of the Faculty of Arts and Sciences, we were able to put comparable machines in the hands of all our new hires up to 2002.

Generated Revenue for the Writing Program. When Kurt and I began to put together our own reader for the required first-year course in 1996, we gave no thought to the role that technology would play in the textbook: At that time—back in the olden days—using e-mail was a novelty, not a regular part of one's workday and surfing the web was of interest only to those who took a particular joy in watching paint dry. For years, in fact, our reader existed as a set of expensive xeroxed copies, because we were leery of the delays, the oversight, and the intrusions involved in traditional publishing.[2] Eventually, however, we were enticed by the quick turnaround time and the editorial control that custom publishing provided, so we decided to put the entire book between one set of covers and make it the required text for all new teachers entering the program in Fall 2000. We arranged to have the book priced to compete with other readers and to have the royalties from all sales at our university deposited tax free in an account the university has set up for the Writing Program. The result: We now have generated the funds necessary to send our teaching faculty to conferences, funds to increase the end-of-the-year awards for outstanding teachers, funds that can be used to bring consultants to campus, funds that, strategically allocated, have been matched by the university to acquire additional hardware and software for the program's teaching faculty.

Michael Goeller, associate director of the business and technical arm of our program, has adopted this strategy and gone a step further, creating RUWrite.com, a referral service designed to help meet the writing needs of the surrounding community. Already, RUWrite has been contacted by a local business that has offered to pay writing tutors $50 per hour to work with struggling executives. And Barclay Barrios, the program's associate director in charge of instructional technology, has created a state of the art interactive CD for students, which has generated additional revenue to support faculty development, web development, and other technological initiatives.

IMPROVED PEDAGOGY

What role does the web play in a writing program? If you had asked me this question in 1999, I would have said, "very little." Now I would say that the web has a central role to play both in the smooth running of a writing program and in the delivery of a transparent, student-centered pedagogy.

Why the change in position?

I became convinced of the web's utility not by being bullied into it or by all the arguments about the liberatory potential of disembodied encounters in cyberspace. In fact, although I realized as this project developed that we needed to create a web presence for the program, I felt the irrepressible urge to cover my ears when advisors from all sides kept telling me how easy it would be to do. Professional web designers, on the other hand, reassured me of what I wanted to hear—that building the kind of Web site I was looking for would be a big, difficult project, but one *they* could finish quickly. If they would build it, I would be able to remain blissfully ignorant about the significance of all those strange words and acronyms: ftp, HTML, javascript, jpeg, and gif. There was only one problem with this plan: Every outside vendor I contacted delivered a bid that hovered around the same figure just for starting the job: $50,000!

I unstopped my ears; I listened to the sound council of the program's instructional technology directors, past and current; and then, by chance, I ran into a friend from college who was abandoning the business world for an acting career and who agreed to slash his consulting rates to help us out. I collected folks interested in the project and we followed the lead of the director of instructional technology, who had a vision of a "student-centered, content-driven" Web site, and the consultant, who kept us focused on the end user, and suddenly we were all in the midst of a genuinely collaborative project. What I started out thinking was going to be little more than a fancy bulletin board quickly evolved into a project that has given the Writing Program a visibility it has never before had at our university: wp.rutgers.edu has attracted the attention of the vice president of the university, who wrote to praise the Web Crew for its outstanding work; it received more than 100,000 hits a month in its first year and more than 400,000 hits a month in its second year; and it was recognized as a finalist in the web design competition at the 17th annual Computers and Writing Conference.

How did this happen? We got people who were teachers first and techno-enthusiasts second (if at all) to contribute to the project. We have a crew that is contentious, opinionated, respectful, obsessed, proud, determined. And our initial goal was clear: We wanted to make available to our students everything they need to know to make their way through the Writing Program's required course. When we completed the first fully populated version of the site (to the degree that anything is ever finished on the web), we had built a Web site that continues to this day to offer practical information about: adding/dropping and contacting teachers for all of our courses; course-specific guided online tutorials with exercises on improving reading comprehension and argumentation; course-specific outlines the program's grading criteria; and sample papers with grades and comments.

THE WORK THAT REMAINS

In ticking off these accomplishments, I do not want to leave the impression that we have turned the tide at my institution and that low-wage writing instruction will soon be a thing of the past. Serious problems remain to be addressed:

- The university's growing reliance on tuition revenue has meant that entering classes continue to increase and this has meant that, after years of reducing the number of sections covered by part-time instructors in the Writing Program, we now find ourselves staffing as many sections with part timers as we did during our peak in the 1990s.
- The full-time instructor positions, although clearly superior to the part-time positions, are not permanent ones. Currently, the reward for 4 years of hard work is to be relieved of your job. State law and the union forbid rehiring or extending the contracts of full-time instructors with the result that every year we lose irreplaceable colleagues simply because they have fulfilled the terms of their contract.
- The workload for full-time instructors (currently seven courses a year) must be reduced and the salaries for full-time instructors and assistant directors in the program must continue to be increased.

These problems, which have long existed in large writing programs, are not likely to be solved by research or scholarship nor is it likely that they will be meaningfully addressed by our union.[3] Rather, I think real headway will be made in the area of wages for part-time and full-time writing instructors off the tenure track only by securing outside funding to supplement the Writing Program's budget. This is my hope, at any rate: that we'll be able to attract donors who are committed to endowing undergraduate teaching fellows and that these endowments will thereby create permanent employment outside the tenure stream for our best teachers at a competitive wage.

Sound too pie in the sky?

In Fall 1999, at the request of the university's foundation office, the Writing Program drew up a proposal seeking outside assistance to improve the salaries of tutors in our Writing Centers, which had been frozen at $9 an hour for the past 13 years! We also requested help developing an online writing lab and increased space for carrying out face-to-face tutoring. Help struggling writers, raise tutor salaries, buy some more computers: Who would find *that* attractive? It turns out that a longtime benefactor of the university and former newspaper owner, Jules Plangere, found our proposal more compelling than any of the others that he was presented with. Indeed, his $2 million endowment of our Writing Center is one of the largest donations to the Faculty of Arts and Sciences by a single donor in the history of the university.

As a pragmatist, I have no teleology to guide me in how to interpret all the changes that have taken place over the past couple of years at my institution: I don't know if all roads lead to revolution or the omega point of intercommunication or some other utopian or dystopian space or anywhere at all. I do know this, however. As a profession, we have tried critique and we have tried despair. It seems to me that, at a time when the economy has placed vast sums of money in the hands of the few and the traditional sources of funding for higher education have been all but depleted, the challenge that lies ahead for us all is to figure out ways to steal opportunity from the jaws of disaster. We might as well try.

It might just turn out that we have nothing to lose but our chains.

ENDNOTES

1. For more on the pragmatic theory of management that has evolved out of these experiences, see Miller ("From Intellectual"; "Writing Program's Assets"; 2004).
2. There isn't room here to discuss the pedagogy that resides at the center of the required course; those interested in this subject may wish to examine *The New Humanities Reader* (Miller and Spellmeyer), where Kurt and I articulate our sense of what students should read in the first year course and how they should be trained to write.
3. To learn more about the ways that the academy is being changed by the macro-economic forces of globalization, see Sheila Slaughter and Larry Leslie (1997).

REFERENCES

Lawrence, Francis. "Inaugural Address" (http://ur.rutgers.edu/medrel/viewArticle. phtml?ArticleID = 818). Accessed June 10, 2001.

Miller, Richard E. "Our Future Donors." *College English* 66 (March 2004): 365-379.

_____. "From Intellectual Wasteland to Resource-Rich Colony: Capitalizing on the Role of Writing Instruction in Higher Education." *WPA Journal.* Spring (2001): 25-40.

_____. "A Writing Program's Assets Reconsidered: Getting Beyond Impassioned Teachers and Enslaved Workers." *Pedagogy.* Spring (2001): 7-15.

_____. and Kurt Spellmeyer, eds. *The New Humanities Reader.* Boston, MA: Houghton Mifflin, 2006.

_____. RUNet 2000. (http://runet2000.rutgers.edu/faqs.html#A2). Accessed June 10, 2001.

Slaughter, Sheila and Larry Leslie. *Academic Capitalism: Politics, Policies, and the Entrepreneurial University.* Baltimore, MD: The Johns Hopkins UP, 1997.

2

COMPOSITION, OR A CASE FOR EXPERIMENTAL CRITICAL WRITING

Janet Carey Eldred
University of Kentucky

Given the tenaciousness of composition as a field,[1] it may seem surprising that someone should feel the compulsion to make a case for it. Yet that is precisely what this chapter will do, not because hegemonic English Departments devalue our subject and our labor, not because legislators and administrators argue loudly for writing "skills" at the same time that they fund a labor system that favors a piecework "delivery" of instruction, but rather because in the face of all these very real pressures, the tendency has been for us, its practitioners, to neglect composition as a genre and, most of all, as a term.[2]

Let me begin with this arguable, post-process premise: Composition as a field could benefit from identifying a *product* as well as a process. Given the time period composition came of age (again), a late 20th-century marked by postmodern thought, the compositions we produce should be hybrids, print of course, but also more forward-looking digital forms, forms rich in dialogism that recognize the disparate subgenres of writing that we, as a field, have come to value. A hybrid form that relies on juxtaposition has the possibility to reconcile—or productively explode—the tensions between those practitioners who promote personal writing and those who advance academic writing (or argument), the tensions between those who conduct field research or studies and those who critique cultures or texts.[3] A hybrid form checks the old saws—that empirical research is necessarily invalid or that postmodern research invents fact.[4] Composition as a form could even be attractively and productively used to "certify" practitioners— whether undergraduates passing a writing requirement, upper-division students concentrating in writing, graduate students earning degrees in rhetoric and composition, adjunct faculty applying to teach composition, or faculty seeking tenure. I realize that this at first might seem like an unattractive proposition. But when I think of people in the field—a number of whom experiment with various kinds of writing—it makes a great deal of sense. The "product" we now compose as scholars always resembles the work produced in some other field: cultural studies, ethnography, textual criticism, or "theory." Yet what we have to offer future scholars is the opportunity to choose methods of inquiry as well as innovative forms to present the results of such inquiry. One would write, publish, study, and teach composition and would do so by selecting and juxtaposing a few of the forms we already know—ethnography, the essay, the critical essay, historical rhetorical scholarship, reports of quantitative data, web and other multimedia productions. Our identity as scholars would be defined by composition's synthetic and associative powers. In short, the form would be— and needs to be—recognizably "ours," an ownership not so difficult to realize when one reads the history of 20th-century composition as a series of practitioners slouching toward this form.

LITERARY NONFICTION AND CREATIVE NONFICTION

"Why don't we write what we teach?" Lynn Bloom poses this important and provocative question in *Composition Studies as a Creative Art*, suggesting that literary nonfiction can provide the field with this formal identification. Literary nonfiction, to its credit, is an expansive form that encompasses, among other subgenres, the personal essay, the profile, even a certain kind of literary criticism. Yet this form, particularly when it veers into the world of creative writing, presents two complications. First, literary nonfiction already belongs to the world of small literary magazines, a world at this point only tangentially related to composition studies, a world with its own established boards and members and conferences and a workshop pedagogy, all of which privilege the aesthetic. As Doug Hesse emphasizes, "a work does not become 'literary nonfiction' because it supports, say, a psychoanalytical or any other kind of reading. Essays become literature as readers attribute to and recognize in them a certain aesthetic and way of construing individual subjectivity—that is, a particular voice and stance toward the world" (326). We can try to simulate this world, but ours will always be a pale imitation—the composition basement, the *Reader's Digest* condensed version, again. Moreover literary nonfiction seems to have an elitist Romantic penchant for individual genius that jars with the central aim of composition, that is, to teach everyone to write.[5] Literary nonfiction, as it has developed (with some notable exceptions), also eschews the political, the essay that has "something to declare."[6] (At best one might say there is a small corner of the belletristic world reserved for political declarations.)

As someone in composition who has written and published literary nonfiction, I want to press this question of genre and generic contexts further with the following prose example, which I think exhibits this tension between the aesthetic and the declaratory, in this case, narration and critical reflection.[7]

Rock, Paper, Scissors

In 1995 and 1996, we adopted two toddlers, two boys, from a Russian orphanage. Although these adoptions strike me as the most heroic and unique acts of my life, they are properly neither. We adopted our children because I am impatient and we wanted badly to be a family, and international adoption seemed—and was—the quickest and surest path. So much for "heroic." "Unique" doesn't fare much better. This year alone, if the patterns from the late '90s hold, somewhere between 15,000-20,000 of the world's "immigrant orphans" will be adopted by U.S. citizens. Over half will come from Russia and China, but many will also come from Korea, India, Romania, Guatemala, and Cambodia, and still a few more from the over 75 countries or regions (Ethiopia, the Caribbean, Sierra Leone) that the U.S. Immigration and Naturalization Service lists.

We are as rock solid a family as any that evolves through the miracle of birth—we are perhaps even stronger than some biological specimens. Yet, we are also an adoptive family in an age that boasts such a thing as "genetic counseling," in an era that can explain a whole life in the tealeaves left behind during the first formative year. In short, genetic and developmental theories press all around us. I can describe the feeling only like this: It is as if we are playing a continual game of rock-paper-scissors, that classic children's introduction to power. You know the rules; they are listed on the World RPS Society website (yes, there really is one), but I will summarize them here. On the count of three, each player simultaneously "throws" one of three options—rock, paper, or scissors. Rock smashes paper to win, paper covers rock to win, and scissors cut paper to win. No one technology, no one strategy is necessarily more powerful than the other. It's a game of relationships and odds. Most often, I open with rock, even though, according to the RPS Society, "Use of rock as an opening move is seen by many players to be a sign of aggression." Regardless, I pound my fist into my open palm. It is a bold, rock-solid statement: our family cannot be shattered.

Yea, yea, yea. Any child familiar with the game can tell you that paper covers rock.

We know this from experience. We see an article in the paper or read a news report headlining what I call the triplets—(FAS) Fetal Alcohol Syndrome or (RAD) Reactive Attachment Disorder, physiological and psychological maladies, each potentially atrocious, each linked with some frequency to Eastern European orphans—and then that flimsiest of mediums, paper, blankets our rock, obliterates our strong foundation. Suddenly, rock-solid love isn't enough; in fact, it makes us weak, vulnerable. We're blind: we can't see what may be right in front of us. Paper, those cautionary tales or horror stories that make the headlines, make every move my sons make, every simple childhood mistake seem not so simple, not so innocent after all.

Case in point:

Shura, my youngest son, went down to the railroad tracks. I dropped him off to play with Sara, his friend from school. I dropped him off, made small talk with Sara's father, pet their dogs, and drove off, leaving Shura and Sara on the swings in the small backyard, a *Good Housekeeping* picture.

Not too long passed, apparently, before they started talking about the railroad tracks and the man who lives there with a Walmart cart. Sara got excited talking, or so I learn later when Shura repeated the story: "There was a woman down there walking, alone. And this man sexed her. Then he killed her."

I don't know who it was—Sara or Shura—who suggested that they, little nine year olds, go down to the tracks, just to see the Walmart cart and what was in it. Anyway, it doesn't matter who instigated because Shura went.

He always follows.

"He's a wanderer," I tell my aunt. "I'm sure other parents in the neighborhood whisper. Kids in our neighborhood don't run wild. They have schedules, have had them since infancy. They belong to clubs."

"Not to the streets," I am thinking of adding dramatically, but my aunt interrupts.

"Isn't that sad?" she asks my uncle. "We used to go outside and play all day, come in when the streetlights went on." They grew up blocks apart in New Bedford.

I am urged on by her reminiscence. "Shura always asks permission to go in the front yard, where he promises to stay, but then a stray dog goes by and he follows it until he sees his friend Ned heading to the park, where they find two other children heading home for a snack, a good one, and there's plenty the friend says, to go around, and so they go."

And so it goes, again and again.

"Oh, your cousin Steve was like that," my aunt reassures me, with all that's unstated: our kids are adopted, genetically uncertain. Natural-born Steve turned out o.k., good job, family man after a carefree and adventurous surfer past. Hell, he married his hippie girlfriend when nobody else did. "But times have changed," she says. She sounds as if she is worried, at least a little.

Still, we are worried about different things. She frets about the general dangers of a world gone awry, about childhood freedom lost in modern times. I worry about some would-be genetic threat lurking just under the skin or about some psychic damage suffered during those "formative years" spent in a Russian orphanage. If she harbors concerns about the triplets, RAD or FAS, I appreciate that she keeps these thoughts to herself. So many people don't, and I've got my own voices. I don't want or need the volume of theirs.

Aloud as I speak to her, I am composing the kinds of things mothers say to each other over coffee, and she is granting me full maternal entitlement, but in my head, against my own will, I'm conjuring notes for a juvenile delinquent's file (*Doesn't recognize boundaries, Puts himself in high-risk situations*), a file that doesn't exist—at least not yet.

Might it someday? Two hours after I dropped Shura off at Sara's, her dad brought him home, not because of the railroad tracks but because he and Sara got in a fight with a kid who pulled a knife. Once they ran back to Sara's, someone called the police and Sara's father drove Shura home. Sara's dad says nothing, but Shura tells us about the kid with the knife, "a real knife," he says breathlessly. He recounts happily the rest of the two hours he's spent with Sara, includes offhandedly the story of the railroad track and the woman who got sexed and killed and the Walmart cart.

"The knife was scary," he says, like the rest of it wasn't, like he's talking about a ride at an amusement park. When I suggest the railroad tracks should have been scary too, he says, "Oh Mom, that's just a myth!"

Later, he remarks, just in passing, that he's told Sara he'll be back at 1:00 the next day. He lights up thinking about it. He fully expects to go, fully expects that I will take him.

He doesn't know it, but he will never go back to Sara's. That night we cut a check for a summer day camp, located four blocks from our house, with hours extending 7:30 a.m.-6:00 p.m., long after we're home from campus. During the school year, he will attend an after-school program, which runs until 6:00.

From here on out, all his days will be structured, all his actions watched, though not by us because we're not good at it. If he shits, someone will know it, just as they did when he was in the orphanage.

You see, at such moments, love is no longer enough. We are shaken, shattered. As someone who works in words, I know what to do next: I will give up on rock and choose paper as my opening move. I have court documents that make me legally the mother of my sons, that make them mine "as if," in the words of the Kentucky Revised Statutes, they were born "of my own flesh." This law has strength, power, "real teeth" as the skeptics like to say. My sons' legal documents bear the names with which we as parents branded them (it was our prerogative). Our sons' parents exist for us only as names on these or other documents. Our papers cover their fleshy, their weighty entitlements; an ocean and a language away, their biological parentage is trumped by our literal claims. Parenthood in a family likes ours derives its power from words: we are because paper makes us so. We haven't the thickness of blood, and so, cannot, should not claim that strength. Yes, yes, yes: as most writers love to assert, it's paper that matters. Paper rules. It rocks.

Until someone brings out scissors.

Like all children who have matriculated from a U.S. preschool, our sons know how to use scissors. Like most children, they have phrases that cut.

Case in point: My elder son Alyosha loves all things Russian and fantasizes incessantly about his native country. His first personal narrative (a second grade assignment) records in complex sentimental seven-year-old terms, his leaving Russia, and in classic personal narrative perspective, his adoption of me.

Leaving Russia

"Alyosha," said Tosha, some one's here to see you. I was in the toy howse that was in the sandbox. I came rite away. I saw a wrmen. I said momy! Before we left we had a prtey because they would mise me so much. I was leaving Russia. In my head I was crying because I was leaving my cutrey. I got on a truck. It took us to a hotal in Moscow. My

new mom and I played gams. On Saturday we on a tran.
It took us to the Aarport. We got on a aarplan. We went to
America. When we got home I went in to one of the room.
It was my room. I jumped in joy. I saw a fire engine bed.
It was mine! I will miss Russia, but I'm glad that Im in
America.

Weeks before writing it, he drew a picture of a long black limou-
sine-type car arriving at a palatial homestead. The caption for it reads,
"The russiens are filly hoem," which in his private seven-year-old
spelling translated to, "The Russians are finally home." He frequently
imagines such trips back—always in grand style—sometimes with me,
increasingly leaving me behind. Although he makes little effort to learn
Russian, despite some opportunities, he expects that when the time
comes, he will instantly once again recognize the language, or that language or not, Russians will simply recognize him as the long lost relation he is. This is why, when he is angry with the stupidity of his mother, he cuts through our literal definitions, denies me the only paper he
deems valuable. "You are not Russian," he pronounces, a statement
unambiguously true.

And that's the game. In choosing my strength, I must guess what
others—and what even we ourselves—will cast. I am prepared. Come
at me with the "love conquers all" or "you're so heroic" stories, and I
will cover you with paper, reminding you that love matters no more for
us that it does for any family made by the sparking of two bodies.
Furrow your brow with RAD and FAS, wave your *New York Times
Magazine* with the "Detached, Disturbed, Unreachable" headline, ask
me with that catch in your voice "Are they (pause) o.k.?" and I will
shred your research to ribbons, excoriating you for your popular, sen-
sationalized science. Pull out your scissors, try to deny me maternity,
and I will smash your efforts with a maternal love as weighty and fierce
as Toni Morrison's Sethe, a woman who would slit her child's throat
before subjecting that baby to injustice.

"This is no way to live," you say.

Perhaps not. It's just a simple game, one I should be able to quit
at any time, but there's paper all around (genetic and developmental
theories abound), so I'll go another round—and another and another.
But I won't lose. I can't lose. I will play it and live it as long as there's
a need to, which is to say, as long as the world's immigrant orphans
continue to find home on our soil and as long as we continue to harbor orphan doubts.

The response one might expect to this when it's presented as a piece of
literary nonfiction is just the one I received from a creative writing publica-

tion (a small literary magazine) whose editorial judgment I greatly admire and in whose pages I have published. One reader remarked, "I admire the essayistic quality of this." But another said: "Interesting treatment, but in my judgment the editorial agenda ends up overpowering the literary one." In the language I've been using here, the readers judged, rightly I would say, that aesthetic concerns are trumped by declaration, and thus that the piece isn't suitable for inclusion in a small literary magazine. This leaves me with a choice: Revision is always possible, but can I—should I—excise my declaration to make a more satisfying literary piece? As a writer who is also an adoptive mother and an academic, would I want the literary to trump the editorial? What would it mean for my children if I did? Were I to make such revisions, what will I have sacrificed for art, or rather, for genre?

I would argue that "Rock, Paper, Scissors" falls short as a piece of literary nonfiction, but stands as an example of a kind of essay recognizable in the field of composition. Finally, creative writing as a collective publishing venue seems very hesitant, almost nervously unable, to embrace a great deal of the inquiry that our field values. Composition studies *does* have a literary, stylistic component, one I wish had a greater presence,[8] but the field's academic roots are varied. The field emerged, or more accurately, it began to flourish in the late 20th-century as a confluence of different disciplines—education, communication, rhetoric, creative writing, literary analysis—all of which share intellectual interests in how people learn and express themselves, but do so through different kinds of written products, among them case studies, high theoretical arguments, and empirical studies—all genres pretty much at odds with a belletristic, essayistic truth.

And yet we crave the personal *and* the aesthetic, the intimate, well-crafted narratives that literary nonfiction and personal essays can provide. We in the academy pay an aesthetic and emotional price for our scholarly distance. Yes, I could (and want to) write about issues that orphans have in composing identities using postmodern theories borrowed from the study of diasporic literatures, but must this necessarily entail masking the central experience behind my inquiry? And must these lines of inquiry be argued separately, published separately in some sort of institutionally reinscribed mind/body split? In order to write for a composition and rhetoric audience, must I remain hidden behind some Oz-like curtain? Can't the "I" (or some other breathing persona or character) emerge?

Creative nonfiction is so attractive at the beginning of the twenty-first century because it allows the personal voice to surface; it has the potential to blend two distinct, institutionalized traditions—journalism and creative writing (including memoir). It's a hybrid—bringing together investigative research with narrative, either first or third person. It seems to solve our genre woes. But there's a problem with adopting creative nonfiction broadly for composition studies' purposes. The academy, except insofar as it houses journalism and creative writing, again doesn't really figure in. The turf wars over ownership of this genre are only beginning (creative writing seems to be ahead). Despite successful forays into creative nonfiction publication venues, composition instructors with a bent toward the belletristic have slim chance of claiming the form, cultural theorists slimmer still, and qualitative researchers slimmest of all, though in theory, all have equal access. In short, creative nonfiction seems to be pushing further and further away from a form with a great deal of potential for the academy: experimental critical writing.

COMPOSITION

We need in the academy more room for *compositions*, those that, as Candace Spigelman describes, either expand creative nonfiction and literary nonfiction to include the academic or, at the very least, open the academic to the powerful examples of lived experience. Such forms blend the richness of our traditions—the narrative essay (first person *and* third), as well as research (whether investigative, critical, qualitative, or quantitative). They adapt the voices of these distinct traditions so that a self-consciously literary voice, or a reporting or declaring voice, or even a confessional, "Romantic" voice finds itself dialogically situated alongside an academic critical voice, a voice that acknowledges and investigates, to borrow my colleague Peter Mortensen's words, "the cultural and narrative forces" that comprise and create it. Where better for such hybrid forms to flourish than in a discipline named *composition*? We've been tempted to look elsewhere, perhaps because of professional insecurity, perhaps because interdisciplinary research has yielded results—good results—in the past (and our rediscovery of journalism and creative writing has proven no different). Yet it now seems the time to look straight ahead of us, even behind us. The answer is before us, it defines us. While literary nonfiction and creative nonfiction have already been adopted by the creative and commercial writing worlds, this hybrid, which the term "composition" expresses, is already recognizably ours, to be placed on our generic shelf right next to the essay, which as Paul Heilker persuasively argues, also rightfully has a place.[9] Compositions (I will avoid the redundancy of using "hybrid" as an adjective) allow us to do the work we in composition studies have always done, although traditionally we have done so in separate pieces in separate publications. Several composition scholars write personal essays—Chris Anderson, Anne Gere, who writes collaboratively with her daughter, Cynthia Gere, Lynn Bloom, Elizabeth Hodges, Min-Zhan Lu, Nancy Sommers, to name just a few—more are perhaps beginning to, but their essays aren't visible to their composition colleagues. They're seen now as extracurricular, a part of the small literary magazine world. And when scholars have written hybrid books (for example, Brenda Brueggemann's *Lend Me Your Ear,* or Keith Gilyard's *Voices of the Self,* or Victor Villanueva's *Bootstraps),* the work is described as "unusual"; its presence is unexpected, its case anomalous.[10] The question is, why? To echo Lynn Bloom again, why don't we write what we teach? Why aren't we more accustomed to reading essays and compositions by teachers and scholars in our professional publications? One could blame the editors of books and journals in the field, but as Bloom notes, "we have met the editors and they are us." We have also, of course, met the peer reviewers, and we have a consistently steady stream of representatives from publishing houses who want to meet with us. We have significant publishing venues (scholarly journals and books, a large—by academic standards—textbook market). And while we currently don't see a great number of pieces by those who teach and study composition, a few are beginning to filter through. One might argue that a journal like *College English* can't accommodate "creative writing." For years, though, it did publish poetry; in retrospect, a section on essays would probably have been as appropriate, if not more so.[11] If we're willing to borrow an essay to include in a reader, say an excerpt from Michael Dorris's *The Broken Cord,* shouldn't we at least be willing to consider Anne and Cynthia Gere's essays on the same topic (Native American children and fetal alcohol syndrome)? We might expect that Gere's perspective would more closely reflect the experience of a life spent teaching composition and, thus, be equally if not more appropriate for a writing classroom. Even if no overt references are made to the teaching of writing (and for now its seems, editors insist on such an overt connection), I would argue that issues that converge on writing instruction surely inform the piece, issues such as how selves are figured by the media, and how individuals who experience the failures of words might create in other art forms to compose different representations. Of course, the inclusion in our journals of something resembling literary nonfiction might beg the disciplinary question, Is it good? After all, if composition teachers are good creative writers, why aren't they publishing elsewhere, where reviewers presumably know quality when they see it? But this, as I've tried to express through my word choice, is odd criteria to apply. It's like asking a journalist to peer review a piece for the *New England Journal of Medicine.* We have a peer review system to determine quality, and we have different standards of what is good *for our rhetorical purposes.*[12] An essay that declares or theorizes or reports data might not find a home in a creative writing journal, but it doesn't necessarily follow that the piece should not be published for readers of composition.

This is not to say that we should see only belletristic essays in our professional journals, although it is possible to imagine such a subsection, just as we've come to expect book reviews and editorial introductions (even cartoon sketches in *Written Communication*!), although none of these forms "typify" these publications. Likewise, other more singular forms of writing—textual analysis, cultural analysis, qualitative studies, the synthesis of scholarship—are specialized, valuable subcategories in composition publications, electronic and print. In fact, I'm arguing quite the reverse: While I am arguing for more space for essays in our professional publications, I am not ready to see the essay, particularly the personal essay, become the composition genre de jour, the current house specialty. Personal essays, whether directly about teaching writing or about issues related to it, can only go so far in advancing our knowledge as professionals and practitioners,[13] only so far in capitalizing on the broad power of composition. Academic inquiry—its methods, its processes, even its much maligned specialized jargon—contributes to our understanding through logics that the personal essay does not deploy. And journalism, at its factual and ethical best, accounts for events happening now and of interest to people now, in this moment. Again, the other forms I am imagining and arguing for and beginning to practice are hybrids that work by juxtaposing the variety of methods we currently recognize, including the "personal" essay.[14]

These issues, of course, relate most directly to our roles as writers and scholars. Teaching the form poses a different set of problems. At its most respected, composition is a monster much looser and baggier than even Henry James could imagine. Patricia Bizzell underscores the challenge when talking about hybrid academic discourse, a form in which students would cite "texts and engage them rigorously, but . . . also talk about their own experiences in ways that feel right to them" ("Hybrid" 19). "In all this," Bizzell explains, "the goal is to help students develop a range of experimental discourses. I don't think we should encourage them to think that each one has a unique, 'authentic voice' sort of hybrid discourse that he or she must discover. Rather, I am encouraging a sort of craft-person attitude toward writing, in which various tools are developed and students learn to deploy them with greater facility" ("Hybrid" 20). Composition in its fullest sense expands this range by adding to personal and textual analysis all our current research methodologies, as well as those provided by journalism. It would take all the collective wisdom of the last half-century to teach composition. But luckily, we have that collective wisdom in our collections of good textbooks, many of which are now out of print. We'd have to cover the *processes* and the *elements* and the *ethics* of narrative[15] (first and third person), academic writing, classical argument, literary writing (particularly style), research, journalism, especially fact collecting and checking, skills that now receive little classroom attention. And since we couldn't possibly do it all at once, we'd have to decide where to start, what kind of assignments we could devise that would move students along the path of producing essays that are academic, in the best critical sense; public, in the sense of investigating, reporting, or declaring; and personal. Of this trio of terms, the much maligned *personal* still needs the most elaboration. To borrow from Phillip Lopate's "Introduction" to *the Art of the Personal Essay,* the traditional personal essay is "approachable and diverting," "intimate," "implicitly democratic . . . in the value it places on experience rather than status distinctions." It is, above all, a literary form that recognizes the "multiplicity of selves" (xxiii). Thus when I employ the word personal here, I'm not talking about pure expression of the sort one might find in a diary, even the most literary of diaries. Instead, personal here entails what James Kinneavy in *A Theory of Discourse* refers to as "expressive," the focus on how a self gets constructed, a focus which can be extended to include how selves get represented (e.g., Mike Rose's *Lives on the Boundary*). What Min-Zhan Lu and Bruce Horner call "the problematic of experience" thus becomes the focus of expressive writing: "what [experience] is, who represents it to whom to what ends, in what manner, and whether and how such representations change that experience" (258). Biographies and ethnographies, in this sense, are deeply personal forms and provide an option for those "who do not wish to represent/live the personal in [their] work" ("Politics of the Personal," 42).[16]

The range of the personal voice also needs elaboration. Both first-person and third-person narrative forms have the potential to be essayistic when marked by the characteristics Lopate and others identify.[17] Yet the personal voice in an essay also has the capability of being critical. As Bakhtin argues, it's this incredible breadth of voice that once attended to exposes the conceptual limitations of individual, atomized selves. It's this potential that is often untapped in the modern essay tradition, which has lapsed into learned irony/skepticism or plain folksiness. Rather than adopting the "ideal of 'light learning'" in the academy, a stance, which according to Lopate, "graciously informs without humiliating or playing the pedantic schoolmaster" (xlii), our hybrid composition can and should embrace learnedness, rejecting the idea that to do so necessarily results in monstrous prose or pedantry. (Indeed, isn't the leisured essayist who need only allude to certain texts to establish his "cultivation," his "well-stocked, liberally-educated mind" [xli-ii], a pedant, a modern dilettante?) Compositions at their best should both embrace higher literacy's promises and exhibit a healthy skepticism of its excessive claims. They should work by yoking fragmented and alienated histories, by fusing together—or juxtaposing—different kinds of writing that we've been schooled and professionalized into keeping separate.

One more clarification is crucial given our pedagogical history. Compositions as I have imagined and sketched the genre would not be merely about moving students along Britton's personal to research trajectory, a curricular model still followed at many colleges. Nor would it be about getting the personal into academic writing (which thanks in large part to feminist scholarship is becoming more acceptable), though that's part of it. It would also be about something perhaps even more difficult— *getting the academic into the personal*, or more accurately, *setting the academic alongside the personal*, creating what Victor Villanueva refers to as "the autobiographical as critique" ("The Politics of the Personal," 51).[18] Artists and professional writers have a deep distrust of academics, a distrust which some in the field of composition studies share. It's not unusual to hear, even in academic writing circles, complaints about "the academic voice" and celebrations of creative nonfiction's return to the "personal voice." Such comments should give us pause. Making room for first-person narrative in our profession and our classrooms is one thing; compelling it in these spaces is quite another. It would lead to the irony Deborah Brandt imagines: "Not too long ago, it was only the institutionally secure who got to write about themselves. Now, it seems, it is only the institutionally secure who do not have to" (58). We are not yet in that situation, nor are we in the situation where the personal is forbidden. Rather, we seem cornered into choices we don't want to make: those wanting to write personal narratives find themselves constrained by the academic, those wanting the academic form feel compelled to reveal personal details. But again, the concept of composition proves the door, the exit that we didn't imagine existed. We don't have to choose between these voices and forms, these ways of knowing, unless we, as a field, continue to shift from one monologic extreme to the other, continue to deny our roots in composition.[19] While it's tempting to either knock down one side or simply erase the division by talking about how the personal can do the work of the academic or vice-versa, it's necessary to sustain the integrity of both genres, something composition as a form can do. As Lu and Horner remind us, there's more than luxury at stake: "we *need* . . . to sustain the tension between experience and discursive understanding" (emphasis added). Not to do so, they argue, "leads to the danger of one discourse speaking in the name of experience against other discourse" (259). It leads, in other words, to the rickety straw figures we know so well by now—the expressivist, the social constructionist. By this point in our field's history, it doesn't require even a feather to knock either down.

From the lofty and millennial distance of 2005, I'm surprised we ever insisted on keeping all our discourses separate. But we have. Or at least I have. And I've learned from the process of separating genres and fusing them. Finally, I'd like to make this immodest proposal: Compositions that blend or fuse the academic with the "personal" (whether construction/representation of self or others), compositions that we might call "experimental critical writing," hold enormous promise to us as individual writers and as a field. They are difficult now to publish because they're deemed "too academic" or "too journalistic" or too "editorial" for small literary magazines that cast a cultivated eye askance at all things academic and pedantic,[20] and frequently, they are judged irrelevant or "too personal" for our academic journals.

All are judgments we can change and are changing, at least in the professional publications now in our collective hands. It seems like a good time to make changes. Outside the academy, nonfiction and memoir are gaining respect again, even market share. Change might be as easy as easing an essay section or a review of nonfiction into our journals. Perhaps it might entail more ambitious projects: we might encourage graduate students to write dissertations that are themselves compositions juxtaposing various genres. We might challenge ourselves and our students to write hybrid dialogic compositions in addition to academic articles or personal essays. We might publish our own *Best Compositions*, much like *Best American Essays* or the *Anchor Essay Annual* series. Our annual volume could come complete with an introduction that comments on the form, and a "Notable Essays" section that includes citations to essays published in small literary magazines as well as more academic publications. We probably, too, should change our indexing practices to allow essays variously placed to be located through traditional search means. With such a change, more of the work that appears in our journals would also be appropriate for the classroom—first year to graduate.

The prospect of such a profound genre shift in the field of composition is daunting, in Spigelman's words, "challenging and risky" (57). Reclaiming a name and an idea we've tried to run from is going to be difficult, but I for one feel compelled to try. I don't know where this allegiance to composition *as a genre* will end up taking me or, practically speaking, what advice I'll end up giving students in my writing classes, but I'm convinced that after undertaking such an inquiry, I'll know more about composition. I will likely emphasize even more the importance of balancing aesthetic concerns with ethical ones. I will likely urge students to pit personal memory against historical memory or community memory—to test memory against different kinds of stylistic representation. Composition as a form thus described, one pleasing to both aesthetic and intellectual sensibilities, might be impossible to achieve (is it possible to satisfy such two different masters?), but the effort—and the possibilities—seem worth it.

ENDNOTES

1. Its history in the United States, at least, is long and rich. We know from the historical research of James Berlin, Robert Connors, Nan Johnson, Tom Miller and Joseph Jones, and Charles Paine that composition as a subject, if not a discipline, has existed for some time. In looking at manuscripts from the antebellum period, Peter Mortensen and I found that authors used the very phrase "composition and rhetoric," alongside other subjects like "chemistry" or "natural history," as a heading for lessons (see *Imagining Rhetoric*). Now, at the beginning of the 21st century, PhD programs in rhetoric and composition are well established, perhaps even flourishing, with PhDs in the field securing that most elusive of things in English Studies, tenure. It is perhaps telling that "advanced composition" as an undergraduate course of studies remains somewhat scarce. While some colleges and universities offer such a course of study, many do not. And where "advanced composition" is offered, the focus of such programs varies widely: rhetoric, technical writing (belletristic), essay writing, editing, journalism, creative nonfiction, and pedagogy all fall under this broad umbrella. PhD programs in composition and rhetoric similarly each have a diverse "brand," yet they seem almost homogeneous in relief to undergraduate programs.
2. Rhetoric, on the other hand, has deservedly flourished as a term and as an object of inquiry. It's unclear whether the revival of rhetoric has to do with appeals to its classical origins, its long-standing ties to democracy, its claims for conflict resolution, or its affinities to philosophy and cultural studies. No matter: it's happily made a comeback.
3. Emerging scholarship addresses attempts to integrate rather than separate these modes. See Bizzell, Eldred, Hindman, Kameen; Kamler; Kirklighter; McComiskey; Schroeder, Fox, and Bizzell; Spigelman; and Welch.
4. See Spellmeyer.
5. I'm borrowing, of course, from Elbow's title. Chris Green explores (and challenges) creative writing pedagogy in his "Materializing the Sublime Reader: Cultural Studies, Reader-Response, and Community Service in the Creative Writing Workshop." Green begins with his experience as a reader of manu

scripts by death row inmates. "The poems were not models of good writing: cliché after cliché pummeled the reader, couplets brashly rhymed, and abstraction after ineffective abstraction was marched out. . . . While we did not accept any of the poems [for publication in a literary magazine], reading them led me to ask how my students might write poems that matter as much. Given the pedagogical configuration of the workshop as I then ran it, I realized that for the most part, I could only help students write poems that looked good in the workshop" (153-54).

6. I am borrowing (and extending) an idea from Julia Alvarez's collection of essays, *Something to Declare*. Publications that invite such "declaring" essays are on the fringes of the creative writing world, which still sees art and politics at odd. Alvarez, for example, could publish her "declaring essays" only after making it as a successful novelist. She earned the right to declare, one might say. Composition studies, on the other hand, is increasingly embracing political engagement. See for example Peter Mortensen's "Going Public," which urges composition scholars and students to write locally about public issues. One might argue that "going public" is the scholarly equivalent to undergraduate service learning.

7. I've presented it here in its print form, although I've also attempted it in web media.

8. I share this value with scholars such as Bishop; Bloom; Elbow; Hesse; Malinowitz; and T. R. Johnson.

9. Specifically Heilker argues that we need to make the essay "an alternative, supplementary form in composition instruction" (xx).

10. Spigelman's work suggests that this perception is changing, at least when scholars employ the expressive in service of academic discourse.

11. Inclusion of essays isn't without precedent. Under Louise Smith, for example, Nancy Sommers published "The Language of Coats," an essay that juxtaposes the experiences of her father's work in the coat industry with her own work as a teacher of writing. Tellingly, this essay was published as an "Editor's Choice" item. Still earlier, in 1993, she published "I Stand Here Writing" in *College English*. Both essays *directly* connect personal experiences with the teaching of writing. Brenda Jo Brueggemann's "On (Almost) Passing," published in the October 1997 of *College English* ably connects issues in the field with her own lived experience.

12. See, for example, Spigelman's criteria (22, 34).

13. Gesa Kirsch and Joy Ritchie, "Beyond the personal." See also the symposium collective, "The Politics of the Personal: Storying Our Lives against the Grain," *College English*. (Contributing authors are Deborah Brant, Ellen Cushman, Anne Gere, Anne Herrington, Richard E. Miller, Victor Villanueva, Min-Zhan Lu, and Gesa Kirsh.)

14. I've used the scare quotations here to foreshadow my argument that the personal essay might best be thought of as a "narrative of lived experience" because it frequently involves representations of others as much as of self.

15. See Lu and Horner; Mortensen and Kirsch.
16. See also Ellen Cushman's contribution to "The Politics of the Personal" symposium: "When a researcher's personal life becomes the object of intense scrutiny, s/he becomes the butterfly that has been exoticized and chased after" (45).
17. See Phillip Lopate's introduction to *The Art of the Personal Essay*, which covers elements such as confession, constructions of self, irony, and egotism. *What Do I Know? Reading, Writing, and Teaching the Essay*, edited by Janis Forman, collects essays by Donald McQuade, Carl Klaus, Richard Marius and others, ranging from topics of the essay's disjunctive form to the its literary status. See also Forché and Gerard, *Writing Creative Nonfiction*.
18. See also his contribution to the edited volume *Personal Effects* (Holdstein and Bleich). Spigelman describes this as "superimposing an academic content" (xvii, 91-95)
19. It leads, in other words, to one school of composition pedagogy claiming as entirely theirs something that they cannot own (Lu and Horner, 259). Finally, there can be no disciplinary ownership of "experience."
20. Even were these pieces to be published, they probably wouldn't be seen by others in the field, unless we create new indexing methods that make them so.

REFERENCES

Alvarez, Julia. *Something to Declare*. New York: Penguin, 1998.

Anderson, Chris. *Edge Effects: Notes from an Oregon Forest*. Iowa City: U of Iowa, 1993.

Berlin, James A. *Rhetoric and Reality: Writing Instruction in American Colleges, 1900-1985*. Carbondale: Southern Illinois UP, 1987.

Bishop, Wendy. "Suddenly Sexy" *College English* 65 (2003): 257-75.

_____ *Teaching Lives: Essays and Stories*. Logan: Utah State UP, 1997.

Bizzell, Patrica. "Basic Writing and the Issue of Correctness; or, What To Do with 'Mixed' Forms of Academic Discourse." *Journal of Basic Writing*. 19.1 (2000): 4-12.

_____ "Hybrid Academic Discourses: What, Why, How." *Composition Studies (Freshman English News)*. 27.2 (1999): 7-21.

Bloom, Lynn Z. *Composition Studies as a Creative Art*. Logan: Utah State UP, 1998.

Brueggemann, Brenda Jo. *Lend Me Your Ear: Rhetorical Constructions of Deafness*. Washington: Gallaudet UP, 1999.

_____ "On (Almost) Passing." *College English* 59.6 (1997): 647-60.

Connors, Robert J. *Composition-Rhetoric: Backgrounds, Theory, and Pedagogy*. Pittsburgh: U of Pittsburgh P, 1997.

Dorris, Michael. *Broken Cord*. New York: Harper Perennial, 1990.

Elbow, Peter. *Everyone Can Write: Essays Toward a Hopeful Theory of Writing and Teaching Writing.* New York: Oxford, 2000.

Eldred, Janet Carey. *Sentimental Attachments: Essays, Creative Nonfiction, and Other Experiments in Composition.* Portsmouth: Heinemann/Boynton Cook, 2005.

Eldred, Janet Carey and Peter Mortensen. *Imagining Rhetoric: Composing Women of the Early United States.* Pittsburgh: U of Pittsburgh P, 2002.

Forché, Carolyn and Philip Gerard. *Writing Creative Nonfiction.* Cincinnati: Story P, 2001.

Forman, Janis, ed. *What Do I know? Reading, Writing, and Teaching the Essay.* Portsmouth: Boynton/Cook, 1996.

Gere, Anne Ruggles (with Cynthia Margaret Gere). "Living with Fetal Alcohol Syndrome/Fetal Alcohol Effect (FAS/FAE)." *Michigan Quarterly Review* 37.3 (1998): 129-49. www.umich.edu/~mqr

Gilyard, Keith. *Voices of the Self: A Study of Language Competence.* Detroit: Wayne State UP, 1991.

Green, Chris. "Materializing the Sublime Reader." *College English* 64.2 (2001): 153-74.

Heilker, Paul. *The Essay: Theory and Pedagogy for an Active Form.* Urbana, IL: NCTE, 1996.

Hesse, Doug. "The Recent Rise of Literary Nonfiction: A Cautionary Assay." *Journal of Advanced Composition* 11.2 (1991): 323-33.

Hindman, Jane E. "Special Focus: Personal Writing." *College English* 64.1 (2001): 34-40.

Hodges, Elizabeth. *What the River Means.* Emerging Writers in Creative Nonfiction Series. Pittsburgh: Duquesne UP, 1998.

Holdstein, Deborah H. and David Bleich, ed. *Personal Effects: The Social Character of Scholarly Writing.* Logan: Utah State UP, 2001.

Johnson, Nan. *Nineteenth-Century Rhetoric in North America.* Carbondale: Southern Illinois UP, 1991.

Johnson, T. R.. *A Rhetoric of Pleasure: Prose Style and Today's Composition Classroom.* Cross Currents: New Perspectives in Rhetoric and Composition. Portsmouth: Boynton/Cook, 2003.

Kameen, Paul. "Re-covering Self in Composition." *College English* 62 (1999): 100–11.

Kamler, Barbara. *Relocating the Personal: A Critical Writing Pedagogy.* Albany: State U of New York P, 2001.

Kinneavy, James. *A Theory of Discourse.* Englewood Cliffs, N.J.: Prentice-Hall, 1977.

Kirklighter, Cristina. *Traversing the Democratic Borders of the Essay.* Albany: State U of New York P, 2002.

Kirsch, Gesa and Joy Ritchie. "Beyond the Personal." *CCC* 46 (1995): 7-29.

Lopate, Phillip. Introduction to *The Art of the Personal Essay.* New York: Anchor, Doubleday, 1995.

Lu, Min-Zhan. *Shanghai Quartet.* Emerging Writers in Creative Nonfiction Series. Pittsburgh: Duquesne, 2001.

Lu, Min-Zhan and Bruce Horner. "The Problematic of Experience: Redefining Critical Work in Ethnography and Pedagogy." *College English* 60.3 (1998): 257-77.

Malinowitz, Harriet. "Business, Pleasure, and the Personal Essay." *College English.* 65.3 (2003): 305-22

McComiskey, Bruce. Review of *Literacy Matters: Writing and Reading the Social Self,* by Robert P. Yagelski. *College Composition and Communication* 53.4 (2002): 751–54.

Miller, Thomas P. and Joseph G. Jones. "Working Out Our History." *College English.* 67.4 (2005): 421-39.

Mortensen, Peter. "Going Public." *College Composition and Communication.* 50.2 (1998): 182-205.

Mortensen, Peter and Gesa E. Kirsch, eds. *Ethics and Representation in Qualitative Studies of Literacy.* Urbana, IL: NCTE, 1996.

Paine, Charles. *The Resistant Writer: Rhetoric as Immunity, 1850 to the Present.* Albany: State U of New York P, 1999.

Rose, Mike. *Lives on the Boundary.* New York: Simon and Schuster, 1989.

"The Politics of the Personal: Storying Our Lives against the Grain." *College English.* 64.1 (2001): 41-62.

Schroeder, Christopher, Helen Fox, and Patricia Bizzell, eds. *Alt Dis: Alternative Discourses and the Academy.* Portsmouth, NH: Boynton/Cook, 2003.

Sommers, Nancy. "Between the Drafts." *College Composition and Communication* 43 (1992): 23-31.

_____ "I Stand Here Ironing." *College English* 55.3 (1993): 420-28.

_____ "The Language of Coats." *College English* 60.4 (1998): 421-25.

Spigelman, Candace. *Personally Speaking: Experience as Evidence in Academic Discourse.* Carbondale: Southern Illinois UP, 2004.

Villanueva, Victor. *Boostraps: From an American Academic of Color.* Urbana, IL: NCTE, 1993.

Welch, Nancy. "Managed Care: An Essay about Irony, Illness, and Teaching." *Genre by Example: Writing What We Teach.* Ed. David Starkey. Portsmouth, NH: Heinemann/Boynton Cook, 2001. 3-17.

3

TECHNOLOGICAL LABOR AND TENURE DECISIONS

MAKING A VIRTUAL CASE VIA ELECTRONIC PORTFOLIOS

Kristine L. Blair

Bowling Green State University

Because technological literacy is so much a part of teacher and student professional development, and because of the changing student populations and student needs that call for distance or distributed teaching and learning forums, it is clear that technology plays a large role in the assessment of student learning outcomes and the demonstration of teaching effectiveness. Thus, technological literacy and technology in teaching need to be common topics in the general assessment of candidates for tenure and promotion. Despite the significant impact of technology on the professoriate at forums such as the American Association of Higher Education's 2001 Conference on Faculty Roles and Rewards, the manner in which candidates continue to be assessed for tenure and promotion focuses on activities and genres that are more traditionally researched based, and print-researched based at that. Indeed, a continuing problem at many institutions is that tenure, promotion, and merit documents continue to privilege print-based scholarship or do not acknowledge the impact of technology on teaching. Yet, in their article "Implementing the Seven Principles: Technology as Lever," Arthur Chickering and Stephen Ehrmann make the case for technology to foster equally effective pedagogies by applying Chickering and Gamson's original principles for good practice in undergraduate education to the use of technology in the classroom. Among those principles are the following: Good practice, they say, encourages contact between students and faculty; develops reciprocity and cooperation among students; uses active learning techniques; gives prompt feedback; and relates learning styles in ways that maintain curricular standards. In their overview of the advances in educational technologies that help to foster some of these goals—including synchronous and asynchronous discussion networks—Chickering and Ehrmann pose the question, "How are we to know whether given technologies are as useful in promoting the Seven Principles and learning?" Such a question, focused as it is on the role of technology, can encourage faculty to analyze and evaluate the relative effectiveness of their instructional strategies through gauging student-learning outcomes in technological settings (whether it be cooperative learning, service learning, problem-based learning, or more lecture -and presentation-based modes of content delivery). Thus, in order to document indicators of teaching effectiveness, many U.S. universities have opted for the teaching portfolio, a collection of multigenred documents that reflect teacher professional development and quality of teaching and learning (Seldin). Although there are clear benefits to any sort of portfolio-based approach, it seems ironic that as we recognize that student work can be created, delivered, and assessed electronically, and often through an electronic portfolio approach, faculty work—even when technological in nature—is all too frequently reviewed in a print forum and not an electronic one.

Despite this continuing problem, this chapter profiles a range of university-wide training and other faculty development programs implemented at Bowling Green State University (BGSU) that support an initiative for electronic teaching portfolios as professional development tools. For Lieberman and Rueter the advantages of electronic portfolios include more technological work being viewed in its original medium, more types of information being displayed, more immediate access and distribution (via the web and CD-ROM), and more visual and audio documentation appealing to diverse reading and learning styles, as opposed to strictly textual evidence. Regardless of these possible benefits, it is clear that institutional education about the potential impact of technology on teaching in general and of electronic portfolios in particularly, is increasingly necessary to the successful recruitment and retention of digital scholar-teachers. Thus, in addition to training and professional development initiatives, this chapter also outlines both candidate and administrative responsibilities in educating peers and reviewers about the role of technology in tenure and promotion. Ultimately, such efforts are a way of providing incentive, support, and reward systems that encourage faculty to utilize technology in ways that genuinely enhance their teaching and overall professional development.

E-PORTFOLIOS: POSSIBILITIES AND CONSTRAINTS

Admittedly, the labor of creating and "reading" a portfolio, particularly an electronic one, creates a range of design and delivery dilemmas. Although technological problems may include the need to provide portfolio readers with appropriate hardware or software to access information on disk, CD, or the web, there is also need to de-emphasize the "bells and whistles" of the portfolio to instead using the opportunity for an electronic-based format to support the same learning outcomes and curricular contexts as its print-based counterpart. Because faculty materials for tenure and promotion are reviewed by committees at all levels, the labor of this review process conforms to normal processes for academic work: Committees sit at tables, review materials, and make judgments. Although such tasks are themselves considered labor-intensive, the concept that a committee member might actually sit at his or her computer, type in a URL or insert a CD-ROM of electronic materials is erroneously considered more laborious, making it harder for the committee to review a candidate's work and perhaps subject that work to backlash. Moreover, because it is important that the candidate's work be evaluated in the medium in which it was produced, it is equally important to solicit internal and external reviewers qualified and prepared to review nontraditional sources of evidence, including Web sites, discussion boards, CD-ROMS, and instructional software. Here, it is important to consider the lessened impact of reviewing a faculty member's online syllabi as "hard copy" in a portfolio, with departmental and college-level review committees unable or unwilling to review materials online and admittedly ill-equipped to do so because of a lack of "local" criteria for evaluating the effectiveness of technological learning spaces.

And although Chickering and Ehrmann, as well as scholars such as Lawrence Ragan, acknowledge that "good teaching is good teaching," whether it be face to face or technologically mediated, there are some distinctions between how such effectiveness may manifest itself between one environment and another. For instance, Dave Madden's online discussion of the "17 Elements of Good Online Courses" notes a range of indicators for effectiveness, including navigability, usability, and instructional considerations ("material should be presented in such a way that it is compatible with a number of learning styles," "students should be able to readily and easily communicate with the instructor online," and "special attention should be given to testing design and procedures" online). Moreover, in "The Electronically Augmented Teaching Portfolio," Lieberman and Rueter contend that technology offers several options for enhancing the tradition-al print-based portfolio, including the ability to "capture information about our teaching that previously was not part of our teaching frame of refer-ence" and allowing "efficient means for storing and critiquing the portfo-lio" itself (47). Ultimately, the limitations of hard copy portfolios include their failure to give a full view of not only the way in which classroom man-agement and assessment strategies manifest themselves electronically but also the sheer technological skill and labor that enables online teaching effectiveness.

Regardless of the archival advantages of an electronic portfolio, tenure and promotion candidates still face difficulties in educating peers and administrators about the impact of technology on teaching, particularly in relation to academic workload. Often, those who are designated as "early adopters" of both face-to-face and online educational technologies are tapped as administrative resources as well. Such individuals are frequently called on to serve on committees and to assist in departmental and univer-sity-wide faculty development initiatives that are certainly rewarding, although not always "rewarded" at tenure and promotion time, given tradi-tional weightings at many universities that privilege research over teaching and especially over service. A notable instance of this occurs in Carrie Leverenz's narrative about her denial of tenure at Florida State University; despite departmental recognition of her work in computer-mediated writ-ing program administration and in dissertation supervision in this area as meritorious, her case was unsuccessful at college and provost level, in part because of Florida State's desire to maintain the standards of its recent Carnegie I status, standards that fall within a traditional print-based para-digm of scholarship.

Such a case suggests that although faculty should be informed about whether and how work with technology and online teaching/scholarship will be considered in the tenure and promotion process, those faculty who engage in virtual and electronic teaching must continue to educate mem-bers of tenure and promotion committees, chairs, and deans about candi-dates' technological work and help departmental and university-level administrators understand that within this context, intellectual rigor may manifest itself in ways that transcend the traditional definitions of teach-ing, research, and service. Because of the limitations of internal committee processes for evaluating technology-based teaching, scholarship, and serv-ice, the Conference on College Composition and Communication (CCCC), in addition to its 1999 guidelines for work with technology, has also devel-oped a website that provides useful case studies of five fictitious candi-dates, with commentary from chairs of personnel committees, department chairs, and deans. Although in a number of cases, significant electronic teaching and scholarly materials were developed, there is little mention of an electronic portfolio as an option for evaluation; in fact, the anonymous commentary from these departmental and university administrators reveal that there continues to be little to go on how to evaluate technological work, regardless of whether it is delivered in a print or electronic format:

> when the Department decided to hire a faculty member who was conducting research on a topic and in a mode never encountered before, the Department, through the chair, had an obligation to define how this research would be evaluated for tenure, preferably through articulating these expectations in tenure and promotion requirements. Likewise, the faculty member who is doing non-traditional work cannot expect that a department in which he or she is breaking ground to accept this work without question. New faculty members are obligated to present in their review portfolio the rationale for their publication choices, relating this rationale to articulated departmental standards. (online)

As this site and the above comment indicates, the responsibility for contextualizing technological labor within the triad of teaching, scholarship, and service rests jointly on the committee and the candidate (CCCC). Similarly, the Modern Language Association (MLA) guidelines for the evaluation of digital teaching and scholarship state the following:

> Faculty members who work with digital media should be prepared to make explicit the results, theoretical underpinnings, and intellectual rigor of their work. They should be prepared, to the same extent that faculty members in other field are held accountable, to show the relevance of their work in terms of the traditional areas of teaching, research, and service. (online)

Although the CCCC site makes it clear that we have a long way to go in creating an amenable climate for electronic portfolios, support of hybrid options that would allow qualified external reviews to comment on actual syllawebs, online articles, and technical expertise would inevitably help to contextualize the impact of technology on preconceived notions of academic labor. As the following comment from one of the case studies contends:

> External review can be very helpful for committees reviewing candidates whose specialties they don't know or understand. The senior composition/computers faculty at other institutions who end up

> reviewing such cases are usually sensitive to issues that Spencer faced.
> . . . With luck they would also be candid about his publications and
> where they stand in the computers 'n' writing firmament, would give
> Spencer's work considerable credibility, not only by praise and evalua-
> tion but most importantly by placing it in context. (online)

Certainly, the series of quotes above may raise concerns among some academics that work in technology must somehow be made to fit existing
guidelines. Within an electronic portfolio model, however, there exists the
opportunity to educate internal and external evaluators about how teaching, scholarship, and service manifest themselves digitally and, as a result,
potentially change the definition of what is valued to account for this continually emerging medium. Because most tenure and promotion guidelines
explicitly indicate that what is being measured is teaching effectiveness,
scholarly production, and to some extent service, an electronic portfolio
can actually be designed, developed, and distributed to display how such
academic labor, as well as measurements for assessing that labor, can and
should manifest themselves digitally. Moreover, designing and delivering
electronic teaching and scholarship for both internal and external review
can help candidates self-assess the extent to which their specific online
pedagogies not only meet university learning outcomes and thus impact
student retention and student success but also meet more theoretical
accounts of active learning and critical pedagogy.

TRAINING AND PROFESSIONAL
DEVELOPMENT PROGRAMS

Whether a tenure and promotion portfolio is print-based or electronic, it is
clear that a candidate is indeed making a persuasive case about the quality of his or her teaching, scholarship, and service contribution. In the case
of teaching with technology, candidates, while they may actually possess
some technological savvy, may not possess the institutional savvy about
ways to discuss, organize, document, and distribute electronic materials in
tenure and promotion. As a result, faculty development units such as
BGSU's Center for Teaching, Learning, & Technology (CTLT) often provide a
range of theoretical and hands-on training for faculty and graduate student
instructors wanting to utilize technology as a teaching and professional
development tool. In Summer 1999, I joined the CTLT staff on a 2-year

appointment as associate director in the area of online pedagogies. As an English professor whose area of expertise included technology and teacher training, I was charged with developing programs that helped not only faculty and graduate students in the humanities but the entire campus, in an effort to create more university-wide forums for discussing both the theoretical and the practical issues surrounding technology and faculty development. The following are a range of existing programs that have been a part of that process and have contributed to the call for more incentive and reward for the use of technology in teaching and learning and the role of electronic portfolios in tenure and promotion.

Technology and Teaching Institutes

In Spring 2000 and Winter 2001, I collaboratively developed a 3-day institute called Developing Online Pedagogies: Integrating the How and the Why for Faculty. As a pilot program, the institute was designed to promote technology infusion in an integrated way and serve as a significant professional development and incentive opportunity for faculty. The institute was designed to help participants define and determine the extent to which technology can enhance teaching and learning within their specific curricular contexts and teaching formats. Hands-on sessions helped participants develop a range of technological skills to integrate and manage an online presence and assess its impact on pedagogical goals. Among the hands-on sessions were the following:

- Developing and Managing an Online Presence with Course Management Tools
- Creating and Converting Syllabi with .html and authoring tools
- Delivering Classroom and Web Presentations through Microsoft PowerPoint
- Scanning and Digital Imaging with Adobe Photoshop
- Storing and Distributing Course Materials with CD-ROM Technology

Participants had the opportunity to bring relevant pedagogical materials for use in sessions and to work on independently during several "open-lab" times. Staff consultants were available during sessions to provide both pedagogical and technological support. In addition, luncheon sessions featured faculty from across the university utilizing online pedagogies and addressed issues such as managing and assessing online courses as well as institutional support and reward for technology-based course development. A final session allowed participants to save to CD-ROM all materials produced during the institute and discussed this technology as one mode of delivery of course content for students as well as the tenure and promotion portfolio. In addition to a notebook of useful documentation and articles related to online teaching and learning, including important issues such as copyright and fair use, participants received a follow-up individual consultation session with suggestions for continuing their online work and to work with technological consultants and faculty experts in the area of technology-infused pedagogies.

Despite the success of this initiative, part of the difficulty for faculty participants was the sheer workload that prevented them from implementing what they learned, particularly if they possessed novice status in technology and teaching. Many of the faculty participating more theoretical sessions addressed the issue of workload, noting, as does Bruce Horner, that asking faculty to take on new responsibilities almost never means that some other role—advising, teaching, scholarship requirements—can be lessened.

Portfolios as Professional Development Tools

In my role at the CTLT, I also developed a series of workshops on the subject of teaching portfolios for faculty and graduate student instructors, one focusing on print-based portfolios and one focusing on electronic portfolios. In the case of the print-based workshop, "Teaching Portfolios as Professional Development Tools," the following general questions were addressed: What is a teaching portfolio? Why should you have one? What documents can/should be included? For whom is such a document produced? A special focus of this session was the "teaching narrative," a vital document that determines what other documents to include as evidence of teaching effectiveness. Participants brainstormed possibilities for their own portfolios based on their particular curricular context.

A second session was titled "Developing your Electronic Portfolio." General questions included: When should a teaching or professional development portfolio be an "electronic portfolio"? Who is the audience for an e-portfolio? How are documents similar to and different from a print-based portfolio? Facilitators overviewed the goals, formats, and delivery options for e-portfolios, including web and CD-ROM and also profiled a range of electronic document formats, including a curriculum vitae in both hypertext markup language (.html) and portable document format (.pdf), and a teaching philosophy in digital video format as a model of the ways an e-portfolio can enhance traditional print-based genres required for tenure and promotion. Participants were asked to bring a copy of their curriculum vitae or some other document in Microsoft Word to get a sense of how such a document could be easily converted to a format appropriate for web or CD delivery.

In addition, because our own institution does not currently accept electronic portfolios only, both sessions demonstrated the integration of print and electronic formats, focusing on specific references to URLs in print-based portfolios as well as inclusion of CDs in the overall hard copy portfolio. Electronic portfolios in CD format were profiled in both sessions as a way of storing and delivering a range of documents, whether they be print-based or more genuinely electronic document formats. Given the sheer bulk of print-based portfolios and the space and bandwidth restrictions of campus and commercial provider web servers, CD-ROM versions of portfolios were stressed as viable for both internal and external levels of review, particularly because external reviews tend to privilege traditional models of scholarship that often exclude a range of teaching performance indicators.

INTERNAL AND EXTERNAL GRANT INITIATIVES

The importance of grant initiatives cannot be stressed strongly enough, for in addition to providing vital resources in the development of technology-infused curricula, grants are seen as a form of scholarship in many tenure and promotion contexts. At Bowling Green, a number of internal and external grant initiatives have helped in this area.

Tech Grants 2000

Promoted as an opportunity to take advantage of new technology infrastructure project at the university, the internal "Tech Grant 2000" program offered a series of three internal grant initiatives designed to help faculty and staff promote creativity in technology to enhance teaching, learning, and business operations: development grants ranging from $1,000 to $10,000 for teaching and learning projects that would be applicable to hardware, software, faculty course reductions, and student/staff technical support; travel grants awarded to faculty and staff for travel to universities and conferences for "best practices" observation of the ways in which technology is used and supported; and laptop grants that allowed faculty and staff to enhance and augment the quality and quantity of technology available to them through their own academic units for both teaching and research. Recipients of these grants totaled more than 150 faculty and staff members, including the CTLT for developing online training tutorials and best practice travel for two of its staff members.

Ohio Learning Network Faculty Professional Development Grant Program

As a staff member at the CTLT, I collaboratively applied for and received a $50,000 Ohio Learning Network grant to help faculty at the university's 2-year branch campus receive training and support for distributed learning initiatives. Because the branch campus is 90 miles away from the main campus where the center is housed, the incentive for this program was the ability to provide onsite and online training for faculty in a way that alleviated the workload for the cadre of primarily pre-tenure faculty awarded mini-grant (similar to the Tech Grant 2000 program) funding through this initiative to develop web-enhanced or fully online courses. Even with the development of such grant programs designed to assist with the technological labor or to release faculty from more traditional forms of academic labor to develop digital teaching and learning spaces, there exist constraints. In the case of the 2-year branch campus faculty, they often served as "one-person programs," the only faculty with expertise in public health or genetics, and thus could not be released from their regular assigned teaching or advising duties. And admittedly, as the principal investigator for the $50,000 grant, this form of scholarship felt less visible to me; despite its regional and campus recognition, it was not the traditional article I was used to writing, and was not necessarily something to discuss with conference colleagues when they asked that perennial question among colleagues that Horner notes: "What are you working on?" And indeed, a number of comments from the CCCC site express conflicting views about whether grants are considered scholarship or service.

Still, there is no doubt that funding as an incentive for technology training and use is vital. Thus, other grant programs included several in the College of Education that focused on technology-infusion in the all courses required by preservice teachers as a type of modeling process for this group. Both internal and external grants awarded for technology-based teaching ultimately bridge the gap between traditional research and teaching functions, thus helping to create a culture that fosters the "scholarship of teaching," a concept beneficial to both current and future faculty, particularly those teaching with technology. Equally important, as more and more faculty adopt technology-based pedagogies, it will become increasingly important to develop policies and templates for helping them to analyze and assess the effectiveness of these pedagogies for the purposes of tenure and promotion. Seth Katz, as part of a special *Kairos* issue on tenure and technology, notes the importance of having a technology-user actively involved in the creation of such documents. For techno-rhetoricians such as Katz, despite his involvement within the process, the constraints of a traditional English department and a traditional tenure process can significantly lessen such impact.

TENURE, PROMOTION, AND TECHNOLOGY-INFUSED COURSE DEVELOPMENT

In her recent article on technology and tenure, Sibylle Gruber contends that technology-related work not only is "collaborative, time-consuming and blurs the distinction between research, teaching, and service" but also is something that promotion and tenure committees "are not comfortable assessing . . . and do not know how to evaluate 'alternative scholarship, teaching, and service" (p. 41). In response to this dilemma, I offer the following range of guiding questions and responsibilities departmental and college review committees should acknowledge in evaluating the role technology plays in teaching, scholarship, and service, as well as in using technology as a medium for such evaluation. Although these guidelines represent a compilation of CCCC and MLA tenure and technology directives, they also have roots in the larger "scholarship of teaching" discussions promoted by organizations such as the American Association of Higher Education. The use of such guidelines is multifaceted. Although candidates themselves can consider these questions as they develop their tenure and promotion dossiers (whether print or electronic), they can also be utilized by departmental promotion and tenure committees to write committee reports and thus have more potential to shape a favorable response at the college and university level.

Guiding Questions

- How can/must existing tenure and promotion guidelines regarding teaching effectiveness account for the changing delivery models of technology-based learning?
- How can the concept of "the scholarship of teaching" contribute to better understanding of the ways in which online teaching contributes to teaching, research, and potentially service?
- What constitutes "evidence" of teaching and learning effectiveness in a technology-infused education model?
- How does relying on a primarily print-based review of candidate files hinder understanding of the impact of technology on teaching and learning?
- How does the level of faculty support for course development (course reductions, reduced class size, technical support and team-development models) impact teaching effectiveness?
- What constituencies on campus must be involved in discussions of technology's role in tenure and promotion decisions (faculty development units, faculty senate, college technology committees, departmental and college tenure and promotion committees)?

Candidate Responsibilities

- Offer commentary within teaching narratives that "guide" internal and external reviewers to weigh and evaluate online course materials and to clearly connect technological initiatives with indicators of student success within that discipline.
- Arrange for "peer observation" and evaluation within an online/distance or any technological setting. (Note that options may include virtual observation/participation of online discussions or chats, quantity and quality of course customization, ease of access and navigation to course materials, the extent to which courses account for multiple learning styles, and so forth.)
- Provide specific evidence, preferably in its original medium, including transcripts of online discussions, web syllabi and electronic course content in various media, and student technology projects.

- Educate departmental and college review committees about existing guidelines within the discipline and through national distance learning organizations that would support the candidate.

Departmental/College Tenure and Promotion Committee Responsibilities

- Review and revise existing student evaluation forms to account for distributed learning models/technology based teaching.
- Commit to review candidate's distance/technology-based teaching in its original medium (video, audio, www, CD-ROM).
- Collaborate with faculty development and instructional technology specialists and department/college technology committees for training of internal reviewers to review online course materials.
- Secure external reviewers knowledgeable about the role of technology in teaching and learning and to provide reviewers with guidelines about departmental/university standards in this area for tenure and promotion.
- Explore options for implementing an electronic teaching portfolio program for technology-based teaching and learning.

Currently, the use of these guidelines on the BGSU campus has been promising. As a member of the 2000-2001 Distance Learning Taskforce, I served on the faculty development and rewards subcommittee and thus was able to share an earlier version of these guidelines with a range of constituent groups that included the vice-provost for Academic Affairs, the executive vice president, as well as the chair of faculty senate for possible discussion by Senate's Faculty Welfare Committee. Although the guidelines have not been formally implemented, the university's desire to enhance its regional presence in distance learning has brought the discussion of faculty support and reward to the foreground and has created a climate for some consideration of the impact of technological labor on candidate's tenure and promotion cases. In the case of the College of Arts and Sciences, for instance, some electronic scholarship and teaching materials are being reviewed on both CD and the web, in addition to the print portfolio binder.

CONCLUSION:
SEEKING INSTITUTIONAL CHANGE

As some of the guidelines presented here indicate, some disciplines have relied on their major professional organizations (e.g., the MLA and the CCCC) help define and assess the role of technology in the curriculum. Yet to ensure institutional recognition of the importance of technology in tenure and promotion decisions, these national standards and guidelines must be contextualized around the role technology places in the localized teaching and learning community. For instance, rather than solely rely on national and disciplinary guidelines, college and academic units can also rely on case studies similar to the CCCC case studies of actual faculty examples of how technology is employed in the teaching, research, and service roles. This is particularly important at both the college and provost levels in which reviewers are outside the discipline and less able to assess how such work is valued within the tenuring unit. And although the positive impact of national and departmental discussion about the impact of tenure and technology is clear, it is important that discussions such as the ones that have taken place in national journals within English studies, for example—the special issues of both *Kairos* and *Computers and Composition*—extend beyond those disciplinary forums to ensure that we're not only talking to ourselves. In many ways, the faculty development initiatives outlined in this chapter have been a way to begin this discussion on the Bowling Green campus in that the workshops, institutes, and grant programs are meant to help faculty and administrators understand the need to support technology-based teaching and learning by recognizing technology's transformative impact on all aspects of instruction: content, delivery, and assessment. Support, however, should extend beyond technological training and support for faculty to also include forums for sharing pedagogies and acknowledging local material conditions that help and hinder faculty and student success in electronic environments. Although a number of workshops addressed this purpose, future options in this area can include local "learning communities" comprised of both faculty and administrators to address technological topics that enhance teaching and learning, a new initiative supported in Ohio, for instance, by the Ohio Learning Network, a branch of the Ohio Board of Regents.

Regardless of present and future initiatives, tenuring units must themselves be prepared to revise traditional teaching review processes, particularly student ratings and peer and supervisor evaluation. For instance, in their discussion of evaluating online courses, Palloff and Pratt stress the importance of considering all aspects of the course, including student performance, course design, online conversation, and other elements that usually don't make their way to the standardized rating form. Because the ultimate goal is to help students meet the learning outcomes expected in a multimedia lab-based, significantly web-enhanced, or fully online course formats, tenure and promotion cases that demonstrate as specifically as possible the extent to which these outcomes were met are most likely to be successful ones. While teaching portfolios, including electronic teaching portfolios, are recommended for all teacher education students by the National Council for the Accreditation of Teacher Education (NCATE), such professional development tools must be extended to university-level educators. Yet in advocating such an initiative, the material conditions of the institution must be addressed, including issues of access, technical support, learning curve, workload, educational philosophy, and institutional rewards. More than any other group, the college professoriate is charged with educating future teachers and working professionals in the newest technologies of literacy and communication and with meeting the diverse needs of learners both inside and outside the traditional boundaries of academe. Electronic portfolios provide an opportunity to both demonstrate our curricular efforts in this arena and to be rewarded for those efforts, although admittedly those of us who support such initiatives may still only be talking to ourselves. As Gruber notes, "We need to keep in mind that transformation can only happen if we and the institution want it to happen . . . To do this, we need to create an environment that opens dialogue, accepts difference, and promotes new and transformative ideas" (53). And as this chapter stresses, working toward these goals is the collaborative institutional responsibility of faculty, administrators, departmental and college tenure/promotion committees, and faculty development units.

REFERENCES

Conference on College Composition and Communication. Tenure and Promotion Cases for Composition Faculty Who Work With Technology. Available: http://www.hu.mtu.edu/~cyselfe/P&TStuff/P&TWeb/Introduction.htm. Site accessed June 2, 2002.

CCCC Committee on Computers and Composition. Promotion and Tenure Guidelines for Work With Technology. *College Composition and Communication.* 51, (1999): 139-142.

Chickering, Arthur, & Stephen Ehrmann. *Implementing the Seven Principles: Technology as Lever*. Washington, DC: American Association of Higher Education, Washington, DC. Available: http://www.aahe.org/technology/ehrmann.htm. Site accessed February 21, 2001.

Chickering, Arthur, & Zelda Gamson. "Seven Principles for Good Practice in Undergraduate Education." *AAHE BULLETIN 39* (1987): 3-7.

Gruber, Sibylle. "Technology and Tenure: Creating Oppositional Discourse in an Offline and Online World." *Computers and Composition.* 17 (2000): 41-55.

Horner, Bruce. *Terms of Work for Composition: A Materialist Critique.* Albany: State University of New York Press, 2000.

Katz, Seth. "One Department's Guidelines for Evaluating Computer-Related Work." *Kairos.* 2 (1997). Available: http://english/ttu.edu/kairos/2.1/coverweb/katz/art2/html. Site accessed June 18, 2001.

Leverenz, Carrie. "Tenure and Promotion in Rhetoric and Composition." *College Composition and Communication.* 52 (2000): 143-47.

Lieberman, Devorah, & James Rueter. The Electronically Augmented Teaching Portfolio. *The Teaching Portfolio: A Practical Guide to Improved Performance and Promotion/Tenure Decisions.* Ed. P. Seldin. Boston, MA: Anker, 1997. 46-57.

Madden, Dave. 17 *Elements of Good Online Courses.* Available: http://www.hcc.hawaii.edu/intranet/committees/FacDevCom/guidebk/online/web-elem.htm. Site accessed February 21, 2001.

Modern Language Association. *Committee on Computers and Emerging Technology in Teaching and Research.* Available: http://www.mla.org/reports/ccet/ccet_frame.htm. Site accessed February 21, 2001.

Palloff, Rena, & Keith Pratt. *Building Learning Communities in Cyberspace: Effective Strategies for the Online Classroom.* San Francisco: Jossey Bass, 1999.

Ragan, Lawrence. Good Teaching is Good Teaching: An Emerging Set of Guiding Principles and Practices for the Design and Development of Distance Education. *Cause and Effect.* 22 (1999). Available: http://www.educause.niss.ac.uk/ir/library/html/cem9915.html. Site accessed February 21, 2001.

Seldin, Peter. *The Teaching Portfolio: A Practical Guide to Improved Performance and Promotion/Tenure Decisions.* Boston, MA: Anker, 1997.

4

ASSESSMENT AS LABOR AND THE LABOR OF ASSESSMENT

Peggy O'Neill
Loyola University
Ellen Schendel
Grand Valley State University
Michael Williamson
Indiana University of Pennsylvania
Brian Huot
Kent State University

Writing assessment is *research*, a form of intellectual inquiry based in research methodologies, depending on one's position as a teacher/scholar/researcher in composition and rhetoric or education and/or measurement (O'Neill, Schendel and Huot; see also Huot). As with other forms of research, assessment involves labor—the work of examining needs, defining problems, collecting data, interpreting results, validating decisions, verifying outcomes, considering consequences, as well as meeting, reading, decision making, copying, e-mailing, coordinating, and preparing among many other activities. Although all research involves work, assessment is typically viewed as an occasion for *more* work in the face of an agenda already full with the primary academic requirements for advancement—scholarship, teaching, and service—because many composition and rhetoric professionals do not think of assessment as part of their work and they are, consequently, not interested or prepared for it. Usually special circumstances force Writing Program Administrators (WPAs) and compositionists to take on assessment—a mandate from administrators to justify the program, an institutional accreditation review, a desire to improve student learning, or a felt-sense that curricula and pedagogy need to be revised. Clearly, when the mandate for assessment is imposed on the writing program or its administrators from those outside of the program—such as university committees, deans, or provosts—assessment is seen as an onerous requirement of WPA work, if not also a form of surveillance, harassment, and regulation by other members of the academic community. After all, assessment requires more labor from those already laboring under heavy teaching and administrative loads, poor working conditions, and/or marginal status (Schell; Schell and Stock).

Besides large-scale assessments such as program review, placement testing, or exit exams, composition instructors also experience the labor of assessment in the everyday teaching of their classes. Managing the paper load—recommendations for how to be more efficient—is a standard topic in preparing future writing teachers (see, e.g., Dethier 76; Lindemann 248; White "Assigning" 145; Hairston 117; Williams 267), and burnout is a very real concern of many composition instructors. Even experienced writing teachers look for ways to reduce the amount of work required to assess their students' writing because, no matter how it is approached, reading, responding to drafts, conferencing, and grading final drafts and portfolios require time and effort. Most writing instructors enjoy teaching writing, but the complaints about the time and effort devoted to the work of assessment seem universal. Although all compositionists understand the necessary and important role that assessment plays in not only teaching writing but also administering a writing program, we often seem to resent the labor it requires. Brock Dethier puts it this way:

> Some of the most depressing moments in the life of a composition instructor come at the end of an eight-hour day of classes and conferences when, instead of being able to leave the job at the office and settle down for *Seinfeld* re-runs, the overworked instructor arrives home to a three-inch stack of papers that need to be returned the next day. (94)

Although writing assessment work often seems like additional, onerous labor imposed on composition, it does not need to be cast in this way. Writing assessment can actually work for compositionists, writing programs, and composition studies. Specifically, we can use assessment to place students into classes, to define curricula, to improve teaching, to improve individual students development as writers, to develop administrative structures, and to argue for better labor conditions for instructors. Programmatic assessment in particular allows us to gather data to consider as we restructure curriculum or revise programmatic goals. Because all of these assessment activities require that we articulate our judgments about what we see, assessment provides a visible representation of what we value as teachers, as programs, and as a profession.

But assessment has also been an important foundation for our profession. In fact, writing assessment, through the establishment of entrance examinations in written composition, was a significant factor in defining Composition Studies (as well as English Studies) as an independent field of academic labor and in helping the institutionalization of composition courses that followed. Writing assessment continues and has become a pervasive, defining activity for composition, whether through placement or proficiency testing, responding to student writing, grading of essays or portfolios, or program evaluation.

In this chapter we begin by exploring the work and history of writing assessment as a kind of narrative about academic work that had profound effects on the disciplinary formation of composition. The assessment of writing has historically performed important roles in defining composition as a discipline and shaping the academy and the community at large—with both positive and negative effects. The significance of writing assessment has not waned; if anything, it has become more influential through the insidiousness of high-stakes writing assessments. Because assessment contributes in important ways to the discipline of composition and to the work we do in the academy, compositionists should be more responsible in undertaking the work of assessment. If we don't do that work, someone else—such as testing companies, psychometricians, or technicians—will do it for us; which means someone else—not writing instructors, not composition researchers and scholars—will define our values, our programs, our discipline.

THE WORK OF ASSESSMENT

Whether we are the person being assessed or the one doing the assessing, the work of assessment and the roles it plays in our daily professional lives are pervasive parts of our labor as compositionists. However, assessment's function in defining what is valuable in our teaching and learning is often invisible. Although instructors may be more conscious of the role assessment plays in our professional lives when participating in explicit assessment tasks such as grading student writing, assigning course grades, or placing students into a writing program, writing instructors and scholars are typically less aware of the intuitive assessments we make of students

based on their appearance, their demeanor, their gender, or their participation in our classes (see, e.g., Haswell and Haswell, Hull et al.). Yet, assessment incorporates all of these formal and not so formal judgments, and
much more. Each time we make a professional judgment about a student,
a course, or a program, we are performing an assessment of one sort or
another. We cannot teach without assessing. Through both formal and
informal methods, assessment is inherent in the work of teaching writing
although it is a type of work often disdained and misunderstood (Belanoff
"Myths," "Toward").

Although important to students' development as writers, assessment is
very much a form of unappreciated, unwanted—even resented—academic
labor. The time and energy—a large percentage of our professional
resources—that go into reading student writing is often invisible to colleagues across the disciplines (including literature colleagues), yet very visible to composition teachers and scholars who spend much of their professional lives involved in it. What's not so visible to compositionists, however,
are the structures, assumptions, and values that inform the assessment
work we do. And, as with all invisible cultural structures, assessment results
in invisible constraints, defining who we are by circumscribing and prescribing labels and roles for our activity as teachers and researchers. Instead
of being writing teachers and scholars, composition instructors are often
defined as mere paper graders.

Besides—and maybe because of—the invisible aspects of writing
assessment, it is also undervalued as academic labor, often assigned to
graduate student teaching assistants (TAs), adjuncts, instructors, and junior
faculty. For example, in research universities, professors from across the
curriculum may give lectures to large classes of 100 students or more, but
TAs grade the students' writings. Clearly, the labor of assessing the value of
student work is not important enough for the professor to do, but it is
acceptable work for TAs who do not have the experience or disciplinary
expertise that the professor has.[1] Furthermore, because it is unappreciated, assessment is not typically recognized as a valid form of *intellectual*
labor. It is viewed as bureaucratic work, an institutional requirement of little consequence to the real work of the professorate. Again, TAs (some who
may be first-year master's students) and adjuncts (some who may have little if any preparation in teaching and assessing writing) are assigned to
deal with student writing because a professor's time is better spent on
more challenging, more important, work—research, scholarship, writing,
lecturing. (The only time assessing student writing is valued is when the
writing is produced by doctoral students.) In writing placement testing, exit
examination, even statewide proficiency testing, the work of reading and

evaluating the student writing is often done by adjunct instructors or graduate students, not the professorial staff. In some cases, when writing assessment is outsourced to testing companies, those doing the reading and evaluation may not even be writing instructors. Most composition and rhetoric scholars have heard colleagues in literature, not to mention those from across the campus, complain about the mindlessness of reading and evaluating student writing, or they have been asked questions such as "How can you stand reading all that student writing?" Partly in response to such attitudes during the last decade, computer-assisted assessments of writing have become more visible. Computer-adapted administration and scoring of multiple-choice tests (such as the Compass and Accuplacer testing programs) have been joined by programs that "read" and score student essays (such as E-rater, WritePlacer Plus, and Intelligent Essay Assessor). As Herrington and Moran explain:

> The firms that are marketing the machine scoring of student writing all explicitly or implicitly define the task of reading, evaluating, and responding to student writing not as a complex, demanding, and rewarding aspect of our teaching, but as a "burden" that should be lifted from our shoulders. (480)

This stance toward student writing and the labor associated with assessing it influences not only the students' learning experiences but also compositionists' professional experiences. Because assessing student writing—whether responding to and grading it in our classrooms or evaluating it as part of large scale testing—is central both to the work of composition instructors and to the development of writing students, the devaluing and under appreciation of it as intellectual labor clearly transfers to those who do it. In short, those professionals who labor in the field of writing assessment—whether that labor involves stacks of student papers from composition courses or reading essays for exit or placement—are considered somehow "less than" those who don't, which contributes to the overall sense of composition as an inferior discipline (e.g., Connors; Miller "Composing"; Spellmeyer).

This positioning of the labor of writing assessment may seem troubling by some but is often explained away by funding constraints within which postsecondary education must function (Miller "Droids"). The assumed, inferior position of assessment in particular and composition in general is actually a much more serious situation with the potential to undermine the values and work that define Composition Studies because of the work that writing assessment does in the academy and the larger culture. Writing assessment has historically played a role as gatekeeper, distinguishing those students who belong in the university from those who do not, or those who deserve to graduate from those who don't. It also works to define what is considered good—or good enough—writing. Good writing is what passes; bad writing is what fails. In other words, the work that assessment does has real consequences for students and society as it defines people as literate or illiterate and functions as a means to distribute resources and opportunities, all of which are significant work. So, why is the work of assessment so disparaged when it is responsible for such important decisions? Why is this work doled out to marginal members of the academy, "lesser" academics, or even outsourced to technicians, technologies, testing companies, and even computer software? Why does the scholarly work of assessment often get cast as administrative instead of as research and scholarship? How can those who labor in assessment transform assessment so it does the work that they value?

The answers to these questions lie in the emergent role of assessment in American education as a response to the increasing diversity within America. Although this is evidenced in the 21st century by the role of writing in many high-stakes, standardized tests such as the SAT II, the Graduate Management Admissions Test, state-mandated tests, and the College Board's inclusion of a writing sample as part of the revised SAT, writing assessment's role in defining who our students will be, which students are considered successful, and what constitutes good writing was just as influential throughout the last half of the 19th century as it is in the beginning of the 21st century.

WRITING ASSESSMENT AND THE EMERGENCE OF COMPOSITION STUDIES

The importance of assessment to the identity of Composition Studies becomes clearer when we look at its historical role. Arthur Applebee describes the ways that writing assessment, both large-scale and classroom-based, has been intertwined with the institutionalization of composition and the development of the contemporary American university system. His exploration, among others (see also Berlin; Brereton; Connors; Kitzhaber; Ohmann) suggests that writing began its function as a gatekeeping mechanism for colleges and universities with the written entrance examinations for college admission. However, the use of written entrance examinations predates their use for college admissions.

The technology of written examinations was initially fostered in the public schools as early as 1840 by Horace Mann to replace the existing oral examinations common during that time period (Witte, Trachsel and Walters). Thus, writing replaced oral language, raising the stakes for the teaching and learning of writing, probably setting the groundwork for the later use of written entrance examinations by colleges. Notably, Mann's argument for written examinations as more thorough, objective, and fair than traditional oral exams echoes claims made for large-scale multiple-choice tests later in the next century. The use of written examinations was intensive labor for students and teachers, and, at the time, essay examinations were used as the primary form of assessment for schooling at all levels. Universities also switched from oral examinations to written entrance examinations during the 19th century. Typically, students had to do such tasks as translate a passage from Latin or write about a Latin text in Latin.

The middle of the 19th century saw Americans engaged in a war among themselves. The Civil War would determine the economic future of the country because it promoted massive industrialization in the northeast and bankrupted the states that seceded. As part of the war, restrictions were eased to allow immigration from western Europe. The new immigrants became workers in the mobilization of industry and conscripts to feed the war of attrition established as the strategy by the federal government. These developments and the war itself caused further changes in the demographics of America throughout the remainder of the 19th century.[2] Americans began an exodus from the country to the city, a movement that continued until the mass exodus from the cities to the suburbs. The increasing use of immigrants from all over the world as a cheap form of labor increased the diversity of American culture itself, while creating an increasing economic distance between the immigrants of the previous century and the new immigrants. During the last part of the 19th century, the surviving native people were cleared from open ranges and isolated in reserved territories, opening the door for the massive westward movement that characterized that moment in American history. At the same time, compulsory, community-based education was introduced as necessary step to educate the children of the many new immigrants to their responsibilities as citizens in an increasingly complex society. In short, the increasing diversity of American culture led to new and different student populations, structuring new and different types of institutions, redefining the role of the schools and higher education, and their curricula, a trend we would argue continues today with new immigrant populations.

Around 1900, the college entrance examination system was revised in response to these changes. In some cases, the goal was to foster these changes in the student population. In other cases, assessment was meant to limit student diversity and limit educational opportunities to the already privileged. The most influential change in terms of the discipline of composition was the introduction of English as an examination area. The earliest entrance exams in English (Princeton in 1819 and Yale in 1822) had been oral and focused on the formal features of language, such as grammar, spelling, and usage (Trachsel). With the introduction of modern subjects such as English into the curriculum, significant differences in college entrance examination requirements appeared (Trachsel 53). Harvard, under the leadership of Charles Eliot, a Harvard graduate and chemistry professor who had earned a doctorate from a German university, was largely responsible for revising the entrance examination system, particularly in terms of English (Brereton; Lunsford; Trachsel). As Kitzhaber argues, Harvard became one of the foremost leaders in educational reform with the admission of English and other modern languages into its curriculum and helped "establish the pattern that nearly all other colleges would be following by the end of the century" (32-33). Eliot, who was president of Harvard from 1869 to 1909, championed English as the language of learning in the new university he was creating. He consciously used the entrance examinations to promote English instruction in the secondary schools and to secure it a place in the college curriculum (Brereton 28; Kitzhaber 33). During this time, writing emerged "as a management tool in both the corporate workplace and in the university classroom" as it was used to "manage and examine the growing student body" (Strickland 458). Although Eliot only had direct oversight of Harvard, the preparatory schools would have to teach their students how to write an acceptable composition in English (rather than Latin) because the students would have to take—and pass—the entrance exam if they were to enter Harvard. This entrance examination in English composition became the cornerstone in the development of the Harvard English program.

Typically, an institution's entrance exams were created and assessed by the professors who taught the courses, but because there were no English or composition professors at this time, Eliot had to decide who would be responsible for these tasks. For the English composition exams, Eliot hired Adam Sherman Hill, a Harvard graduate who had studied law and worked in journalism with Horace Greeley (Brereton). Importantly, the examination in English—as with the teaching of the courses—was handled by Hill, someone who had experience as a professional writer but not someone trained as a scholar. Eliot's move to make English the language of learning in the university coincided with the adoption of the German model of the university, which endorsed the scientific method, research, postgraduate study, and specialization, among other things. In other words, although other fields of study were demanding advanced degrees, developing research agendas, and rewarding scholarship, someone prized for his professional experience and expertise—not academic training or scholarship—was hired to introduce composition into the university curriculum. As Brereton explains, Hill was initially hired as an assistant to Frances James Child, Harvard's Boylston Chair of Rhetoric, who was a German-trained PhD "who preferred collecting ballads and researching literature to reading student themes" (9). In fact, when Child was almost lured away by Johns Hopkins University, Harvard managed to keep him by promising he would not have to read student themes anymore and made him the first Harvard professor of English, not rhetoric (Kitzhaber 33). In other words, assessing student writing was directly related to not only the separation of the study of composition and rhetoric from the study of English literature but also of the privileging of literary scholarship over the teaching and evaluation of student writing.

Hill, who had already initiated the entrance exam in composition, was named to the Boylston Chair, and he continued to manage the writing program, which he developed into a comprehensive 4-year curriculum. Although he became widely influential, especially through his popular textbook and the assistants he eventually hired, he never became a scholar or researcher, and he did not hire scholars; yet scholarship and research were becoming the foundation of the modern American university. Thus, composition was not only located outside the scholarly mission of the university, the assessment of student writing was seen as a burdensome activity not fit for scholars but rather assigned to itinerant teachers and scholars-in-training.

In the classroom, writing assessment was necessarily driven by efficiency due to the tremendous workloads of teachers. As Connors, Brereton, and others demonstrate, composition teaching was labor-intensive. A single teacher was often responsible for the instruction of up to 200 students: "At Harvard in 1892, Barrett Wendell read daily and fortnightly themes from 170 students—over 24,000 papers each year" (Connors 191). Such a workload produced several deleterious effects for composition and assessment. The production of so much student writing coupled with the principles of scientific management popular at this time—efficiency and containment of labor costs—necessitated a division of labor in English "between the head and hands, intellectual work and mechanical work" (Strickland 460). Writing, which was used for examination and surveillance, was cast as mechanical labor. Connors notes that the prestige, authority, and influence a professor of rhetoric might have enjoyed at the beginning of the 19th century, as a keeper of standards and English-language expert, is almost completely diminished by the end of the century owing to the impossible workload and the onerous task of teachers as gatekeepers and writing assessors. Although Strickland's analysis differs somewhat from Connors, the consequences are not so different: Strickland likens composition teachers to secretaries, whose work was considered routine and mechanical (their managers performed the intellectual work):

> Just as secretarial work became more clearly separated from managerial work and thus promised little possibility of promotion into those ranks, so did composition teaching, in the process of becoming more clearly separated from literature teaching, come to be more associated with non-tenure-track positions. (466)

The effects of this decision by Eliot to hire Hill, who continued to run the composition program for more than 30 years, coupled with the enormous workload associated with assessing student writing, is arguably still influencing how the teaching and assessing of writing is positioned in academe today. For example, Harvard's program—the oldest independent writing program in American higher education, responsible for the teaching of the only course required of all Harvard undergraduates—is completely staffed with non-tenured instructors and administrators (O'Neill and Schendel). In fact, only a handful of administrative positions are permanent employees; all of the classroom instructors are "preceptors" with an employment cap of 5 years. Even Harvard Professor Patrick Ford, who serves on the interdisciplinary faculty committee that oversees their program, acknowledges the problems with the staffing and positioning of writing in the academy:

> In one respect, Expos [the Harvard writing program] is not unlike the situation of writing in many universities. It is not a department and its faculty are called by the strange name 'preceptor.' I support changing this to 'lecturer,' but that doesn't seem likely to happen. Fortunately, salaries have improved somewhat for preceptors but are still below that of lecturer. Teachers of writing have been professionals for some years now, but there remains almost everywhere a suspicion on the part of 'real' scholars that writing and writing pedagogy lie outside of the main preoccupations of the academy. This is not likely to change, in my view. (qtd. in O'Neill and Schendel, p. 199)

So, although Harvard and many others think that writing is so important that it is required of all students, it doesn't think it is relevant to the research and scholarly mission of the university. This positioning of composition, we believe, is directly connected to the labor involved in assessing student writing: writing assessment performs certain work in the academy, yet the academy does not reward that kind of work.

Unfortunately, this conception of assessment has remained a constant in the use of writing assessment at American colleges and universities. Eliot's insistence on English as the language of higher education, to replace the role of Latin, and his attempts to improve the secondary schools' teaching of written English caused him to use writing assessment as a tool to accomplish these ends. As is now also the case, the increasing pressure to improve education and the diversification of American culture led to the regulatory uses of assessment.

STANDARDIZING ENTRANCE EXAMS AND ASSESSMENT

During the 19th century when Eliot and others were reshaping American higher education, each university created its own system of entrance exams, which controlled admissions and influenced prep school curricula. This created a climate of inconvenience and inefficiency due largely to the labor involved with scoring and the apparent duplication of effort necessary for each university to develop and administer its own examinations. It also made it difficult for students who needed to prepare and sit for multiple exams if they wanted to apply to more than one university. The first move toward standardizing the entrance exams in English occurred with the National Education Association appointing the Committee of Ten in 1892. The committee recommended the English exam "should be uniform in kind throughout the country" (qtd. in Trachsel 54). The committee also maintained that ability in written expression could only be brought into play through demonstrating content knowledge and that for the English exam literary knowledge was appropriate (Trachsel 54). One form of efficiency emerged as some college preparatory schools specialized in preparing students for the examinations of one institution rather than another (Diederich). In 1905, in order to address these problems, or inefficiencies, the College Entrance Examination Board (CEEB) was founded to prepare and administer examinations for "selective" colleges who could then decide upon which students it would admit based upon their scores, among other criteria. The creation of the CEEB certainly seemed to make good sense because it clearly made entrance examinations more uniform, more efficient, less labor-intensive for colleges, and more convenient for examinees. In short, the effort involved in preparing tests and students reflects an early awareness of the desire for an efficient use of labor and technology.

The CEEB conducted essay examinations up through the 1930s. In 1937, they introduced the SAT for students who wished to apply for scholarships because the new exams did not require students to write a series of essays and could be administered and scored more easily, providing scores more quickly than the essay exams. Comparatively, essay exams were administered after school was out and took more time to score, so schools did not receive student scores until the middle of the summer. Within a couple of years, the scholarship stipulation for the SAT was lifted (Fuess). By the end of the 1930s, increasingly more students were sitting for the SAT, and fewer were opting for the traditional essay exams because the SAT involved less time and effort. When the country went to war in late 1941, the leadership of the CEEB seized the opportunity to shelve the traditional exams altogether. There was, of course, some resistance to this move. The CEEB's reaction to this resistance can be summed up in the words of its secretary, John Stalnaker:

> The type of test so highly valued by teachers of English, which requires the candidate to write a theme or essay, is not a worth-while testing device. Whether or not the writing of essays deserves the place it has in the secondary school curriculum may be equally questioned. Eventually, it is hoped, sufficient evidence may be accumulated to outlaw forever the "write a theme-on" type of examination. (qtd. in Fuess 158)

The board's stance was supported by a technological orientation questioning the scientific integrity of the traditional essay exams. In trying to account for why it took so long for the CEEB to move toward the indirect testing of writing through the use of multiple-choice tests of grammar, usage, and mechanics, Orville Palmer of Educational Testing Service (ETS) writes,

> The Board regretted the authority of a large and conservative segment of the English teaching profession which sincerely believed that the

writing of essays and other free response exercises constituted the only
direct means of obtaining evidence as to a student's ability to write and
understand his own language. (11)

Palmer's history of the "Sixty Years of English Testing" goes on to elaborate
how "more complex testing techniques" were eventually developed (11-
12). This thumbnail history of writing assessment to around 1940 illustrates George Madhaus' point about the emergent technological orientation
of assessment in general:

> Changes over the last two centuries in the predominant ways of exam-
> ining student achievement—from the oral mode, to the written essay,
> to the short-answer form, to the multiple choice format, to the
> machine-scorable answer sheet and finally to computer-adaptive—
> have all been geared toward increasing efficiency and making the
> assessment systems more manageable, standardized, easy to adminis-
> ter, objective, reliable, comparable and inexpensive. ("Technological"
> 82)

According to Madhaus ("A National"), testing, as we now know it, is
largely a creation of the 20th century. Assessment specialists eager to
achieve scientific status for their work applied statistical explanations and
other technological apparatuses to social and psychological phenomena
like intelligence and aptitude. Along with the statistical machinery of psy-
chometrics, testing was also pushed toward a technological approach since
there was increasing pressure to develop means to test the greatest possible number of people in the shortest possible time at the least possible
expense. Although assessments continued to evolve technologically, there
was little if any critical relationship about their uses and consequences.
Madhaus ("A National") contends that through the 20th century we have
seen an evolution in the way we can define technology: "something put
together for a purpose, to satisfy a pressing and immediate need, or to
solve a problem" (12-13).

The development of standardized assessments are linked to Alfred
Binet's scripted interview developed in the late 1890s to help decide which
French school children would not profit from a public school education.
The interviewer made one decision that resulted in a specific school path
for an individual. Although Binet's approach to IQ testing did not result in
labels, it did categorize the students as either needing additional help to
succeed in school or not because, as Foucault points out, assessments
define and inscribe individuals carving out spaces and prescribing labels,

such as normal or average. However, in the United States, Binet's procedure underwent a radical, technological transformation. The Stanford revision of Binet's work was the first to assign numbers on an IQ scale to such labels as moron, idiot, and genius. As Bourdieu and Passeron point out, educational assessments replicate a culture of schooling and the culture at large—they tend to reinforce pedagogies that privilege teachers over students, rote learning over critical thinking, as the reinforcement of the dominant (often racist, often classist, often sexist) ideologies of a society. F. Allan Hanson notes that assessment in general defines who we are as humans, through everything from medical tests to driving tests, from the SATs to IQ tests. Assessments classify and define, constraining individuals within existing cultural structures.

It is both discomforting and important to note that the work of Foucault, Bourdieu and Passeron, and Hanson clearly indicates that our use of writing assessment, both in and out of our own classrooms, replicates what has always been the case for assessment: It is a way of classifying, sorting, and labeling students. This is problematic because composition has become a field that increasingly focuses on ways to help students become agents of change within their culture. We are in the business of helping people to become rhetoricians within and outside of the university, claiming power that comes with language and rhetoric and writing, rather than being positioned by discourse. As a field, we try to work *against* rigid notions of dominance and power in our classrooms, the culture at large, and our writing assessments in favor of giving students space to think critically within the university and in the world.

But writing assessments are technologies, as Madaus points out. In fact, any form of writing is a technology, because tools are used to create language. As technologies, writing assessments are imbued with the values of the culture in which they are constructed and used. For example, a placement system reflects the following:

- The values of the larger society in which the university is positioned and perhaps that society's values about assessment and standards.
- Local values about the work of assessment.
- Local values about the work of schooling in general and literacy instruction in particular.

For Passeron and Bourdieu, assessments are technologies that replicate the ideologies behind educational systems—and they do so smoothly and efficiently, without drawing attention to the fact that they are technologies of replication rather than of change. And because the "best" assessments are often viewed as those that are highly efficient, they are often viewed uncritically within the contexts in which they are used. After all, it takes much more effort and time to critically examine the use of a given assessment system than it does to simply allow the assessment to do its work. The problem is that this very invisibility allows their continued use, even if the assessments are insensitive to students or teachers or result in negative consequences for the community in which they are used. Defining assessment as a scientific endeavor—rather than as a political and ideological act—has set limits on discussions about assessment. Instead of questioning the ways a given assessment positions human agents, the discussion often focuses on the more quantitative, technical aspects of an assessment. For example, according to Edward White, any form of assessment must be reliable to be "fair." But this relationship between reliability (a property of a test) and fairness (a value judgment) obscures the larger issue of the appropriateness of the assessment's results and the impact those results have on people and education.

Likewise, Nicholas Lemann's history of the SAT and ETS outlines the progressive agenda of using the technology of testing to measure people's abilities and create a meritocracy in which the "New Mandarins" would assume leadership in a bright future for America. Lemann's work highlights how the history of assessment is deeply rooted in dangerous assumptions of the kind of work assessment can do to better society and how that history permeates even contemporary discussions about assessment. For example, the biological determinism that early tests validated fit right in with a view that certain races were superior to others. Currently this determinism can be seen in the fact that SAT scores correlate with family income. But Lemann's work also demonstrates how dangerous a noncritical view of assessment technology can be; although efficient, although reliable, a test can also do detrimental work within particular contexts, limiting access to certain groups of people for certain privileged opportunities, like admission to selective colleges or universities.

CONCLUSION

Clearly, this vision of a meritocracy—leadership based on those most intellectually capable—echoes Plato's view of an oligarchy. The notion of merit, as opposed to inheritance, is at the heart of the sense of fair play and "rugged individuality," a reflection of Horatio Alger in the 19th century and the contemporary infomercial selling opportunities for wealth. But, is the playing field really level with respect to the assessment of merit? Is writing assessment for programmatic or individual decisions used to promote those most capable? And how is "capable" being defined and who benefits from this definition? Is it possible for people outside the mainstream of American culture to actually take a role in leadership?

In the face of characterizations of writing assessments as technological replications that discipline and define individuals, it is also important to (re)view writing assessment as a way of doing the intellectual work of a writing program, a writing classroom, and Composition Studies. To view assessment as intellectual work may help us to define it in new ways that are antithetical to the principles on which it has been developed and fostered but that are more consistent with the principles many contemporary compositionists espouse. Intellectual work is, after all, anything but efficient, reliable, cheap, or anything else that writing and other forms of assessment have worked to become.

If anything, the labor involved with writing assessment has asserted the value of reading and responding to student writing, as generations of writing teachers have demonstrated. We have asserted the value of humans interacting with other humans, an unpopular stand against apparently objective scientific proof demonstrating the subjectivity and, hence, unfair results of human responses to texts. It is the very human element, however, that is most important in writing because writing—and therefore the evaluation of it—is ultimately about communication between writers and readers. As Herrington and Moran explain, the "expectation of active response is fundamental to the act of writing. Even if the response is not communicated by the reader to the writer, as is the case with the placement-testing situation, the writer assumes she will have some impact on a reader's thought and feelings" (496-97). When that reader becomes a cog in a machine—or even worse, when the machine becomes the reader as with programs such as Erater or the Intelligent Essay Assessor programs—the very act of writing is corrupted. When a college or university uses machine scoring of student essays, it sends two messages: "Human readers are unreliable, quirky expensive, and finally irrelevant; and students' writing matters only in a very narrow range: Its length, its vocabulary, its correctness, or its congruence with the mathematics of space" (Herrington and Moran 497).

We believe that using machines to assess student essays sends another message as well: Evaluating student writing is not worthwhile, not legitimate, not intellectual labor. Although the history of composition has already cast the assessment of student writing and the field of writing assessment in this way, there has been enough resistance to see the possibility of recasting writing assessment as valued, disciplinary-defining scholarship (see, e.g., Slevin).

It is easy to see in this short historical narrative how assessment emerged as a regulatory tool, a gate-keeping device. When colleges adopted an exit examination system based in writing, of necessity schools preparing students for college would have to move toward the use of writing in their curricula. The influence of these standardized forms of writing assessment also influence the work we do in our own classrooms as we prepare our students for proficiency exams, essay exams across the disciplines, entrance exams or other types of assessments. In turn, our assessments also work to assess us—our work is often evaluated by the work our students do. The systems of examination in which we all labor has worked to ensure that those who belonged succeeded and those who did not were denied admission. Compositionists have been challenging this system while at the same time we have often been used to perpetuate it. By paying more attention to work of assessment—legitimate intellectual and social work—we might be able to bring the values that we espouse in line with the values promoted by assessment.

ENDNOTES

1. This notion of assessment as work not fitting the professorate was recently made visible in a conversation one of us had with a representative for the Compass test (a placement exam that consists of an untimed editing test students complete on computer) who asked, "Don't you want your faculty doing more important work?"
2. Connors and Traschel, among other scholars, report on the social and political factors that influenced literacy during the last half of the 19th century.

REFERENCES

Applebee, Arthur. *Tradition and Reform in the Teaching of English: A History.* Urbana, IL: NCTE, 1974.

Belanoff, Pat. The Myths of Assessment." *Journal of Basic Writing.* 10 (1991): 54-66.

_____. "Towards an Ethics of Grading." *Foregrounding Ethical Awareness in Composition and English Studies.* Eds. Fontaine, Sheryl I. and Susan M. Hunter. Portsmouth, NH: Heinemann, 1998. 174-96.

Berlin, James. *Rhetoric and Reality: Writing Instruction in American Colleges, 1900-1985.* Carbondale: Southern Illinois UP, 1987.

Bourdieu, Pierre and Jean Claude Passeron. *Reproduction: In Education, Society, and Culture.* London: Sage, 1977.

Brereton, John C., ed. *The Origins of Composition Studies in the American College 1875-1925: A Documentary History.* Pittsburgh: U of Pittsburgh P, 1995.

Connors, Robert J. *Composition-Rhetoric: Backgrounds, Theory, and Pedagogy.* Pittsburgh: U of Pittsburgh P, 1997.

Dethier, Brock. *The Composition Instructor's Survival Guide.* Portsmouth, NH: Boynton/Cook Heinemann, 1999.

Diederich, Paul. "Turning Fords Into Lincolns: Reminiscences on Teaching and Assessing Writing." *Research in the Teaching of English.* 30 (1996): 352-60.

Foucault, Michel. *Discipline and Punish: The Birth of the Prison.* Trans. Alan Sheridan. New York: Vintage Books, 1977.

Fuess, Claude. *The College Board: Its First Fifty Years.* New York: College Entrance Examination Board, 1967.

Hairston, Maxine. "On Not Being a Composition Slave." In *Training the New Teacher of College Composition.* Ed Charles W. Bridges, Urbana, IL: NCTE, 1986. 117-24.

Hanson, F. Allan. *Testing Testing: The Social Consequences of the Examined Life.* Berkeley: U of California P, 1993.

Haswell, Richard H. and Janis Tedesco Haswell. "Gender Bias and Critique of Student Writing." *Assessing Writing.* 3 (1996): 31-84.

Herrington, Anne and Charles Moran. "What Happens When Machines Read Our Students' Writing?" *College English.* 63 (2001): 480-99.

Hull, Glynda, Mike Rose, Kay Losey Fraser, and Marisa Castellano. "Remediation as Social Construct: Perspectives from an Analysis of Classroom Discourse." *College Composition and Communication.* 42.3 (1991): 299-329

Huot, Brian. *(Re)Articulating Writing Assessment for Teaching and Learning.* Logan: Utah State UP, 2002.

Kitzhaber, Albert R. *Rhetoric in American Colleges 1850-1900.* Dallas: Southern Methodist UP, 1990.

Lemann, Nicholas. *The Big Test: The Secret History of the American Meritocracy.* New York: Farrar, Straus and Giroux, 1999.

Lindemann, Erika. *A Rhetoric for Writing Teachers.* 4th ed. New York: Oxford UP, 2001.

Lunsford, Andrea A. "The Past—and Future—of Writing Assessment." *Writing Assessment: Issues and Strategies.* Eds. Karen L. Greenburg., Karen L. Wiener, and Richard A. Donovan. New York: Longman, 1986. 1-12.

Madhaus, George F. "A National Testing System: Manna From Above? An Hstorical/Technological Perspective." *Educational Assessment.* 1 (1993): 9-26.

_____. "A Technological and Historical Consideration of Equity Issues Associated With Proposals to Change the Nations's Testing Policy." *Harvard Educational Review* 64 (1994): 76-95.

Miller, Richard E. "Composing English Studies: Toward a Social History of the Discipline." *College Composition and Communication*. 45.2 (1994): 164-79.

_____. "Let's Do the Numbers: Comp Droids and the Prophet of Doom." *MLA Profession* (1996): 96-105

Ohmann, Richard. *English in America: A Radical View of the Profession.* New York: Oxford, UP, 1976.

O'Neill, Peggy, Ellen Schendel, and Brian Huot. "Defining Assessment as Research: Moving from Obligations to Opportunities." *WPA: Writing Program Administration*. 26(2002): 10-26.

O'Neill, Peggy and Ellen Schendel. "Locating Writing Programs in Research Universities." *Field of Dreams.* Eds. Peggy O'Neill, Angela Crow, and Larry W. Burton. Logan: Utah State UP, 2002. 186-212.

Palmer, Orville. "Sixty Years of English Testing." *College Board Review.* 42(1960): 8-14.

Plato. *The Republic.* Trans. Desmond Lee. 1955. 2nd Edition. London: Penguin, 1987.

Schell, Eileen E. *Gypsy Academics and Mother-Teachers: Gender, Contingent Labor, and Writing Instruction.* Portsmouth, NH: Boynton/Cook, 1998.

Schell, Eileen E. and Patti Lambert Stock. *Moving a Mountain: Transforming the Role of Contingent Faculty in Composition Studies and Higher Education.* Urbana, IL: NCTE, 2001.

Slevin, James F. "Engaging Intellectual Work: The Faculty's Role in Assessment." *College English.* 63 (2001): 288-305.

Spellmeyer, Kurt. "Marginal Prospects." *Writing Program Administration.* 21.2/3 (1998):162-82.

Strickland, Donna. "Taking Dictation: The Emergence of Writing Programs and the Cultural Contradictions of Composition Teaching." *College English.* 63 (2001): 457-79.

Trachsel, Mary. *Institutionalizing Literacy: The Historical Role of College Entrance Exams in English.* Carbondale: Southern Illinois University Press, 1992.

White, Edward M. *Assigning, Responding, Evaluating: A Writing Teacher's Guide.* 3rd ed. Boston: Bedford St. Martin's, 1999.

Williams, James D. *Preparing to Teach Writing: Research, Theory, and Practice.* 2nd Ed. Mahwah, NJ: Erlbaum, 1998.

Witte, Stephen P., Mary Trachsel, and Keith Walters, "Literacy and the Direct Assessment of Writing: A Diachronic Perspective." *Writing Assessment: Issues and Strategies.* Eds. Karen Greenberg, Harvey S Wiener, and Richard A. Donovan. New York: Longman, 1986. 13-34.

PART TWO

Mediating Technology-Shaped Identities

5

WAC FOR CYBORGS

DISCURSIVE THOUGHT
IN INFORMATION RICH ENVIRONMENTS

Charles Bazerman

University of California, Santa Barbara

It isn't easy being a cyborg these days. The human wetware constantly needs rewiring to remain compatible with the latest software and hardware options. When I was a young cyborg, back in the 1950s, the work component of my cognitive and affective system mainly needed compatibility with the well evolved and fairly stable print world. The entertainment component needed compatibility mainly with passive reception of audio and video delivered at the pace of unaugmented life—although people were already complaining that their lives were being fragmented by too many choices and commercial interruptions.

Through my education I wired myself well to the print world, as organized and delivered through the university system of disciplinary knowledge production, distribution, and use. I rose through the ranks until I got to support newer cyborgs as they wired themselves into the knowledge system. I thought the best way to provide access to educational opportunity was to unpack all I had learned about operating in the print world, thereby demystifying the cultural capital that middle-class life and elite education had afforded me. Others could then use those skills for their own purposes in relation to their own experiences and knowledge.

As I gained experience teaching, I met an ever-wider set of cyborgs with different orientations, motives, resources, and compatibilities with different parts of the knowledge system. My familiarity with the knowledge system expanded, as well. Technology upgrades required some minor personal rewiring, but xerography, word processing, even early email were easy to assimilate within my existing ways of working and thinking.

But the last 10 years have heightened cyborg challenges for me as it did for others. The human component needed major reconfiguration to work with the external knowledge systems and multidimensional communicative relationships that are becoming standard in many professions, as various people have started to explore. Sherry Turkle, for example, has examined changing identity and self-conception through close relation with the computer (*Second Self*) and computer-mediated communication and forums (*Life on the Screen*). The work on cognitive and affective change in children spending many hours on video games, particularly as those games model police training to overcome anxiety and focus attention in firearms situations, suggest some of the issues. I, along with others, have started to explore some of the changes in participation frames and social organizations being afforded by web-mediated activities (see, e.g., Yates and Van Maanen and Bazerman "Genre").

One human cyborgian challenge for most students, academics, and professionals results from the accessibility to and machine analyzability of large data sets. Of course, large accumulations of data are not new to this generation. Detailed astronomical data go back millennia, as do maps and other forms of geographical recording. Modern accounting practices go back to the 15th century, and since then have generated extensive commercial records. Colonial empires, the development of science, the modern bureaucratic state, systematic agriculture, the large corporation, transportation systems—all have increased the need and means for gathering and keeping extensive data. For the most part, however, these extensive files of data would only be examined and used by people trained and experienced in the area. Often, such experience included experience of the material realities recorded by the data. Extraction and manipulation of the data were also often done manually, often by the same people who collected and would use the data. Displays of the data, by and large, were close to the original form—complex graphic and tabular display only came gradually for the most expert users. Consider, for example, the ways numerical and graphic displays in science articles only flowered in arcaneness in the last 200 years (Bazerman *Shaping*). Or consider that vertical filing cabinets are less than 150 years old, and the Hollerith system of data extraction (the precurser to the IBM card) is only about 120 years old (see Yates; Lubar).

Nonspecialist use of data sets, historically, then, was limited and often required training—as with reading maps and train schedules.

In schools, too, for many reasons, the amount and form of information students had access to and had to make sense of was limited. In 18th-century elementary classrooms students might have access to the alphabet and a few words and phrases on a hornbook—and that was it. Later, a few textbooks of the McGuffey sort entered the picture. Until the advent of the computer, even in well-funded school districts, students received information primarily predigested in a series of subject matter textbooks—where the selection and meaning and activities were all set out. Students had to address only the most limited problems with defined data, as in arithmetic exercises or end-of-the-chapter history questions. Even the advanced learning in the talmudic tradition involved only a few books, with all the multiple voices on each passage visually available on the same page. Similarly, in Western higher education, students frequently did not need to know much beyond the professor's lecture and the notes they took on it, perhaps supplemented by assigned reading. Even reliance on the material for prerequisite courses may have been sporadic.

Occasionally, students at all levels, might be sent to the library to locate other resources, but as a whole the knowledge universe has remained tightly circumscribed, controlled, and already interpreted. The thing most like a data set I remember from my 1950s childhood were tables of logarithms and trigonometric functions—whose use and meaning were determined by algorithmic procedures. They were treated mechanically and not as matters for interpretation or understanding. The main place where an open-ended richness was to be found was in the library—and the ill-defined research paper became the one potential site of inquiry and discovery. When I began to teach and study writing in higher education I was quickly attracted to the research paper, which then led me into fundamental question of knowledge use, understanding, and production in disciplinary contexts. Coming to know the literate system of knowledge texts—how to find your way around a library and a disciplinary literature—was to learn how to access and think about what the academy had to offer. Immersion in disciplinary databases was something that only the most advanced students would get to, often only in graduate education, and perhaps only in the more advanced years of graduate work.

This collection, interpretation, and use of data defines much of professional practice. The competence to find one's way within relevant data, to know how to manipulate and think about it, licenses the professional as professional, in industry and public practice as well as in the academy. The problems of making sense of data for professionals is not trivial, but professionals have whole careers to work their way into the competence—a competence that often distinguishes the skill and presumed intelligence of people at the highest levels. The search for data starts from a basis of contextual knowledge about the subject matter, the kinds of data typically available in the field, and the typical uses of data. The data search or gathering also starts from a set of purposes and projects that would be aided by the data. Also needed early in the process is knowledge of where the appropriate data is to be found and how to access it. Because the data often are not direct representations of the phenomenon being considered, but only some indicator or surrogate for the phenomenon (e.g., test scores to indicate learning, questionnaire responses to indicate attitudes), the savvy researcher understands the relationship between the mapping device and the territory. Furthermore, the knowledgeable inquirer needs to know the kinds of manipulations and analyses he or she can legitimately and conveniently make of the data in order to answer more subtle questions than can be answered directly by unprocessed data.

Now computers and the Internet have changed the game radically. Data are exchanged rapidly and cheaply among colleagues, and extensive electronic archives are set up and easily accessed and/or distributed. Many electronic instruments also collect extensive data easily with limited human set-up, guidance, and examination. We are awash with data.

Furthermore, because manipulations are now also frequently and complexly automated, even before the user sees the data, at some point knowledge of how the system manipulates and transforms the data is important for the expert to understand. The power of computing has facilitated the building of complex models of complex systems, such as of global warming or a nation's economy. The outputs of these complex models are highly transformed from the original data, and again an inquirer is more enabled the more he or she understands of what the model does. Similarly, forms of representation, such as tables or graphs, have long involved transformations of data into new forms that make them readable in different ways, ways that highlight different aspects and meanings of the data. The data user again needs to understand the consequences of the forms of data representation. The electronic world has made that problem even greater through bit-mapping, which allows many new and creative forms of visual and audio display that are many removes in appearance from the original phenomena, as when the stock market becomes a field of wheat or a flock of birds. These forms of representation, both old and new, are usually in the service of finding and displaying meaningful patterns and significant consequences; the skill in finding the most powerful of such meanings is one of the key attributes of experts.

Coordinately, expertise of many professions has been more explicitly defined around the ability to manipulate large amounts of data, and students are often given access to large amounts of data much earlier in their careers. Students not only have access to massive amounts of information, the information is often in undigested form or not placed within the frame of the learning task at hand. Often enough students get access to the exact same data bases that the professionals use. One project I work with, for example, is preparing for Internet access for elementary school children (along with every other age and level of student and scholar) to a massive video oral history archive of holocaust testimony consisting of more than 120,000 hours of digitized video. This contact with the real-world experience of the holocaust is to be used, for, among other purposes, inquiry-based tolerance education. This project is the first step of gaining other testimonies of similar experiences, and more generally of providing electronic access to all oral history and other historical archives. Historical archives were until recently rare, expensive, hard to collect, hard to get to—only credentialed scholars might be granted admission, and then they had to wear white gloves. Now first graders may have access to the same material. How can they use it well? How can kids make sense of the material? How can this material be part of their educational development? How will they adapt to growing up in such a data-rich environment?

Historically, the making sense of data has been associated with skills of expression and writing. Books and then journals were the repository of knowledge; libraries and universities were the places within which people explored and came to find the meaning in information, and writing was the vehicle largely by which they came to express, synthesize, and evaluate information. The greatest experts in information-rich fields were typically those who write about the knowledge of their field, at least to other specialists, and sometimes to wider audiences. As writing teachers we soon come to understand how much we are in the center of the process of students coming to intelligent terms with what they are learning and by which they come to be competent professional knowledge users. Our profession's extensive concern with academic writing, the research paper, critical writing, Writing Across the Curriculum (WAC), and Writing In the Disciplines indicate our profession's awareness of how much writing is intertwined with knowledge, information, and meaning-making.

However, with the easy accessibility of data and the attractiveness of exposing students to more extensive data earlier in their education, the need for students to articulate what they have found and to make sense of it has become greater and more pressing. They need the tools of more sophisticated writing earlier on and more universally. Not just the few who make their way over many hurdles that both train and exclude to become experts have to cope with data, but all students with little prior relevant experience have to understand the following:

- The purposes of consulting data
- The relevant contexts for their inquiry
- Access to the data
- Planning a methodical inquiry
- The logics of the data and the data systems, including complex models that produce secondary data
- The forms in which data are represented
- Manipulation and analysis of the data
- The human meaning of the data
- The patterns and concepts that suggest interpretation of the data
- The role that knowledge takes within their lives.

The problems of the traditional sort have been exacerbated by the tremendous power of computation. Databases are larger, accessible from a greater distance, and more likely to have little to do with students' immediate experience. Even more, the computer may manipulate the data in ways that may not be apparent to the user. The input data may be very different from what a user is likely to see. Techniques like bitmapping have extended the transformation of the representation far in excess of traditional graphing techniques. Various search, tracking, and analytic tools as well allow students and other users to do many things to the data. How can students make sense of what they are finding, what they are doing, what the data means? Students have to do a lot more thinking, at a higher level, as they provide them more to think about and as the machines do a lot of the preliminary thinking, or even appear to substitute their thinking for human thought. How can we integrate machine thinking with our thinking? What parts of the thinking is it appropriate to let the machines do? How can we think about what the machines have done? How can machines support our thinking? How do machines displace or narrow our thinking? How can we train people to be up to the challenge of figuring out what their knowledge and information means? For the time being, until someone comes up with another stronger task-appropriate thinking and articulating tool, writing must carry a strong educational burden, and student writing must be supported in useful ways.

As university courses make greater use of professional databases for introductory and midlevel courses, WAC and Electronic Communication

Across the Curriculum initiatives provide opportunities for us to explore how writing might help students develop the understanding they need to access, work with, and come to conclusions from the data. At UCSB, I have had the good fortune over the last several years to consult with Professor William Prothero on his large freshman course Geology 4: Introduction to Oceanography. Since 1994 in lecture, lab, and at-home assignments, he has introduced students to the use and interpretation of geological and oceanographic databases in order to develop their abilities in the subject matter and more generally to think scientifically. From the beginning, he has been interested in incorporating writing as a way to help students develop and express their thinking, and I have consulted with him on the organization of the writing activities. Professors Greg Kelly and Allison Takao have also studied this project, including examination of the arguments students make in their writing (Kelly and Takao; Takao, Prothero, and Kelly). Currently, another graduate student, C. Julie Esch, under my supervision, has been studying how students learn to associate data with higher level generalizations, and she has been developing some additions to the course materials, activity, instruction, and guidance for teaching assistants (TAs) to support student writing.

The most thorough integration of writing now occurs in the first third of the course, as students are introduced to oceanographic data and are asked to develop a seven- to eight-page mid-term paper. In the paper the students are asked to observe, identify, classify, and describe earth data and then argue how they relate to the theory of plate tectonics. The data, which is made available for lab and home use on a CD, "Our Dynamic Planet," consists of the ETOPO5 data set of land and sea floor elevations, the Smithsonian Global Volcanoes data set, the earthquake data set from the World-Wide Network of Seismic Stations, and a Heat Flow Data Set provided by Professor Carol Stein of Northwestern University. These are the same data sets used by professional earth scientists. These data are displayed not as raw numbers, but in map formatted graphic displays and as cross-section profiles.

By use of tools and tutorials developed by Professor Prothero over the years, students are guided in accessing and manipulating the data sets. To help students identify features from the mapped displays the CD-based lab provides them with several games. Through the games, the students learn to identify three-dimensional objects from two-dimensional displays, to associate elevation profiles with descriptive names, to identify key data items, to make some basic inferences, and, most subtly of all, to determine which selection of the data will be most useful in answering their questions. Simultaneously, they are introduced to the basics of plate tectonic theory and how various identifiable topographic features are created by tectonic processes. The theory is regularly tied back to the mapped data.

These tools and training devices were developed in response to student difficulties in handling and interpreting the basic data sets. When I first discussed this project with Professor Prothero about 5 years ago, he already had most of these pieces in place, including the long mid-term paper, supported by a 10-page guide for writing a scientific paper with a short checklist on proper format. He was concerned, however, that students in their papers, were not able to demonstrate adequate scientific reasoning, which for him meant coming up with arguments supported by good reasons and appropriate data. I suggested to him standard WAC advice—he should provide some smaller, less ambitious paper assignments and students should have an opportunity for peer-editing groups before turning in the assignments. I also suggested that he provide some rubrics and questions to guide the peer reviewing sessions. He then developed a three-page, small area description assignment. In this assignment, students had to work with a limited section of the mapped data to identify the geologic features in it and explain how the features might be related to a plate boundary. The paper was to consist of only one page of text, one page of figures, and one page of a self-assessment checklist. He also developed an author feedback form to guide peer-group discussions. He has also expanded the guide to writing a scientific paper to almost 20 pages.

Although adding the preliminary shorter assignment did seem to improve student writing, Professor Prothero was still concerned that many students were not understanding how to support their general claims well with data. There was the further problem that the geology graduate TAs were not providing consistent or pedagogically helpful correction and commentary on student papers, despite a detailed grading rubric. He still sensed there was something more to be articulated what good scientific writing consisted of, in this context.

To start to see where student arguments were succeeding and failing, Professors Kelly and Takao analyzed a sample of the student papers, using a model of argumentation that considered the different epistemic levels of argument and how those levels were integrated. To analytically specify Bruno Latour and Steve Woolgar's sequence of different levels of epistemic certainty a claim might reach, they followed my suggestion to adapt James Britton's seven types of transactional argument as a tool for analyzing sentence types. Britton et al. identify the various levels of transactional discourse as record, report, generalized narrative, analogic (low level of generalization), analogic, analogic-tautologic (speculative), and tautologic (argument carried out fully on the level of abstractions). Many years ago, I had played around with using these categories as sentence-level descriptors to help students recognize how different sentences and paragraphs might be integrated through hierarchically arranged levels of generalization or intellectual abstraction. Although I found the taxonomy worked well as a revision heuristic, I did not pursue it at that time. Kelly and Takao adapted this taxonomy to identify epistemic levels of sentences using the task-specific categories, going from the most concrete to the most theoretical:

- Data charts, representations, locations, and age of islands
- Topographical features identified
- Relational aspects of geologic structures
- Geologic theory or model illustrated with real earth samples
- General geologic theory or model
- General geologic knowledge not specified to data presented.

The better rated papers, they found, had far more statements at all levels, with a substantial number of sentences at the middle epistemic levels to bridge between the most concrete and the most abstract. Furthermore they found there were specific reference linkages among claims made at different levels, with few big jumps of level in the links. Figure 5.1, for example, is the map of the sentences in one of the papers that was highly rated wholistically by disciplinary graders.

On the lower rated papers, however, there were fewer sentences at all levels, with particular absence at the lower or middle epistemic levels. Furthermore, there were fewer linkages between claims, and what linkages there were jumped across levels. Figure 5.2, for example, maps the epistemic levels and linkages of a paper rated poorly by disciplinary assessors.

This mapping of epistemic levels and linkages made visible some key aspects of arguing well, although expert evaluation of the sample suggested that other factors such as problem formulation, focus, and accurate inferencing were also important. Other issues that seem important are the understanding the argumentative power of different and multiple sorts of data and the use of figures. Nonetheless, the findings on the levels of claims model were strong enough to warrant explicit instruction and guidance about the kind of claims that needed to be made and how they should be linked. C. Julie Esch then developed several interventions on this theme, which were incorporated into the Spring 2000 version of the course. First was an exercise in the lab book that helped students identify in sample essays statements at different epistemic levels and linkages made between those levels. Students were to do this exercise before writing the small area description. Second, she developed an author self-analysis form Third, she

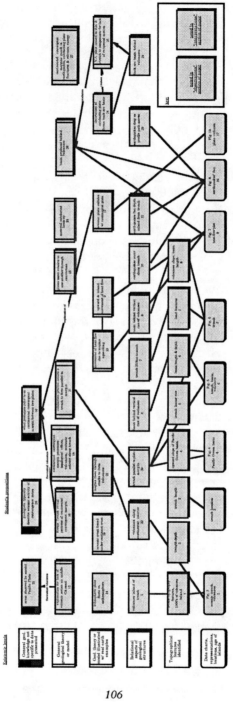

FIGURE 5.1. Epistemic levels in a highly rated paper (From Kelly and Takao).

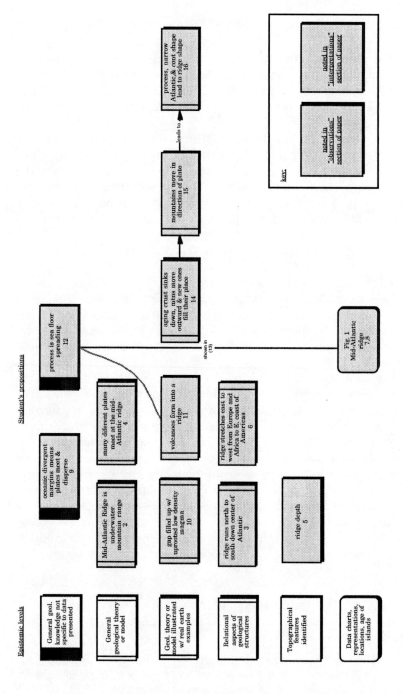

FIGURE 5.2. Epistemic levels in a lower rated paper (From Kelly and Takao).

revised the feedback form used in peer-group sessions to reflect the epistemic levels model. These levels and rubrics were then used to orient TAs and modify grading rubrics. During TA training, Esch introduced the TAs to the model and related writing issues. Students reported this support was extremely helpful.

Such studies suggest the kind of difficulties students have in making sense of and arguing from data with some theoretical sophistication. When students write, their lack of understanding of the meaning of data and the relation to larger ideas becomes evident. This project also suggests how we may begin to provide more specific writing support that will give students the kind of help they need to cope with the complex intellectual and human demands the information is placing on them.

If we really believe that writing is the vehicle for understanding, learning, and human meaning-making, then these are the fields on which we now need to play. The work is demanding and the interdisciplinary collaboration is serious. But the consequences are large. The kinds of courses with which we have been working are being funded at high levels with the hope that they will be models for a new generation of courses, if not themselves directly reproduced. The production of cyborgs is now a large- scale proposition.

Educational programs that mix humans with machines highlight the fact that human intelligence is a major component of cyborgian intelligence. The future of cyborgian intelligence requires we go beyond just making smarter machines or even making more user-friendly interfaces that allow humans to work easily with the machine enhancements. Humans too must develop to act intelligently in coordination with their machine supplements. Writing is one of the major vehicles by which people actively develop their thought. By incorporating writing in our new forms of supported thought, we help people figure out what all this new information and knowledge means and what it is useful for. We also help them maintain connection with the complex resources of human intelligence and wisdom that we have developed over millennia of literacy.

REFERENCES

Bazerman, Charles. "Genre and Identity: Citizenship in the Age of the Internet and the Age of Global Capitalism." *The Rhetoric and Ideology of Genre.* Eds. Richard Coe and Tanya Teslenko. Cresskill, NJ: Hampton Press, 2002. 13-38.

_____. *Shaping Written Knowledge: The Genre and Activity of the Experimental Article in Science.* Madison: University of Wisconsin Press, 1988.

Britton, James, Tony Burgess, Nancy Martin, Alex McLeod, and Harold Rosen.*The Development of Writing Abilities.* London: Macmillan, 1975.

Kelly, Greg J. and Allison Takao. "Epistemic levels in argument: An analysis of university oceanography students' use of evidence in writing." *Science Education.* 86 (2002): 314-342.

Latour, Bruno and Steve Woolgar. *Laboratory Life: The Construction of Scientific Facts.* Beverly Hills CA: Sage, 1979.

Lubar, Steven D. *InfoCulture: The Smithsonian Book of Information Age Inventions.* Boston: Houghton Mifflin, 1993.

Takao, Allison Y., William Prothero, and Greg J. Kelly. "Applying argumentation analysis to assess the quality of university oceanography students' scientific writing." *Journal of Geoscience Education.* 50 (2002): 40-48.

Turkle, Sherry. *Life on the Screen: Identity in the Age of the Internet.* New York: Simon & Schuster, 1995.

_____. *The Second Self: Computers and the Human Spirit.* New York: Simon and Schuster, 1984.

Yates, JoAnne. *Control Through Communication: The Rise of System in American Management.* Baltimore, MD: Johns Hopkins University Press, 1989.

_____. John Van Maanen, ed. *Information Technology and Organizational Transformation: History, Rhetoric, and Practice* Thousand Oaks, CA: Sage, 2001.

6

"WHATEVER BEINGS": THE COMING (EDUCATIONAL) COMMUNITY

Victor J. Vitanza
Clemson University

[Background scene: Workers applauding students on trucks as they make their way to Tiananmen Square, June '89, Beijing.]

PREAMBLE

[Background: Paper white]

In this paper—this is (a) paper, it is not the multimedia presentation that it originally was[1]—I explain, develop, and assess the values of what is becoming said (by/e) Georgio Agamben and others in relation to the changes that are *taking place*—literally and punceptually, taking place (taking, as in confiscating conceptual *topoi*)—in our (coming) educational community. The West and East. I am concerned specifically with the changes

111

in terms of subjectivity, language, and community, or in roughly ancient terms of ethos, logos, and pathos. For Agamben, subjectivity (of the sub-ject–object, master–slave relations) is changing to a third-term, un/namely, "whatever beings" or "radical singularities." (This "whatever" is better understood as a being of the repressed excluded middle.) If subjectivity is changing, then, language and community are changing as well. In affect, the unfundamental puncept, as Jean-Luc Nancy states it—Nancy and Agamben travel in the same plane of intensities—is that "a thinking of sub-ject thwarts a thinking of community" (*Inoperative Community* 23). Such a thought, of course, appears completely perverse in the light of the work done toward developing effective political subjects to bring about neces-sary change. For some time now, however, a significant number of political theorists have argued against subjects (subjectivities) as the building blocks of communities for political struggles. Most notably, it has been Deleuze and Guattari who have argued, "There is no fixed subject unless there is repression" (*Anti-Oedipus* 26). So it figures that if what is wanted is a less repressed, less suppressed, and less, if any at all, politically oppressed sub-jects, then, the very problem is in the material, emotional, and intellectual conditions for the possibilities of sub-jectivity, which is a sub-ject that is only one better than ob-jects (thrown before) and two better than ab-jects (out-casts). And yet, although there might be some agreement on subjec-tivity as being determined by way of the negative—after all, the word *sub-ject*, like *under-stand*, is a stance, status, State signifier word—there has been little agreement about what term, if a term, should take its place, allowing for new conditions and possibilities. Deleuze and Guattari's vari-ous suggestions—from the schizo to becoming minoritarian—have had a major influence, but differences, in what a new political "agency" would be, still remain. The paraconcept frequently used now, which can be found in Deleuze and Guattari's work, is *singularity*. But again, the differences of thought are often waged in terms of the differences among body, will, and desire, while still other terms or, in some cases, metaphors (puncepts) are offered.

Which brings us back to Agamben and his *own* (communitarian) *views* on political agencies. For Agamben, instead of subjects, as I have said, there are "whatever beings" or "whatever singularities." But it is not the naming but ways of placing these political agents in (coming) communities that is of the utmost importance and that I would like to examine, if only here in a passing mannerism. Whereas the old dream was thought in terms of *realms* of beings (suggesting infinitude and immanence); now it is, with Nancy and Agamben and yet others, *relations* of beings (suggesting fini-tude, or an infinite radical finitude and imminence).

This word "imminence" has a special meaning. Perhaps we have seen its use earlier in Deleuze and Guattari's writings on a "plane of immi-nence,"[2] which always and strongly suggests an ever-present readiness to happen, a potentiality that is in place, though not in the place established by negation. With the word "potentialities," we get to another paraconcept that is important in relation to my second interest, technology.

For Agamben, it is not "technology" per se that is driving the change in subjectivity to singularities; it is, as I surmise it from a neo-Heideggerian view, less the withdrawal of Being (which would be from a realm of being) and more so now the diminishing of the negative itself and a coming of nothing (which is without negation).[3] I would surmise, therefore, that it is *being* itself that withdraws to the threshold to become whatever beings in their various singularities (which would establish the conditions for the pos-sibilities of a relation of beings). It is this withdrawal that, again I am sur-mising, so changes the very nature of potentialities (*dynamis*) and, conse-quently, actuality (*energeia*). In the coming community, potentialities will have been in a statelessness of exuberance (always already ready to reestab-lish relations). It is this withdrawal of the negative that gives us the Hegelian view of the absolutely essential be-coming now absolutely unessential. We will take up with Agambin's reworking of this turn in thinking.[4]

Often, we think of the Greek term *"techne"* as if, even though we know better, it meant technology as historically determined by the industrial rev-olution. And only that revolution and at the expense of evolution or invo-lution.[5] We must not continue to look through this Victorian-Edwardian-Marxist lens, for it only blinds us to what is *confiscating place*. Agamben reminds us that it is not technology but *"techne"* or, better put, *"dynamis"* and *"potentia"* that drive us in what we have called history. With the with-drawal of the negative (determinate negation), *potentia* (nothing) "can" more fully now allow for third terms, in be tweens, the remainders (i.e., all the countless excluded middles) that were "produced" by the ontotheolog-ical and Humanist (including Judeo-Christian-Islamic, Atheist, Agnostic, Sophistic, Marxist) traditions.

The taking of place (and time, for time surveys space) is difficult if not impossible to determine since *the thing (das Ding)* that is taking place does not show up on any determinate-thinking's register. At best, what can point to the taking of place/s (*topoi*) is a potential misrepresentative antidote: Is it happening? Has it happened? Yes. Hark, such a misrepresentation has presented itself recently, as it has in many countless similar and other places, in Patricia Harkin's proffered criticism of students. Hossier stu-dents? Only? Is this a local crit? She says, "When the postmodern Hoosier rhetor [student] has a contradiction pointed out [in an argument], then, she is less likely to contemplate the cognitive dissonance as a spur to invention and more likely simply to say 'whatever'." Harkin quips: "The postmodern Hoosier reinvents the 'whatever' genre." This quip, however, is an ingenious statement, which we have yet to appreciate. Soon, however, according to Agamben, we will live in a perpetual statelessness, in the coming (educational) community, of such ingenuities.

It is not that we have a generation gap between students and teachers or that we have a *mis en abyme* in this misrepresentation that calls on us to generate bridging terms. It is rather that we live chaste, yet not chastized (for this chastizing would only be reactionary) lives in relation to the task of thinking. It can only be the caseless that these misrepresentations fill our so-called, yet anemic universe of discourses. Leaving possible worlds untapped. Whatever whatevers uninvented from. Or by(e) way of.

Whatever is not a genre, though it can be reinscribed as such, but only at the perpetual risk of remaining blind and chaste to it. *Whatever* is just something else, some thing or occasion that has been, heretofore, excluded by the conditions for what is considered possible, and yet that perpetually knocks on every door in our neighborhoods and gated communities. But never mind.

Whatever has become the paraconceptual restarting places—taking places and providing strange ones—for what Agamben refers to as "the coming community." What this so-called postmodern Hoosier rhetor-student, like so many other students, is harkening, perhaps unbeknowst to them (to all of the so-called *us* of our academik community) is Behold, *Whatever*!

The task of thinking—when it is dis/engaging in an *a*pedagogy[6] and allowing for the emergence of puncepts (appropriating the places of concepts)—is to welcome the event (*Ereignis*). But how is anyone to welcome this event, such as it is, when concealed! Or always already cancelled (reinscribed) out by what presently goes for the task of thinking (by way of the three principles of logic that inform traditional philosophy and rhetoric: Identity, noncontradiction, and excluded middle)? Nevermind! Is there any hope as long as there is the Right and the so-called Left. There can (as in capability, *dynamis*, potentialities) be hope in what is far left of what is humanisticly possible. With a setless of compossibilities that compose a radically infinite finitude (Ronell, *Finitude's Score*; Davis).[7] Enough of this neo-Hedieggerian spin.[8] And a movement towards a proper improper Agambean spin, but with a reminder that I now will begin to quasi-render into paraliteracy what was a multimedia presentashun. Print cultures and Electronic cultures and the hybridity, in be tweeness of them can produce peculiar texts.

THREE QUOTES AND A VIDEO CLIP:
DISSEMINATING ORIENTATIONS

[Background: Hexidecimal Custard with a blend of Mustard]

I am working here with these three quotes, one of which I've already presented, but will add a dia(dis)logic scene from a film trailer to complete it.

"When the postmodern Hoosier rhetor has a contradiction pointed out to her, then, she is less likely to contemplate the cognitive dissonance as a spur to invention and more likely simply to say 'whatever'. . . . The postmodern Hoosier reinvents the 'whatever' genre."

As written by Patricia Harkin in "Rhetoric, Poetics, and Cultures as an Articulation Project" in *JAC* 17.3 (1997): 494-96.

The Video Clip:

The Teach says: "Act three, scene 2. You know you've got to pass English to graduate."

The student says: "I know." . . .

Quick cut . . .

Student says to student: "Gurl, you best keep yo' mouth shut!" . . .

W h a t e v e rrrrrrrrrrrrrrr

As (a) Scene from the Film *Whatever*.

A man who is after the truth sets out to be a man of learning; a man who wants to give free play to his subjectivity sets out, perhaps, to be a writer. But what[ever] is a man to do who is after something that lies between?

As spoken by Ulrich in Robert Musil's *The Man Without Qualities* 302.

What could be the politics of whatever singularity, that is, of a being whose community is mediated not by any condition of belonging (being red, being Italian, being Communist) nor by the simple absence of conditions (a negative community, such as that recently proposed in France by Maurice Blanchot), but by belonging itself? A herald from Beijing carries the elements of a response.

As written by Agamben in *The Coming Community* 85.

So let's (not) Whatever! to the Question of the In Be Tween and Whatever Be(ij)ings . . .

SCATTERED NOTES, TOWARD A VIDEO TRAILER
FOR A FILM/IC THAT WILL NEVER BE RELEASED

A. [Background Image: Closeup, overly amplified, splotchy image of Robert Crumb.]

I'm still interested in the Question of Third Subjectivities. I've worked on this paraproject previously. Perhaps all of my lives. I tend to look for experimental subjectivities in what I have referred to as Third places. Outside binairies. Not Male. Not Female. But whatever else might remain. And an exuberance of others remains!

What I have been interested in, like others, is specifically how to transform sub-jectivity into its radical finitude while not denegating it beyond its being an effectual political agent. (And yet, let us not Oedipally lose sight, no longer a sub-jectivty or agent as classically, humanistically, or Marxist-ickly thought to have to be!) I have tried to focus, at times, on a protean subject, and at other times, on a subjectivity that many people with what goes for good taste would find repulsive. (It's not that I am after bad taste, nor above it, but in an affront of it.) Yes, I've learned much from Hélène Cixous and Clarice Lispector (their passions according to G.H., their notes on libidinalized education). Their monst(o)rosities!

Although I am interested in monsters and specifically the cyborg as a conceptual starting place to think through the problem of subjectivity (cyborgs are a product of technological thinking), I am more interested now—than ever before, as I've said—in Giorgio Agamben's "whatever beings" (which are productions of *techne*, *dynamis*, or potentialities). In dis/order to even begin to talk about *techne*, Agamben has had to revalue the concept through neoplatonists and earlier (than Chicago) neoaris-totelians, all very heretical ones. His major source is the great excluded middle ages.[9]

So I will thematize what I am going to think about here in my notes . . . connections . . . for a video of a film/ic that will be produced but never, ever released: I will be thinking in terms of

    1. Subjects (active)   < - >   2. Objects (passive)
    3. "whatever beings" (radical passivity).[10]

Yes, I will be thinking with the Thirds-Turds. But this three is not a synthe-sis, but what goes for a most radical form of dissensus. And yet, not an abject, not really still "shit" (Kristeva, *Abjection* 3-4; Butler, *Gender Trouble* 133-34). It is a third-turd more radical in its infinite finitude than any that has been, heretofore, thought, as . . . well . . . Whatever!

B. And Yet, Neither Subject nor Object [Background splotchy image of Robert Crumb]

To com*PLI*cate (refold) matters, I am beginning to think also of "third objects." In other words, I am not now—in any, but this event—referring to the object of the subject < - > object relationship, but one of the third order, or perhaps, otherwise put, dis/order. There are so many of these objects like this one: . . . Now again, in my multimedia presentation I offered a gif-ani-mation of myself (< IMG SRC = "vvpeek.gif" >), which anyone can still download for free from the Web (see URL in footnote 1).[11] This animation is an object of the third dis/order that will believe *for* whoever takes (down-loads) it. That is, whoever-cum-whatever takes it as, say, a neopagan god-less and an obtuse remainder of all future gods and as "loveable" and as giv-ing off a "useless expenditure" of tics and Tourette "gestures" (cf. Barthes, "Third Sense" 56-57; Agamben, *Means Without Ends* 49-62). But the main thingless is that this *obtuse* animation *wills to believe for you* when placed on your uncanny, canny page. ("vvpeek.gif" is not a virus, although viral.)

Or this one: Again, in my presentation, I offered, as another exemplar, a two-page advertisement for Macromedia, which inscribes in a two-page spread in *Wired* magazine a living room—like any living but especially a MOO living room—as (third) objects. Every thing in this so-called living room is marked as an object of HTML, < IMG SRC = "dog.gif" >. All objects are computer objects. Man. Sofa. Books. Table. TV. Window. Lamp. The whole room, including < IMG SRC = "room.gif" >. All is turned into, fur-nished as, objects. (It's called object-oriented programming.) With these simple tag names. . . .

In discussions of ideology, let us recall Marx's notion that while we as subjects no longer believe, our commodity objects believe for us (*Capital I* 166-67). In discussions of seduction, Jean Baudrillard writes, "It's no longer the subject that desires; it's the object that seduces" (*Fatal Strategies* 111). In technology, Sherry Turkle tells us that there is a new kind of object in a third culture: "I believe," she writes, "in a new kind of computational object—the relational object" that "requires (and promises) emotional nur-turance" ("third culture" 1). The list goes on.

But although I find these third "objects" interesting, I am less and less interested in the cause-effect relationship between technology and ideology, but remain ever concerned about the timeless when both subjects < - > objects disappear into thirds.

Which means, I am more interested in returning to *techne*, *dynamis*, and *potentialties*, which is what Agamben is most interested in, in terms of "whatever beings" . . . while I have simultaneously a growing interest in the Question of . . . Let me just call it . . . The Question of Hygiene.

C. An Interruption (abruption, eruption) . . . [Background color, off white, near vanilla, but in 3-ply]

Allow me to interrupt abruptly this statement concerning my intentions and stop for a moment to consider predecessors, those who I have studied and who have had an influence on me. Though perhaps a rather perverse influence. I mention in passing only two people, but two widely separated in geographies and cultures. My thoughts about this presentation began with my readings of Giorgio Agamben and then Steven North.

In his closing prophetic statements in "The Death of Paradigm Hope," North attempts to rethink "research": Specifically, how "the object of inquiry, 'composition,' will have lost its (imagined) identity," how "researchers of all kinds will have simply posted their studies directly through one or another network clearinghouse, eliminating those last vestiges of paradigm hope, editors and referees, in favor of a kind of free market of ideas," and how research on composition will be "revalued" (204-205).

The keywords and phrases here for me are "object of inquiry," "loss of identity," "paradigm hope," and "revalued."

Steve, as well as Giorgio, is talking about subject/object relations in a community, in a discipline or a field. Steve and Giorgio are talking about work and labor . . . in the coming community. And how they will be revalued. And both talk about paradigms. But whereas Steve points to a future that he cannot fully fathom (he simply suggests that technology will change everything), Giorgio is highly suggestive and indifferent toward technology (he returns us toward a rethinking of *techne*, *dynamis*, potentialities and he asks us to think of the other meaning of "paradigm" as *alongside*).

What I'm going to do is take Steve's abrupt ending—after all, he's mostly interested in speaking of the Death, End, and Future of the field, although spends little time on the future— . . . I'm going to take Steve's abrupt ending and enfold it into Giorgio's discussions on the coming community that opens up the conditions for entities that are cast outside, *alongside*. Unlike Steve, I would fathom the future perfect of the coming educational community and our work and labor in it.

Therefore, I am going to talk about—as called to do—"labor, workplace, and technology," but it may not sound to y/our ears that, in fact, I am talking about them at all. I will especially focus on *techne* and *dynamis* (potentiality) and in something that I will refer to as Adjacencies, or in Agamben's phrase "whatever beings." . . .

Let's cut back to the Question of Hygene:

D. The Q of Hygiene (contd.)
[Background image: Tiananmen, June '89. PLA Officer speaking (quoting) to the people.]

The Q of Hygiene has become of ironic interest to me after reading Dominique Laporte's *History of Shit*. I like Laporte's suggestion

> that the management of human waste is crucial to our *identities as modern individuals* [subjects, Faces] including the organization of the city, the rise of the nation-state, the development of capitalism [a.k.a. *caca*pitalism], and the mandate for clear and proper language [rhetoric as Inter/Face, Inter/Face as rhetoric]. . . . Laporte argues, we are thoroughly mired in [waste, shit], particularly when we appear our most clean and hygienic. (from back, inside jacket; emphasis mine).

Like the Ancient Romans, we build whatever receptacles! . . .

Think of the Q of Hygiene (the policies we institute to deflect our byproducts and flush off our waste) as being intimately related to the eternal return of the . . . "Whatever." I use this expression "Whatever" for it signifies, in my estimation and Agamben's, all that itself has been excluded. What will return—does return—are "whatever beings." And these "whatever beings" will comprise the coming community. Without Qualities. Without Content. . . .

Now, again, I had a video for my presentation of a commode flushing over and over again. Since this is an image—naturally animated—in most homes and institutions, just think of what I am referring to here in terms of Laporte, next time you flush away that part of your body that is your abjection. I'm writing both literally and, yes, litorally. And . . .

I began this . . . whatever this is! . . . with . . . the quote from Patricia Harkin about "The postmodern Hoosier, who reinvents the 'whatever' genre"; the quote from Robert Musil about the "in be Tween"; and the quote from Agamben on the "herald from Beijing [who] carries the elements of a response" to the question of political resistance. The quote from Harkin is illustrative of a critic's greatest insight—as Paul DeMan would say—amidst her/our greatest blindness.

When I made this statement at the conference, Patty asked me afterword, publicly, what she might have said to the student. My reply was to ask not what the student meant by "whatever," for whatever is immune to meaning. Rather, to ask, How goes whatever? Or rather, How goes the *sense* of whatever? Surfing the Bonsai Pipeline, I discovered what I would come to see as a transitional (though the change will occur sporadically through *abruptions* as it is occurring now) *wide image* video of the student (in this exemplar, a female "student" in a Web Soap Opera) and what it might have said, if asked, to Harkin:

Well, so Asley, How goes "Whatever"? What is your sense of "Whatever"? Asley in the video from the Web Soap, says:

> See, I don't really know what "whatever" is either. Because whenever I try to explain the word, I have to use the word in the meaning. I don't know. I looked it up once. Pronunciation *What Ev' Er*. Ahhhh, it's a relative clause. It's a number of things like books, papers, magazines, whatever. I don't understand it. It just . . . whatever! Whatever! It doesn't matter. You don't care, I guess. Whatever means like . . . You can do whatever you want. See what I mean! Godddd. Whatever! (Trailer for the Web soap *Whatever*)

What I find charming (secrete-ly dis-[h]arming) is that Asley, so trained by teachers in terms of responses to teachers, pretends to hear the question as What is? (either pragmatic or ontological). Students have every ri(gh)te to distrust us. Asley's response is nothing but a sudsy put-on, though c/harming.

The quote from Musil is not self-explainable. Either. The expression "in between" in the novel *The Man Without Qualities* is exceptionally difficult to grasp. The man without qualities in the novel, who is Ulrich, is an *essayist* in that he lives the life of an *essay*; that is, he practices *essayisms*. (I call what I am practicing the genre of "Notes," but it, too, is an essay. I am a writer of essays, not just as Montaigne was, but also as Ulrich is a character of and in *essayisms, essayistic spaces*.) Musil has Ulrich, the essayist, living "the floating life within," which is one or a radical many "*between* [emphasis mine] religion and knowledge, between example and doctrine, between *amor intellectualis* and poetry" (301). Ulrich is "simply [a man who has] gone out on an adventure and lost [his] way" in dis/order to be unfounded (301).

The quote from Agamben, however, is where I want to focus and then disperse what I have to say. (By the way, Agamben calls on Musil's Ulrich and the man without qualities and content, so we will not be excluding Ulrich and his concern for the in be tween.)

E. Extracting content—from a man without content— from Agamben's text The Coming Community, is . . . impossible, for it is written in an aphoristic manner. [The background image is of the Goddess of Liberty, Tiananmen, Spring, '89.]

Agamben lives, in his essayist lives, in be tween, while waiting, yet writing for a transvaluing of values. But what Agamben has to say is also of a coming in threes. The first (abruption) is Agamben's return to, his rebeginnings by way of the past—a future anterior process—to rethink *techne, dynamis*, and potentialities. I am going to slight this first issue with a too brief discussion, for I want to emphasize the second issue of whatever beings and political resistance without being reactionary.

In considering labor, work, and technology (or rather—and there's a categorical in-difference—*techne*, I am not considering technology but *techne*), I am mentioning in passing that I am assuming a full discussion of the paradigmatic shifts in economy (being, becoming; thinking, writing, reading; libido [as in Lyotard *Libidinal Economics*], recognition [as in Lordship/Bondage], etc.). These shifts occur as potentiality is freed from the negative. And what I am assuming, consequently, is a radical paradigmatic shift from

1. a Nation-State Economy (a restricted economy) through
2. a Global Economy (a liminal one) to
3. a General Economy (a "general, libidinal economy").

The difference between the first and third, as Bataille, Derrida, and Cixous explain, is the difference between lack (scarcity) and excess (exuberance). As the economy shifts, there is a diminishing of the negative (negation, negativity) and a collapsing of traditional partitions and boundaries. The diminishing of the negative affects everything; for example, in a general libidinal economy there's no longer

1. one sex (male), or
2. two sexes (M/F), but
3. an exuberance of sexes (M, F, Hermaphrodites, Merms, Ferms, etc. [See geneticist Anne Fausto-Sterling.]).

When the negative loses its control over *techne, dynamis,* and potentialites, the negative topoi of species-genus-differentiae (diaeresis) no longer sort out in order to hold things in place. Hence, whatever beings are not

1. particular (species) nor
2. general (genus); instead, they are
3. a setless of radical (whatever) singularities or a "manner" (*maneries*) (See *Coming Community* 27).

Things just flow and mix noncategorically, and yet, *in relation to* each other (67). Cutting semiotically across taboos. Remember Cixous in *Three Steps on the Ladder of Writing* writes about being "'immund,' to be unclean with joy" 117), establishing heretofore unacceptable relations. Remember what Henry Miller quotes from "the great blind Milton" and perversely *elaborates* on in *Tropic of Cancer:* "Yes, I said to myself, I too love everything that flows: rivers, sewers, lava, semen, blood, bile, words, sentences," establishing heretofore unacceptable relations (257; cf. Deleuze and Guattari, *Anti-Oedipus* 132-33).

A General Economy causes all things to flow and mix in perverse ways—contrary to culture (nomos, -oi)—which is a compromise formation against nature (physis)—. . . causes all things to flow but in a new dis/concert. When the flow begins, as Hegel says,

> All identity dissolves away, for the utmost disparity now occupies the scene; what is absolutely essential is now absolutely unessential, being-for-self is now external to itself: the pure "I" itself is absolutely disrupted. . . . [S]ubject and predicate are utterly indifferent, immediate beings which have nothing to do with one another, which have no necessary unity, so much so that each is the power of a separate independent personality. [. . .] It is this absolute and universal perversion and alienation of the actual world and of thought; it is *pure culture.* What is learnt in this world is that neither the actuality of power and wealth, nor their specific *Notions,* "good" and "bad," or the conscious-

ness of "good" and "bad" . . . possess truth; on the contrary, all these moments become inverted, one changing into the other, and each is the opposite of itself. (Hegel, *Phenomenology of Spirit* 314-17; Hegel's emphasis; qt. by Agamben, *Man Without Content* 24-25)

Here we have explained, in Hegel's notion of "pure culture," the para-concept of *in-difference*. Which is not to be taken as indifference in the sense of apathy or political quietude. But as *indifferentiae*. Agamben writes:

> Decisive here is the idea of an *inessential* commonality, a solidarity [cf. Blanchot] that in no way concerns an essence. *Taking-place, the communication of singularities in the attribute of extension, does not unite them in essence, but scatters them in existence.*
>
> Whatever is constituted not by the indifference of common nature with respect to singularities, but by the indifference of the common and the proper, or the genus and the species, of the essential and the accidental. Whatever is the thing *with all its properties*, none of which, however, constitutes difference. In-difference with respect to properties is what individuates and disseminates singularities, makes them loveable (*quodlibetable*). (*The Coming Community* 18-19; Agamben's emphasis).

What we gain with *indifferentiae* are "Whatevers"! Adjacencies! (Who are without identity, species or genus, for they are radical singularities. Leftovers. Far leftover from what was presumed humanisticly possible.) But whatevers are *loveable*. They may be, from our vantage point in the present political community that speaks of solidarity, a bit like *idiots*, perhaps *idiot savants* (see Agamben, *Coming Community* 20).

Roland Barthes, I think, gives us an intimation of a whatever being: In his discussion of "The Third Meaning [Sense]," Barthes examines what he thinks are three levels of meaning in films: The *informational*, the *symbolic*, and what he calls a puzzling third level of meaning [sense], the *obtuse* level. But this is really a meaning [sense] without meaning [sense], very contrary, perverse, to the informational and symbolic meanings. Actually, the word "meaning" in the translation of the title and the text is not meaning but should be *sense*. This third level Barthes locates in, though rare, stills from Eisenstein's films. He writes:

> The obtuse [sense] appears to extend outside culture, knowledge, information; analytically, it has something derisory about it: opening out into the infinity of language, it can come through as limited in the eyes

of analytic reason; it belongs to the family of pun, buffoonery, useless expenditure [cf. Bataille]. Indifferent to moral or aesthetic categories (the trivial, the futile, the false, the pastiche) [cf. Hegel, Agamben]. (55)

As Barthes continues, he appears to be describing—future-perfectly, met-aleptically—what Agamben refers to as whatever beings and their libidinal economy and politics: These obtuse people of Eisenstein, Barthes tells us, are "loveable," they are "contrary to beautiful" (e.g., a hermaphrodite) (59). The obtuse sense is "indifferent" (61, 63) and "a luxury, an expenditure with no exchange" (62; cf. Bataille, *The Accursed Share*). He adds: "This luxury does not *yet* belong to today's politics but nevertheless *already* to tomorrow's" (63). Yes, to the coming community.

Barthes explains why the obtuse meaning of a whatever being cannot be defined in terms of meaning, which is not meaning but sense to begin with: "The obtuse meaning is a signifier without a signified, hence the difficulty in naming it [recall Asley]. . . . If the obtuse meaning cannot be described, that is because, in contrast to the obvious meaning, it does not copy anything—how do you describe something that does not represent anything?" (61). He continues to distinguish the *film*, which is concerned with informational and symbolic meanings, with the *filmic*, which "cannot be described" (64). The obtuse sense *is the filmic*. This is all so idio(ma)tic, *n'est pas*? It's a Franco-Sicilian scandal ([fortunate?] stumbling block).

Let us not misjudge Asley (in her im/possible reply to the question, What does Whatever mean?) as a generationally geographically stupid student so quickly (cf. Ronell, *Stupidity*)!

Are we yet in a better position to understand—than heretofore—how these notes, for a video trailer, *are processually for a film/ic* that will never be released! . . . These notes cannot but remain in be tween ties, tying, without any technological application[12] that has the capacity *to tween* them from where they are not to where they might possibly be. These NOTes do not want to be tweened as such. But unfortunately they can be reinscribed into a form of rational-spacial tweening from where they are not to where they would not be—forming a knot—given the right counter-derisory formula, that would expel their potentialities. Purge them. Once again.

But nevermind. For they, too, forever, will return. If purged, they but return! Cycling back through *dynamis*, potentialities. And will take on, reinscribble-inscrabble in re/turn the tying and (k)noting and untying to form a heretofore unseen, yet remaining unscene, political community of obtuse (idiot, stupid) singularities. Jean-Luc Nancy, following Agamben, tells us:

One would thus demand a politics [poly-tics, Tourette or otherwise] without dénouement—which perhaps also implies a politics without theatrical model, or a theater that would be neither tragic or comic nor a dramatization of foundation—a politics of the incessant tying up of singularities with each other, over each other, and through each other, without any *end* [Nancy's emphasis] other than the enchainment of (k)nots, without any structure other than their interconnection or inter-dependence, and without any possibility of calling any single (k)not or the totality of (k)nots self-sufficient (for there would be 'totality' only in the enchain[ing] itself).

   Such a politics consists . . . in testifying that there is singularity only where a singularity ties itself up with other singularities [recall *relations of being*], but that there is no tie except where the tie is taken up again, recast, and retied without end, nowhere purely tied and untied. No where founded and nowhere destined, always older than the law and younger than sense. Politics would henceforth be neither a substance nor a form but, first of all, *a gesture* [my emphasis]: the very gesture of the tying and enchainment of each to each, tying each time unicities (individuals, groups, nations, or peoples) that have no unity other than the unity of the (k)not. . . . This politics requires an entire ontology of being as tying. (*Sense of the World* 111-12)[13]

What *techne, dynamis,* and potentialities have become (are becoming), therefore, in our pure culture that is not a culture, nor nature—for "pure culture" is

in be tween (excluded middle, nonetheless, with its trace)

(the **virgule** as an incipently-potentially present third becoming, ever becoming a politics of beings as tying [///])

nature///culture— . . .

. . . what *techne, dynamis,* and potentialities have become is in-different. (Agamben's paramodel of the subject-cum-whatever of in-difference is Bartleby, the scrivener. [See *Coming Community* 35-38; *Potentialities* 243-71.])

F   The Film/ic Spectacle
[Background color white]

Whatever Beings!? !? !?
   Agamben writes: Whatever beings perversely "experience their own linguistic being—not this or that content of language, but language itself,

not this or that true proposition, but the very fact that one speaks" (83). The *spectacle* (accomplished nihilism)[14] does not speak for them; whatever beings speak without and beyond the spectacle. In language itself! They chew—as Kenneth Burke, Agamben, and Nancy would say—the phatic communion.

But the news footage of Tiananmen! [In the multimedia presentation, I showed four videos of the events at Tiananmen Square, May-June '89.] Is this not the SPECTACLE! The festival and carnage at TS!

And yet, Whose spectacle? Is this whatever beings' spectacle or ours, under our western eyes? Whatever beings can play to the powers (or impotence) of The Spectacle, our spectacles, and yet not be a part of it all. The students wave their flags, gesturing, along side the Goddess of Liberty Statue (which is collapsing in the video) and "we, " watching the TV news footage, believed—perhaps still believe—that the students along with the workers wanted "our" Liberty, "our" Freedom, "our" democracy!

Look, and yet How?

Have we not seen such "scenes" before! Paris '68, Nanterre '68, Chicago '68, etc. But are we not seeing spectaclizing—theorEYEzing—with our own spectacles and events! How, then, to see these *events*, if events! How then to presume to identify these happenings, if happenings! How, then, a politics?

Agamben asks—just as "we" (who live with predispositions and the State) would ask—:

> What could be the politics of whatever singularity [Abruption, interruption, in the multimedia rendition, with electronic graffiti[15]], that is, of a being whose community is mediated not by any condition of belonging (being red, being Italian, being Communist [being Hoosier Rhetor!]) [Abruption, interruption, with electronic graffiti] nor by the simple absence of conditions . . . but by belonging itself? [Agamben's emphasis] [Abruption, interruption, with electronic graffiti] A herald from Beijing [italics mine] carries the elements of a response. (85)

In *belonging itself*! But for "us" this belonging—or any thing called a politics based/less on this belonging—is so difficult to understand since it is a belonging without a predisposition or State, a politics without taking a stand; after all, the very word "understand" itself is a stasis, status, State word! (See Burke, *Grammar of Motives* 21, 23.)

Whatever singularities, according to Agamben, have no understandings! They do not ask or demand or fight for *recognition*! Among themselves. Or with "us."

Whatever beings are post-Lacanian, post-Zizekean subjects that are not subjects but whatever singularities. (They are What comes after the subject.[16]) Yes, "a herald from Beijing carries the elements of a response" to our question concerning "What could be the politics of whatever singularities"? Unlike Lacanian subjects, unlike Oedipal subjects, whatever beings do not make any demands or presuppositions.

Nancy (a repetition and a partial fulfillment) tells us:

> What one needs to think through . . . is a politics of the *seizure of speech* [emphasis mine], not of multiple wills competing to define a Sense, but of each one who makes sense, that is, ties (k)nots, from birth to death, and nothing else, and for nothing: the (k)not itself is neither a sense nor a goal nor a subject, even and above all if one wants to call it 'the law.' It is quite the contrary of what one calls today, in the magazines, the 'search for meaning' with which our time is driving itself crazy. It is the 'wandering *labor of sense* [emphasis mine].' And, without complacency, one can read the sumptuous graphical singularities and fleeting semantics of *graffiti* [Nancy's emphasis] as one mode of inscription of this 'wandering labor'—a crude and desperate mode, no doubt, but one that is therefore all the more demanding [without making demands] (*Sense* 115-16).[17]

Agamben reflects more on the Question of "What Politics?" and writes:

> What was most striking about the demonstrations of the Chinese May [Tiananmen] was the relative absence of determinate contents in their demands (democracy and freedom are notions too generic and broadly defined to constitute the real object of a conflict. [. . .] The novelty of the coming politics is that it will no longer be a struggle for the conquest or control of the State, but a struggle between the State and the non-State (humanity), an insurmountable disjunction between whatever singularity and the State organization. This has nothing to do with the simple affirmation of the social in opposition to the State that has often found expression in the protest movements of recent years. Whatever singularities cannot form a *societas* because they do not possess any identity to vindicate nor any bond of belonging for which to seek recognition. (85-86)

The keywords are "determinate contents," "demands," "identity," and "recognition." The presence of these words and the absence of what they conceptualEYEze in the students signal that the Hegelean and Kojevean principles of subject/object in a struggle unto death for recognition are no longer present—they are without quality and content—since the determinate negative has been set aside for the absolute negative, in other words, since subjectivity/objectivity has been set aside for a third of whatever singularity, or sovereignty.

[Recall the news footage of the young Chinese man who stood down three tanks in Beijing during the student protests.]

Agamben continues:

What the State cannot tolerate in any way . . . is that the singularities form a community without affirming an identity, that humans co-belong without any representable condition of belonging (even in the form of a simple presupposition). . . . A being radically devoid of any representable identity [without references] would be absolutely irrelevant to the State. . . . Whatever singularity . . . is the principal enemy of the State. Wherever these singularities peacefully demonstrate their being in common there will be a Tiananmen, and, sooner or later, the tanks will appear. (86-87)

This is NOT an *individual* stopping a tank; this is a radical *singularity*, who is a being in common with other radical singularities. He is a man without qualities, without content! To this day, this young man is unknown. Like Bartleby, he is "'a man without references, someone who appears suddenly and then disappears, without reference to himself or anything else'" (Agamben, *Potentialities* 244). (But of course it is too easy to reinscribe this disappearance of the young man as an act of brutal oppression, which it is on the part of the State, or as a romantization, which it is on the part of history.)

Our media-State spectacles see an *individual* who stops the tanks t.here! (What a romantisEYEzation this would be yet is!)

. . . Now allow this non sequitur of a parallel statement—yes, I am making a statement!—and thereby allow yourself to realEYEze that . . .

If we are similarly predisposed as the Media or even contra-predisposed, "Our" critical-Pedagogical spectacles (would) then see a postmodern Hoosier or WHATEVER rhetor in our classes—in the form of some sort of romantic youthful rebel or some spinoff avatar of Bartleby—resisting our interrogations concerning contradictions with a mere . . . "Whatever!"

A being, called a "postmodern Hoosier rhetor," or whatever, radically devoid of any representable identity except some local name applied to (a.parent.ly) politically uneducable beings (idio[ma]t.ics), would be absolutely irrelevant to the State and, as we see here, the Ideological Pedagogical Counter-State Apparatuses (that which would critique and puri- fy the State of its social contradictions, that which would *will* the redemp- tion of the past).

The Will is so tormented, however, that it has been transformed into *ressentiment* (see *Potentialities* 267). Whatever beings intuit this predispo- sition of the Will. They see this torment having been built into technology itself. Whatever beings embody resi*stance*. They go with potentialities, no longer preferring the Nothing of the State but desiring "the only ethical experience," which is "the experience of being (one's own) potentiality, of being (one's own) possibility" (*Coming Community* 44). Agamben tells us:

> Common and proper, genus and individual are only the two slopes dropping down from either side of the watershed of whatever: As with Prince Myshkin in Dostoyevsky's *Idiot*, who can effortlessly imitate any- one's handwriting and sign any signature . . . the particular and the generic become indifferent, and precisely this is the 'idiocy,' [the obtuse- ness, the filmic] in other words, the particularity of the whatever. (20)

And yet, let us pull this together now and remember that *although* "whatever is the figure of pure singularity," *although* it "has no identity," and *although* "it is not determinate with respect to a concept"—all of which Agamben reminds us—"neither is it simply indeterminate; rather it is determined only through its [third] relation [of adjacency] to an *idea*, that is, to the totality of its possibilities" (67; Agamben's emphasis). In other words, there are more than only two slopes as possibilities. There is a third of radical finitude.

T.Here, then, are two very different "communities," one blind to and in collision with the other coming (whatever) community:

- one dead, practicing a maieutics of stillbirths;
- the other, in its incipient formlessness, mutating into ever more radical, "loveable" (*quodlibetable*) singularities (19).

"Our" students refuse *to labor* and *to work* as we instruct them to.

They may play with technology and may use the equivalent of FAX + machines as the whatever beings in Beijing did in the spring and summer of 1989, sending out electronic flyers about what was (a) happening(?)! But they are more so, near completely so, creatures of potentiality. Theirs is a radical passivity! They—like Bartleby—prefer not to not (i.e., to negate in order to critique).

And then, when asked, "What is it that you want?" (*Che Vuoi?*) by the aging political-pedagogical always-already Oedipal Fathers and Mothers, whatever singularities prefer not to answer. After all has been said and undone, they are whatever beings. They prefer not to be in the present reactionary, resentful community. Prefer not to be complicit in employing the principle that excludes.

They prefer the coming community. in be tween! alongside!

In the "interworld" (*Coming*, 97).

In Limbo (5-7).[18]

Living there, abandoned by God and Satan, Media Generals and State Pedagogues, *abandoned beyond good and evil*[19] (therefore, without any foundations, naive or cynical ones called "provisionary" or "strategic foundations"!), and with "guilt and justice behind them . . . the life that begins on earth after the last day is simply [whatever] life" (6-7; italics mine).

ENDNOTES

1. The multimedia (video, audio, animations) version of this paper can be seen online at http://www.uta.edu/english/V/test/agamben/.
2. There is, of course, no "plane of imminence," phrased as such, in Deleuze and Guattari. However, there is a sense of such. See *Thousand Plateaus* 265-66, where they make a distinction between the plane of organization or development and the plain of consistency or composition. They describe the latter as "no longer [having] any forms or developments of forms, nor are there subjects or formation of subjects. There is no structure, more than there is genesis. There are only relations of movement and rest, speed and slowness between unformed elements, or at least between elements that are relatively unformed, molecules and particles of all kinds. There are only haecceities, affects, subjectless individuations that constitute collective assemblages. Nothing develops, but things arrive late or early, and form this or that assemblage depending on their compositions of speed. Nothing subjectifies, but haecceities form according to compositions of nonsubjectified powers or affects" (266). See Deleuze's discussions in *Pure Immanence: Essays on A Life*.
3. I have discussed the problems inherent in subjectivity in *Negation, Subjectivity, and The History of Rhetoric*.
4. It is the case that both Georges Bataille and Maurice Blanchot were, in turn, influenced by Hegel and had, in return, an influence on Agamben.
5. Revolution and evolution at the conceptual and material levels are better known than "involution" (or becoming). For the latter, see Deleuze and Guattari's discussion in *Thousand Plateaus* 238-39. In addition, I grant that my

interpretation of Agamben's reading of technology could be seen as a casuistic stretching of Agamben's point concerning *techne* (not technology) and potentialities. My interpretation is based on a reading of Agamben's *Potentialities*. Concerning the impact of technology on cultures, cf. Virilio's *Open Sky*, especially "The Third Interval" (9-21). Also of importance to this discussion of *techne* (not technology) is Mark Hansen's *Embodying Technesis: Technology Beyond Writing*, which would take issue, in part, with the distinction *techne* (not technology) as I unfold it here in passing. But finally, the issue of "*techne* (not technology)" plays a secondary role here in relation to what is happening to subjectivity and community in their movement toward whatever beings.

6. Apedagogy is a term that I take, with its various senses, from Lyotard (*Political Writings* 58).

7. What would reconstitute hope, Agamben makes clear: "We can have hope only in what is without remedy. That things are thus and thus—this is still in the world. But that this is irreparable, that this *thus* is without remedy, that we can contemplate it as such—this is the only passage outside the world. (The innermost character of salvation is that we are saved only at the point when we no longer want to be. At this point, there is salvation—but not for us" (102; Agamben's emphasis).

8. I have more fully discussed the relationship between Heidegger and Agamben in "Two Gestures."

9. Agamben's discussions in *Potentialities* (e.g., 184, 214-19) attempt to recapture the sources of the "mystical" Aristotle, which have been all but erased in the production of an Aristotle who is in part the originator of a rational view of the world.

10. The term "radical passivity" is Thomas Wall's, in a book of the same title.

11. Although there is a certain uncertain humor in what I am saying here, there is the same in terms of seriousness. In making an animated image of myself, I am not only offering a third object but also am alluding to Agamben's discussion of advertising in the section of *Coming Community* titled "Dim Stockings." He writes: "What was technologized was not the body, but its image. . . . To appropriate the historic transformations of human nature that capitalism wants to limit to the spectacle, to link together image and body in a space where they can no longer be separated, and thus to forge the whatever body, whose *physis* is resemblance—this is the good that humanity must learn how to wrest from commodities in their decline. Advertising and pornography, which escort the commodity to the grave like hired mourners, are the unknowing midwives of this new body of humanity" (50).

12. Tweening is a technical term in computer applications such as Macromedia's *Flash* that are programmed for animations. Tweening allows for the application to automatically take an animated object (person, dog, etc.) from one point in time and space to another point, as in starting a walk to finishing a walk.

13. Nancy continues to discuss a second attribute for a politics and that is "the seizure of speech, not of multiple wills competing to define a Sense, but of

each one who makes sense, that is, ties (k)nots, from birth to death, and nothing else, and for nothing: the *(k)not* itself neither a sense nor a goal nor a subject, even and above all if one wants to call it 'the law'" (*Sense* 116). And then most importantly—given tying and seizure of speech—Nancy writes: "The tying up of singular events of sense does not arise from either of these two models, but from access to the concatenation of acts of speech, even if—or rather, *because*—this concatenation is not completeable, is infinitely reTICulated [capital letters mine], infinitely interrupted and retied, and even if—or because—these acts of speech tend toward the most naked function of language, toward what one calls its phatic [communicative] function: the maintenance of a relation that communicates no sense other than the relation itself" (*Sense* 117).

14. See Agamben's discussion of the Situationists and Debord's *Society of the Spectacle* in *Means Without Ends* 73-89.
15. These bracketed interpolations are electronic animations undisclosed here but present in the Web version.
16. See Cadava, Connor, Nancy's *Who Comes After the Subject?*
17. I exaggerate (abruptly, erruptively).
18. Agamben asks, "Where do whatever singularities come from? Where is their realm." The title of this first section (and answer) is "From Limbo." About being in Limbo, Agamben writes: "The greatest punishment—the lack of the vision of God—turns into a natural joy: Irremediably lost, they persist without pain in *divine abandon*. God has not forgotten them, but rather they have always already forgotten God; and in the face of their forgetfulness, God's forgetting is impotent" (6; italics mine).
19. See Vitanza, "The Hermeneutics of Abandonment." Part 3 of "Abandonment" is presently being drafted. (There is no Part 2.)
20. In the multimedia rendition, outtakes from the video trailer for a Film/ic that will not be released are standing ready to be dispersed. See them at the URL given in footnote 1.

REFERENCES

Agamben, Giorgio. *The Coming Community*. Minneapolis: U of Minnesota P, 1993.
_____. *The Man Without Content*. Trans. Georgia Albert. Stanford, CA: Stanford UP, 1999.
_____. *Means Without Ends: Notes on Politics*. Trans. Vincenzo Binetti and Cesare Casarino. Minneapolis: U of Minnesota P, 2000.
_____. *Potentialities: Collected Essays in Philosophy*. Ed. and Trans., Daniel Heller-Roazen, Stanford, CA: Stanford UP, 1999.
Barthes, Roland. "The Third Meaning [Sense]." *Image Music Text*. Trans. Stephen Heath. New York: Hill and Wang, 1977. 52-68.

Bataille, Georges. *The Accursed Share*. Vol. 1. Trans. Robert Hurley. New York: Zone Books, 1988.

Baudrillard, Jean. *Fatal Strategies*. Trans. Philip Beitchman and W. G. J. Niesluchowski. Brooklyn, NY: Semiotext(e), 1990.

Burke, Kenneth. *Grammar of Motives*. Berkeley: U of California P, 1969.

Butler, Judith. *Gender Trouble*. New York: Routledge, 1990.

Cixous, Hélène. *Three Steps on the Ladder of Writing*. New York: Columbia UP, 1993.

Davis, D. Diane. "Finitude's Clamor: Or, Notes toward a Communitarian Literacy." *CCC*. 53.1 (2001): 119-45.

Deleuze, Gilles. *Pure Immanence: Essays on A Life*. New York: Zone Books, 2001.

Deleuze, Gilles, and Felix Guattari. *Anti-Oedipus*. Minneapolis: U of Minnesota P, 1983.

_____. *A. Thousand Plateaus*. Trans. Brian Massumi. Minneapolis: U of Minnesota P, 1987.

Fausto-Sterling, Anne. "The Five Sexes: Why Male and Female Are Not Enough." *The Sciences*. (March/April 1993): 20-25.

Hansen, Mark. *Embodying Technesis: Technology Beyond Writing*. Ann Arbor: U of Michigan P, 2000.

Harkin, Patricia. "Rhetoric, Poetics, and Cultures as an Articulation Project." *JAC*. 17.3 (1997): 494-96.

Hegel, G. W. F. *Phenomenology of Spirit*. Trans. A. V. Miller. Oxford: Oxford UP, 1977.

Kristeva, Julia. *Powers of Horror: An Essay on Abjection*. Trans. Leon S. Roudiez. New York: Columbia UP, 1982.

Laporte, Dominique. *History of Shit*. Trans. Nadia Benabid and Rodolphe el-Khoury. Cambridge, MA: MIT UP, 2000.

Lyotard, Jean-François. *Libidinal Economy*. Trans. Iain Hamilton Grant. Bloomington: Indiana UP, 1993.

_____. *Political Writings*. Trans. Bill Readings and Kevin Paul Geiman. Minneapolis: U of Minnesota P, 1993.

Marx, Karl. *Capital*. Vol. 1. New York: Vintage, 1977.

Musil, Robert. *The Man Without Qualities*. Vol. 1. Trans. Eithne Wilkins and Ernst Kaiser. New York: Capricorn, 1965.

Nancy, Jean-Luc. *The Inoperative Community*. Trans. Peter Conor et al. Minneapolis: The U of Minnesota P, 1991.

_____. *The Sense of the World*. Trans. Jeffrey S. Librett. Minneapolis: The U of Minnesota P, 1997.

North, Stephen M. "The Death of Paradigm Hope, the End of Paradigm Guilt, and the Future of (Research in) Composition." In *Composition in the Twenty-First Century: Crisis and Change*. Eds. Lynn Z. Bloom, Donald A. Daiker, Edward M. White. Carbondale: Southern Illinois UP, 1996.

Ronell, Avital. *Finitude's Score*. Lincoln: U of Nebraska P, 1994.

_____. *Stupidity*. Urbana: U of Illinois P, 2002.

Turkle, Sherry. "A New Kind of Object." *Edge*. http://www.edge.org/3rd_culture/story/101.html.

Vitanza, Victor J. "The Hermeneutics of Abandonment." *parallax*. 4.4 (1998): 123-139.

———. *Negation, Subjectivity, and The History of Rhetoric*. Albany: SUNY UP, 1997.

———. "Two Gestures." *EBR*, vol. 3 (2003). http://www.electronicbookreview .com/ v3/servlet/ebr?command = view_essay&essay_id = vitanzaaltx

Virilio, Paul. *Open Sky*. Trans. Juilie Rose. New York: Verso, 1997.

Who Comes After the Subject? Edited by Cadava, Eduardo, Peter Connor, and Jean-Luc Nancy. New York: Routledge, 1991.

7

'OUTING' THE INSTITUTION

(RE)WRITING TECHNOLOGIES
WITH A RHETORIC OF FEMALE-TO-MALE DRAG

Tara Pauliny

University of Wisconsin, Oshkosh

As demonstrated by the numerous articles, books, and journals that deal with the intersection of composition and technology, it is clear that any technological addition to either the classroom or the larger university is not a neutral act, but a fundamental alteration of these sites.[1] The introduction of computers in the writing classroom, for instance, has produced a new genre of pedagogy, compelled changes in class size, and revised the day-to-day interactions of students and teachers. Likewise, the larger world of the university has been widely affected by advances in technology: Web sites now serve as information centers and advertisements for institutions, distanced learning classes have become expected additions to course offerings, a school's technological resources are often a major consideration for prospective students, and, as we have all experienced, most campus communication now takes place via e-mail. Technology, as both a tool and a theoretical structure, has become—for better or for worse—such an inescapable force in the everyday life of the university that even when an instructor merely doesn't "do" e-mail, he or she runs the risk of missing vital information or, more importantly, being regarded as entrenched in the past.

Keeping pace with the ever pressing advances of technology, therefore, has most often meant considering and reacting to technology's electronic incarnations. As such, English Studies has responded with discussions of and research about technology in the computer-based composition classroom, the construction of student and teacher identity on the Internet, student correspondence via e-mail, and the discursive possibilities of hypertext. Together, these pedagogical investigations form a diverse and significant area of English Studies laden with theoretical possibilities.

Another theoretical possibility, however, is the investigation of nondigital and nonelectronic modes of technology—the consideration of technology as an ideological and epistemological force, for instance. For, when technology is unmoored from its more traditional definition, it can be understood as a kind of cultural tool or performative force. The technological, therefore, can be located not only in physical objects—computers, the World Wide Web, e-texts—but in metaphysical concepts as well. Assuming such a construction, technology can be characterized as a "screen" or "projected image" through and on which power fluctuates, and markers of identity can thus be termed technological because it is in their name that power operates (Halberstam and Livingston 2).

Following this logic, it is reasonable to recognize the concept that has come to be called "the body," as a technology itself. The body, after all, is certainly an object and an idea on which images of gender, sex, power, and the like have been corporealized. What is significant here is that, as Judith Halberstam and Ira Livingston note in the introduction to their collection *Posthuman Bodies*, conceptualizing the body in this technological way effectively "queers" the body: it "fragments it, frames it, cuts it" (16). In other words, formulating the body, (or in their term the *posthuman* body), as a technology is to recognize its ideological potential. This understanding of the body does not see it as a "slave to masterdiscourses" or an empty vessel waiting to be filled with dominant culture's prescriptive norms, but as a fluttering and flickering screen that "emerge[s] at nodes where bodies, bodies of discourse, and discourses of bodies intersect to foreclose any easy distinction between actor and stage, between sender/receiver, channel, code, message, context" (2). Bodies pulsate with signification and brim with persuasive power. Furthermore, as Donna Haraway argues, formulating the body in this way does not offer a "fixed location in a reified body" but "nodes in fields, inflections in orientations." Embodiment, as she sees it, "is significant prosthesis" (2).[2] To be technological then, is to be projected and shifting. It is to be a body—or a subject—constructed not of "natural" parts or even of "normal expectations," but of prosthetic mechanisms that can be deployed, added, altered, or removed in attempts to achieve particular purposes.

The specific prosthetic technology I introduce in this essay is what I call the "rhetorical technology of female-to-male (FTM) drag," or the rhetorical deployment by women of language structures, dress, behaviors, and/or physical postures traditionally coded either specifically masculine—or those unmarked codes that reflect highly privileged positions. This particular bodily technology of FTM drag is rhetorical because it functions on the level of argumentation. It is an analytic that allows for the deciphering, examining, and questioning of particular sites, objects, and constructions. And although this rhetorical technology may not be "hard-wired," it is a technology that produces representations and arguments. As both a tool and a theory, rhetorical FTM drag changes the elements of any situation in which it is deployed.

An important distinction to note, however, between the performance of the rhetorical technology of FTM drag outside a staged context, is that the presentation drag becomes less overt. So, rather than performing "as a man"—like drag kings who dress in "men's" clothes and use markers of masculinity to shape their act—women who perform FTM drag within the university perform activities "of a man." That is, they transgress boundaries of power and privilege, taking it upon themselves to decide course content, research topics, and levels of appropriate behavior. This rhetorical practice thus uses markers of power not only to represent images of subjects' identities, but to draw out the gendered, raced, sexed, classed, and sexualized hierarchical codes that construct institutional identities. Like the "posthuman becoming-subject" who "vibrates across and among an assemblage of semi-autonomous collectives it knows it can never either be coextensive with nor altogether separate from," the rhetorical technology of FTM drag moves across and through boundaries of gender, sex, race, and privilege; it never wholly *becomes* or any of these categories (Halberstam and Livingston 14). Instead, FTM drag technology appropriates and imitates the seemingly "original" markers of bodily categories and reveals these "originals" as copies themselves.[3]

The rhetorical technology of FTM drag thereby emphasizes the ways women can engage with and utilize "masculine" or "privileged" codes in potentially disruptive ways; it provides a unique insight into how women in the academy negotiate their own identity categories and how the institution simultaneously attempts to manage and control such identities. The analysis of FTM drag does not attempt to usurp the position of the dominant, however, but to disperse its hegemony and expose its seemingly solid foundation as makeshift and theatrical. As performances of FTM drag therefore, some women's classroom and scholarly practices may be seen as processes that build arguments about authority, ethos, class, audience, and the heteronormative and racial assumptions of the academy. For in the always rhetorical and performative contexts of teacher and student, speaker and audience, writer and reader, performer and onlooker, FTM drag becomes a way to understand how women use masculinity and the un-named markers of power to authorize themselves and affect their various audiences. Furthermore, because FTM drag considers as "masculine" any position or activity that has the advantage of being un-marked, un-named, or inherently the most powerful, it can also be utilized as a device to understand how non-normative identity performances unmask or "out" the regulatory structure of the university. This revised version of technology is thus a way to decipher the intricate web of relatedness between identity categories, social expectations, disciplinary boundaries, and the myriad elements that work to produce power relationships. Seen not only as a tool, but also as the very means by which arguments about identity and power are constructed and disseminated, images of the body—and even the body "itself"—can be considered a technological force both complicit in and resistant to the maintenance and subversion of institutionalized power.

* * *

In her text *Female Masculinity*, Judith Halberstam conceptualizes masculinity in Western society as that which "inevitably conjures up notions of power and legitimacy and privilege," as that which often represents a symbolic reference "to the power of the state and to uneven distributions of wealth," and as that which "extend[s] outward into patriarchy and inward[s] into the family" (Halberstam 2). However, as masculinity "represents the power of inheritance, the consequence of the traffic in women, and the promise of social privilege [. . .] many other lines of identification traverse the terrain of masculinity, dividing its power into complicated differentials of class, race, sexuality, and gender" (2). Ultimately, Halberstam argues that "the shapes and forms of modern masculinity are best showcased within female masculinity" (3). Beginning with Halberstam's definition, then, I extend her concept of female masculinity to include women's cooption and inhabitation of those positions and privileges traditionally considered the domain of white men in Western society. Whereas Halberstam uses "the topic of female masculinity to explore a queer subject position that can successfully challenge hegemonic models of gender conformity," I understand the rhetorical technology of FTM drag as a form of female masculinity that queers[4] the hierarchical power structure of the university (9). FTM drag not only "challenges models of gender conformity," but also challenges the institutional and disciplinary binaries that restrict women's participation in, and identity construction by, the university.

To illustrate these points, I offer two scenarios. Together, these show how a rhetorical technology of FTM drag can uncover the inner workings of the university's institutional hierarchies. The first scenario, taken from a second-level writing classroom, explains how easily a disruption of the institution's power structure can be thwarted, whereas the second scenario demonstrates how the institution might respond to such a disruption.

SCENARIO 1

During Summer 2000 I taught my university's second-level writing class in a computer classroom. This class met twice a week for 2 hours and enrolled 20 students. During this same time, the Writing Program Administrators from the university's First-Year Writing Program were planning the annual teacher-training workshop. As part of that preparation they asked to videotape my teaching so the tape could be excerpted and used during the training course. I agreed, and the taping proceeded without incident. Out of curiosity, however, I watched the tape a few weeks later. To my surprise and concern, I discovered that the self I always thought I performed as a teacher was a very different self from that which appeared on the screen. I typically think of myself, at least in some ways, as having a masculine presence in the classroom. Although I do not officially "out" myself to my students, I have always assumed that from my self-presentation (my very short hair; my consistent outfit of pants, plain shirt, and flat shoes; the absence of make-up; the nontraditional course material I assign; and the overt attention paid to sexuality, gender, and power in my classes) that students either thought I was a lesbian or at least recognized my deviance from traditionally coded "feminine" dress and behavior.

As I sat down to watch this tape, then, I was confident that I would see Halberstam's version of "female masculinity" on the video.[5] Instead, what I saw was a rather traditionally coded feminine teaching performance emanating from what I believed to be a less-than-traditional teacher: although

I looked somewhat unconventional, I was also nurturing, took most of the responsibility for the discussion and even group work, made sure to ease students' discomfort, and responded to their frustrations with the texts by reassuring them or even providing suggested ways to read or interpret. So although my appearance was not traditionally feminine, I read my actions as such. I saw myself as reflecting the by-now-archetypal "feminized" composition instructor. Like those theorists who have identified the influence of gender and power, within both English Studies and larger culture, I saw my teacherly persona as feminized and my classroom as the epitome of this pedagogical phenomenon.[6]

I located my pedagogical performance within the feminization trope that conceives of identity as male/female or feminine/masculine, has a theoretical understanding of composition's devalued relationship to English departments and the larger university, and notes that women and men have different access to institutionalized power and privilege. This rubric characterizes composition as the "female"—read second-tier, devalued, service-oriented—counterpart to the "real" discipline of literary studies, and recognizes that composition instructors are expected to conform to these roles (even male compositionists, for example, are seen as more "nurturing" or less "rigorous" than their literature colleagues).[7]

Like those teachers described by Sue Ellen Holbrook, Nancy Schneidewind, and Susan Miller, I de-centered the authority of my classroom, and reified a pedagogical identity "deeply embedded in traditional views of women's roles" (Miller 122). Consequently, I read my performance as one that failed to push the boundaries of gender, power, or the discipline. I saw it in the terms prescribed by composition studies and articulated it to myself accordingly. As a self-defined queer teacher whose intention was to blur the boundaries of authority and lay bare the structures on which power was draped, I thus regarded my work in the classroom as unsuccessful because it failed to deviate from the "ideological constructions that tie [composition instructors and female teachers in general] to fantasized functions and activities" traditionally accorded to women (Miller 123). Success of the employment of a rhetoric of FTM drag in the classroom, it seemed to me, would not look feminized at all, but rather would look much like it does on stage: dynamic and overt. My adoption of feminized composition behaviors, I believed, fell short of this framework.

As I reflected on my interpretation of this scene and started to re-read it, however, I began to see my performance differently. Instead of viewing it as a direct enactment of the trope of feminization, I recognized that my reading of the video was being driven by the powerful rubric of feminization. The 15-minute classroom performance that originally looked traditional to me, did not actually tell the whole story of the course. By relying on this established theory, I neglected to place this short scene in the context of the entire course; I allowed the disciplinary entrenchment of feminization to direct my interpretation and I thus confined my judgment to the field of its parameters.

If I had looked beyond this binary of masculine–feminine and authoritative–subordinate, however, I would have seen quite a different picture. For rather than focusing solely on my bodily performance (my relaxed and feminine posture, encouraging nods, and nurturing smile), I could have recognized that the genre and content of my course as a whole actually disrupted the coherent narrative fostered by the larger university. By substituting an analytic of the rhetorical technology of FTM drag for the feminization of composition, the intricate plays of pedagogical power could become visible. No longer relegated to binaries of dominant–subordinate, this classroom moment resisted its own suppression. My performance, therefore, was not an example of how a feminized instructor is complicit with the power structure of the academy, but became for me, a means by which to understand how easily thwarted any infiltration of such a structure can be. By conceptualizing FTM drag in the classroom not in terms of bodily performance (as it is analyzed when performed on stage by drag kings), but in terms of continual and sustained disruptions of hierarchialized power, it becomes clear that such a technological intervention uncovers, rather than upholds, the power structures of the university.

Reading this first scenario as an example of the rhetorical technology of FTM drag then, is to identify the ways I utilize "masculine"—read privileged—positions of power and simultaneously subvert and critique those un-marked positions. For instance, as a White instructor I inhabit the privileged position of my un-marked race. Whiteness authorizes me and legitimates my place as the instructor of the class. My race invisibly upholds my position of power and empowers me even as my position as a woman marks me as paradoxically inferior. Likewise, my status as a middle-class White woman also authorizes my privileged position. So although I may be vulnerable because of my potential queerness and my gender, my invisible class and race markers mediate these subordinate positions. Judging the success of my classroom performance, then, depends not only on whether I became feminized, but how my varied identities complicated such a flat trope. The queer analytic of FTM drag thus demands that the entire content and context of the course be considered. Identity performance cannot be relegated to bodily expression, but is expanded to genre, content, and outcomes. Likewise, my identity as an instructor is defined by the textual content I assign, the diverse genres my students write and read, and the expectations I have for them as critical readers of culture. The success of my course depends not on my students' recognition of me as a queer woman, but on their ability to question how such terms of identification come to be invested with or emptied of cultural capital. When my students are able to understand how power flows and coalesces at various points related to race, class, gender, and religion, I have been a successful queer teacher.

Outing myself as a lesbian, therefore, is not necessary for me to effect a queer pedagogy. Rather, the consistent, varied, and sustained covert (and occasionally overt) disruption of norms, expectations, and demands make pedagogy queer. Because queerness privileges fluidity and indeterminacy, by not "outing" myself, but rather allowing my nonhierarchical classroom construction to "out" the structure of the academy itself, my classroom becomes a space where students cannot easily relegate my identity to a binary of either gay or straight, masculine or feminine. Instead, the course's privileging of difference, investigation of power dynamics, and continual challenging of students' world-views queer the classroom. Juxtaposing a constructive and affirming teaching persona with an indeterminate sexuality, nontraditional course content, and assignments that foster critical thinking and cultural analysis, compels students to look beyond simple explanations or overgeneralized theories. The rhetorical technology of FTM drag encourages students to evaluate not only their own thoughts, but to question the validity of cultural and institutional expectations. FTM drag thus unsettles disciplinary tropes and allows for a subtle reading of the structured system of university authority.

By taking the instance of this particular class and applying a queer FTM rubric, we can understand how powerful the normative demands of the university are and how continual and diverse subversions of that structure need to be. This scenario, coupled with my evolving response, highlight how difficult it is to interrupt the disciplinary power of the university. Because the institution has numerous ways to protect itself (including theoretical tropes), an "outing" of such a system needs to be sustained, varied, and often quite subtle.

To illustrate this resilience and tenacity of the university, I offer my second scenario. This scenario provides a counterpoint to the first, for rather than exposing how easily the institution can suppress any disruption of itself, this example exposes how the institution (through its representatives) might respond to such a disruption. Again, issues of genre, context, and identity are important here, because it is when these boundaries are transgressed that the institution responds by entrenching itself in a defensive position.

SCENARIO 2

Approximately a year after I watched the videotape of my teaching, I presented a paper at a university-wide graduate student research competition. Delivering a section of my dissertation that analyzed the rhetorical performance of Dréd, a Haitian-American FTM drag king, I hoped to engage my audience in an analysis of gender binaries and queer rhetoric. Within the paper I first conceptualized Dréd's act as one that appropriated and embodied certain discourses of desire, and I then rhetorically analyzed these appeals according to the arguments they made about gender, sexuality, and race.[8]

From all outward signs the presentation went well: I was the only person to finish within the prescribed 12-minute limit; my audience of graduate students and two professors—who were also serving as judges—nodded and took notes as I spoke; afterward, everyone was eager to ask me questions and express their interest in my work. In the follow-up critique session, however, during which time both the judges and session participants provided feedback to each presenter, I was shocked by what I heard. Instead of posing questions about my methods or analysis, my responders seemed enthralled by what they apparently perceived as the "sexual" aspects of my paper. They spent the majority of my critique time discussing my introduction, which gave a brief, first-person account of Dréd's performance. Overwhelmingly, they seemed to agree that this narrative and highly descriptive preface provided an effective departure from traditional academic writing and that it conjured a clear image of Dréd's act. One of my fellow presenters even commented that the pictures evoked by my description exactly matched the photos I later showed of the actual performance. What surprised me about all this was not their interest in or positive response to my introduction, but where the conversation led. For rather than moving from this initial discussion to a more detailed critique and examination of the rest of my piece, our discussion turned to popular images of sexual titillation. Directly on the heels of these comments, one of the judges asked me how my work related to "pornography" and jokingly told me, in front of this same audience, that if I didn't "make it" in academe, I could always be a soft-porn writer. With this, everyone laughed, and we moved onto the next critique.

Barring any other explanation, it seems to me that the institution's anxieties about queerness and its threat to the hegemonic power structure surfaced swiftly and clearly in these responses. For rather than commenting academically on my work, the judges equated my theorization of sexuality with any and all forms of sex. Consequently, it became acceptable for them to relate my work to pornography, and in a postpresentation conversation later that day, "out" me as a lesbian. Because the genre of my introduction deviated from traditional notions of academic prose and the content failed to conform to expected parameters, my work was judged academically unrecognizable. As representatives of institutional power, then, the judges claimed the right not only to "out" me as a gay woman, but also to ignore the academic content of my presentation.

By examining this scenario through an analytic of rhetorical/technological FTM drag the audience's responses can be read not simply as the unprofessional or inadequate critical comments of individuals, but more importantly as the defensive stance of an invaded institution. The tenor and content of their comments become markers of what Halberstam and Livingston name a "rhetorical crisis" in which

> one minute he'll lay down the law of the jungle to you and the next minute he'll be aghast when everything isn't tastefulness, gentility, and rationality. The privilege of blindness to these contradictions is part of the arrogance of entrenched power; no doubt it will always be ready to sacrifice everything, beginning with its subalterns, in order to go to the grave with the privilege of this blindness, with the delusion of its own disinterestedness or internal consistence, the proud fiction of its self-sacrificing fatherliness or motherliness. (Halberstam and Livingston 9)

Retreating to binaries of academic–popular, gay–straight, and expert–amateur, the judges reflect the tendency of power to reproduce itself and dismiss that which challenges it. As individuals whose authority is conferred by the institution, which reflects prevailing cultural norms, and is further upheld by their whiteness and maleness, their response to my work exemplified the institution's ability to protect itself. What this scenario represents, then, is the university's attempt to reproduce itself through masculinity/authorized subject positions.

The defensive posture of the judges was not confined to my work, however. Another presenter, an African-American female student, was faced with similar problematic responses. After her analysis of the (mis)treatment of race in Judy Blume novels, the audience responded by commenting that she faults Blume for, on the one hand, ignoring non-White races, and on the other hand, complaining about the representation Blume does give Black characters. They were confused, they claimed, and asked what, exactly, did she want from Blume? Following this query, a fellow presenter asked if she was arguing that Judy Blume was a racist, and one of the judges suggested the presenter might be "reading too much into these books." Similarly, during the question and answer session of my talk, this same judge also accused me of "reading race" into Dréd's performance (even though, as you'll remember, Dréd is Black). After I responded that any performance is always marked by race, he continued his line of questioning, ultimately arguing that he thought a White drag king could simply perform gender and not perform race if she chose to do so.[9]

Perhaps not surprisingly, these kinds of questions were not asked of the other presenters. Even, for example, when one White female speaker (who won first place in the competition) discussed a specific language pattern of Cantonese females without analyzing gender or race, the judges had no comments about these issues. Likewise, when the second- and third-place winners were finished their presentations (about Eastern European language relationships and Caesar's diary as an imperialist document), the judges' comments were restricted to content-specific issues. Although each of the other presenters was critiqued in various ways by the judges, I received no substantive response when I inquired about the faults of my project. Instead, their responses reverted to vague positive comments about the high quality of all the work presented. As can be seen in the following e-mail excerpts, the judges appeared unable or unwilling to respond to my work critically or to evaluate it according to the academic guidelines prescribed by the contest. The following excerpts are taken from a short e-mail exchange I had with them in which I asked for specific feedback about the quality of my project, particular areas I could improve, and where my presentation failed to meet the forum's criteria.

> You're [sic] paper and presentation were extremely interesting, provocative and entertaining. I suspect that what I have to express to you about my reasoning and the deliberations [the other judge] and I went through will not be very satisfying to you. I certainly don't think I can frame a response in terms of "criteria you failed to meet" [. . . . I] know this is going to be frustrating to you, but I honestly cannot think of anything about your presentation that I would suggest you do differently. Both [the other judge] and I thought it was a superb presentation, as I know you gathered from our positive comments. The decision to award the prizes to three other papers was not a reflection of any problem in your paper or presentation.[. . .] As I've said, I know this is not the kind of helpful input you were hoping for, but I honestly cannot think of any criticism I would make either of your paper or your presentation.[10]

Understanding this series of events through the matrix of the rhetorical technology of FTM drag, suggests that my presentation offered a threat
to the institutionalized hierarchy of the university. The subversive intent of
my work coupled with my appropriation of unmarked privileged identities
made the work unacceptable or anomalous to the judges. My recognition
and annunciation of myself as a marked subject (woman, gay, graduate student), along with my work's critical attention to these categories, effectively "outed" the power invested in such categorizations.

So when the argument of my work was ignored and its content equated with sex, the markers on which academic authority is based became
clear and sex became a kind of academic currency. As a means to devalue
my work and separate it from an academic context, sex became "a channel for something besides its own drive for pleasure" (Halberstam and
Livingston 8). The judges protective responses to my queries work to reinforce the idea that recognizably academic work is that which adheres to,
rather than diverges from, accepted genres; it is that which leaves unques-
tioned or even unacknowledged, the categories through which power
flows; and which actively, if not overtly, reinscribes hierarchies of gender,
genre, content, and race. To produce work that diverges from these parameters is to unmask these markers as artificial and flawed. Therefore,
because my performance of the academic seemed more like a masquerade
than a legitimate enaction, it raised suspicion and evoked a reactionary
response.

It might seem, then, that my original intention had failed. After all,
rather than engaging my audience in an academic critique of gender
norms and an examination of a woman's persuasive use of masculinity, my
work was relegated to the sphere of humorous quips and reactionary dis-
missals. My personal identity became a topic of discussion, and the larger
context of my work was evaded; rather than producing a nuanced reading
of the interaction of identity and power, my presentation was regarded as
an amusing diversion. If, however, I read this scene as an engagement with
the rhetorical technology of FTM drag, these answers are not so easy to
come by. The very fact that my performance elicited such a virulent
response is evidence of its potentially subversive effect. It may not have
changed the power structure of the university, but it just might have
revealed the level at which institutional norms are embedded.

* * *

Although there are undoubtedly numerous ways to read these two events (including discomfort with nontraditional material, an unwillingness to engage with postmodern identity theory, or quite simply as sexual harassment), I read them as moments in which queer performances expose the gendered, raced, heteronormative, and ideological structures that uphold the authority of the university and its representatives. In these two instances, my gendered and sexual identity became juxtaposed with the very systems of authority and power that constructs university hierarchies and determines my place within them. My presentation as a simultaneously masculine (empowered, authorized, un-marked), and feminine (subordinate, vulnerable, marked), teacher of writing and female graduate student induced a state of heightened anxiety for both myself and my audiences. By exposing the silent workings of institutionalized power, these examples illustrate that the institution is not a monolith at all, but an intricate web of constructed identities, expectations, and social norms. Because my performance in these two events deviated from academic norms and pushed the expected definitions of both teacher and student, my own constructed and shifting identity was exposed along with the unstable nature of the institution. Put another way, my unlikely pairing of tradition and subversion effectively "outed" the carnival nature of the university.

To use Mikhail Bakhtin's term, the rhetorical technology of FTM drag is similar to the "carnival consciousness" because like the carnival, FTM drag is "a concept inherently concerned with generation and change," and defined as a "complex system of meaning," that "simultaneously ridicules and celebrates, crowns and decrowns, elevates and debases" (Morris 16). FTM drag represents a performance of queer identity that is not only related to the individual or her body, but to "the body of all people" (21). In other words, just as the carnival is connected to a social system, identity is connected to political, sexual, gendered, raced, and classed groups. Furthermore, this connection between the carnival and identity performance is especially relevant because both are engaged in a process of "liberating human consciousness from a vertical hierarchical perception of the world and of opening up the possibility for a horizontal historical understanding of change" (21-22). The rhetorical technology of FTM drag thus allows identity performances, and responses to those performances, to be read as heteroglossic because it recognizes the relationship that exists between these performances and the various institutions effected by them. As a queer identity is invested in upsetting the status quo and querying the traditional, stable, and dualistic nature of self-construction, so too is queer pedagogy and institutional performance.

It is not surprising then, that when I watched myself perform a part of my identity on tape, I saw a fractured, partial part of myself. What I originally took as the "whole" of my pedagogical performance—the seemingly clear representation of a feminized instructor—when viewed in the context of my entire, quarter-length performance, became only a small section of my identity. My use of certain "feminine" markers, therefore, did not stand alone, but was forced into dialogue with the other, less reducible, markers of identity.

My presentation of masculinity became less legible or overt then, because it manifested itself in non-bodily ways and was in competition with the disciplinary and cultural conversation that marks me as feminine and my classroom space as feminized. It was not that my attempt at performing FTM drag failed, but that it forced an alternate kind of reading. So although masculinity or the performance of masculinity may be more apparent within certain contexts (at a drag show, for instance), it is not as obvious when the context makes continuous and intense normative demands.

Because FTM drag purposely displays the unnatural connection between sex and gender, it also exaggerates the deprivileged position inhabited by the "performer." Suddenly, the numerous positions that make me professionally vulnerable (graduate student, female, teaching assistant) are glaring. My performance takes place against a traditional, White, male, and heterosexual backdrop, and makes my place as Other readily apparent. So, although I see FTM drag as a way to understand the manner by which some women use masculinity to authorize themselves and affect their audiences, it is also a way to understand how the use of nontraditional or normative displays of gender and authority cannot simply or easily be transplanted into the composition classroom or the university at large.

By making the queer tangible (if at least for a moment), the scenarios I describe here destabilized what have traditionally and utopically been deemed rigidly determined academic spaces. The pedagogical space of the classroom and the competitive space of the graduate forum were disrupted by the queer—indeterminate, masculine and feminine, lesbian and passive —identity I displayed. By thus seeing this engagement with institutionalized power as an act of "outing," I conceive of it as a forced and potentially unwelcome announcement. After all, "outing" yourself is very different from being "outed" by someone else. To be "outed" implies that a potentially dangerous secret has been revealed; a code of silence has been broken, and a person left vulnerable. Taken metaphorically into the realm of the university, this "outing," or exposure of a secret identity has equally as unsettling consequences. For just as unsolicited and unapproved "outing" has often been condemned by members of the gay community in the United States, the exposure of the inner-workings of the university is also frowned on. Although it is acceptable—and certainly not new or surprising in our postmodern times—to reflect on the gendered and raced nature of the academy and its reproduction of privilege, it is still risky to deviate from the expected codes of academic behavior. But beside the potential "real" consequences of lost jobs or promotions, "outing" the normative demands and problematic structures of the university poses a serious threat to the hegemony of authority the university promotes. For if the local sites of the university—the classroom, meeting room, presentation competition—function to uncover rather than uphold such structures of coherence, the very authority on which the university rests is in jeopardy.

I raise this point not to make the blanket claim that incidents such as those I present above undo the power of the university and disrupt its normative agency, but to take these two examples as occasions to understand more fully the place identity, and more specifically, queer identity, has in the construction of university-sanctioned power. In the introduction of *PoMoSexuals*, we are told that "multiple subjectivities [. . .] encourage overlapping and sometimes contradictory realities" (Queen and Schimel 21). Read with these above scenarios in mind, this analysis suggests that the conjunction of subversive identities and the appropriation of privileged positions work to highlight the biased reality that is closeted by the university. My identities as a teacher, graduate student, and scholar, therefore, are not stable or easily contained. Any position I inhabit is effected by and defined in relation to other positions I hold in addition to those restricted to me. Put another way, my identity and that of the university is constantly being queered.

When I engage in masculine or privileged strategies within the academy, therefore, those tactics, or technologies, are always in dialogue with other accoutrements of identity as well as the situation in which they are performed. Ultimately, I think, they are queer devices that "are not pacifist [but embrace] instead the 'by any means necessary' approach: self defense and more. [They are . . .] a Foucauldian tactic of 'discipline and punish,' inspiring fear without actually laying a finger on anyone" (Halberstam and Livingston 15). As such a tactic, the technology of rhetorical FTM drag does indeed "inspire fear" at the institutional level, but it also inspires critical thought, and the disruption of normative boundaries at a variety of levels. Importantly, FTM drag is a technology that argues against norms and induces a disturbance of power.

ACKNOWLEDGMENTS

I am privileged to have the personal and academic support of many generous and insightful colleagues and mentors. A number of these people read,
responded to, and talked with me about this chapter and deserve my
thanks. Members of Ohio State's Winter 2000 dissertation seminar and the
seminar's instructor, Debra Moddelmog, critiqued an early draft of this
chapter; members of an informal dissertation group: Melissa Ianetta,
Emma Perry Loss, Kristen Risley, and Lisa Tatonetti provided thoughtful
criticism, suggestions for revision, and much needed laughter; and Kay
Halasek worked closely with me through all stages of this project. While
making copious notes of outlines and changes, wrestling with my thesis,
and generally sharing my enthusiasm and commitment to this chapter,
Kay, as always, made this work fun and productive.

ENDNOTES

1. One example of this kind of work can be found on the Computers and
    Composition Web site < corax.cwrl.utexas.edu/cac/ > . This site includes arti-
    cles, discussion forums, and links to issues related to the intersection of com-
    position and computer technology.
2. As quoted in Halberstam and Livingston (2). Originally appears in Haraway,
    Simians, Cyborgs and Women.
3. My theorization of this point is influenced by and indebted to Judith Butler's
    understanding of these issues. I am thinking specifically here about her essay
    "Imitation and Gender Insubordination," in *Inside/Out: Lesbian Theories, Gay
    Theories.* Halberstam likewise references Butler when she discusses female
    masculinity. In her introduction, for instance, she quotes Butler's theorization
    of heteronormativity and its relationship to alternate identity categories.
    Halberstam notes Butler's argument that

    > the parodic or imitative effect of gay identities works neither to copy
    > nor to emulate heterosexuality, but rather, to expose heterosexuality
    > as an incessant and *panicked* imitation of its own naturalized idealiza-
    > tion. [. . .] This inversion is powerful because of the way it intervenes
    > in the construction of gendered subjectivity at the point where it
    > becomes a model of humanness. It interrupts a linear continuity
    > among gender, heterosexual norms, and human sexuality by showing
    > how heavily heterosexuality and gender depend on gay identities to

idealize, humanize, and naturalize their own definitions. This dependence is too often left out of accounts of the "Other" that stress marginalization. While clear and present oppression of "Others" is by no means to be understated, the Other is also the matrix against which the self is made to appear and from which it can never be extracted; the "conservation of Otherness" dictates that any "assimilation" or "incorporation" will also be a transfiguration. (Halberstam 5)

4.   By queer, I mean to suggest "not only the disruption of the binary of heterosexual normalcy on the one hand and homosexual defiance on the other, but [the] desire 'to bring the hetero/homo opposition to the point of collapse'" (145). Outing the queerness of the university, then, is disruptive because it denies stability. It does not present a clear picture of a lesbian academic, an "unruly" woman, or even a feminized instructor. Instead, it offers a muddled or amalgamated view of identity. It argues, in effect, for the indeterminability of identity and the contextual and technological nature of gendered performances. See Luhmann, Suzanne. "Queering/Querying Pedagogy? Or, Pedagogy is a Pretty Queer Thing."

5.   It is worth noting here, that Halberstam argues that "masculinity must not and cannot and should not reduce down to the male body and its effects" (Halberstam 1). Rather, she claims that "[f]ar from being an imitation of maleness, female masculinity actually affords us a glimpse of how masculinity is constructed as masculinity." Masculinity is not merely an expression of "maleness" or the gender that matches the sex. The "myths and fantasies about masculinity that have ensured that masculinity and maleness are profoundly difficult to pry apart." And the "widespread indifference to female masculinity" she suggests "has clearly ideological motivations and has sustained the complex social structures that wed masculinity to maleness and to power and domination"(2).

6.   See, for example, Susan Miller, *Textual Carnivals*; Susan Jarratt, "Feminism and Composition: The Case for Conflict" in *Contending with Words*; Louise Wetherbee Phelps and Janet Emig, eds., *Feminine Principles and Women's Experience in American Composition and Rhetoric*; Susan Jarratt and Lynn Worsham, eds. *Feminism and Composition Studies*; and Jan Zlotnik Schmidt *Women/Writing/Teaching*.

7.   Susan Miller's chapter entitled, "The Sad Woman in the Basement," which appears in *Textual Carnivals: The Politics of Composition,* details this trope.

8.   This presentation represents a section of a larger essay entitled "Erotic Arguments and Persuasive Acts: Discourses of Desire and the Rhetoric of Female-to-Male Drag" (Pauliny).

9.   As neither the presentations nor the question and answer/critique session were recorded in any way, these are not direct quotes, but represent the general quality and content of responses as I remember them. It is not my intention to directly quote any individual audience member or judge with these passages, but to portray their responses as a whole.

10. Although in this instance I am quoting directly, I do so not necessarily to fault the particular authors of these correspondences, but to illustrate how these comments align with my overarching analysis of the situation. My intent here is to demonstrate how the university's protective response reveals itself repeatedly. It is the discourse of nonresponse I am interested in here. For, as with the question session and critique session, these e-mails construct a divide between the academic and the popular—or, more to the point—the "accepted-as-academic" and the "not-accepted-as-academic." Because these judges could not or would not respond to my work in a critical or even specific way, they ostensibly deny its right to be judged at all.

REFERENCES

Butler, Judith. "Imitation and Genders Insubordination." *Inside/Out: Lesbian Theories, Gay Theories*. Ed. Diana Fuss. New York: Routledge, 1991.

Halberstam, Judith. *Female Masculinity*. Durham and London: Duke UP, 1998.

———. and Ira Livingston. eds. "Introduction." *Posthuman Bodies*. Bloomington and Indianapolis, Indiana UP, 1995. 1-19.

Haraway, Donna. *Simians, Cyborgs and Women*. New York: Routledge, 1991.

Jarratt, Susan. "Feminism and Composition: The Case for Conflict." *Contending with Words: Composition and Rhetoric in a Postmodern Age*. Patricia Harkin and John Schilb, Eds. New York: MLA, 1991. 105-123.

Luhmann, Suzanne. "Queering/Querying Pedagogy? Or, Pedagogy Is a Pretty Queer Thing." *Queer Theory in Education*. Ed. William F. Pinar. Mahwah, NJ: Erlbaum, 1998. 142-155.

Miller, Susan. *Textual Carnivals: The Politics of Composition*. Carbondale and Edwardsville: Southern Illinois UP, 1991.

Morris, Pam. ed. "Introduction." *The Bakhtin Reader: Selected Writing of Bakhtin, Medvedev, Voloshinov*. London: Edward Arnold, 1994.1-24.

Pauliny, Tara. "Erotic Arguments and Persuasive Acts: Discourses of Desire and the Rhetoric of FTM Drag." *Journal of Homosexuality*. 43.3-4 (2002): 221-248.

Phelps, Louise Wetherbee and Janet Emig, eds. *Feminine Principles and Women's Experience in American Composition and Rhetoric*. Pittsburgh: U of Pittsburgh P, 1995.

Queen, Carol and Lawrence Schimel. Eds. *PoMoSexuals: Challenging Assumptions about Gender and Sexuality*. San Francisco: Cleis Press, 1997.

Schmidt, Jan Zlotnik. *Women/Writing/Teaching*. Albany: SUNY P, 1998.

Worsham, Lynn and Susan Jarratt, eds. *Feminism and Composition Studies: In Other Words*. New York: MLA, 1998.

8

(CYBER)CONSPIRACY THEORIES?

AFRICAN-AMERICAN STUDENTS IN THE COMPUTERIZED WRITING ENVIRONMENT

Samantha Blackmon

Purdue University

In his 1992 *JAC* essay Thomas Fox writes:

> [S]chools have failed to make good on the promise that literacy instruction in the schools will reward African-American students socially and economically. Equally serious is the fact that schools have failed to change the perception (and reality in most cases) that for African-American students literacy instruction entails "deculturation without true assimilation." (http://nosferatu.cas.usf.edu/JAC/122/fox.html)

In this chapter I argue that this is not only the case in traditional Composition classrooms, but that this is something that is replicated in the computerized classroom to a greater extent. Ironically, although computers and the World Wide Web are being hailed as the great equalizer for students in the computerized classroom, African-American students are finding themselves further marginalized. Kira Pirofski finds the following:

> Minority and low income students who are not provided programming, networking, and word processing courses will have compromised educational, economic, and employment possibilities.
>
> Availability of computers and computer literacy skills are not only important in terms of future educational prospects and employment but

also needed so that school children achieve a sense of competence and mastery (http://www.literacyandtechnology.org/v2n1/pirofski.html).

In order to benefit from all of the "advantages" of American economic society, these students must not only have material access to the machinery but must also be competent, comfortable, and confident.[1]

Minority students are often expected to ignore their own cultural markers and history in order to become "cyber human." For the purposes of this chapter I am define *cyber human* as a raceless, sexless, genderless, classless entity that, because of its lack of descriptive features, is the same as every other person in the virtual world. In order to achieve the status of cyber human, these students must become raceless in the real-world in that they must ignore things that conflict with the sensibilities of their real world racial(ized) selves if they are to accept and interact with the technology. For example, in order to ignore the racist, sexist, and classist nature of certain webbed communities (and I argue technology itself), one must also ignore their own positions within one or more of their own real-world discourse communities (racial, ethnic, sexual, or socioeconomic).

Signithia Fordham defines *racelessness* as the denial of other-cultural affiliation, a denial of the collective, the rejection of fictive kinship (which can be demonstrated and fostered through dress, music, and language) in favor of America's dominant ideology (Villanueva 39). For Fordham, fictive kinship is the connection between a person and his or her race. This connection is fostered by and exhibited through physical and auditory markers. According to Victor Villanueva, choosing to be raceless (and to give up these markers) while accepting the ideology of the dominant bears the price of a loss of fictive kinship without the gain of full acceptance by the majority (48). It is this loss of one culture, through an actual lack of fictive kinship (in this case on the Internet), while not being fully integrated into another that Villanueva calls being "tonto" in both cultures (42).

Many African-American students find no fictive kinship in the computerized world in general or the computerized writing environment specifically. They feel that, as a race, they are misrepresented on and excluded from the Internet (more on this later). In this chapter, I offer the voices of students enrolled in my first-year composition class at a large, urban university. This course met solely in the computer classroom and students were expected to utilize the available technology in all nontimed assignments. The focus of this class was the interrogation of difference as it was presented in popular culture. We began the semester working with and through an understanding of what a discourse community was and what it meant to belong to a variety of discourse communities. This was done by reading a variety of essays that dealt with the experiences of different races, genders, and sexual orientations. As the semester went on, students were asked to focus on one of their discourse communities per week and take an in-depth look at the history and culture of said community in a written assignment. As the weeks passed and students were building a portfolio of discourse community assignments, they were asked to begin to think about how and why different discourse community relationships in their lives affected one another even when they seemed to be contradictory.

THE TEXTS

This section of the course was comprised of 11 White, 1 Arab-American, and 6 African-American students at a university that maintains a student population that is about 23% African-American and 30% non-African-American minority (http://www.wayne.edu/stu_profile.html). A survey[2] of 189 students conducted at Wayne State University in Detroit, Michigan found that 84% of the 86 White and 65% of the 52 African-American students surveyed reported using a computer at home. Of the White students, 73% reported connecting to the Internet from home at least once a week, whereas this number dropped significantly to 29% for African-American students. It is also startling to see that 33% of the African-American students (vs. 12% of their White counterparts) surveyed had never used e-mail (http://www.english.wayne.edu/data). This study of Wayne State University's student population can not be taken as representative of all American culture, but it is a part of the larger picture. Indeed, the national averages show more disparity. The United States Department of Commerce's October 2000 report, *Falling Through the Net: Towards Digital Inclusion* shows that 55.7% of Caucasian households and 32.6% of African-American households own a computer (http://www.esa.doc.gov/fttn00.htm). This shows that Whites are 1.7 times more likely to have access to computers in the home than African-Americans whereas at Wayne State University they were only 1.3 times more likely.

I offer the texts of three African-American students in a first-year writing course. These texts deal with the students' perceptions (or realities) of the representation of the African-American race on the Web as an example of this phenomenon.

In his written response, Marcus, an African-American, male student,[3] writes about what he feels is negative about the way that he feels he is represented on the web as a African-American male. Marcus writes:

> It seems young Black men are only associated with rap. . . . Young Black males, such as myself, need to start making websites [sic] that aren't music based. We need to start making websites that educate people of other things that young Black males are involved in (ex. Big Brothers, Big Sisters).

For Marcus there is no real connection between who he is as a "young Black male" and the way that he sees young Black males represented on the Web. He does seem to feel that he is being at worst "deculturated" (à la Tom Fox) and at best culturally minimized in such a way that makes it seem as if he *is* "rap music" and all of the negative stereotypes that come along with it rather than a "big brother" committed to the education and positive socialization of Black male children.

This is not a phenomenon that is exclusive to African-American male students. Kim, 19-year-old African-American female student, responds to the way that she sees herself represented on the web in the following way:

> Most of the websites that I have seen that are about African-Americans like me[4] seem to concentrate on sports. They talk about how great sports are and how we are great at them. . . . But that isn't me. I don't play sports, I don't even like sports.

Kim feels that, as an African-American, she is being misrepresented. She recognizes a cultural myth that is not her reality. She is being reduced to a cultural base that is not accurate.

If, as Fox claims, "literacy instruction entails the deculturation without true assimilation" the same rules are at play in the web based literacy instruction of African-American students (http://nosferatu.cas.usf.edu/JAC/122/fox.html). They are being asked to see themselves as either rappers or sports stars or as a part of the raceless, White majority, which is represented on the web in a more detailed way. Let me be specific here that this representation of the raceless majority is not tied to an actual declaration of whiteness, but rather to the fact that in the absence of a specific race, White is considered the "default."

It is most often those sites that declare their whiteness that are problematic in that they want to erase the presence of the African-American race (and other racial minorities) as a whole not only virtually but physically as well. Since the boom of the World Wide Web, hate-group membership in the United States has grown astronomically. According to the Anti-Defamation League Online:

> . . . the [neo-Nazi] National Alliance [which has a strong online presence] has leaped to prominence again. In the last several years, dozens of violent crimes, including murders, bombings and robberies, have been traced to NA members or appear to have been inspired by the group's propaganda. At the same time, the National Alliance's membership base has experienced dramatic growth, with its numbers more than doubling since 1992. (http://www.adl.org/explosion_of_hate/introduction.html)

Through this new "equalizing" medium, hate groups have found a way to reach more potential members. This increasingly visible presence of whiteness and prejudice, and the history of oppression that it evokes, on the World Wide Web can add to the feeling of exclusion from and distrust of the web specifically and technology generically for African-American students.

As Marcus states, perhaps the way to combat the negative and inaccurate representations of African-Americans on the web is for students to build their own positive depictions of African-American people and culture. Although the more technologically savvy of us know this to be possible, students who historically lack access to technology may not be aware of the "freedom" of the web. Although many African-American students now have the ability to do simple technological tasks such as word processing, many have no knowledge of things such as web-page building and publishing. The lack of knowledge of these things seems to lead to the fallacious assumption that the web (like all other aspects of society) is governed and controlled by the majority.

Justin, another male, African-American student, believes that regardless of the attempts by African-Americans to make themselves present on the web, there is a White, higher power that will continue to control exactly who and what people see on the web. Justin writes:

> I'm sure things could be changed for the worse. At least Black people are allowed to even have websites [sic]. I'm sure the Internet world is run mostly by Whites and they have the power to allow and not allow people to make websites [sic].

It is this vague but omnipresent fear of purposeful exclusion that stops many African-American students from achieving the same level of technological comfort and mastery that they believe their nonminority counterparts experience. These students seem to believe that even though the real world is filled with the exclusion and misrepresentation of African-American culture that they have a better chance at equality here in the "real world" than in the virtual world because they are not being forced to participate in a medium that is not only exclusionary but unfamiliar. So for them, the "real world" becomes the lesser of two evils.

At a time when computers may not be as cost prohibitive, African-American students are still playing a game of "catch up" when it comes to expertise in applications and web building. In his essay "The Computer Race Goes to Class", Jonathan Sterne argues:

> if white people in the United States had a distinct advantage over people of color in learning computing and gaining access to computers, then that would go a long way toward explaining why the Internet remains predominately white (though it is far from entirely white). (191)

It is this unequal ability that can lead to students such as Justin believing that there is some sort of White web board designating who and what can be published on the web. The history of oppression that haunts African-Americans in the United States has followed African-American students into the computerized classroom and although these students may have increased physical access to technology, many times their knowledge of the technology is inferior to that of their White counterparts because of the historical inequity of access. It is this inequity of access that leaves Marcus, Kim, and Justin feeling that they are misrepresented or unrepresented on the World Wide Web, either intentionally or unintentionally, and thus leaves them with little interest in it.

According to Sterne, the problem of computer access that led to unequal computer literacy, and now to problems of representation on the web, began in the 1980s, when computers where first entering American public schools. Federal defunding of public schools led to inequity in resources and greater inequality among different school districts depending on location and local tax bases. With less federal funding to balance resources between richer and poorer school districts, school districts were forced to rely more heavily on funding from property tax revenue and thus susceptible to existing inequities in housing (Sterne 193). It is here that the educational system had failed these students, yet again, by not ensuring equal access to the social and economic rewards that are promised to all students who become literate.

While observing the interaction of these three African-American students in the computerized writing environment I found it sadly ironic that although these students felt that, as African-Americans, they were falling behind others in the virtual world, two of them consistently chose to resort to pen and ink rather than keyboard and monitor for in-class writing assignments, even while Marcus wrote in his response that he believes that "computers are good though because I think that people like to type rather than write."

THE STUDENTS

As a computer classroom teacher, I had noticed that the attrition rate of African-American students in these classes was more than double that of the traditional classroom. For me, the fact that difference in the numbers of African-American students and the numbers of White students who had access to computers at home was not as great as the attrition rates suggested that the problem was not with material access but with something more profound, something that computers and writing teachers had been overlooking, I call this something historical access. In the past 10 years, computers and composition as a field has been focusing on how to bridge the digital divide in terms of material access. Our main concern has been how to give all students equal physical access to technology.

Since the advent of the sub-$1,000 computer and the increase of the number of computers in schools across the country and community free access points (such as community centers, libraries, and universities), our focus has shifted farther away from issues of access and closer to the nuts and bolts of issues of teaching with technology such as application usage, classroom configuration, and assessment. Although these are very important issues, embarrassingly little research has been done on historical access, the access that students have to technology based on prior knowledge of and access to technology as well as the access that students allow themselves based on past personal and cultural experiences with both computer technology and the hegemonic power structure that it is seen as representing. In other words, it not only depends on the students' past experiences with computers and the Internet, but also on their level of comfort with (and trust in) the racial relationships in the United States (both past and present). We have not asked what if students don't want to use technology, why they don't want to use technology, and what effect the denial of technology (and of other educational "equalizers") for decades has had on minority and lower class students.

In *Defending Access: A Critique of Standards in Higher Education*, Tom Fox argues:

> [w]hen students have been granted access and still fail this failure is usually blamed on the individual and their problems (maturity, pre-paredness, psychology, etc.) rather than looking at the social and cul-tural situations that surround the student. (11)

If we assume that because minority students have material access to com-puters they should be able to perform at the same level of computer com-petence as their majority counterparts, we once again fail to make good on the promise of a better life.

I argue that this is the case because even in a time when more minor-ity students have material access to technology, they are still technological-ly tentative. Although they have a working knowledge of the technology, there is always an underlying distrust of the rationale behind the technolo-gy itself. The technology is something that had historically been withheld from them because of material circumstances and in a time when they are being forced to use it they are distrustful of not only the reasons for this requirement but also of those who have a more than working knowledge of it.

An example of the reasons behind this distrust can be seen in the his-tory of African-American workers in the Bell Phone System in the mid-20th century. In response to a series of Consent Decrees signed with the U.S. government from 1973 to 1975, AT&T agreed to pay workers $39 mil-lion in wage compensation and to completely reorganize personnel proce-dures in order to reduce racial and sexual job segregation. The decree gave AT&T 6 years to hire, transfer, and promote a "target" number of minori-ties and women into higher paying positions. The Bell System created the Upgrade and Transfer Program (UTP) in order to achieve this goal (Green 122-123).

Under the UTP, White women moved more rapidly and in higher num-bers into the higher level position than their minority counterparts. African-American women were moved into operator and other low-skilled service positions that paid more money than their previous positions but less than those of their White counterparts. The underlying reason for the increase in African-American operators seems to have been the fact that as technol-ogy improved and fewer operators were needed to place overseas calls, these operator positions were being phased out. Between 1973 and 1979, the number of operators in the Bell System decreased by 28.7% and service workers by 53.8% (Green 124). So, in essence, although adhering to the terms of the Consent Decree, Bell was able to hire and promote more women and minorities while essentially continuing to discriminate against and decrease the number of African-American women in its company.

Another example of previous occasions when African-Americans and other minorities were given cause to distrust both technology and those who used it can be seen in the struggle of reproductive rights in the United States. From 1933 to 1973, under the auspices of the Eugenics Commission of North Carolina, 7,686 women with "mental defects" were sterilized, and about 5,000 of these women were African-American. In 1974, eighteen women came forward and charged that they had been sterilized in the early 1970s by obstetrician Dr. Clovis Pierce of South Carolina. Pierce regularly sterilized Medicaid patients who had two or more children. He "persuaded" them to do so by refusing to deliver the babies of these pregnant women until they agreed to post birth sterilization. As the only obstetrician in town, the women had little choice as they would typically have neither money nor transportation to travel to other towns for prenatal treatment. At his trial, Pierce was supported by the South Carolina Medical Association, which ruled that doctors "have a moral and legal right to insist on sterilization permission before accepting a patient, if it is done on the initial visit" (Davis 216-217). This was followed by Congress' passage of the Hyde Amendment in 1977, which withdrew federal funding for abortions (causing many states to follow suit) while still providing funds for "voluntary" sterilizations (Davis 206). This amendment effectively robbed minority and impoverished women of their right to legal and safe abortions.[5]

Memories of the abuse of medical and other technologies in U.S. history (i.e., The Tuskegee Experiment, which from 1932 to 1972 watched African-American men wither and die from untreated syphilis in the name of "research") permeate African-American consciousness. To ignore the cultural factors at work and the scars left from centuries of racial oppression and abuse serves to continue to perpetuate the ethnic violence of North American history by erasing not only the racial component but by erasing the history itself. It is this erasure of historical oppression that continues to oppress minority students even today and lends itself to the creation of conspiracy theories and a fear of technology.

This technological trepidation is furthered by the fact that these African-American students do not see themselves adequately represented in the media that are produced by technology. They regularly see and hear about Web sites dedicated to African-American vocal artists and athletes, but never see a representation of common folk. Is this to say that these sites don't exist? No, it is the perception that these sites don't exist (and that the World Wide Web is a Eurocentric and exclusionary place) that makes this theory of Eurocentrism and exclusion a part of the students' reality. I argue that it is this theory of purposeful exclusion from the World Wide Web that causes African-American students to fail to "connect" with the technology and to be able to successful complete a course that has this technology as its basis.

The student texts that I offer draw on Elspeth Stuckey's argument, in *The Violence of Literacy*, that rather than being libratory, as promised:

> Literacy, like communication, is a matter of access, a matter of oppor-
> tunity, a matter of economic security-a total matter. The violence of lit-
> eracy is the violence of the milieu it comes from, promises, recapitu-
> lates. It is attached inextricably to the world of food, shelter, and
> human equality. When literacy harbors violence, society harbors vio-
> lence. To elucidate the violence of literacy is to understand the distance
> it forces between people and the possibilities for their lives. (94)

The stories that the student texts tell document the attachment to both the material and political conditions that Stuckey discusses. The texts show how the everyday violence of the real world, the violence of racial erasure, comes into computer-assisted writing and literacy.

So, what are we as scholars and teachers to do with this information? Although issues of physical access are readily debated in educational cir-cles, we do not look at cultural factors in computerized composition class-rooms in the same way that we have previously looked at them in tradi-tional composition classrooms because we are still under the assumption that technology can be the great equalizer in the classroom and because many of us who are heavily invested in computers and education are hes-itant to acknowledge and critique its shortcomings for fear of it reflecting negatively on us or devaluing our professional positions.

I argue that we can no longer ignore the very real cultural issues that are still at play in our classrooms because they are equally important to those in the traditional classroom. In much the same way that we have asked students to acknowledge and interrogate questions of access we must also ask them to interrogate issues of representation, to think about how and why minorities are seemingly being asked to give up their own cultures in lieu of the raceless culture of the web and what the repercus-sions of this could be. If we are teaching in computer classrooms we should give students the opportunity to question "who" as well as "why." We should make critique a part of the curriculum, ask students who might have a certain degree of privilege in the classroom, ask them why this is, and how it might be made more equal. Although students may not come up with the answers to these questions, they will be forced to think actively about them.

We must give these students a reason to go online. Contrary to what the computer companies, like Compaq and IBM, want the public to believe, the desire to "hook up" to the Internet and "jack in" to the experiences of cyberspace is not present at birth (see Nakamura 18-20 for advertising images). As teachers, we should give students the opportunity to critique not only the course but the educational institution itself and ask them to go online and find support for their arguments, to prove their point. This will serve to make them active in their own educations while (possibly) arguing against it.

Although the active critique of cyberspace technology and its use in the classroom falls short of physically making any change to the content of the web (or its perceived content), it does take a step in the right direction in that we are making those who can make a change aware of the cultural inequity that exists. It can also serve as a source of support and validation for the minority students who are victims of this inequity. Thus, giving them the increased sense of self-worth that seems to be diminished by misrepresentation, deculturation, or basic hate speech that is present in the virtual realm. It is when students have a sense of equality and comfort regardless of culture, race, gender, or sexual orientation that we have an environment (be it virtual or real) that is conducive to teaching and learning. It is then and only then that we have any chance of making good on the promise that along with literacy comes social and economic rewards.

ENDNOTES

1. My argument here is that in order to be competent and to master something one *must* be comfortable with it as well.
2. This survey, conducted in February 1999, had a sample of 189 students in 10 sections of various composition-based courses. There were two sections of basic writing, two sections of intermediate writing, four sections of first-year composition, and two sections of the writing-intensive Introduction to Fiction course. The ethnic breakdown of the students surveyed was 86 White, 52 African-American, 10 biracial, 14 Asian/Indian, 8 Arabic, 7 Hispanic, 4 who identified as other, and 5 who abstained from identifying themselves.

3. The quotes offered here were collected from critical response assignments on representation and the World Wide Web written by African-American students. The names of the students quoted here have been changed.
4. Here I believe Kim considers not just race but age as well.
5. In the several years preceding the decriminalization of abortions, 80 % of the women who died from illegal abortions in the state of New York were Black and Puerto Rican (Davis 204).

REFERENCES

Davis, Angela Y. *Women, Race & Class*. New York: Vintage Books, 1983.

Explosion of Hate: The Growing Danger of the National Alliance, Anti-Defamation League. < http://www.adl.org/explosion_of_hate/introduction.html > .

Falling Through the Net: Toward Digital Inclusion, U.S. Department of Commerce. < http://www.esa.doc.gov/fttn00.htm > . Site accessed October 2000.

Fox, Thomas. *Defending Access: A Critique of Standards in Higher Education*. Portsmouth, NH: Boynton/Cook, 1999.

_____. "Repositioning the Profession: Teaching Writing to African-American Students." *JAC Online* 12.2 (1992). < http://nosferatu.cas.usf.edu/JAC/122/fox.html > . Site accessed November 16, 2001.

Green, Venus. "Race and Technology: African-American Women in the Bell System, 1945-1980." *Technology and Culture: An International Quarterly of the Society of the History of Technology*. Supplement to April 1995, v. 36.

Kitchens, Marshall. "Computer Access, Ability, and Equality in the College Composition Classroom." *Access, Ability, and Equity*. < http://www.english.wayne.edu/data/index.html > . Site accessed November 16, 2001.

Nakamura, Lisa. "'Where Do You Want to Go Today': Cybernetic Tourism, the Internet, and Transnationality." *Race in Cyberspace*. Ed. Beth Kolko, Lisa Nakamura, and Gilbert B. Rodman. New York: Routledge, 2000.

Pirofski, Kira Isak. "Are All Schools Equally Wired? An Overview of the Digital Divide in Elementary and Secondary Schools in the United States". *The Journal of Literacy and Technology*. Winter 2002. < http://www.literacyand technology.org/v2n1/pirofski.html >

Sterne, Jonathan. "The Computer Race Goes to Class: How Computers in Schools Helped Shape the Racial Topography of the Internet." *Race in Cyberspace*. Ed. Beth Kolko, Lisa Nakamura, and Gilbert B. Rodman. New York: Routledge, 2000.

Stuckey, J. Elspeth. *The Violence of Literacy*. Portsmouth, NH: Boynton, 1991.

Villanueva, Victor. *Bootstraps: From an American Academic of Color*. Urbana, IL: National Council of Teachers of English, 1993.

"Wayne State Student Profile." *Student Profile*. http://www.wayne.edu/stu_profile.html > . Site accessed November 16, 2001.

PART THREE

*Exploring Possibilities
for Agency in
Institutional Settings*

9

AGENCIES, ECOLOGIES, AND THE MUNDANE ARTIFACTS IN OUR MIDST

Stuart Blythe

Indiana University-Purdue University Fort Wayne

Human beings first learned to walk on two feet; then they mastered fire; after that, anthropologists tell us, they invented bylaws and elected a recording secretary.

—Cullen Murphy

I was an interface in my first job after college. As an assistant director in a college admissions office, I spent much of my time explaining admission guidelines to prospective students and their parents. I worked in a cubicle next to the registrar, who explained campus policies regarding the use of space to faculty and staff. Several cubicles down, the director of financial aid spent much of his time explaining federal and state guidelines to others. Each of us measured our worth by our ability to explain written texts to people, to direct them to the appropriate decision-making authority, and to coach them on ways to receive favorable judgments. In the cases where one of us was the authority, we hoped we were making decisions that were fair both to the one seeking a decision and to the institution that employed us, and those decisions were usually recorded on appropriate forms. The director of admissions had a healthy attitude about our jobs. We were all bureaucrats, he told me, and the job of a good bureaucrat is to help others find their way through the maze of paperwork and decision makers that an institution presents. In this way, a bureaucrat helps others meet their goals vis-à-vis the institution. A good bureaucrat is an interface.

My first job taught me that institutions are maintained in large part through the creation and interpretation of written documents such as charters, contracts, policies, applications, organizational charts, reports, and other records. For many, being able to interact with an institution means being able to read its texts and, in some cases, to contribute to the writing of them. One might say, in fact, that being able to "read" an organization involves a type of literacy—a type of literacy to which we should attend. If much of an institution's existence depends on writing and reading, then our insights as teachers and scholars of writing afford us a unique and valuable perspective on organizational life (see Porter et al.). We should develop such perspectives for our students' sakes as well as our own.

The need to understand how organizations operate is so crucial that the U.S. Department of Labor has defined "understanding social, organizational, and technological systems, monitoring and correcting performance, and designing or improving systems" as a basic "competency" (Meyer and Bernhardt 87). Many of our graduates, regardless of their major, will be employed in organizations as complex as the one in which I began my career. Many of them will produce the texts that play a part in maintaining an organization. Even if they are to be self-employed, students will have to interact daily with local institutions such as a bureau of motor vehicles or a local bureaucracy that licenses small businesses. Students (and we) should recognize how organizations operate, critique that operation, find points where the working of an organization may be altered (points that are often discursive, as explained later), and recognize their role (perhaps even their complicity at times) in maintaining organizations. Students should learn, in other words, that organizations have what Iris Marion Young calls "structural inequalities" built into them, and that people may either maintain or attempt to alter those inequalities as they create and enforce written policies (35).

My intent in this chapter is to expand on the work begun by Jim Porter, Patricia Sullivan, Libby Miles, Jeff Grabill, and me, and described in the article "Institutional Critique: A Rhetorical Methodology for Change." I do so by considering possibilities for agency in institutional settings. Such possibilities depend on understanding how institutions are maintained, the role that writing and reading plays in that maintenance, and how maintenance processes offer opportunities for hope and resistance. To illustrate, I bring together several stories that have been told in publications and conferences. I do all this for at least three reasons: We must recognize (a) our complicity in maintaining organizations, including the "structural inequalities" that Young writes of, (b) the way that writing is used (both in the process of composition and in the reading of other texts) to maintain organizations, and (c) ways of "re-writing" institutions for more democratic, just ends. What we must develop, in other words, is a concept of institutional agency, but *agency* is a troubled term.

THE TROUBLED CONCEPT OF AGENCY

The concept of agency has taken a beating from all sides in the past few decades. If we understand the term as the degree to which any human may exert control over his or her own life, retain the ability to act in meaningful and purposeful ways, and change things to meet his or her preferences, then we must admit that agency seems like an elusive quality. Our belief in our ability to change conditions where we work and live has been undermined by a host of developments large and small. It is difficult enough to feel empowered given our knowledge of 20th-century history with its totalitarian cultures and institutions such as Stalin's Soviet Union, Hitler's Germany, and Pol Pot's Cambodia; menacing technological developments such as nuclear warfare and the state apparatus necessary to guard against its use; the growing power of corporations; the widespread destruction of the environment (whether it be the South American rainforests or a small patch of wetland in one's own county); and the failure of large-scale movements such as the French student-worker revolt against the Gaullist government in 1968. It is also inevitable for us as teachers of writing to worry about agency when we think about students' control over their own language and texts, about our roles within the institutions through which we work, and about our relationships to computer technology. It is difficult to feel empowered when we see nontenure-track associate faculty paid an unlivable wage and made faceless in cramped office spaces where several individuals may share one desk.

As if that were not enough, our sense of agency has also been challenged by recent theories of authorship and the development of new writing technologies. (John Trimbur documents the former development in an article in *JAC: A Journal of Advanced Composition*.) Agency in composition has typically been construed as a student's control over self-definition and language. Such a sense of control requires a foundational discourse on which a student can base a stable sense of self. The impasse is caused by the anti-foundationalist belief that no foundational discourse exists; rather, many competing discourses exist. Donald Jones, citing Lester Faigley, illustrates the problem:

> When a subject is situated "among many competing discourses that precede [it]," Faigley cautions, "the notion of 'participation' becomes problematic in its implication that the subject can control its location and moves within a discourse" ([Faigley] 226-27). The autonomous writer of foundationalism becomes a situated object, something "subjected" to the influences of the dominant discourses. These influences reduce the subject to "an effect rather than a cause of discourse" so subjectivity becomes a debilitating pun, and agency, an illusion. ([Faigley] 9). (n.p.)

If a person is always subjected to competing discourses, and if a person cannot transcend them, then an impasse is reached. A "dead end [is] created when agency cannot be explained fully in theory," Jones writes (n.p.). Such threats to a writer's sense of agency have in turn been supported by the continuing development of digital communication technologies. In fact, George Landow, among others, has noted the compatibility of digital technologies and postmodern literary theory. It is easy to question notions of authorship in a world where text is easily copied and repurposed, and where writing so often goes unattributed.

Thus, we have instability brought about by a double whammy of cultural and technological change. "When technologies accompany cultural changes," Robert Johnson writes in *User-Centered Technology*, "it often is not clear who or what is controlling or influencing the change, and the appearance that humans have lost control is a commonly rendered conclusion" (87-88). Given these circumstances, it is tempting to give up on any sense of agency, but that would be a disheartening, disenfranchising option.

Numerous writers in English Studies have offered solutions to the problem of agency; however, solutions often focus on helping each student discern her "true" preference, rather than what she was conditioned to prefer. For Alan France, for instance, agency is the ability to "translate public knowledge into personal meaning" (164), and the purpose of English Studies is to teach students to negotiate between cultural forces and their own feelings and preferences. Likewise, Donna LeCourt wants students to recognize how their subjectivity is written by the "norms of discourse" inherent in a given rhetorical situation, such as an academic essay (277).

The critical praxis she espouses seeks to prompt students to discover how rhetorical conventions constrain the expression of a "free-standing self" (282). Agency is therefore presented as a very personal thing; a matter of making informed decisions. It is defined primarily as the ability to "communicate" and define one's sense of self.

Although the individualistic sense of agency espoused by writers such as France and LeCourt may be very appropriate for a first-year composition or undergraduate literature course, it is not the conception of agency one needs in order to focus on affecting institutional conditions. The people in the following stories, for example, may have known their "true self," but that could not have helped when it came to modifying conditions to meet their preferences:

- Mary Dieli, the first usability manager of the Microsoft Corporation wanted to establish "users and user testing as a more integral part of the software development process" (Porter et al. 610-611). Such a move would not only lead to better products, she believed, but would better the position of her department within the corporation.

- Members of an HIV/AIDS Planning Council in Atlanta, Georgia, wanted to involve a greater range of clients in its planning activities, resulting in greater representation during the establishment of program priorities such as housing and pharmaceutical subsidies. The fear was that current decisions were too closely tied to the racial, gendered, classed make up of the planning council, which was primarily white, male, and middle to upper middle class (Grabill 37-42).

- Workers in an abortion clinic were forced to distribute a state-supported brochure in which "the state presumably attempts to fix the meaning of abortion as the interruption of fetal development, not as a medical procedure" (Haas 225). Essentially, the workers were forced to distribute a message with which they disagreed.

- Cindy Moore, at the time a newly minted Writing Program Administrator, noticed that the associate faculty with whom she worked used almost identical syllabi and that those faculty members were reluctant (if not downright afraid) to experiment with lesson plans, etc. Although Moore wanted associate faculty to feel free to adapt syllabi as they saw fit, they referred dogmatically to the procedures and policies listed in a writing program handbook and seemed unwilling to exercise any agency at all.

In these cases, individuals and small groups seemed to know what they wanted. What they did not know was how to effect the changes they desired. (Whether one truly knows one's desires strikes me as an unanswerable, unproductive question.) The institutions within which the agents worked seemed to constrain their actions too much, or they disenfranchised groups of people.

- Microsoft Corporation was failing to recognize users and the usability division during its production processes, which perhaps led to software that articulated users in unwanted ways and definitely threatened the positions of those who aligned themselves with the usability division.
- Members of the HIV/AIDS Planning Council in Atlanta could have continued to make decisions that ignored the needs of large segments of the HIV/AIDS population in that city, which in turn could have funneled resources toward one population while bypassing others.
- Workers in an abortion clinic were being forced by the state to define abortion in ways that contradicted their medical training and personal beliefs, which constrained not only their ability to act as they saw fit, but also a client's ability to make an uncoerced choice about her medical options.
- Associate writing faculty felt forced to teach to a syllabus that ignored individual strengths and prohibited innovation.

The outlook seemed bleak in these cases. The people seeking change could have opted out of the situation, but that would simply involve running away from a problem. Nor could the people resort to revolutionary or authoritarian force. As Young points out, that is "only rarely a live option" (35). What was needed in each case was a way of prompting change in the organization.

FACING THE PARADOX OF AGENCY

Common approaches to agency in writing studies do not help in the cases mentioned so far because such approaches bracket the individual from other groups. Rather, one should focus on ways that agency operates within larger structures. After all, agency has a dual nature. "Agency, as I see it," Trimbur writes:

> is the way people . . . articulate (in the double sense of the term) their desires, needs, and projects, *giving voice* to their lived experience as they *join* their productive labors to the institutions and social structures they live within. (287)

Agency involves a "lack of constraint," by which people are free to make meaningful decisions and take purposeful action; simultaneously, it involves the ability to function "as part of something larger"—as, for example, our positions within institutions of higher education enable us to teach and write. That is the paradox of agency: We gain it not by being an autonomous individual, but by being part of something larger, by being a part of systems that constrain and enable simultaneously. This dual nature holds true for technological and institutional systems alike. Computers have enabled us to accomplish many things. Simultaneously, "In recognizing ourselves as computer users," Johndan Johnson-Eilola writes, "we are also articulated (at least partially) as the used, the variable piece of the machine that closes the circuit, like a key in the ignition of a car" (n.p.) Likewise, we are part of what makes institutions operate.

Attempts to identify social, discursive influences so as to bracket them off, to sift through them and identify one's "true" preferences, establishes a false dichotomy between individuals and communities because it lets people speak of communities as if they were separate things. In fact, just as we anthropomorphize technology, we commonly anthropomorphize collectives and speak of them as if they acted with intent. Too often, we speak of organizations as "other." Many United States voters think of government as "other," rather than a collection of fellow citizens. Oftentimes, individuals think of institutions as other, as if their work were not part of the maintenance of the organization. (Faculty members often engage in this type of thinking in regard to the institutions that employ them.) What we need is a theory of agency that does not posit a heroic individual fighting against big institutions. Nor do we need simply to teach students how to become cogs in a machine. What we need is some sense of how agency can be exercised within organizations. Given the training of writing scholars, we also need to examine more carefully the ways people use writing (the process of writing, as well as people's reactions to and uses of written documents) to cause changes in an organization.

INSTITUTIONS AS ECOLOGIES AND TECHNOLOGIES

If agency inevitably involves constraints, how does one work within them to modify conditions? In thinking about agency and our work and our students, I suggest that two apparently contradictory metaphors are valuable. Institutions can be thought of as both ecologies and technologies. I hope that the value of entertaining these two metaphors simultaneously will become apparent through the remainder of this chapter.

Institutions can be thought of as ecologies. In the words of Bonnie Nardi and Vickie O'Day, many organizations are *information ecologies*, which they define as "a system of people, practices, values, and technologies in a particular local environment" (49). They use the notion of an ecology metaphorically, "to evoke an image of biological ecologies with their complex dynamics and diverse species and opportunistic niches for growth" (50). An information ecology is highly situated, similar to Porter et al.'s sense of micro-institutions. "Like a biological ecology," Nardi and O'Day write, "an information ecology is marked by strong interrelationships and dependencies among its different parts" (51). Through such a metaphor, they hope to emphasize that human activity often takes place within local systems. "An ecology is complex," they write, "but it does not have the overwhelming breadth of the large-scale systems and dynamics [Jacques] Ellul and others describe. An ecology responds to local environmental changes and local interventions" (50).

By thinking of information ecologies, we remind ourselves that we are all integral parts of specific organizations (such as a college campus). Just as an ecological view of the environment prompts us to see the environment as a set of interrelated systems (e.g., bird population depends on insect population, which depends on plant populations, which depend on weather conditions, etc.), so does an ecological view of organizations prompt us to see a given local institution as a series of interrelated systems. If changes in one system brings changes in others, then one's actions can have ripple effects in an organization, but how does one effect more than random change?

The institution-as-technology metaphor complements the institution-as-ecology metaphor by suggesting strategies for purposeful change. Consider first the metaphor itself. Consider that a technology presents a gathering of artifacts and processes designed to enable users to accomplish a desired task. A bicycle presents a collection of gears, ball bearings, wheels, and so on, all of which enable a person (with the proper know-how) to get from one point to another with less time and effort than on foot; a computer presents a collection of chips, wiring, code, and the like, that enables humans (with the proper know-how) to store data and calculate numbers at a magnitude and speed that would be impossible for the human mind alone; likewise, an institution presents a collection of bricks and mortar, written documents, personnel, and so on, designed to enable people (again, with the proper know-how) to accomplish certain tasks. In a library, for example, one often finds librarians fulfilling diversified roles (e.g., children's librarians, reference librarians), patrons, print technologies (e.g., books, journals), digital technologies (e.g., databases, web pages, CD-ROMs), and other resources. A library is a kind of technology that enables users (with the appropriate know-how) to access information that would be harder to access otherwise.

If we accept the institution-as-technology metaphor, then arguments against technological determinism also can be made against institutional determinism. Writers such as Andrew Feenberg and Wiebe Bijker, for example, argue that agency in the face of apparent technological determinism seems possible when one sees technology as a constant process of development. As Bijker, Thomas Hughes, and Trevor Pinch point out, we can talk about technologies in the following three ways:

1. As physical artifacts (e.g., an automobile or a computer).
2. As activities or processes (e.g., the steps needed for making steel or a computer chip).
3. As know-how (e.g., ability to design an automobile or chip).

It is when we look at a technology as an artifact that technological determinism seems the most probable explanation because a technology is difficult to resist once it is in place. However, when we realize that technology also involves processes of development, and the know-how to carry it all out, then we can begin to see points where humans have the ability to change things.

Feenberg and Bijker both argue that designers are constantly faced with decisions for which there are no clear answers. It is not that design processes must move inexorably toward one determined outcome. (See Fig. 9.1. The diamonds represent points where decisions must be made. Notice that each decision leads to a more efficient technology over time.) Rather, there are many instances where designers have no clearly rational, efficient choice, or where other factors affect designers' decisions. At these points of ambivalence or contingency, designers must make decisions that are as often based on social and political factors as they are on economic or technological ones. (See Fig. 9.2. Again, the diamonds represent points where decisions must be made. In this version, however, decisions do not always lead to more efficient technologies.) Bijker's book, *Of Bicycles, Bakelites, and Bulbs*, is devoted in part to illustrating the role of contingency through three historical case studies.

What is true for technological indeterminacy is true for institutions. As writers such as Anthony Giddens and Porter et al. realize, institutions can be viewed in the same three ways suggested by Bijker, Hughes, and Pinch:

1. As objects (buildings filled with documents, etc.).
2. As activities or processes (the policies and procedures that constantly reproduce an institution).
3. As know-how (the ability to implement those policies and procedures).

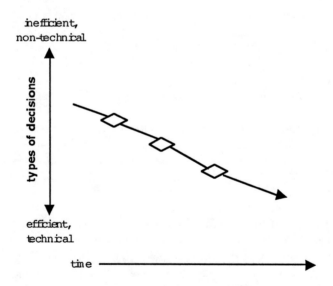

FIGURE 9.1.   Technological determinism states that design decisions are made on purely efficient, rational grounds, leading to inevitable design outcomes. Designs become more efficient over time.

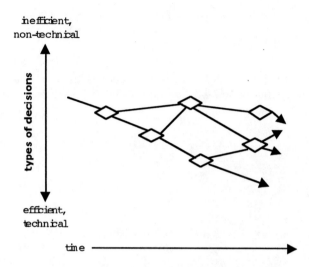

FIGURE 9.2.   Some claim that technological decisions are just as often made on political and social issues as on purely efficient, rational ones. Thus, the outcome of design is undetermined.

Institutions are embodied in part by bricks and mortar, and money, and printed forms, and policies, *and the people that uphold them.* These people and objects are part of the way an institution is articulated and maintains a recognizable form over time. Reinforced by the resources and rules that guide behavior, those practices constantly reproduce the system, which is maintained through regulations which are in turn reinforced by sanctions or rewards (see Fig. 9.3 for an illustration of the process). "Without the joint behavior in which members engage," write Teresa M. Harrison and Susan M. Katz, "there is no organization. . . . Organizations must be re-created every day. Because re-creation is essential to their nature, organizations are more accurately viewed as processes rather than as things" (19-20).

Moreover, we should recognize that most institutional maintenance practices involve reading and writing. Consider, for instance, how much negotiation and interpretation surround policy. A person must make some conscious decisions when implementing policy, as Stephen Ball suggests:

> Policies do not normally tell you what to do; they create circumstances in which the range of options available in deciding what to do is narrowed or changed or particular goals or outcomes are set. A response

must still be put together, constructed in context, offset against or bal-
anced by other expectations. All of this involves creative social action
of some kind. (n.p.)

To those versed in postmodern theories of reading, the possibility that policy must be interpreted, and will be interpreted differently by different people, should not be surprising.

FIGURE 9.3.   **(A)** A system is
not a large, unchangeable
thing.

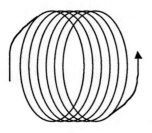

(B) It is maintained through
dynamic   processes,   and
although a system maintains
its basic "shape" over time . . .

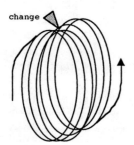

(C) small changes in maintenance processes can ripple
through a system, thus having
larger consequences.

APPLYING ECOLOGICAL AND TECHNOLOGICAL METAPHORS TO SPECIFIC STORIES

Earlier, I presented several stories in which individuals faced unacceptable institutional constraints. What these stories have in common is the way agents learn to create agency by recognizing that small-scale actions can have large-scale consequences. The agents have recognized what Giddens calls the "interdependence of action"—"a relationship in which changes in one or more component parts initiate changes in other component parts" (73). In essence, they have discovered a phenomenon akin to the butterfly effect. (Here we return to an ecological metaphor.) Just as chaos theory suggests that a butterfly flapping its wings in a South American rainforest may ultimately affect weather patterns in the northern hemisphere, so in these stories do agents hope that a small alteration will have larger systemic ramifications. Therefore, the agents look for what James Gleick calls "point[s] of crisis that could magnify small changes" (23):

- Mary Dieli spearheaded a change in Microsoft's corporate documentation. That is, she "worked very hard to get the term 'usability' included on the company's generic product development chart" thereby establishing audience awareness and audience research "as a value and a procedural norm" within the corporation (Porter et al. 610-611). The hope, as expressed by the story tellers, is that eventually such a seemingly small rhetorical change can sensitize the institution "to users, to people, systemically from within" (611). Moreover, the rhetorical change strengthens the position of the usability department, making it more integral to product development.
- Members of an "ad hoc" client involvement committee of the HIV/AIDS Planning Council argued to have their status changed to a "task force," which in turn makes the work of that group "part of the public record" which must be "acted upon (usually in terms of a vote)" (Grabill 43). The hope, again, is that a change in the designation of an institutional unit (in part, a change in the Council's organizational chart) will further sensitize the institution "to users, to people, systemically from within."

- Workers in the abortion clinic undermined "attempts by the state to exercise semiotic power" by committing "seemingly trivial acts"—such as "clipping the [state's] fetal development pamphlet underneath other informational materials" (Haas 225). That is, they downplayed the importance of the pamphlet by burying it within a collection of other documents, thus allowing them to continue to frame abortion as a medical procedure rather than as a disruption of pregnancy.
- Cindy Moore focused on rewriting the writing program handbook and also on changing the way it was presented to associate faculty. In many cases, she began to qualify statements by changing words like "must" to phrases like "should consider." In others, she dropped certain restrictions altogether in the faith that the faculty would act in the best interests of the students. She also dropped the practice of asking job applicants to read the handbook and write a response to it as part of the hiring process.

What these agents sought were ways to make seemingly insignificant changes to such things as organizational charts, written procedures, and other institutional documents, or to change the way such a document was presented and received.

Change was possible because systems, like weather patterns, are dynamic and tangible things, rather than static, monolithic entities. Except for total institutions (such as prisons), people often have what Giddens calls the "power to do otherwise." Thus, agency is gained within institutions in part by recognizing that people who must maintain an institution constantly face situations of ambiguity similar to those faced by technologists. That's why Giddens' concept of transformative capacity—an agent's ability to "intervene in events in the world, thus producing definite outcomes" (88)—relies on a concept akin to Feenberg's concept of ambivalence and Bijker's of contingency.

Writing is often the nexus in which human agency and institutional constraints get played out. Porter et al.'s concept of rhetorical action is a type of transformative capacity that involves a rewriting of the resources by which an institution is maintained, whether it be to rewrite the policies that help reproduce institutional structures, or to revise the way an institution uses space. For example, Porter et al. cite changes in product development charts and the addition of a usability lab within a department of English— the latter being a change in physical space that marks a change in the status of professional writing within a traditional department of English. To bring it all together: Because ambiguity and contingency appear inevitably within any process of development or maintenance, it is at these points that agents exercise their transformative capacity. One way for institutional agents to affect change is to focus on written documents—either how they are written or how they are interpreted. Rhetorical action is a way of exercising transformative capacity because so much of an institution and its maintenance involves reading and writing.

WHAT THESE STORIES CAN TELL US

There are perhaps several lessons we can take from these stories. First, they warn us not to ignore the mundane texts in our midst. Second, they tell us something about how texts derive power. And third, they illustrate a number of tactics for changing systemic conditions that are constituted in part by these texts.

They Warn Us Not to Ignore Mundane Texts

Johnson writes, "We often point to those technologies that have had very visible and sweeping cultural effects like the printing press, the steam engine, or the computer"; however, "Some mundane technologies, maybe less visible but no less essential, have had equally strong cultural effects" (89). Perhaps the same thing could be said about texts, which are, after all, a type of technology. We understand the power of well-known texts such as The American Declaration of Independence or the Gettysburg Address. (Garry Wills argues in *Lincoln at Gettysburg* that the latter speech—specifically, the written transcripts that circulated in periodicals afterward—helped redefine people's understanding of the United States. He notes, for example, that people stopped using the plural with the United States—the United States *are*—and began using the singular—*is*—shortly after the address.) But what about texts that are less obvious, more mundane? Some mundane documents may have similar effects. I am talking about documents that set parameters for our labor and for the labor of those who work with us—including secretaries, students, editors, and so on. Consider the power of a job description or a performance evaluation or the written procedure for conducting such an evaluation; consider the power of a faculty enchiridion or other written policies, of an accounting report, of a writing program handbook

They Tell Us Something About How Texts Derive Power

Texts can derive power in three ways: in the way they are written, presented, and received. The writing program handbook mentioned by Moore illustrates all three. Consider the way it was written. The handbook stated, for example, that instructors "should" cancel no more than two class periods for conferences, which left associate faculty thinking they could hold no more than one or two conferences per semester unless they wanted to overload their own schedules. One associate faculty member told Moore that she (the associate faculty member) wanted to conference with students after every paper but that she couldn't because of this "two-class" rule. The handbook also stated that students "must write five papers," which left some associate faculty feeling that they could not assign, say, four slightly longer papers while devoting more time to revision.

The potential to read the handbook as a list of rules rather than guidelines was increased by the way it was presented to those teaching in the composition program. According to Moore, the handbook was used more as a "central text" than a "reference" for associate faculty. Any applicant to teach in the composition program was asked to read the handbook and write a reflective response to it before a decision to hire would be made. However, the reception of the handbook was still tempered by the status of the people reading it. Moore noted, for example, that tenure-track faculty viewed the handbook as a collection of guidelines, whereas associate faculty read it as a set of restrictions. Whereas nontenure-track associate faculty read "should" as "must," tenure-track faculty read it more liberally. For the latter group, the perceived penalty for fudging with the guidelines was much lower than for the former. Therefore, the text had less power over some than others because people of differing rank received the book differently.

They Illustrate a Number of Tactics for Changing Systemic Conditions

If texts derive power in three ways, as illustrated in the previous section, then change can be focused at one or more of them. Some may argue for a rewriting of those documents. In some cases (as in the HIV/AIDS planning council and Microsoft cases) the agents who want change lack the power to rewrite institutional artifacts and processes themselves. Rather, they must argue to those in power in order to get a change accepted. Others (as in Moore's case) have the power to start rewriting texts themselves. In cases where agents have no control over rewriting a text (and where those in control will not acquiesce to such revision), agents may focus on the way a text is distributed and received. The workers in the abortion clinic, for instance, had no choice in the wording of the brochure. Nor could they choose not to distribute it without serious penalty. What they could do was change the way it was distributed by burying it under other texts. Likewise, before she could revise the handbook, Moore changed the way it was received by claiming that it was "in revision" when someone asked for it, and by not making the reading of it a condition of the hiring process.

CONCLUSION

It strikes me that concepts of agency have not kept pace with concepts of writing. Our conception of writing has become highly situated, even ecological, whereas our conception of agency remains highly decontextualized and individualistic. Those who write about activity theory (e.g., Russell), systems theory (e.g., Suchan and Dulek, Bouldin and Odell), and ecology (e.g., Cooper and Holzman) all see writing as a phenomenon that emerges from the interplay of numerous interrelated variables. Writing is understood best when scholars attempt to identify and relate those variables. Most approaches to agency, however, attempt to isolate them. I hope that my arguments here may prompt some to begin redefining our sense of agency as a highly situated, ecological construct.

Let me close with two caveats: First, the stories shared here should not be misread as narratives of liberal individualism. Individuals seldom act autonomously. Remember that actions are constrained by the systems in which we work. Only in Moore's case did anyone have power enough to change things unilaterally. (Even there, others still had to interpret the revisions that she made.) In the other cases, people had to convince others to accept a small change. Or, in the case of the workers in the abortion clinic, the people simply had to change the way the text was presented. These are not grand narratives of one person's fight against a system. (In the HIV/AID case, remember, we are talking about one ad hoc group seeking more formal recognition from another group.) These are stories about political action. I am reminded of an interview with Al Gore during the 2000

Presidential elections. The interviewer first paraphrases Gore: To deal in politics means "[t]o walk the line between idealism and compromise"; then he gets quoted: "you find the limits of the possible and you push" (Henneberger 9A).

Second, through such stories, we may overestimate the power of writing (as might be understandable given our training). As scholars and teachers of writing, we are inclined to see power in writing processes and written artifacts because that is what we are good at seeing and it is in our best interests to illustrate its value. But other factors are equally as important as writing. Money, for instance. No policy, no matter how well written, will be worth much if people cannot afford the resources to support it. There are certain physical and temporal realities to consider as well. Are associate faculty given adequate space in which to work? Can potential participants in a planning council get themselves to a meeting if they have children and jobs and must rely on public transportation? And then, of course, there can be threats of violence.

Writing is not always (perhaps it is only occasionally) an answer to a systemic problem. And yet, from the stories I have mentioned, I think it sometimes is a key to change. Therefore, keeping in mind its limitations, we should consider whether and when recognizing such stories helps each of us find agency in sometimes hostile environments. "[O]ur responsibilities as teachers of technical communication must go beyond simply teaching students the skills of creating a communication product," write Harrison and Katz. "We must emphasize to students that communication contributes to the ongoing constitution of the organization and the world it embodies" (27). This claim is true for more than technical communication.

REFERENCES

Ball, Stephen J. "Policy Sociology and Critical Social Research: A Personal Review of Recent Education Policy and Policy Research." *British Educational Research Journal*. 23 (1997): 257-274.

Bijker, Wiebe. *Of Bicycles, Bakelites, and Bulbs: Towards a Theory of Sociotechnical Change*. Cambridge, MA: MIT Press, 1995.

_____, Thomas P. Hughes, and Trevor Pinch. *The Social Construction of Technological Systems: New Directions in the Sociology and History of Technology*. Cambridge, MA: MIT Press, 1987.

Bouldin, Tyler, and Lee Odell. "Surveying the Field and Looking Ahead: A Systems Theory Perspective on Research and Writing in the Workplace." *Writing in the*

Workplace: New Research Perspectives. Ed. Rachel Spilka. Carbondale: Southern Illinois UP, 1993. 268-281.

Cooper, Marilyn, and Michael Holzman. *Writing as Social Action.* Portsmouth, NH: Boynton/Cook-Heinemann, 1989.

Faigley, Lester. *Fragments of Rationality: Postmodernism and the Subject of Composition.* Pittsburgh: University of Pittsburgh Press, 1992.

Feenberg, Andrew. *Critical Theory of Technology.* New York: Oxford UP, 1991.

France, Alan. "Dialectics of Self: Structure and Agency as the Subject of English." *College English.* 62(2000): 145-165.

Giddens, Anthony. *Central Problems in Social Theory: Action, Structure, and Contradiction in Social Analysis.* Berkeley: University of California Press, 1979.

Gleick, James. *Chaos: Making a New Science.* New York: Penguin, 1987.

Grabill, Jeffrey T. "Shaping Local HIV/AIDS Services Policy through Activist Research: The Problem of Client Involvement." *Technical Communication Quarterly.* 9.1(2000): 29-52.

Haas, Christina. "On the Relationship between Old and New Technologies." *Computers and Composition.* 16.2(1999): 209-228.

Harrison, Teresa M., and Susan M. Katz. "On Taking Organizations Seriously: Organizations as Social Contexts for Technical Communication." *Foundations for Teaching Technical Communication: Theory, Practice, and Program Design.* Eds. Katherine Staples and Cezar Ornatowski. Greenwich, CT: Ablex, 1997. 17-30.

Henneberger, Melinda. "Early Career Had Marks of Struggle: Biography Reveals a Man with Regrets, Ambition." *The News-Sentinel* [Fort Wayne, IN] 1 Nov. 2000: 1A, 9A.

Johnson, Robert. *User-Centered Technology: A Rhetorical Theory for Computers and Other Mundane Artifacts.* Albany: SUNY Press, 1998.

Johnson-Eilola, Johndan. "Little Machines: Rearticulating Hypertext Users." 1995 Conference on College Composition and Communication, Washington, DC. 20 Aug. 2000

Jones, Donald C. "Beyond the Postmodern Impasse of Agency: The Resounding Relevance of John Dewey's Tacit Tradition." *JAC: A Journal of Composition Theory.* 16 (1996). 2000.

Landow, George P. *Hypertext: The Convergence of Contemporary Critical Theory and Technology.* Baltimore, MD: Johns Hopkins UP, 1991.

LeCourt, Donna. "Critical Pedagogy in the Computer Classroom: Politicizing the Writing Space." *Computers and Composition.* 15 (1998): 275-295.

Meyer, Paul R., and Stephen A. Bernhardt. "Workplace Realities and the Technical Communication Curriculum: A Call for Change." *Foundations for Teaching Technical Communication: Theory, Practice, and Program Design.* Eds. Katherine Staples and Cezar Ornatowski. Greenwich, CT: Ablex, 1997. 85-98.

Murphy, Cullen. "Who's in Charge?" *The Atlantic Monthly;* May 2001; Volume 287, No. 5; 18-20.

Nardi, Bonnie A. and Vicki O'Day. *Information Ecologies: Using Technology with Heart*. Cambridge, MA: MIT Press, 1999.

Porter, James E., Patricia Sullivan, Stuart Blythe, Jeffrey T. Grabill, and Libby Miles. "Institutional Critique: A Rhetorical Methodology for Change." *College Composition and Communication*. 51.4 (2000): 610-642.

Russell, David. "Activity Theory and Its Implications for Writing Instruction." Ed. Joseph Petraglia. *Reconceiving Writing, Rethinking Writing Instruction*. Mahwah, NJ: Erlbaum, 1995. 51-77.

Suchan, Jim, and Ron Dulek. "From Text to Context: An Open Systems Approach to Research in Written Business Communication." *Journal of Business Communication*. 35 (1998): 87-110.

Trimbur, John. "Agency and the Death of the Author: A Partial Defense of Modernism." *JAC: A Journal of Composition Theory*. 20 (2000): 283-298.

Wills, Garry. *Lincoln at Gettysburg: The Words that Remade America*. New York: Simon & Schuster, 1992.

Young, Iris Marion. *Inclusion and Democracy*. New York: Oxford UP, 2000.

10

ROOTS AND ROUTES
TO AGENCY

SPACE, ACCESS, AND STANDARDS
OF PARTICIPATION

Annette Harris Powell

University of Louisville

As a field, we continue to wrestle with defining agency, and in computers and composition, specifically, we have been concerned with how we might get students to realize agency in technologized contexts. Many discussions of agency in composition have been centered on critical pedagogy and resistance as ways to empower students (Berlin, Bizzell, Aronowitz and Giroux, Shor). In considering how composition matters in the lives of our students, agency does not necessarily explain everything. Given that "practices" speak to who we are and where we've been, and that practices enable certain effects, why focus simply on agency? Lawrence Grossberg argues, "There can be no universal theory of agency; agency can only be described in its contextual enactments" (123). Recognizing individual, daily practices and the meaning attached to these practices is more effective in promoting social change. Composition, in traditional and computerized classrooms, matters most to our students if their literate practices, the meanings that are valued in their communities are validated in our classrooms. To enact a socially meaningful agency that entails power and ownership is to engage practice. How do we get our students to realize agency in technologized contexts? In "Interrupting Our Way to Agency," Nedra

Reynolds argues, "Agency is not simply about finding one's own voice but also about intervening in discourses of the everyday and cultivating rhetorical tactics that make interruption and resistance an important part of any conversation" (59). Agency is often fleeting; students' everyday practices do not actively "interrupt" and disrupt traditional discourses, often they are not heard or their voices are dismissed, and they do not realize the much-theorized agency that we claim to value.

I argue that the significance we have attributed to agency, in many ways, distracts us from enacting and designing material practices that might actually have an effect on somebody besides us (and besides our already existing constituencies within the academy). Similarly, Ellen Messer-Davidow makes the point that "If we continue to argue that academic knowledge is a system of ideas, values, and practices shaped by ideological, material, and social forces, then the pertinent question is: can we merely choose among knowledges, or will we have to struggle?" (300). Messer-Davidow argues that we must put "know-how"—"the capacity to expedite"—to work reconnecting inquiry and action (301). By focusing more on action and less on critique, we will indeed have to "struggle" as we begin to reconsider standards of participation that ensure that students enact an agency that is useful to them. This chapter offers my reflections on agency and participation in computer-assisted learning environments and in online spaces (listservs, web pages). My discussion foregrounds my participation in two sessions (both 2 weeks) of a technology camp for middle school students.

A VEHICLE FOR AGENCY?

During Summer 2001, middle school students from underserved populations participated in a technology camp housed in the computer classrooms of a large urban university run by five compositionists (a tenured professor and four graduate students, including me).[1] The observations I share are part of a larger project in which I focus on complicating notions of access and what it means to be technologically literate. Objectives for this camp included giving students experience in introductory computer skills, word processing, web authoring, web research, and page design principles and programs. Additionally, we anticipated helping students from underserved communities to become more familiar with technology so that they would not fall into the digital divide, providing them with a space for this and a bit of fun at the same time, as well as introducing these students to a college campus and some of what goes on there. We also hoped to get students to critically explore technology as more than something to consume, but also as a tool for (re)producing, themselves, their culture, and the world around them. I would say that one of the primary goals, although perhaps unarticulated, was that students might see this camp and the technology as an opportunity to give voice to their values and cultures. The camp curriculum consisted of a variety of assignments including technology literacy autobiographies, photoessays, creative annotations, Interviews of community members, and parody ads. To facilitate these assignments, we conducted workshops on photography, visual representation, interview principles, web design principles, taking and scanning digital photos, and publishing them to the web, among other things. Ultimately, camp participants' selected work would be added to the 'zine and published to the web.

In both sessions of the camp, students were especially interested in chatrooms and downloading music from the web, activities unsponsored by camp instructors, although not forbidden. In Session 1, the students were very technology literate; they required no lesson plan or teaching in order to get into mp3s or to navigate the web. However, creating a web page and putting their 'zine on the web was not impressive or particularly interesting to many of these students. The technology they were interested in mastering—Flash and running videos—was not available in our computer classroom, however. The students in Session 2 also knew a lot about getting in and out of chatrooms and the like, but their basic literacy skills and social skills were lacking. A lot of energy was spent trying to get kids in this session to focus on the other technology-related activities we wanted them to do—scanning images, *doing* their writing, putting their writing online, and so on. Based on their chat conversations and practices, they were, however, very interested in race and identity construction online.

There were a couple of specific things that happened during both camp sessions during an instructor-sponsored photoessay assignment and unsponsored chatroom activities (which I discuss later) that encouraged me to rethink agency. I focus on the photoessay assignment because it was one of the assignments we felt would facilitate students' agency, and we thought it would be something that they would enjoy.[2] The photoessay provided an opportunity for students to "represent" their lives. Students were given disposable cameras and told to photograph their lives and communities. Their photoessays were later published to the web as part of their E-zine. As one of the beginning activities, it acted as somewhat of an ice-breaker, while providing students an opportunity to tell us something about themselves. For the most part, they enjoyed taking the pictures, scanning them, and sharing them with each other and us. The assignment seemed to be very successful. However, in looking at the photoessay pages, I had to ask myself what these students intended to represent of their lives and how this assignment really served them. Did the subject positions these students created aid or hinder their agency?

In "Really Useful Knowledge," Marilyn Cooper writes "We came to understand that writers cannot and do not achieve agency in writing by subduing language to their selves but rather by using language to construct subject positions. Agency in writing depends not on owning or taking responsibility for a text but on understanding how to construct subject positions" (339). Although Cooper does not say it explicitly, she seems to get at the idea of agency as practice. With the photos that students in both sessions of the camp took and selected, they constructed subject positions that illustrated not only the social practices in which they engage in their home communities, but also the bleak economic circumstances in which some of them lived. Several of the photos showed younger siblings or cousins partially clad and dirty, other family members sitting in a kitchen surrounded by dirty dishes and food cluttering counters and tables, and family/friends sitting on run-down porches with various junked items. Although they were, in fact, constructing positions, I don't think many of them had any meta-awareness. What, if anything, did they think about what they were showing? Although it was clear to us that social and institutional structures create positions for these students, I don't think it was clear to them. At least one or two instructors commented on what they saw in the photos. The question on my mind, which I hesitated to ask at the time was, how, if at all, does what we see in the pictures alter our interactions with or approaches to these students? In other words, what is the real *effect* of what they have chosen to share with us? And ultimately, how have their representations been agentic?

Although some would argue that voicing or "representing" is most critical in the process of agency, as evidenced by the camp participants, it seems that most 12-year-olds voice through practice. Throughout Sessions 1 and 2, both groups' self-expression was evidenced in how the students chose to construct their 'zines. They spent a good deal of time debating the music that should be linked to the 'zine's music page, the jokes they wanted to include on their joke page, and the kinds of icons they thought were "boring" and those they thought were "tight," (good) and so on. In fact, at one point there was some debate between one of the instructors and the students. This instructor did not want the students to publish certain jokes because she found them to be in poor taste, although the students thought they were exactly what jokes are supposed to be, funny. In another instance, students were upset by what they saw as our attempt to control the layout of their 'zine. When asked what they liked best/least, and what they might change about the camp, one student responded, "Camp, I like it. I think it's fun. It's real fun. But some things I don't like that you all have a tendency to do—because like when we work with this one teacher, we decide a picture should go to one section and she says it's going in another. And I don't feel she listens to our opinion. It's about her. We decided we wanted certain backgrounds, but she decided she didn't want that background." Although responses such as the one related by this student certainly interfered with these students' agency, in some ways, what's important isn't what you articulate as much as what comes out of your practice. What came out of the photoessay assignment for these kids, other than it was fun? What were they enacting unconsciously, or were they consciously deciding to portray their lives the way they did? Before students began taking their photos, we might have begun the assignment by using other pictures to demonstrate a reading of pictures in the way we read other texts. Because they might not be have been aware of how people construct and so that they would be more conscious of how their pictures might be read, we could have discussed the assumptions or inferences that people often make. *This* kind of action is helping students to develop critical agency. We could have spent some time talking with them about those structures that position them and asked them to consider certain questions as they put together their photoessays: For example, we could have asked: How do you *want* to represent yourself? Why do you want to include these two pictures? What does this picture say about you? What will people who look at your selected photos think about them, about you? Had we done this, we might have avoided perpetuating simplistic notions of agency.

Additionally, we might have asked ourselves: *What effect do these students' practices have on us?* What are we going to do with what they have represented of themselves and their lives? Although I believe individual agency (coming to voice, a vote in decisions that affect us) to be valuable and certainly the critical starting point, I am concerned with what comes next, so I envision a kind of agency that is public, visible, and leads to social and/or institutional change. Because social material context shapes notions (and uses) of space, including technology, how we think about space and technology determines our relationship to it. If we are to realize the potential for parity and participation, we have to re-examine how we build community in technologized spaces. How we build these spaces, and the terms on which we ask people to participate in these spaces, however, continues to be a source of contention

PARTICIPATORY SPACES

We must purposefully build these virtual spaces, in much the same way that we deliberately construct them in real space. Jurgen Habermas' model of the bourgeois public sphere is said to represent the ultimate public space in which "private persons' come together to discuss issues of "public concern" or "common interests." Ideally, this leads to rational discourse and mutual agreement within a given community. A number of scholars argue, however, that Habermas' model is an idealized notion of the public sphere that fails to consider competing interests (Frazer). For example, historian Evelyn Higginbotham documents how African-American women were forced to construct access to an alternative Black public sphere when admission to the "official" liberal public sphere during the 1880–1920 period was denied. For many, the Black Church served as a public space for critical discussion and debate of social and political issues of the day as well as a space for educational training and promotion. According to Higginbotham, the Black Church provided a space for African-American women to "articulate a public discourse critical of women's subordination" (9). Analogizing from Higginbotham's point, perhaps the true public sphere would be one in which we are all encouraged to bring our individual practices. Similarly, Patricia Hill Collins theorizes space as a bond, arguing that there are certain "institutional sites" (churches, African-American community organizations) that represent "safe spaces" that enable self-expression and self-definition (95). Such safe spaces yield natural embraces, rather than a negotiation of difference. Although there is a normalized discourse, it is implicitly agreed on by the participants. This implicitness is based on shared social material context. Culture, discourse, access is all constructed by the participants, and access is meaningful because they participate in the making of the experience. For Nancy Frazer, "participation means being able to speak in 'one's own cultural voice,' thereby simultaneously constructing and expressing one's cultural identity through idiom and style" (88). People of color, especially, continue to seek participation in the spaces theorized above, both online and in real space.

The students in our technology camp were no exception. During both sessions, many of them spent a good deal of time in various chatrooms. In fact, this was a significant part of the underlife of the camp. They used the technology and space in ways that we had not anticipated. For example, for the majority of these students, race was a significant factor in their online literacy activities. Their discussions online focused, to a large degree, on race and identity construction (e.g., how they were visualized in this space). And, although they actively changed their appearance—they had green eyes or became girls or boys, at will—race remained the constant factor in their online identities. It seemed that this discursive space was very comfortable for them and they were very aware of how they manipulated their self-representations.

So then, it seems that how we view a given space depends to a large degree on who occupies it, how we use it, the language used in it, and the ideology we attribute to the space in question. This has important implications for online discourse because our construction of both the physical and cultural spaces of the academy as well as of cyberspace determines what can and does take place there. So, contrary to popular narratives, cyberspace is not unlimited and boundless. But, rather than lament the competing narratives of technology as an agent of social change and technology as embedded with hegemonic ideologies, we might consider the complicated sociopsychological barriers that limit access and increase the disconnect. In *Imagined Communities*, Benedict Anderson argues that with the rise of mass-produced print culture, individuals are now able to travel the distance between space and time, to connect to people with whom they had no personal acquaintance. With the World Wide Web as such an imagined community, I urge examination of the kind of community that it symbolizes. In some ways, the web's conception as virtual or imaginary works as a theoretical foil, engaging notions of "imagined communities" as a movement toward embrace of the "other." One of the dangers of virtual imagining, however, is that it facilitates avoidance of the real. Although we should trust our imaginations, we must also be critical of them. Although our imagination and our visual representations can work to challenge oppressive constructions of race, gender, sexuality, and so on, without interaction, without contextualization they stand alone. Discursive representations become nothing more than one-dimensional constructions of self, thereby flattening the possible "layers of interpretation" (Hawisher and Sullivan 285). Yet, as Margaret Morse suggests, computer and television screens are not one-way, rather, they act as "membranes" for filtering culture—ideology, events, and customs or practices. People adopt culture for their own uses but they are also influenced by said culture. However, though we may control the physical images in the medium, without dialogue, we have very little control over how people interpret these images. What takes place in virtual space, then, is much the same as that which occurs in real space. Difference continues to be nothing more than a rhetorical construction, neutralized by a lack of contextualization.

PROBLMATIZING SPACE AND ACCESS

Crucial to the consideration of access is the presumption of human agency and the ability for us to construct technology in a way that is meaningful to us. Much of the literature on the web and the digital divide (differential access to computers and Internet technologies) focuses on technical access, that is, inequalities of access, and the differences (education, class, gender, age) between the individuals who use the web. A more complicated articulation of access counters the notion of access as primarily concerned with infrastructure or resources, or the notion of access as a one-time fix. Jeff Grabill employs Jim Porter's three-part framework—infrastructural or resource access, literacy (skills and expertise), and community or social acceptance—to illustrate how computers and composition scholars can invigorate the discourse surrounding access. Grabill finds that in the site he studied, although there was a "presence of computers, at significant infrastructural levels, [students] are still denied access because their teacher (let alone the students themselves) was denied equally fundamental access to the decision-making processes that affect the technologies they can and cannot use" (309).

As Grabill suggests, without meaningful access and the ability to construct computer technology as writing technologies (307) such that it contributes to knowledge making that is local, relevant, and valuable, critical human agency is tenuous at best. The individual and the community must be able to employ technology to achieve their economic, social, and cultural objectives. Access is not a proxy; there must be participation in order for it to be meaningful—to be truly representative of human agency. Online space must be theorized in ways that foster an agency that allows one to define and to construct technology, and to determine the terms of one's participation. Access is effective when distinct identities are recognized, and new perspectives are welcomed and valued.

Toward this end, we need to work at complicating the layers of literate and social practices that mediate access to technology. I argue for complicating access on two levels: First, we need to recognize what I call substantive, rather than procedural access. Procedural access is simple access to a computer. A substantive, effective access must be more than a gateway to a space with entrenched boundaries, but a real bridge to meaningful exchanges that result in the construction of new spaces. Thus, substantive access is participation in the communities created in the public sphere—that is, the opportunity to share, to respond to, and to test our real or perceived notions of the world, without neutralizing our subjectivities. Second, we need to work at establishing the difference between access and agency. Too often there is slippage between the two terms; achieved access seems to suggest only successful consumption, rather than production. Although, it should be noted that consumption is not always uncritical. As Morse suggests, nothing is consumed without resistance, adaptation, and change. Agency, in relation to access, I define as the ability to determine the terms of one's participation in a particular medium, to help define and construct the technology, and to use it in the production of a culture that is useful and meaningful in the context of one's material social condition. Although access itself is certainly important, it is crucial that we understand that many, perhaps, are experiencing technology in very different ways than we are thinking about it. As Selfe and Selfe assert, "within the virtual space represented by these interfaces, and elsewhere within computer systems, the values of our culture—ideological, political, economic, and educational—are mapped both implicitly, and explicitly, constituting a complex set of material relations among culture, technology, and technology users" (485). Our attitudes toward technology dictate our relationship to it, and that relationship is determined by materiality (social, economic, class, political)—in sum, geographic location both physically, emotionally, and culturally.

Most people would agree that technology and space, virtual or real, are already and always ideological; they are not empty containers, so to speak. The theorizing of online space as somehow separate from face-to-face space is analogous to the theorizing of an academic–real-world split. In some ways, this might be helpful for our thinking about some specific thing, but the problem is when that heuristic division comes to represent the thing itself. We attribute certain characteristics to all social spaces, use particular kinds of language in those spaces, and observe certain conventions when entering them. For example, cyberspace is not the traditional public square or open marketplace dedicated to the free flow of ideas. The "blank space" has its own costs: Access is controlled by systematic exclusions. Not everyone gets in, and those who do must speak a certain language or adhere to certain conventions and perform certain rhetorical moves. According to Sarah Sloane, "embedded in most writers' encounters with digital technology are the visible traces of conventions, structures, and styles of communicating" (51), so when we travel in cyberspace, we bring our practices and prejudices, our individual ideologies, and in turn, we are shaped by the ideology within—that ideology alters our subjectivity.

Although we have moved beyond the egalitarian narratives and utopian claims of the web as an ideal social space, we continue to move quickly without particular attention to the concrete effects the web may have on various discourse communities. Hawisher and Sullivan note "As women have more control over writing their own visualizations online, we see some women representing themselves complexly in creative, rhetorically effective ways. . . . Multiple and competing visuals, animation, mythological drawings, and even sound all command the viewer's attention" (288). Yet, even Hawisher and Sullivan acknowledge that the visual is only one component necessary to effect "visual discourse online." They go on to say, "In its profusion of visual images, the World Wide Web is doing little more than imitating the material world we all inhabit" (289). As Cooper suggests, students use technology to enact agency "by using language to construct subject positions" (339). Home page design, for example, enables students to use the interface to add their image or vision of themselves to the array of cultural pictures that web pages represent. In this instance, technology provides a site for resistance, an opportunity to contest social, cultural, political assumptions in favor of images or texts that they consider more representative. To some degree, there is agency in the design of web pages as participants have the tools to actively engage in self-representation and manipulation of the technology.

However, although the web provides a medium for individuals to construct rich personal narratives, it is not enough to just do this. I agree that we need to pay attention to the visual but if the "multiply rich selves" (Hawisher and Sullivan) that we construct do no more than imitate the material world, then re-constructing the self electronically does little more than replicate the stasis underlying social discourse in the material world. Listservs, as another example, are constructed spaces that have been touted by some as democratizing agents of voice that allow more people to participate in the discussion. Grabill notes that those who have great expectations for Computer Mediated Communication (CMC) embrace "claims that e-mail environments support more democratic and egalitarian spaces for communication, open discussion, greater collaboration, and access to more and better information" (301). But, whereas CMC theory argues its stabilizing function, and even though in the case of listservs selected individuals are invited to participate, hierarchies still exist. In "Technological Fronts," Addison and Hilligoss construct e-space as a "front"—it operates as a metaphor for "sites of struggle": "What is constant, perhaps, is that the act of identifying oneself as lesbian is complex, often emotionally charged, and, even in feminist or otherwise 'safe' spaces, a political statement and site of potential disruption" (21). They argue that with topics falling outside the norm, people who don't feel comfortable discussing are ignored and ultimately silenced, and the normalizing function of technology is accomplished. "Norms" and "normal" are coded in our culture as White, male, heterosexual, and so on. This is another way for the virtual world to avoid representing or welcoming the subaltern. Thus, the notion of silence needs to be complicated much more. We need to examine the ways in which social materials are laid over the physical space; how does this affect voice and the dialogue that we might engage in this space? Because the same group chooses the medium and decides the discourse, the discourse continues to be normalized. Addison and Hilligoss, citing Richard Sclove argue that in this regard, the medium, technology, "continues to function as a tool for the maintenance of exclusionary and oppressive cultural practices despite an individual group's liberatory aims" (22). Without problematizing the potential for technology to alienate and obscure we perpetuate the marginalizing discourse, as we see in Addison and Hilligoss' experience as participants in an online study of academic women and computers. To combat this, we need to consider the difference between procedural and substantive access. The latter involves moving away from idealistic notions that reinvigorate stereotypes, engaging in dialogue, engaging difference, and rejecting neutrality.

Although there is no consensus on the connection between CMC communities and the physical, sociopolitical communities of users offline (Barber and Jones), there is agreement that virtual communities grow out of "real-world interests and needs" that compel people to go online (Barber and Jones 11). I question, however, whether virtual communities are any different from real-world ones. If we look at the spatial configuration of cities and suburbs, we see a striking similarity to cyberspace, existing as "'maps of contestable worlds,' which carry social and material consequences" (Comstock). Urban/suburban landscapes are planned or imagined with certain practices built into their function; thus, "the meanings we attach to landscapes are crucial" (Monberg 7). As Richard Sennett argues, urban centers, unlike the suburbs, represent myriad "contextual interactions." Suburbia symbolizes "the fullest, most unadulterated embodiment of contemporary culture; it is a manifestation of such fundamental characteristics of American society as conspicuous consumption . . . [and] upward mobility" (47) promoting the same mythology of individualism, progress, and self-actualization fostered by CMC theory. And as John Monberg perceptively argues, "because reality is permitted to intrude only in carefully crafted preestablished paths, suburbs promote a brutal simplification of human activities. Experience is impoverished because we lose the opportunity to test our received [or perceived] understandings of the world more fully" (445). As with these highly acontextual discursive interactions in the "streets," those online fail to provide substantive access because absent the exchange of dialogue and ideas, we are not able to "test" because there is no base of experience. There is no substantive access because these cyber-suburbs promote little, if any, exchange and interrogation based on different ideas or values.

Our pedagogy must incorporate discussion of images/issues that disrupt hegemonic narratives. Absent the push for deconstruction of simple representations and the push to de-regulate normalized discourse, we continue to misunderstand the status quo. In much the same way, visual representations of identity remain just that, visual representations—often unexamined, accepted or rejected wholesale, sometimes because we don't care to engage the dialectic or because we claim the inability to relate to a particular subject position. Thus, even self-constructed representations need interrogation to ensure the meaning that shapes critical social dialogue. When we remain silent on these issues, in many ways, we succumb to a kind of technological determinism. We need to examine the ways in which social materials (cultural assumptions, pre-existing determinations) are laid over the virtual space of the web, and how this affects the voice and the dialogue that we might engage in this space. Race, for example, continues to be fundamental in sociopolitical, economic, and cultural organization. So, although many cling to the rhetoric of neutrality and colorblindness, for the most part, in our daily lives, our self-conception and our relationships with each other are constructed around race. In other words, in physical space, and by extension, in the composition classroom where we treat sociopolitical issues that are very much a part of our daily lives, racial, ethnic, and cultural identity is not as fluid as it is argued to be on the web. Furthermore, because we have prior knowledge of everyone's social identity, to some extent, our responses are often tentative and contingent.

In this way, we need to constantly reflect on the kinds of CMC communities we are building in our classrooms; do they/will they come to resemble the classic city/suburban split that we see in so many American towns? Anderson argues, "all communities larger than primordial villages of face-to-face contact (and perhaps even these) are imagined. Communities are to be distinguished, not by their falsity or genuineness, but by the style in which they are imagined" (6). We imagine communities, virtual and real, as social spaces where we might find others like us. Because we imagine cyberspace as community, the presumption is that it will represent a set of social practices and related meanings. We need to be sure that all practices are included.

As noted by Jonathan Sterne in "The Computer Race Goes to Class," "the politics of access are not simply a matter of getting more people online. It is also a matter of how, when, and *on what terms people are com-*

ing online and what they discover upon arrival" (209 italics added). It's important that people of various races, genders, sexual orientations, and so on, be able to hold on to their identities and not be assimilated into a "white space" that the virtual world seems often to offer—their practices must be sustained. In the context of agency and power, it is impossible to obtain agency when doing it on someone else's terms. And although the web represents myriad possibilities for social interaction and integration, and creates/maintains relationships that might not otherwise exist, in order to realize the full potential for virtual space, critical to the consideration of public access and the presumption of human agency is the ability for us to construct technology in a way that is meaningful to us.

During the technology camp, one of the objectives that we did not realize was the desire to engage these students in critical reflective conversations of what they were doing. As expressed by the student during a group interview, our response to the way they wanted to use the technology was frustrating to some of them, and perhaps, interfered with their agency. In Session 2, in particular, some of the students resisted the activities we had centered around the construction of their 'zine. A number of them came to the camp with a fair amount of experience in chatrooms. Even those who did not have previous experience or access at home quickly caught on, with help from their peers. To promote substantive access and a more meaningful agency, we might have asked ourselves: What can we do to help them be more critical, reflective, and productive in their use, to have more agency with these activities? As I indicate in the chapter title, I believe that one route to agency is through roots, the historical and cultural lines of our practice. Initially, we could have begun with these students' every day practices (de Certeau)—using the technology as they do on their own, downloading mp3s, visiting gaming sites, and chatting on the web—and helped them develop more agentic positions. To take advantage of these students' fascination with chatrooms, we could have printed the chat transcripts and used them to facilitate discussions on race and online identity. From there, we could have structured more activities; the camp could have grown more organically. Such a pedagogical principle can be applied to any teaching with technology.

Postcolonial theorist Gayatri Spivak asks, "Can the Subaltern speak?" Of course they can speak. Essentially, she asks, can we hear them? And if we do hear them, do they have to have adapted to a specific discourse or culture? Usually, if we get to the point where we hear the subaltern, they are speaking in a way that we can understand. In the instance of this camp, our hearing was limited for a number of reasons, one of which was the complexity of this site. As a result, the students' voicing had limited effect.

To hear them is to acknowledge their roots, their lived experiences, their practices within, not separate and apart from existing structures. Hearing them really only matters if it results in action. There must be a response. A socially meaningful, ubiquitous agency provides the opportunity to enact practices that grow out of our real-lived experiences—to embrace a given space, to enact culturally and socially specific practices.

For these students, the agency that might have resulted would have been contextual, very visible, and as Reynolds advocates, *active* and *disruptive*. Such an agency enables us to not only be heard, but also enables us to disrupt existing structures. After all, while coming to voice is a critical and important first step, and in itself empowering, voicing only has social effects if someone hears us and then acts on what they've heard in order to promote change.

ACCESS AND AGENCY FOR THE FUTURE

As we begin to examine the issues related to access and agency, and we look at who is making decisions, and how access will be designed and implemented, we are faced with questions about who is best suited to do the work that this entails, and which methodologies will be most effective. Grabill stresses that "public institutions will play a critical role in assuring public access to the economic and social benefits of the Information Age, especially for those who do not have computers at home" (303-04). The business of collapsing the space between academy and community to address the technological challenges facing us in the 21st century will require a collaborative effort to (a) develop research models that facilitate community–academy collaboration; and (b) work with communities to develop and implement their literacy/technology objectives.

In working to reconnect inquiry and practice, we need community-based narratives that focus on the meanings of computer technologies within the larger themes of literacy in the lives of those outside the academy. In other words, space must be contextualized. We cannot afford to consider only the infrastructure; we must also pay attention to how the rhetoric of technology functions in relation to other social and political institutions. In view of the complicated ways in which ideologies co-exist or clash in society, this is especially important because it is in this space that some significant choices get made. And of course, people do not divorce themselves from the ideologies that they embrace; they use them when creating and participating in the development and the implementation of technology, though often not cognizant that they are doing so.

As Selfe notes in *Technology and Literacy in the Twenty First Century*, there are a number of very public and political dialogues about the "technological challenges" facing America:

> [They] . . . are significant because they help shape America's ongoing relationship with technology, the ways in which citizens think of human agency within the relationship, and the ways in which Americans put computers to work in the service of those social projects that are most important to the nation's commonweal. (4)

Thus, to a large degree, the narratives that we create and the agency that can be enacted depend on how that space has been defined by the media, instructors, employers, and society as a whole as well as our role as participants in the defining process. Social factors (context) shape space, so what goes on in society directly impacts how space is constructed. Disciplinary discussions of agency must make conscious steps to disrupt the tradition of keeping limited practices intact. These narrowly conceived practices do not move toward social change but maintenance of the status quo in the academy. We need not speak of agency so arbitrarily, but explicitly, as it relates to specific practices and how those practices inhabit certain spaces. The questions we need to consider are: Who is allowed admittance to the spaces in which these conversations take place; who is sitting at the table when decisions are being made; and who has the economic resources to participate? Those with the authority to facilitate change (researchers, educators, policymakers) need to consider whom we will hear and whom we will allow ourselves to hear.

ENDNOTES

1. Demographics—Camp I—Race (African American—12; Caucasian—5; Asian—1); Gender (Male—5, Female—13); Camp II—African American—9; Caucasian—7); Gender (Male—11; Female—5)
2. See Mary Brydon-Miller for a discussion of how the use of images aids individuals in representing their lives and interests to a wider community.

REFERENCES

Addison, Joanne and Susan Hilligoss. "Technological Fronts: Lesbian Lives 'On the Line'." *Feminist Cyberscapes: Mapping Gendered Academic Spaces.* Eds. Kristine Blair and Pamela Takayoshi. Stamford, CT: Ablex, 1999. 21-40.

Anderson, Benedict. *Imagined Communities: Reflections on the Origin and Spread of Nationalism.* London: Verso, 1992.

Aronowitz, Stanley, and Henry Giroux. *Education Still Under Siege.* Westport, CT: Bergin & Garvey, 1993.

Barber, John T. and Stephen Jones. "More Than You Think: African Americans on the World Wide Web." *The Information Society and the Black Community.* Eds. John T. Barber and Alice A. Tait. Westport, CT: Praeger Publishers, 2001. 3-30.

Berlin, James A. *Rhetorics, Poetics, and Cultures: Refiguring College English Studies.* Urbana, IL: NCTE, 1996.

Bizzell, Patricia. *Academic Discourse and Critical Consciousness.* Pittsburgh: U of Pittsburgh P, 1992.

Brydon-Miller, Mary. "A Glimpse of a Lighthouse: Participatory Action Research, Post-Colonial Theory, and Work in Refugee Communities." *Cort.* 9(2001): 254-76.

Collins, Patricia Hill. *Black Feminist Thought: Knowledge, Consciousness, and the Politics of Empowerment.* New York: Routledge, 1991.

Comstock, Michelle. "Critical Technological Literacy." Handout from CCCC, 2000 Preconvention Workshop.

Cooper, Marilyn. "Really Useful Knowledge: A Cultural Studies Agenda for Writing Centers." *Writing Center Theory and Practice.* Eds. Robert W. Barnett and Jacob S. Blummer. Boston: Allyn and Bacon, 2001. 335-349.

de Certeau, Michel. *The Practice of Everyday Life.* Berkeley: University of California Press, 1984.

Frazer, Nancy. *Justice Interruptus: Critical Reflections on the "Postsocialist" Condition.* New York: Routledge, 1997.

Grabill, Jeffrey T. "Utopic Visions, The Technopoor, and Public Access: Writing Technologies in a Community Literacy Program." *Computers and Composition.* 15 (1998): 297-315.

Grossberg, Lawrence. "Articulation and Culture." *We Gotta Get Out of This Place: Popular Conservatism and Postmodern Culture.* London: Routledge, 1992.

Habermas, Jurgen. *The Structural Transformation of the Public Sphere: An Inquiry into a Category of Bourgeois Society.* Trans. Thomas Burger with Frederick Lawrence. Cambridge, MA: MIT Press, 1989.

Hawisher, Gail and Patricia A. Sullivan. "Fleeting Images: Women Visually Writing the Web. *Passions, Pedagogies and 21st Century Technologies.* Eds. Gail E. Hawisher and Cynthia L. Selfe. Logan: Utah State UP, 1999. 268-91.

Higginbotham, Evenlyn Brooks. *Righteous Discontent: The Women's Movement in the Black Baptist Church.* Cambridge, MA: Harvard UP, 1993.

Messer-Davidow, Ellen. "Know-How." *(En)Gendering Knowledge: Feminists in Academe.* Eds. Joan E. Hartman and Ellen Messer-Davidow. Knoxville: University of Tennessee P, 1991. 281-309.

Monberg, John. "Making the Public Count: A Comparative Case Study of Emergent Information Technology-Based Publics." *Communication Theory.* 84(1998): 426-54.

Porter, James E. *Rhetorical Ethics and Internetworked Writing.* Greenwich, CT: Ablex Publishing, 1998.

Reynolds, Nedra. "Interrupting Our Way to Agency: Feminist Cultural Studies and Composition." *Feminism and Composition Studies: In Other Words.* Eds. Susan Jarratt and Lynn Worsham. New York: MLA, 1998.

Selfe, Cynthia. *Technology and Literacy in the Twenty-First Century: The Importance of Paying Attention.* Carbondale: Southern Illinois UP, 1999.

_____. and Richard J. Selfe, Jr. "The Politics of the Interface: Power and Its Exercise in Electronic Contact Zones." *College Composition and Communication.* 45.4 (1994): 480-504.

Sennett, Richard. *The Uses of Disorder: Personal Identity and City Life.* New York: W.W. Norton & Co., 1992.

Shor, Ira. "When Students Have Power: Negotiating Authority in a Critical Pedagogy." *JAC: A Journal of Composition Theory.* 17 (1997): 525-29.

Sloane, Sarah J. "The Haunting Story of J: Genealogy As A Critical Category in Understanding How a Writer Composes." *Passions Pedagogies and 21st Century Technologies.* Eds. Gail E. Hawisher and Cynthia L. Selfe. Logan: Utah State UP, 1999. 49-65.

Spivak, Gayatri. "Can The Subaltern Speak?" *Marxism and the Interpretation of Culture.* Eds. Cary Nelson and Lawrence Grossberg. Minneapolis: University of Minnesota Press, 1989. 271-313.

Sterne, Jonathan. "The Computer Race Goes to Class." *Race in Cyberspace.* Eds. Beth E. Kolko, Lisa Nakamura, and Gilbert B. Rodman. New York: Routledge, 2000. 191-212.

11

(MIS)CONCEPTIONS

PEDAGOGICAL LABOR AND
LEARNING ENHANCEMENT PROGRAMS

Joseph Zeppetello
Marist College

This chapter was triggered by some of the following events, all of which happened in the course of a few weeks. The CEO of a small educational software company approached me and wanted me to write some "content" for his distance education template for English composition. I met with him and his chief programmer, and the conversation went something like this:

CEO	"We need something, content, to fill out our templates. You know, different lesson plans—just write it. We'll put it in the templates."
Me	"You mean grammar lessons?"
CEO	"Exactly. Then we need you to give us some essay questions. We need you to supply some information so that we can program the essay corrector"
Me	"You mean that students can write essays in the distance education template?"
CEO	"Yes. It even corrects them."
Me	"Really? How?"

CEO	"By identifying keywords, and by looking for word groups. It even assigns a grade. You can override the grade though, of course."
Me	"I'm glad to hear that."
CEO	"Yes. Once you set up the course, you won't have to do anything but check your e-mail once in a while. The students work completely on their own. No more need for teachers."[1]

I later was reading a business plan for another software company specializing in distance education, and a few lines struck me as interesting.

"I consider myself to be a pedagogy [*sic*]. The teacher says you'll never replace him/her. I think that you can."[2]

A week or so later I was contacted by a representative/sales consultant from the Educational Testing Service, which is a prestigious organization that prepares standardized tests used by school systems throughout the country. The representative encouraged me to visit a Web site, and I found out firsthand what online writing evaluation software was all about. The screen gave me a specific question, and then directed me to write an essay in the dialogue box provided. The grader did not seem to understand my essay, and said that my sentences were too long. We have all heard the lore of a professor typing sections of literature from canonical texts into these essay graders only to have the program give the passage a failing grade.

These three incidents underscore a fundamental problem between those who design learning enhancement software—the programmers, and those who use the software—the educators. It is a fundamental misperception of the nature of pedagogical labor, and infuses our society as a whole, but seems very prevalent among computer programmers, especially in relation to the labor of composition instruction. This chapter explores this impasse generated by a common misunderstanding of what it is that compositionists do, and what they need from educational software developers.

It's too easy for us to quickly blame programmers and software development specialists for having an incomplete understanding of what we do as compositionists. After all, I am not sure what it is a programmer does. I do think, however, that we need to look at our own definitions of composition labor right here in our field to find at least one source of the misunderstanding regarding our labor. Bruce Horner, in *Terms of Work for Composition: A Materialist Critique,* offers some insights as he applies a materialist critique to the labor of composition. In an article in the September 2000 issue of *The Journal of the Conference on College Composi-*

tion and Communication, Michael Murphy gives some powerful insights on the nature of being a professional compositionist in "New Faculty for a New University: Toward a Full-Time Teaching-Intensive Faculty Track in Composition."

Although Horner tends to work more on a theoretical level than Murphy, both have some fundamental insights into the nature of composition and its place in the academy. Horner points out that valued work in the academy has been traditionally the creation of text, mostly esoteric and academic, what he calls "intellectuality as a commodity" (12). Academics themselves, he argues, have encouraged others to think of this work as outside of, or separated from, the material social conditions of its production (xvii). This type of work, however, is in a crisis of a certain nature in that less and less of it is getting funded in academia or in the world of art, another area that claims at times to be outside of the material social historical conditions (13-14). This claim can lead to what Horner calls torsion between the (class) alternatives of capitalization and proletarianization (13). This torsion is manifested in the conflicting roles that academics play between the ideological commitment of putting their labor outside of material conditions, and the contrary commitment of achieving important career milestones by publishing a "reasonable" number of essays or longer texts. A career in composition lands squarely between the horns of this dilemma. This can lead to two possible alternatives. Either the career compositionist spends time writing about the teaching of writing, and ends up, in what Bartholomae notes, as a career in composition "that has everything to do with status and identity in English and little to do with the . . . evaluation of student writing" (qtd. in Horner 15). In other words, we end up with experts who write about the teaching of writing, but who never actually teach writing. The other extreme is found in the compositionist who never leaves the classroom, and is interested in only what knowledge can be used in the day-to-day realities of the teaching experience. The former will achieve tenure, and perhaps prestige, at the sacrifice of removing herself from the classroom, the latter will marginalize him or herself with what may seem to others as a stubborn adherence to a craft, and very likely be denied tenure if he or she is even on a tenure track.

The work of composition, however, even at its most esoteric, is in the area of applied pedagogy—namely teaching, and is an area that traditionally has not been valued by the academy. Therein we find the problem. Even the scholarship of composition tends to not stray far from teaching. A collection of essays, *Cross-talk in Comp Theory,* edited by Victor Villanueva, contains around 40 essays, most of which deal at some point with the teaching of writing. I know of no other subdivision of the

Humanities that parallels this. Compositionists, then, are in a double bind. If they focus on the commodification of knowledge in the production of text, they are seen as scholars who are a bit pedestrian at best, certainly they do not soar to the heights of *truly academic* scholars, and if they stick close to the classroom, they are marginalized almost as Fordist (Faigley 10-13) assembly line workers. Couple this disvalue of both the labor of teaching and the area of scholarship with the tendency of composition programs to be staffed by part-time faculty, and the nature of the problem of the work of composition begins to emerge.

Both Horner and Murphy point out how, invariably, discussions of composition labor (i.e., part-time, low-wage per-diem employees) turn into discussions of issues of academic freedom, academic work versus teaching, tenure, and so on (Horner 24-26; Murphy 17-19). Full-time faculty invariably argue for the creation of more tenure-track lines, budget conscious administrators try to cut costs by proposing nontenure lines or more part-time positions. Arguments break out along deeply entrenched binaries. We argue tenure versus nontenure, academic freedom versus academic drudgery, or non-freedom, material work versus nonmaterial work. What tends to get lost in these sorts of discussions are the facts that academic freedom is a nonissue if you don't have the capital to pursue it; tenure or nontenure makes little difference to a marginalized teacher looking for full-time work, and the production of books and articles, whether material or nonmaterial labor, is almost impossible under the conditions of work for part-time employees. As Horner writes: "Academic freedom without the material means to practice it means little" (25). Murphy points out that "[T]enure rights, although clearly one of the greatest contemporary sources of tension between university administrators and *traditional faculty*, also work as something of a smoke screen in the part-time faculty discussion" (19).

What I am getting at here is that before we blame outsiders for getting a skewed version of the labor of composition, we need to take a look at how we in the academy deal with composition labor. Although I think we engage in conversations regarding the above binaries with the best of intentions, the binaries themselves get in the way of helping us really resolve these labor issues. As long as we look on the labor of composition as a form of drudgery to be avoided with a convenient course release at the first opportunity, or something to be—however regrettably—farmed out (subcontracted?) to part-time instructors, as long as we keep the discussion of part-time instructors within the borders of these binaries, we will give the appearance that composition labor is an addendum to the academy that can easily be replaced by the proper algorithm, or distance education interface.

I am not arguing that we stop putting on the pressure for more full-time tenure-track Composition/Rhetoric positions, or that we simply give up on important issues of academic freedom; I am just asking that we begin to think of the possibility that compositionists are professionals who contribute an important service to the academy, and that we consider them to be professional instructors. We must also value the composition course. As Joseph Harris puts it, "We—tenure-stream faulty in composition and English—need to regularly teach first-year writing" (63). If we are not willing to teach a composition course at least once a year, then how can we allow others to teach only composition and nothing else for an entire career? If the teaching of writing is such an odious task, then perhaps we need to take Sharon Crowley's advice and simply get rid of the course altogether.[3] Although Crowley presents a compelling case for the elimination of first-year writing, and I do not have space here for a full-blown critique, my problem with the abolitionist position is that that I do not think that my administration would give me much grief if I were to propose the elimination of the first-year writing program. It does not see the requirement so much as a revenue generator as a temporary solution to a problem that may be fixed some day when our institution attracts the "right" sort of student. In fact, there are members of our professional schools who might canonize me if I were to get rid of what they see as "another annoying Core requirement."

I believe that our own unwillingness to address the compositionist as a professional instructor in the field of composition, as one who applies theory and transforms it into practice, whether the theory comes from Elbow, Flower, Sommers, Trimbur, or Bartholomae, or anyone along this not exhaustive continuum, is what perpetuates the misunderstanding of the work of composition that I find evidenced above.

Consider the view from the outside. A person with no knowledge of composition studies is hired to create a template for distance education, or educational enhancement software to be used by higher education. After asking questions regarding the nature of composition instruction of various faculty members, the programmer diligently compiles a list of problems that need to be solved. Perhaps they are listed in this order: (a) Students don't know grammar, (b) essay correction takes up a tremendous amount of time, (c) students can't read with good critical skills. Because the programmer is not a composition professional, and probably avoided composition like the plague in undergraduate school, and, furthermore, is trained as a linear problem solver, all that we can expect is that the program developed will address these and whatever other elements happen to be on the list. Furthermore, unless the programmer is totally blind and deaf to certain political realities, it's almost a foregone conclusion that he or she will see the work of the part-time compositionist as marginal at best, performed by instructors who earn about as much in a semester as he or she makes in a week. In other words, the programmer is going to see that such instructors perform cheap Fordist-style labor, which can be easily replaced by a machine. Is it any wonder then that programmers come back to us with programs that "teach grammar," "correct essays," or give multiple choice questions directed at fragmented readings? They are giving us exactly what we ask for, whether covertly or overtly.

I am not arguing that there are no useful distance education programs, or multimedia learning enhancement tools. Anyone who is passing familiar with the work of Cynthia Selfe or Gail Hawisher can understand the importance of technology in the classroom, and the redefinition of the space of the classroom by technology. Many institutions, including my own, already have distance education in place for composition courses, and many instructors make use of valuable learning enhancement tools. In fact, I developed an online College Writing course in 2003, and have taught it at least once a year since. It is my contention that successful learning enhancement software, far from aiming at eliminating the teacher, tends to focus on the teacher as an important component of the distance education, or electronically enhanced, classroom. In fact, my institution has found that, in many cases, distance education courses bring with them *added* and *increased* work for teachers, especially in the development stages. A teacher developing an online course needs to rethink his or her entire pedagogical methodology. For one thing, the teacher may never meet his or her students face to face. A teacher needs to be creative in directing discussions through threaded chat rooms, and must increase the timeline regarding posting reading materials and assignments. Far from *replacing* the teacher, distance education increases some elements of a teacher's workload. More than once I've had students e-mail me on a Saturday afternoon with a paper, and expect comments by Monday morning. (They don't get them.) Because using electronic media to enhance our instruction requires us to rethink our pedagogical labor, I propose that we should also rethink and restructure attitudes toward the labor of composition itself.

The misunderstanding regarding composition pedagogy cited at the beginning of this chapter is not caused so much by outsiders looking in, as by the image that the academy presents to those outsiders. We need to change this image. Horner calls for us to revision the teaching of writing as the teaching of writing as material and social practice (232). We need to present the writing instructor as a person doing valuable work for the academy and for society, and not necessarily as one teaching a useful job preparation skill. Murphy calls for a teaching-intensive full-time faculty to be seen as an alternative to the traditional research-centered faculty (33). He further defines them as active consumers of research, but not necessarily its producers (34). Instead of the traditional credentialing processes of tenure, we need to find alternative and newer forms of credentials (34). Harris seems to feel that, at least, tenure stream faculty must maintain a presence in the first-year composition course (59-63). Most of all, however, we need to find better ways to bring compositionists into the academy as professionals, as valuable members of the academic teaching community and as full-fledged partners in the labor of the academy. Although none of the above solutions offers any direct link to distance education or learning enhancement software, all of them can help reshape the message we give outsiders as to what we do as compositionists.

This leads to my last point, one that was mentioned by a member of the audience who first heard this chapter as a presentation at the Watson Conference. If we do not define our needs to software engineers developing learning enhancement programs, others will. In other words, the learning enhancement programs now on the market tend to be very good at testing and quantifying results of those tests, an ability much valued by college administrators. I do not want to paint the administrator as the enemy. In fact, I am partly an administrator myself, or as Harris quotes James Sledd, a "boss compositionist" (44). I see this struggle as one that, if we do not rise to the occasion, others in the institution will, and they will be more than willing to give us the software they feel we need.

It is only when we ourselves value the labor of compositionists, and bring them out of the margins of academic professionals, that we can expect those we work with from outside the academy to understand the true value and nature of our work. Then, and only then, will we get learning enhancement programs and distance educational tools that make pedagogical sense.

ENDNOTES

1. This conversation was with the CEO of DistanceEd.Com. But I think it may be representative of the attitude of many people in the distance education business.
2. Team Synergy business plan. Again, I am not singling out these two companies. I think the attitude demonstrated by them is typical, and feel that they are not entirely to blame.

3.   For an in-depth look at the arguments to dispense with the first-year composi-
     tion course, see Sharon Crowley's *Composition in the University: Historical and
     Polemical Essays.*

REFERENCES

Crowley, Sharon. *Composition in the University: Historical and Polemical Essays.*
     Pittsburgh: U of Pittsburgh P, 1998.
Faigley, Lester. *Fragments of Rationality, Postmodernity and the Subject of
     Composition.* Pittsburgh: U of Pittsburgh P, 1992.
Harris, Joseph. "Meet the New Boss, Same as the Old Boss: Class Consciousness in
     Composition." *The Journal of the Conference on College Composition and
     Communication.* 52.1 (2000): 43-68.
Horner, Bruce. *Terms of Work for Composition: A Materialist Critique.* Albany: SUNY
     Press, 2000.
Murphy, Michael. "New Faculty for a New University: Toward a Full-Time Teaching-
     Intensive Faculty Track in Composition." *The Journal of the Conference on
     College Composition and Communication.* 52.1 (2000): 14-42.
Villanueva, Victor, Ed. *Crosstalk in Comp Theory: A Reader*, 2nd ed. Urbana, IL: NCTE
     Press, 2003.

12

LABOR PRACTICES AND THE USE VALUE OF TECHNOLOGIES

Marilyn M. Cooper
Michigan Technological University

In Richard Powers' novel *Plowing the Dark* an artist, Adie Klarpol, is lured into working on a computer-assisted virtual environment by a friend. Later, amazed by her enthusiasm for the project, the friend comments, "Oh Lord . . . What have we done? We've taken a decent, law-abiding hater of technology . . ." Adie replies, "Oh, I still hate technology. I'm just learning how to make it please me" (Powers 131). Adie relates to the technology by making it please her as an artist; she works in collaboration with a team of programmers and other researchers who freely borrow ideas and code from each other to create "rooms" that none of them on their own could make; best of all, the members of this team push each other to make their creations useful. When Adie first shows her virtual art museum to other team members, they point out that "it doesn't do anything," "it doesn't transform the ordinary" (Powers 164, 165). In working to make the technology please them, they are focusing on its use value, the human needs it serves, which they are beginning to suspect are revolutionary—although, of course, they cannot completely ignore its exchange value, the value it will acquire in its circulation on the market.

"To discover the various uses of things is the work of history," says Karl Marx at the very beginning of *Capital*. I was inspired to think of Marx's concept of use value in connection with labor practices and educational technologies in composition by Bruce Horner's *Terms of Work for Composition,* in which he argues that faculty should be "fighting for education's use value" (208). In this chapter, I argue that the use value of educational technologies is discovered in the situated everyday work of faculty, staff, students, and administrators, and that such work, largely ignored within academia, needs to be taken into account in reforming academic labor practices. I suggest in particular that giving such "teams" of academic workers more autonomy as well as more support results in better educational technologies, better working conditions for academics, and better education for students.

When I say educational technologies, I am thinking of such things as educational computer software but also of the less obviously technological educational technologies of curriculum, pedagogies, courses, even textbooks. I take as my main example InterChange, which is widely used in composition classes and was initially developed in the 1980s by graduate students working in the University of Texas English Department Computer Research Lab. Like the virtual environment in Powers' novel, InterChange was a group project: Paul LeBlanc details the history of its development in *Writing Teachers Writing Software* and notes, "Paul Taylor is actually the principal developer of *Interchange,* though as typical of development in the Daedalus Group, many of its members would influence the final shape of the program" (LeBlanc 46).

According to the stories told by LeBlanc and by Taylor in his dissertation, Taylor had been working in the research lab with Wayne Butler, Locke Carter, and Fred Kemp, and when Kemp came back from the 1987 CCCC inspired by Trent Batson's Electronic Networks for Interaction project and convinced that synchronous conferencing software "would be a powerful tool for collaborative learning and discourse analysis" (Taylor 57), they started working on developing their own program. Taylor wrote the prototype, and they tried it out with Carter's first-year English class in April 1987. Taylor describes the classroom debut of InterChange (at that point named Forum):

> I introduced the program to the class and explained that the software
> might have a few bugs because it had been programmed in "only two
> days." Then the students began to send messages to each other.
> Regrettably, the transcript of that session has been lost, but the conver-
> sation generally addressed the software itself. Some students com-
> plained about the program's slow speed and aggravating tendency to
> disrupt reading by displaying new messages; a few others wondered
> why anyone would want to engage in this activity. Gradually their
> thoughts turned to the pleasant spring weather and how they would
> rather be outside instead of confined to a windowless computer room

in the basement of the undergraduate library. For the most part, the technology failed to fire their imaginations; one student summed up his response with a message saying, "I think Paul wasted a couple of days." (Taylor 58)

The technology failed to fire their imaginations; it did not please them; they saw no use for it, no reason why anyone would want to engage in this activity. But over time, as Kemp, Carter, Taylor, Butler, and others continued to revise and use the program in their classes, the use value of InterChange was discovered, along with features such as pop-up editing windows to write in and ways to save transcripts of the discussions. Butler recalls the process: "We'd come back from class and say, 'We need a larger window here' or 'It needs to be quicker this way,' and then we'd make the changes and try it out again the next day" (qtd. in LeBlanc 49).

Butler described to me, in an email message, how this process continued:

> InterChange grew directly out of the classroom. We were the teachers developing the prototypes and testing them in our classrooms on a daily basis, patching code on the fly, making up pedagogy as needed, all guided by a fuzzy vision of collaborative learning, the writing process, and discourse theories. As more and more teachers began using it in its commercial version, we got lots of feedback from our professional peers and colleagues and tried, whenever possible, to incorporate those ideas.

A number of professors at UT Austin were among the pioneering users of InterChange. Lester Faigley, writing about his use of the software in writing classes in 1988 and 1989, noted that

> *InterChange* makes possible a utopian vision of class discussion where everyone with minimal keyboard skills can participate and where the links of knowledge construction are more likely to run from student to student rather than from teacher to student. This equality of participation, however, does not necessarily lead to "community building" as some teachers have theorized, following Kenneth Bruffee's model of collaborative learning, where conversation leads to cooperation. (Faigley 185)

Instead, Faigley argues, "electronic written discussions create dissensus because they give voice to diversity" (190), and he noted too that "in both classes students claimed and used classroom space for their own purposes" (197).

Thus, a lot of people contributed to the development of the uses of InterChange in the writing classroom: not only the graduate student teachers who set the process in motion but also their students, their professors and colleagues in composition studies, other teachers and students outside the University of Texas—and also, of course, the administration of the university whose refusal to grant the group ownership of the programs they were developing impelled them to move their research into a private facility and to rewrite and rename all the programs.

Questions of property rights and exchange value inescapably intrude in any discussion of the discovery of use value, and they bring with them questions concerning labor practices. LeBlanc observes that "published research is still the 'currency of the realm,' as Wresch puts it, and will be necessary if [Computer-Aided Composition] developers wish their work to be the basis for promotion, tenure, or even release time" (113). Capitalism converts everything to exchange value, including labor: Instead of being a process of discovering uses, work is turned into a measured quantity of labor that can be exchanged. Thus, teachers developing educational software can commodify their labor through marketing the software or through research which can be exchanged for advancement or release time. In a rational market, use value and exchange value would coincide—people would pay more for products and services with more use value—and so using exchange value as a measure of the full value of a product or a service would not be problematic. But markets are not rational systems, and use and exchange value are often out of synch: Things with a lot of use value (housework, for example, or child care) have little or no exchange value, and things with high exchange value (collectables like Beanie Babies or Precious Moments, for example) have little or no—or even negative—use value.

In the case of labor practices, work that has little exchange value is often unrecognized as work at all, even if it has a lot of use value. Horner quotes from Ken Kusterer whose study of "unskilled workers" revealed how they devote a lot of energy to "learning the working knowledge and building the work relationships that add to their own control over work processes," and how "managers—not recognizing that knowledge, and concerned only with increasing exchange value (profits), frequently take actions that . . . 'undermine or eliminate entirely the resources that the workers have used to render their jobs meaningful and to turn their work activity into life activity'" (Horner, Traditions 371-72, quoting Kusterer). As is demonstrated by the case of these workers, use value can derive from the needs the labor fulfills for those who perform it as well as from fulfilling the needs of others: They make their work please them, as well as doing something that may be useful to others.

Now, returning to the example of InterChange, I'd like to take a closer look at how use value is discovered. I want to emphasize how the uses of InterChange did not precede its history of development, how the final shape of the software and the uses it would serve were not determined at the beginning by its developers but rather were discovered over time in ongoing interactions among software developers, teachers, and students in particular technological and social environments.

The modernist notion that a technology is created to serve a predetermined purpose has been critiqued by Andrew Feenberg; he argues that "what singles out an artifact is not some intrinsic property such as 'efficiency' or 'effectiveness' but its relationship to the social environment." Using the example of the French Teletel system, he explains how "that relationship is negotiated among inventors, civil servants, businessmen, consumers, and many other social groups in a process that ultimately defines a specific product adapted to a specific mix of social demands" (Feenberg 154).

Through this process, however, a technology achieves closure; it appears as "an artifact that can be treated as a finished whole" (154). Like the reification of the processes of labor in the commodity, the closure of the technological artifact eclipses the work that went into its development. Feenberg says, "Before a new technology achieves closure, its social character is evident, but once it is well established, its development appears purely technical, even inevitable to a naïve backward glance" (154). His example of the French Teletel system demonstrates how the uses a particular technology develops can differ radically from the intentions of its inventors: Introduced as a system to enable private households to access information, it was converted by users to a communication medium, mostly devoted at first to "personal" messaging and later adapted to such uses as talking with politicians, taking electronic classes, consulting psychologists about personal problems, and organizing a national student strike (Feenberg 150-52). Feenberg comments,

> In its final configuration, Teletel was largely shaped by the users' preferences. . . . Alongside the expected applications, users invented a new form of human communication to suit the need for social play and encounter in an impersonal, bureaucratic society. In so doing, ordinary people overrode the intentions of planners and designers and converted a postindustrial information resource into a postmodern social environment. (165-66)

It is a familiar pattern, as Feenberg notes: Just as the introducers of the telephone complained about its redefinition as a social rather than a commercial technology, the introducers of Teletel grumble about its misuse for personal interaction—and, in the case of InterChange, we have seen how some writing teachers recoil at the uses their students find for synchronous conferences in their classrooms (see Faigley). But although the pattern is familiar, the dominant ideologies of technology and capitalism impel us to see not only these misuses but also intended uses of technologies as inevitable, and to ignore the work that went into discovering them. We see technologies as discrete products created by discrete individuals to serve discrete purposes. Or, as Marx says, "a definite social relation between men . . . assumes, in their eyes, the fantastic form of a relation between things" (72).

In his more recent book *Questioning Technology,* Feenberg discusses how the notion of function assumes this fantastic form, obscuring the essentially social nature of technologies. The function of a technology is not seen as something that is developed in social context, through the uses people make of it, but rather is seen as a property of the technology itself. Although other qualities of a technology—aesthetic or emotional qualities, for example—are recognized as the product of a relation between the technology and its users (and context of use),

> function looks like a non-relational property of technology "in itself." But in reality function is just as social as the rest. For example, the sharpness of a knife is indeed a measurable physical property, but sharpness is only a function rather than a hazard or a matter of pure indifference through a social construction. . . . As mere physical objects abstracted from all relations, artifacts have no function and hence no properly technological character at all. *(Questioning,* 213)

Marx and Feenberg help us begin to understand how the protracted, complex, and largely unplanned (unplannable) development of the use value of an educational technology like InterChange might be collapsed into a matter of a few smart graduate student teachers producing a software package for writing classes, a product whose function is built in and whose success is naturally measured by its exchange value. In some contexts this might not matter, but seeing a technology as a discrete product also leads to seeing the process of the discovery of the use value of such technologies as an incidental social process that need not be supported.

This is just the point Horner makes in his discussion of the commodification of intellectual labor in courses. As he points out:

the contributions to the work and the very constitution of any course made by individual faculty, specific students, and less easily identifiable factors of institutional, regional, and national history and circumstance are erased in course catalogues, as are the specific meanings that specific actors in actual course sections take from the concrete activities in which they engage for "the course." (Horner 9-10)

Courses are seen discrete products, developed in response to curricular decisions. Just as the administration of the University of Texas saw the early version of InterChange as a commodity whose value was created wholly through the use of university resources (the Computer Research Lab, the salaries of the graduate student teachers), universities, in Horner's words, confuse "the exchange value of [programmatic] work for its full potential use value" (26). As Horner observes, a faculty member might get credit for creating a "'new' course or 'innovative methods,'" but not for "teaching an assigned course for ten years or teaching four sections a term" (5).

But as we can see with InterChange, the work of discovering the use value of educational technologies is not finite; the closure of the technological artifact is largely a mystification. Early on, Daedalus set up a user community discussion list, Teach@daedalus.com, to get feedback from teachers that they could incorporate into the software. And later in *Wings: A Newsletter for Users of the Daedalus Integrated Writing Environment,* teachers and students regularly reported on what uses they found for InterChange and other Daedalus products. In the Fall/Spring 1997-1998 issue, Jeffry Schantz describes how he uses "the printed InterChange transcripts [of previous class discussion of a controversial topic] as the basis for constructing formal structured arguments," and he claims that "The beauty of InterChange, then, is that it allows a hands-on exploration of the entire process a writer should work through in order to construct an effective argument" (5). In the Fall 1995 issue, Anne Agee describes how faculty working in the Humanities Computer Center at Anne Arundel Community College used InterChange to create a collaborative teaching journal that "provided not only some interesting insights on our research but also a wonderful opportunity to learn from and support each other as we worked on developing pedgaogies suitable to the computer classroom" (9).

Work like this does not transform the purpose of InterChange in the way that the Teletel users changed the purpose of that system, but it does contribute to the ongoing process of the discovery of the use value of InterChange, the process of making the software serve the needs of teachers and students. It is also clear in the example of InterChange—and in the development of any educational technology—that these are always group projects, involving not only academic faculty, staff, and administrators, but also, crucially, students and the various companies that produce software (and even textbooks), and sometimes parents, alumni, legislators, and the general public.

What this recognition of the development of use value as a process calls for is a different way of understanding how work gets done. Instead of seeing technologies as discrete products of individual designers, we need to understand workers, technologies, and the environment in which and with which they interact as ongoing systems of relations. It is both a new and an old way of understanding work. From a Marxist perspective it might be seen as dereification, a return to an organic relation among workers, their labor, their products, their communities, the relations that preceded the rise of capitalism with its imperative to derive profit from commodification. From the perspective of postindustrial globalized economics, it can be seen as an aspect of what James Gee, Glynda Hull and Colin Lankshear call the new work order, the reorganizing of work relations into nonhierarchical and flexible teams who jointly design, produce, and redesign products in response to their understanding of the desires and needs of consumers. In their analysis, however, Gee, Hull, and Lankshear point out that the ideals of the new work order are far from being achieved, and the advantages of the new model are being obviated by management clinging to hierarchical practices of control. What they see in industry is equally true in educational workplaces.

As both scholars and educational reporters have observed, the changes in the structure and operation of institutions of higher education that began in 1970 and intensified in the late 1990s and early 2000s reflect not a temporary economic crisis but rather the application of corporate management strategies to the "business" of higher education. Colleges and universities are no longer seen as exempt from market forces and are being forced to respond to the demands of the new capitalism, or, as David Harvey calls it, the regime of flexible accumulation. Richard Ohmann explains:

> This "regime of flexible accumulation" has also been labeled "knowledge society," and that term may be critical for grasping the place of higher education in the new order. For if knowledge is now not only an accomplice in the making of other goods but itself the most dynamic sector of production, we could expect intense efforts on the part of business to guide its development, control its uses, and profit from its creation and sale. (142)

As Ohmann also points out, "boards of regents and trustees, legislative bodies, conservative foundations and interest groups, corporations, and so on want to make teachers and knowledge workers in general more responsive to their purposes, and they have power enough to advance that project" (140). The corporatization of higher education proceeds in many ways, including distance education, outsourcing of support services, and exclusive contracts with soft drink and Internet access providers, but also more crucially by creating a more flexible work force and limiting teachers' control over the curriculum and their work conditions. As David Downing, Mark Hurlbert, and Paula Mathieu explain,

> The "flexible" university has witnessed a huge and expensive growth in administrative ranks designed to direct curricula, downsize or eliminate programs, plan niche marketing, carry out corporate-university partnerships, and regulate "admissions, retention, scholarships, discretionary accounts, and hirings, as well." At the same time, tenured faculty lines continue to decrease while temporary, part-time, and graduate employees do the bulk of the undergraduate teaching. (8; quoting Martin, 11)

Ohmann argues that these changes are not unique to higher education but are part of "a single, broad, uneven historical process" (119) that has challenged the autonomy and privilege of the professional managerial class, including not only middle managers but also doctors, lawyers, and college professors. What this means for education, he observes, is that "the curriculum is passing out of the faculty's control into a market where effective demand is directly or indirectly created by business" (111).

Despite the overall bleakness of his analysis, Ohmann also repeatedly insists that it is possible to "fight to retake the university for education," and that "this fight and the one for decent working conditions might enforce each other" (135). He dismisses any attempts to reestablish the professional managerial class as a means to this end, pointing out that it was the academic disciplines that helped transform knowledge into a commodity through transmuting expertise into intellectual assets and that in this economic climate arguments that "People with Advanced Degrees" should be protected from market forces would be "laughable" (123). David Downing agrees that "the traditional mechanism of resisting market forces: *disciplinarity*" (30) is unlikely to succeed, arguing that "the domination within institutional evaluation practices of disciplinary discourse has often meant the crippling and devaluing of some of our most crucial concrete labor practices" including teaching (27), and that, in any case, the disciplinary status of English studies has always been shaky. Downing elaborates:

> the power of disciplinarity is such that various kinds of textual and
> rhetorical innovations, multimedia studies, pedagogical experimenta-
> tion, collaborative teaching and research projects, and community lit-
> eracy endeavors will continue to be subordinated in value even though
> they may have considerable social and market value for some forms of
> business. (32)

Instead of continuing to defend faculty as a protected class through appeals
to professionalization and disciplinarity, both Downing and Ohmann call
for faculty to make alliances across disciplinary and occupational boundaries. Downing suggests that in English studies, designing curricula that
more fully integrate reading and writing will help resist the isolation of "a
large segment of our professional ranks whose labor never quite counts for
much under strictly disciplinary criteria" (34). Ohmann suggests a broadly
based "movement to end market perils for all workers, and stop capital's
appropriation of human knowledge for profit" (123) along with an ongoing
"ideological critique of oppressive social relations" (149).

Like Ohmann and Downing, I see little hope in resisting the regime of
flexible accumulation and its restructuring of higher education, but I also
believe, with them, that it is nevertheless possible to retake the university
for education. Their suggestions for ways to achieve this goal, moreover,
adumbrate the strategy I am attempting to develop here through connecting my analysis of the work of discovering the use value of an educational
technology with Gee, Hull, and Lankshear's analysis of the new work order.
New power structures offer new opportunities for resistance and subversion, and the reliance of flexible accumulation on the self-directing work of
teams suggests a new ground on which to argue for the autonomy and solidarity of workers. Just as Gee, Hull, and Lankshear discovered in their
study of the teams at work at an electronic assembly plant that the team
structure might improve both production processes and working conditions if management granted the workers more autonomy, I suggest that
recognizing and supporting the collaborative work of developing educational technologies might improve both the quality of education and the working conditions of teachers, while at the same time offering the basis for an
argument for changes in education that might be persuasive to those outside as well as inside the university.

Gee, Hull, and Lankshear base their portrait of the theory of the new
work order on the very popular management books that appeared in the
early 1990s. By now, the story is very familiar. In response to saturated
markets and global competition, businesses had to become more flexible
and leaner, able to create ever more perfect products for niche markets.

Changing the organizational structure of businesses was seen as a way of reducing costs and improving products: Instead of a chain of middle managers translating the decisions of upper management into detailed directions for workers who carried them out, the managers were dispensed with and the workers were given the responsibility of figuring out how to produce the best products. All workers were expected to "add value" through making the decisions and doing the work that directly improved products and productivity. As Gee, Hull, and Lankshear explain it:

> Workers will be transformed into committed "partners" who engage in meaningful work, fully understand and control their jobs, supervise themselves, and actively seek to improve their performance through communicating clearly their knowledge and needs. (29)

But as Gee, Hull, and Lankshear also explain, the new work order struggles with a central paradox:

> fast capitalists texts point to having trust in workers/partners and allowing them to have 'real control' over their work. However, fast capitalist texts rarely contain any notion of empowering employees to assess and (re)frame the *goals* of the organization or to generate a more powerful *role* for themselves in the decision-making processes dealing with such matters as, say, job tenure or whether or not to 'downsize' or 'go offshore'. (34-35)

So although the new work order seems to offer workers more control over their work along with increased responsibility, at the same time, upper management determines the ultimate goals of the business thus effectively restricting the power of workers. Gee, Hull, and Lankshear note that in these books, words like "control," "empowerment," "collaboration," "teams," "name things nearly all of us like but which, on reflection are seen to mean slightly (and sometimes *very*) different things . . . than they might mean to many of us" (29). The consequence is that any instantiation of the new work order is extremely vulnerable to workers' insight into the "real" intentions of management to get them to work harder for less pay and take responsibility for things that are actually out of their control.

  In their study of teams at work in an electronics assembly plant in the Silicon Valley, Gee, Hull, and Lankshear discover how this paradox and deceptive language undermine workers' vision of themselves as "partners" and how workers' clear understanding of the limits of their power prevent the teams from achieving the goals of improved products and productivity that the team structure was designed to address. In their transcripts of team meetings, they noted that workers frequently identified problems in the work process and complained about them and assigned blame for them, but rarely if ever made a decision about what to do about problems or acted on a decision. In one team meeting they observed, workers joked and complained about a new rule that dictated that all jobs had to be carried out by at least two workers on the line, a rule that in some situations made the work go slower. Gee, Hull, and Lankshear comment, "there was no suggestion, no discussion whatsoever that management be apprised of the difficulty and advised to change the rule" (122). When they asked the lead worker about why the workers weren't authorized to decide when to apply the rule, he "merely shrugged and said with some resignation, 'Management decides'" (122).

Another example of how limited teams were in their ability to control and make decisions about their work was the fact that they were absolutely prohibited from making changes in the manufacturing process instructions (MPIs) written by the engineers even though it was understood that these instructions were often wrong and if followed would lead to products that wouldn't work or processes that took longer. Some teams tacitly corrected such mistakes by assembling the product so that it would work even though this hurt their productivity scores; other teams refused to make changes they knew were needed. Gee, Hull, and Lankshear conclude:

> the most robust explanation [for this behavior] has to do with the culture of the company itself and its apparent desire to "empower" workers while continuing to tightly control them. . . . The identities that workers constructed, and the identities that the company appeared to value for its workers, despite its investment in 'self-directed' work teams, foregrounded a willingness to follow instructions and accept change without question, rather than to ask questions and problem-solve. (121)

In this company, which was apparently sincerely committed to worker empowerment, workers were effectively prohibited from "adding value" even in the areas where they were the ones with the knowledge to do so.

As a final example of the central paradox at the heart of the new work order, Gee, Hull, and Lankshear relate how a quarterly competition at this company in which teams made presentations to management on how they had solved a problem was won by a team who simply re-presented a problem from the year before. In fact, of the three final teams, the only team that presented a new problem finished last, again demonstrating the hollowness of the company's commitment to rewarding workers on the basis of their ability to add value. When the researchers interviewed Carlos, the leader of the last-place team, he commented, "Well, the idea of teamwork is, you know, very good, but . . . management should give us the tools, the support, encouragement" (128).

As Gee, Hull, and Lankshear's study of the work of the teams at this company demonstrates, and as my analysis of the development of the InterChange software also demonstrates, the idea of teamwork is very good. The principal work of creating the value of products or technologies is done most effectively and efficiently in systems of relationships, relationships among engineers, line-workers, and users of electronic equipment, for example, or relationships among programmers, teachers, and students who are using educational software. Recognizing that it is these whole systems, rather than an elite few designers, that are the locus of value adding is a true insight of the new work order, and one that Carlos and other workers might call on management to actually subscribe to by giving teams real decision-making power and the necessary tools, support, and encouragement.

For the most part, the new work order exists at present as a deceptive rhetoric: Relying on a modernist notion of discrete individual creation, businesses as well as colleges and universities increasingly segment workers into two tiers: the few, elite "knowledge workers" who add value, and the great mass of implementers who carry out instructions and whose work has such little value that it need not be supported. The only reason it works at all is that the only value that workers are required to add is exchange value: products need only to attract buyers, not actually work; a college degree needs only to get its recipient a good job, not provide the recipient any knowledge to use as a worker or citizen. It is an open question whether a business or an institution of higher learning or a society that ignores use value is sustainable, however.

We may be able to challenge the current corporatization of institutions of higher education most effectively by challenging them to fulfill the promises of the new work order. If, as the theory of the new work order suggests, the most successful institutions are those that encourage faculty and staff input into decision making and goal-setting ("shared governance"), we can argue that the goals of our institutions need to include increasing the use value of a college degree. As Horner argues, "If the dominant recognizes only exchange value . . . we can effect resistance only by calling attention to other values not manifest in circulation" (27). The collaborative work of creating use value, even though it is currently not much recognized or rewarded, is recognizably important work: It is important to us individually—it is the work through which we make technologies please us but it is also important to those we work for, students and the public who support us and expect something of use out of our work. This is the work that creates the quality in quality education, that creates good programs—not only software but also academic programs—that serve the needs of our students and of our society.

We need to work for labor practices that ensure the conditions under which we can do this work. To de-emphasize exchange value, we need to focus less on questions of individual status and rewards and disciplinarity and more on professional practices and the working conditions of *all* the faculty and staff who together discover the use value of these programs. Good programs, like good software, don't spring full-grown from the brains of one or two tenured composition specialists. *All* faculty, not just tenured and tenure-track, need the long-term contracts, teaching loads, office space, and technological support that enable them to participate in the time-consuming work of program building.

Efforts to professionalize composition studies as a means of securing good jobs for all have predictably failed in the regime of flexible accumulation. Disciplinarity, with its emphasis on the commodification of knowledge as research and its support of a two-tiered faculty through tenure standards that call for ever-increasing levels of research and neglect of teaching and service, is no help in securing good working conditions for all. Bill Hendricks has pointed out that disciplines' tacit assumption of labor as individual effort has obscured the obvious and more promising strategy of unionization:

> In common with many liberal academic enterprises, Composition, because it has serious difficulty imagining what *collective* self-interest might be, tends to counterpose against the bad guy of *individual* self-interest the good guy of professional responsibility and solicitude, a social-work perspective that keeps organized labor out of sight. (91)

And as I have been arguing here, Hendricks argues that instead of taking disciplinary positions on whether and when and how writing should be taught in colleges and universities across the nation, we should instead demand that "those who must produce"—those teams of teachers, students, writing center coaches, educational software programmers, computer lab administrators—be given the autonomy and the support to decide how best to teach writing in their particular situations (Hendricks 85-87).

In the conclusion to his study of faculty union contracts, Gary Rhoades also points out that that a promising way to argue for improving work conditions for faculty is to show how such conditions relate to concerns more directly relevant to the public, concerns "such as the educational and economic needs of a broad range of students" and "public interest concern with quality and service in education" (277, 278). Efforts to negotiate more faculty involvement in decisions about the direction of universities and colleges, programmatic decisions, and decisions about technology use, and efforts to "enhance the working conditions and role of part-time faculty as full-fledged members of the institution" (278) can be articulated to our own and the public's concern for quality education for our students. By focusing on use value, on the systems of relations that create use value, on building alliances among faculty, staff, students, alumni, the general public, and other workers, we can retake the university for education.

REFERENCES

Agee, Anne. "Using InterChange as a Teachers' Journal." *Wings*. 3(1995): 8-10.

Downing, David B. "Beyond Disciplinary English: Integrating Reading and Writing by Reforming Academic Labor." In Downing et al.

──────. Claude Mark Hurlbert, and Paula Mathieu, eds. *Beyond English Inc.: Curricular Reform in a Global Economy*. Portsmouth, NH: Heinemann-Boynton/Cook, 2002.

Faigley, Lester. *Fragments of Rationality: Postmodernity and the Subject of Composition*. Pittsburgh: U of Pittsburgh P, 1992.

Feenberg, Andrew. *Alternative Modernity: The Technical Turn in Philosophy and Social Theory*. Berkeley: U of California P, 1995.

──────. *Questioning Technology*. London: Routledge, 1999.

Gee, James Paul, Glynda Hull, and Colin Lankshear. *The New Work Order: Behind the Language of the New Capitalism*. Boulder, CO: Westview, 1996.

Hendricks, Bill. "Making a Place for Labor: Composition and Unions." *Tenured Bosses and Disposable Teachers: Writing Instruction in the Managed University*. Eds. Marc Bousquet, Tony Scott, and Leo Parascondola. Carbondale: Southern Illinois UP, 2004. 83-99.

Horner, Bruce. *Terms of Work for Composition: A Materialist Critique*. Albany: SUNY P, 2000.

──────. "Traditions and Professionalization: Reconceiving Work in Composition." *College Composition and Communication*. 51 (2000): 366-98.

Kusterer, Ken C. *Know-how on the Job: The Important Working Knowledge of "Unskilled" Workers*. Boulder, CO: Westview, 1978.

LeBlanc, Paul J. *Writing Teachers Writing Software: Creating Our Place in the Electronic Age*. Urbana, IL: NCTE, 1993.

Martin, Randy, ed. *Chalk Lines: The Politics of Work in the Managed University.* Durham, NC: Duke UP, 1998.

Marx Karl. *Capital: A Critique of Political Economy. Vol. 1: The Process of Captialist Production.* Ed. Frederick Engels. Trans. Samuel Moore and Edward Aveling. New York: International, 1967.

Ohmann, Richard. *Politics of Knowledge: The Commercialization of the University, the Professions, & Print Culture.* Middletown, CT: Wesleyan UP, 2003.

Powers, Richard. *Plowing the Dark.* New York: Farrar, Straus, and Giroux, 2000.

Rhoades, Gary. *Managed Professionals: Unionized Faculty and Restructuring Academic Labor.* Albany: SUNY P, 1998.

Schantz, Jeffry D. "InterChange as an Aid to Discussing Argument." *Wings.* 5 (1997-98): 5.

Taylor, Paul. *Computer Conferencing and Chaos: A Study in Fractal Discourse.* PhD dissertation, University of Texas at Austin, 1993.

13

LITERACY WORK
IN E-LEARNING FACTORIES

HOW STORIES IN POPULAR BUSINESS
IMAGINE OUR FUTURE

Patricia Sullivan
Purdue University

A speculation of sorts, this chapter takes seriously the stories told[1] in popular business books—what Gee, Hull, and Lankshear call "fast capitalist texts"[2]—about e-learning and the future of online literacy education in college (and at work). It examines some stories that popular business tells about e-learning (particularly learning to write) in contrast with stories that some educators have told. Because most of these narratives are speculations about the future rather than reports of current programs, the stories constitute narrative visions of electronic learning (particularly because e-learning often will occur in workplaces under the aegis of training). Furthermore, these narratives position the labor of teachers and the processes (and places) of future learning. Although the visions in these stories fall victim to the optimistic excesses accompanying most narratives of future technologies, they do have a sort of charm. And, in my mind, charm unexamined is particularly dangerous.

Computers and writing already uses storytelling as one way to imagine teaching with emerging technologies, offering stories of use to establish a common ground for the discussion of a particular writing technology: writers (and conference presenters) who are advocating a new technology offer stories to help the readers (and listeners) who are inexperienced with that new technology imagine it and criticize it (see Webb, Bryson and DeCastell, and also Sullivan, for discussions of technology narratives in education). Proponents of new writing technologies routinely tell readers (and listeners) stories about that new technology's prowess as a way to promote (and probe) how that technology might fit into our thinking, writing, or teaching. Factual, futuristic, and hypothetical stories about emerging technology tales have contributed to the making of disciplinary practice. It makes some sense then, to expect that current stories about distance learning via technology might routinely contribute to the imagining of e-learning. But, as is our custom, computers and writing entertains only those disciplinary stories that talk of writing and communication instruction. This chapter widens our attention to e-learning stories told about any subject area, examining more than our own stories about technology use in distance learning. How, I ask, are our authority, agency, labor, geography, and pedagogies positioned by stories found in popular business literature (in contrast with how those same factors are positioned in stories told by educators)? My reason for focusing on popular business pronouncements, in addition to the charm I mentioned earlier, lies with the ways that these stories expose economies of e-learning. Because e-learning was viewed as a market for learning products, it gained a prominence in general business discussions of the late 1990s (before the dot-com bust); because e-learning has been touted as a cost-saving approach to producing knowledge companies in a down-turned economy (after the dot-com bust), it has maintained a prominence in management and training circles.

COLLEGE AND CORPORATE ECONOMIC LANDSCAPES FOR E-LEARNING

Before examining the narratives in detail, it seems reasonable to clarify the e-learning landscape in which these stories live.

How Do Colleges Construct e-Learning Economies?

Distance education is available in 84% of American colleges, with public colleges more likely than private colleges to offer distance education classes (Savukinas). *The Condition of Education 2002* has noted that despite the growth of distance education offerings, fewer than 1 in 10 undergraduates enroll in a distance education class.[3] But, it also noted that by 1999, more enrollees participated in Internet classes (60%) than classes delivered with live or prerecorded audio or television. Furthermore, the report noted that master's students were more likely than undergraduates to complete an entire degree through distance education. So, e-learning is growing in college settings.

College teachers already are positioned differently by the institutional geography of distance education programs than they are by their traditional classroom/departmental work. Because a distance education program is usually begun at university or college levels rather than at departmental or program levels (where we typically operate), distance learning admittedly enters teachers' lives from a different institutional direction. Because distance learning has increasingly been embraced by universities as an educational economy that they must confront and try to control, teachers cannot afford to ignore it, but they also have little guidance on where to focus their attention. The economy of distance learning in a technology-rich society, however, has not been straightforward. Steve Ryan et al., for example, have argued in *The Virtual University* that no one route to virtual universities is clearly marked as ideal: some teachers have involved the Internet into their classes for pedagogical support and have moved major segments of their courses online; Some universities have seen online coursework as a way to expand their offerings in tough economic times (e.g., that will not fund expansion of physical classroom space); some universities and companies have partnered to develop full-scale virtual universities to compete with traditional universities and/or meet lifelong learning needs. In each case, these authors remind us the economics and pedagogies develop in different ways.

In computers and writing, our talk about e-learning fits most closely with Ryan et al.'s first scenario, the one where an energetic teacher investigates technological support for a particular pedagogy, sometimes working without much support (or oversight).[4] We normally are so insulated from budgets (and budgetary controls) that writing programs are not nearly so likely to study the costs of e-learning classes/programs as are educators in higher education administration. Bates reminds us that determining the costs for e-learning is not straightforward, with one complicating factor being the interaction needed among students and teachers: didactic courses that require little student–student and teacher–student interaction are likely to have high development costs but modest delivery costs, and it is the type of course targeted for early development in distance learning programs. We suspect that is one reason writing courses are not among the early development courses.

We can learn more about the factors of costing courses from studies in education that compare traditional and e-learning course costs (Maher et al., Morgan, Turoff "Education"). Maher et al., for example, in their quest to determine whether technology can reduce the cost of education, divide e-learning costs into acquiring (what it costs to implement a course/program) and using (what it costs to offer each course), and then they examine five cost categories: instructor time; staff and programmer time to put the course online; hardware and software costs of the online course; space costs; teaching assistant time. Interestingly, from an economic perspective, they exclude analysis of these other costs—departmental administration, faculty space, and infrastructure costs (security, library, student housing, computer labs)—ostensibly because analogous studies exclude those costs. As we might expect, Maher et al. found that the online course began to save money in the second year, as it cost nearly $20,000 more in the first year but more than $6,000 less in the second year.[5]

Brian Morgan has developed an online aid for developing cost estimates for e-learning courses based on his research into the development and deployment costs for web-based courses at Marshall University. His categories for figuring the costs of e-learning include development, teaching, and technology/infrastructure budgets[6] and are derived through a 3-year study of the Marshall distance learning program (which lost $160,000 over seven semesters).

Why, you might ask, when many distance learning ventures are not (instant) successes, and when studies of costs show that a substantial start-up investment is needed before the program can be run, would colleges continue to add e-learning to their offerings? For land grant universities, distance education can be justified by the mission to provide practical education for the residents of the state. For urban universities, reaching students who must work during normal class hours can make distance education a mission component. But, one senses that the new interest is driven by technology because the number of colleges offering distance education has grown from 44% in 1997–1998 to a projected 84% in 2002 (Department of Education), a fact underscored by the popularity of Internet delivery. There is a more defensive economic reason for this growth as well. Higher education is very expensive, a fact that shows through the ways that state schools are buffeted by the economic health of their states. But, whereas much of a university does not make money, some units are extremely profitable—the executive MBA is a prime example—because these programs use few resources, attract students who are willing (and able, or their companies are) to pay high tuition, and have relatively stable curricula that is case-based and deliverable online. In fact, because many prospective MBA students would rather stay in their homes and jobs as they pursue the degree, this degree often is targeted in the emerging distance learning business. But, degrees such as the MBA fund college courses that cost a great deal more to offer than they earn (e.g., nuclear engineering labs). So, colleges must develop distance education versions of the more profitable courses as a defensive strategy or watch those courses be siphoned away by other colleges or for-profit e-learning companies.

The money involved ultimately reminds us why universities feel they must respond: if the market for e-learning and training is large, someone will develop a product for the market. Furthermore, if businesses that teach for profit siphon off the universities' money-making degrees, they undermine the economic health of universities that still must support the more expensive degree programs but now with a more limited revenue base.

How Do Corporations Construct e-Learning Economies?

Outside the academy the main target of e-learning is the revisioning of corporate training, which finds e-learning attractive from the perspectives of economic savings and manpower savings.

The training dollars spent are extensive. *The 2000 ASTD International Comparison Report* found that employers worldwide spent an average of $627 per employee in 1998, with the United States spending the most ($724 per employee), and providing some training for 75.8% of its employees. The training looks to be using face-to-face methods (78.5% classroom training to 8.5% delivered online), and to be done by corporate trainers (as the United States sends fewer employees outside of the company for training than does the rest of the world), but the training expenditures for e-learning are growing. Jacqueline Savukinas reports in *Digital Economy 2002* that corporate training expenditures increased 24% between 1994 and 1999 (60). She further quotes estimates for the distance learning market for external training to grow from $558 million in 1998 to $2.3 billion in 2000 (63). Savukinas' estimates, which are drawn from government surveys and address only the smallest part of the training budget (external training), pale beside those offered by some other industry experts: Pfeffer and Sutton, for example, claim that $60 billion is spent yearly on management training. Regardless of the dizzying differences in numbers, all numbers point to training's economic importance.

We should expect, given's industry's focus on the monetary bottom line, that the lure of technology in training is mostly tied to savings in training costs. If a professional has to take a week-long course, not only does the company have to pay for the instruction, it also has to shoulder 40 hours of missed work, and sometimes has to pay travel expenses to a remote site. If, however, that professional can take a comparable course via the web, tuition is the only cost because the employee can be made to complete the course at home. The potential savings in money and productivity delivered by e-learning, then, are not trivial. In 1999, Ira Sanger reported that IBM had estimated that it saves $400,000 for every 1,000 classroom days that are converted into electronic web-based training. At that time, IBM expected to deliver 30% of internal training courses online at a cost savings of more than $120 million a year. Training delivered via technology is definitely an attractive market.

Furthermore, the economic savings calculations for corporate e-learning do not always stop with lower tuition, freed classroom space, lower trainer/teacher wages, less travel, and saved employee work time. Cisco Corporation, a vocal advocate of e-learning, extends the savings calculations to the factory floor as it measured the impact of moving its e-learning to the production line in 1999 as resulting in a $1 million per quarter improved process and an 80% increase in speed to competence (Galagan). Although the impact of writing and communication training could never be so directly linked to production processes, Cisco's economic reasoning is likely to spur even more enthusiasm for e-learning in manufacturing.

How Does e-Learning Fit Into the Older Distance Education and Training Scenarios?

James Martin alerts us to ways in which technology might rearrange traditional power relationships in the learning business. In his discussion of continuous learning, Martin argues that automated training is needed for its advantages, namely: Its content comes from the best teachers and experts world-wise; its process allows students to study at home or in the evening, fast-forward through what they know, and repeat what they need; its delivery is always available, just in time, and without travel (254). If we interpret Martin's characteristics inside our own frames, we find that agency resides either in the machine or in the interaction between student and machine, but is not attributed to the institution providing training or to the teachers who have had their expertise automated. Knowledge morphs into information (a more innocuous term) and is constructed as a commodity even in settings (by this I mean the workplace) where it would seem that know-how is normally more important than factual knowledge. This reconstruction of learning shifts power to technology in ways that has to threaten both the expertise of teachers and the credentialing of academic institutions.

Still, those of us in writing doubtless feel safe. For the most part, composition instruction is a low priority for those who aim to market e-learning or use technology to refigure learning. As we know, writing instruction is labor-intensive. When universities approach distance learning as a business, their views about academic labor[7] often become quite Fordist (i.e., as they look for automation or assembly line possibilities, they focus ways that tools—the computer, the book—can reduce the amount of human labor and cost per unit produced). Because writing instruction resists a mass production model more effectively than some subjects do, it is rarely featured in (or even included in) e-learning initiatives.

The *pragmatic* question for composition studies is, no doubt, why should we be concerned by the struggles to control distance education and e-learning? We know that when the general fiscal health of the university is degraded, our working conditions decline, so the consideration is self-interested. But, until papers can be graded by machines, our teaching jobs seem safe enough (if open to incremental deskilling). Of course, economic questions are hardly ever straightforward, and for those of us who are interested in institutional critique the opportunity to gain another perspective on the deployment of power—in this case the power of the marketplace on the activities of the university—e-learning proves an interesting case.

STORIES OF OUR COMING WORK: BUSINESS VERSIONS

Suppose, for a few minutes, that popular business narratives reflect/predict the future structures for e-learning and that e-learning will become an important way that writing is taught/learned. What sorts of refiguring of our notions of teaching, learning, learning spaces, and even work might teachers and program administrators expect? This discussion offers some preliminary thoughts on this question as it examines some narratives taken from some popular business books[8] posing some straightforward questions about how these narratives position teachers, learners, instructional spaces, and technology. What roles do teachers play in these stories? Who are the learners and how do they proceed through the e-learning experiences that are depicted in these narratives? Where does the learning take place? What technologies are used and to what extent are they mere tools and to what extent are they impresarios of innovation? Questions such as these help us to consider how these business narratives will position academics as laborers in distance learning factories (oh, yes, those factories once were universities), how such stories project economies for e-learning inside institutions and at work.

I might offer some general commentary on the assumptions underpinning these stories. The discussions often assumed that lifelong learning is necessary for workers. Evidencing a mistrust of public education's abilities to prepare workers, and a fear that failing education was more problematic in today's information age, the stories also assumed that education is key to the knowledge-driven corporation. John Chambers, CEO of Cisco Corporation, puts it this way:

> There are two global equalizers in life—the Internet and education. Although the United States has one of the best university programs in the world, education at the K-12 level is broken. I believe that if we don't fix that for our children, the competitive advantage that the United States enjoys today could change. Jobs of the future are going to go to the best-educated workforce, no matter where that workforce is. Leaders around the world get that and that the Internet is going to be the key to survival, including Tony Blair of the United Kingdom, Jiang Zemin of China, and Lee Tung-hui of Taiwan.
>
> Given that, I think we need to do what's best for the next generation. E-learning helps eliminate barriers of time, distance, and socioeconomic status, so individuals are empowered to take charge of their own lifelong learning. (2001, interviewed in Galagan 50)

The last paragraph is almost universally echoed throughout this literature—and it sounds familiar to us that technology is thought to eliminate barriers and make time, distance, race, and class disappear. Duration offers a bit of an industrial take on technology's benefits, focusing on learning that happens through all of adulthood and giving learning responsibility to the learner.

Most chapters I read included examples or extended stories (and often those stories were hypothetical because they spoke of the future of e-learning). In addition to more general assumptions about learning and work, the stories featured more pointed assumptions about e-learning processes and outcomes. First, after start-up costs were recovered and learner resistances were overcome, writers expected e-learning to deliver a substantial cost savings over current training options/costs. Second, they counted on the Internet to deliver courses at any time of the day or night, freeing the employee to learn as she/he wanted and better integrate learning into her/his life. Third, they expected that the Internet also could be counted on to put learners in contact with other enthused learners globally. Fourth, they held that e-learning courseware would personalize the instruction as a way to make it more relevant (and I suspect by that they mean easy) to the learner. Fifth, they diminished the role of teacher and the teacher function that remained often was highly roboticized as machines corrected assignments, students taught other students, and experts in industry were consulted via e-mail. They also offered more pragmatic claims about e-learning as a training mechanism. To their minds, the interactivity possible on the Internet makes it a viable delivery system, the 24-hour accessibility of the Internet allows the company to push training into the employee's "free" (read unpaid here) time, assessment is a key to judging quality and effectiveness, and cooperative ventures with other companies and universities can lower cost and risk. Interesting to me, these business stories often were told about college instead of about workplace learning, a geographical (cultural) fact that makes me think that the authors expected that readers would be more comfortable with examples that did not resemble their working lives too closely.

The questions I posed here can be addressed by examining how the stories speak of teachers, learners/students, instructional spaces, learning technologies, subject matter being learned, and learning institutions. By identifying how these components of instruction/learning operate in four of the stories I found, I hope to shed light on the economies of e-learning that were operating in these stories and to offer imaginaries of learning that conflict with our current ways of work.

Teachers

Not all of the stories in these books retain teachers. The stories in James Canton's *Technofutures* offer a prime example of the death of the teacher. In Canton's example of global collaborative groups (written in 1999 and set in 2007), four students located in Argentina, Wales, Tokyo, and Milan collaboratively develop courseware that they will sell to fund their education. Essentially, their work (notice I do not say "learning" here because learning is backgrounded, whereas work is foregrounded) is group-driven. Although these collaborators do ask for guidance at one time in the narrative, they do not consider asking their teachers in Toledo (the institution name is not given). Instead, they search the Internet to find robotics experts in Beijing and Barcelona, leaving the instructors to function only as evaluators of the completed project. Teaching is only mentioned in relation to the presentation of final projects: "A real-time performance, designed by the students, entertains and educates the other students who log on from 200 countries worldwide" (146). It is particularly noteworthy that students work together as a team and then "educate" other students world-wide even turning their course projects into software they can license to subsequent students. By contrast, almost no instructors are given names, nor are they considered subject-matter experts, but instead, they merely function as graders and credit givers. Because students are developing courseware, it seems plausible that the instructors may be in the process of becoming totally erased.

Not all of the narratives portray teachers as almost totally disconnected from teaching and learning. But even in the more positive views of teachers, those instructors are at least partially cyborgized—in many stories, at least part of the teacher function is automated or reassigned to the computer, to the students, or to social interaction. In true cyborg fashion, however, some human dimensions remain. Take a description of the integration of computers into classes done by Babson College and held up by Seybold as a model for institutions embarked on improving their accountability to students. The electronic campus facilitates all the meaningful educational interactions. Students register for a course in order for "a set of automated processes [to] spring into action" (153). Those include registration, entry into the electronic classroom, student profile, and discussion forums. Already in place online are the professor's syllabus, reading list, schedules, and homework. We might imagine that the teacher is not so needed at Babson, as educational actions and places and people are mapped in/onto an electronic campus that stores and distributes this information according to permissions. Trappings of the teacher function—most notably syllabi, readings, homework, and discussions—are stored and deployed in the electronic campus—giving that network control over the teacher's work. The traces of course work usually done (owned) by teachers is detached from particular teachers. Actually, only one teacher has a name in any of these stories, Francois, the "online edu-agent" who speaks "impeccable French" and provides Rafaela coaching that is invaluable in navigating through her communication blocks. Because the story implies that Francois is a bot, the irony that a bot is the only teacher with a name is hard to diminish.

The non-bot teachers are sometimes portrayed as "drags" on new e-learning systems. Thomas, for example, describes a lively "electronic peer discussion" that yields for the student "nuggets of information she finds useful" and draws her into "heated debate that propels both the subject being discussed and the way this education is being delivered through unexplored territory ripe with innovations." It is clear that the delivery system—which puts students into contact with one another at 10 p.m.—is the innovation in teaching. This technology innovation seems to capture the teacher's function as catalyst to learning. To further isolate teachers from this innovation, not only are no teachers involved in the discussion, but they also seem to worry that it leads to plagiarism. Thomas abuts this story with one of a student who must stop work, drive to a fax machine, and send handwritten work to the professor who believes email invites cheating. This student, Thomas concludes, "is not happy with the logistics of this course." And we expect that the student blames the teacher's mistrust of technology for the problems.

Students/Learners

Students or learners (or, in the case of Canton's collaborators, workers) take center stage in most of these narratives. They always have names and they usually take charge of their educations, but their motivations to study/learn were hardly ever stated or probed.

Rafaela Tong, for example, was a manager of material sciences who decided "she needs to brush up on communication skills and signs up for a virtual learning course from Ascenta Corp." She takes the class from her den at night (after putting her daughter, Mary, to sleep and powering down Mary's android playmate). She watches a simulated scene where her boss and colleagues discuss her communication problems, then she charts her weaknesses and then works on "relating to other people in the virtual class who then score her on her ability to retain and communication accurate information . . . her online edu-agent, Francois, explains in impeccable French how she has scored low in two or three key areas." Even though Rafaela takes charge of her education, and fits it into her full home life, she places her trust in the series of color-coded questions about her needs, the simulation selected to answer them, the edu-agent, and her fellow classmates. She makes a decision to purchase and participate, but she gives over authority for the learning over to others: She is an education participant.

Activity is a key distinction between students and teachers. Although the learners are interactive, engaged, engulfed in heated debate, and making decisions about what to post, the teachers are represented by syllabi, reading lists, assignments, evaluation sheets, and bad attitudes toward technology. Although not one of these narratives credits instructors with ground-breaking work in the construction of online pedagogy, students fare

much better. In Thomas' story, the students wander into innovation socially through "heated debate." Interestingly, however, the students are not
portrayed as needing "genius" or special traits to generate learning innovations; all they need is active and spirited participation.

Learners are portrayed as active, then, and sometimes/often they
become their own teachers. This often is wrought through participation,
social interaction, or collaboration. But you also find portraits of learners
who rely on technology, for example, in the discussion of an IBM ad
(reported in Brown and Duguid) which sketches a 19th-century Italian
countryside and peoples it with an old man who has just finished his doctoral thesis by using the Indiana University library (which—surprise, surprise—has been digitized). He and technology (and I suppose IBM) have
partnered to complete this requirement without leaving his quaint setting
to venture to the wilds of Indiana. It is not clear what institution granted
his degree, or in what discipline he completed his doctrate (this strikes me
as unrealistic as every new PhD I have known has wanted to talk about the
substance of her or his work). Instead, the story focuses more on the Heidi-
like setting and the individual's accomplishment that has been rendered
through technology. Ultimately, then, a student's agency is connected with
her or his decision to purchase, trust, or use technology.

Instructional Spaces

The instructional spaces often are vague in these stories, although it is clear
that the students and teachers are not meeting in traditional classrooms
but are cybermediated in some fashion. We don't know, for example,
where Grandpa was as he was learning (although the ad intimates he was
in a farmhouse at the end of some road in the Appenine Mountains). The
collaborators discussed above were synchronously and electronically
linked across continents. The students in a 10 p.m. peer discussion were
scattered through living spaces. Rafaela, although physically in her den,
was virtually connected to her cyberclass through her virtual reality glasses and her data glove. In each of the stories, the instructional space seems
to be mediated by technology or created by it. Students/learners are not
meeting face to face, but rather they are working at home or in other informal spaces: No computer labs, libraries, or work desks are mentioned.

It is almost as if the software existed in some space, the course materials were funneled through the software, and the students (in concert with
the software) entered that software space and took charge of all of the
learning. No traditional classroom spaces existed in the stories, and the

cyberclassrooms were constituted in ad hoc ways (because the students self-selected into them in ways not open to students entering traditional classes) and classes were informal and timed in contrast with traditional classes (as in the online discussions held late at night).

Technologies

The learners are active, but the technology is in charge. The technology makes possible global classes detached from geographic space and traditional temporal space. It tailors courses to fit each learner's needs, which it has uncovered through diagnostic questioning. It orients students to college through its electronic representations of campus, class, and the student's day. It facilitates, mediates, sponsors, advises, envelops.

Could these stories exist without the technology in them? A resounding "No." A question more to the point: Will coming technologies produce events such as the ones depicted? Of course, because these stories aim to provide goals for developers and thereby feed the technology dream machine, it is not totally fair to propose a technology reality check. The IBM ad, for example, suggests that the Indiana University library has been (or could reasonably be) digitized so that a student in Italy can use the library's resources to complete a dissertation from a chalet in the Alps (a point that Brown and Duguid point out is not possible in the granddaughter's lifetime with the current technology). But, if we are going to preserve the books that are disintegrating on our research libraries' shelves, having the technology goal of digitizing the Indiana University library is a wonderful goal. In another story, a group of global collaborators had no trouble speaking to one another, because "simultaneous language translation enables them to communicate transnationally verbatim in real time" (Canton 146). Although this, too, is not possible currently, it poses a lofty and admirable goal. Some of the other stories, however, seem to offer less important technology goals. Rafaela Tong's virtual reality class suggests that a simulation using real characters from her workplace was always already available or spontaneously generateable if she happened to need it. It seems more voyeuristic than necessary to duplicate one's workplace in a simulation: What if Rafaela began to hold her colleagues responsible for events that happened in the simulation? The potential for interpersonal problems from that sim is high.

Dream machine not withstanding, the technology is portrayed as impresario of learning—providing a global, synchronous cyberspace; populating the Internet with edu-agents; storing all the world's knowledge in

ways that even the most remote person can access it; remaking the physical campus intro an online one; shifting the time for learning to whatever
is convenient.

Subject Matter

As stated at the start, writing is not often the subject matter of the learning
in these stories, even though many depend on writing for learning.
Interestingly, too, the stories do not dwell on any particular subject matter
very often. We don't know what the 10 p.m. talkers are discussing; Rafaela
is supposed to be working on interpersonal communication, but she is
more focused on the gossip revealed by her simulation; Grandpa doesn't
reveal his area of expertise; the international collaborators are working on
robotic designs for an auto plant, but only technology information is
revealed; and the Babson story covers all subjects.

These stories suggest a universality for the e-learning; it could facilitate
learning in any subject area. So, to some extent, we have to infer that the
storytellers would include writing instruction in their learning universe. But,
the more chilling impact of this universal attitude to subject matter, is this:
If any subject can be fit into a particular e-learning approach or software,
then resources have to be funneled through the technology before they are
assigned to any subject matter. In a real way, the differences among subjects
are minimized and devalued; this could lead to a loss of teaching diversity.

Sponsoring Institutions

Institutions hardly fare much better than teachers do. Canton's collaboration story does not mention the institution sponsoring the course until his
sentence describing the teachers: "When the project is complete, it's submitted for evaluation to course instructors at a university in Toledo, Ohio,
where the students are enrolled" (146). In this case, the institution is a cred-
it-granting machine. When institutions are named—Babson College,
Indiana University, and Ascenta Corporation—the institutions are connected to infrastructure—for Babson, it's the course management software; for
Indiana, it's the library; for Ascenta, it's the virtual reality courseware. The
connections do not try to trade on the ethos of their institutional identities;
still, I assume IBM featured Indiana University because of its outstanding
research library. Only Babson is foregrounded as a school, and none of
these organizations is discussed at length or lauded or even run by people

(we don't get a sense of people running institutions any more than we get the sense that teachers are people). Readers get the sense that many other institutional names might be substituted without it mattering much. The institutions are not critical to the e-learning; rather they are a setting or an afterthought.

STORIES OF OUR COMING WORK: EDUCATION VERSIONS

Are futuristic e-learning stories solely the province of popular business books? Actually, futuristic or hypothetical e-learning stories are also told by educators, although they move in a little different direction. In this section, I examine e-learning stories by Chris Anson and by Murray Turoff, focusing on their treatments of teachers, students, instructional spaces, technology, subject matter, and sponsoring institutions.[9]

Teachers

We would expect teachers to retain more authority in e-learning stories fashioned by other teachers, and they do get more mention. But, the teachers are not usually in charge in these stories either. Anson's story of Jennifer follows her around campus as she "attends" classes. The teachers she encounters are a "world-famous historian (now living overseas)" (266); "a recitation coordinator (a non-tenure-track education specialist" (266); her composition instructor, "one of many part-time instructors/tutors hired by the semester to 'telecommute' to the institution from their homes" (267); "a world-famous psychologist" (267); and "several tas" (for her history course) (267). Her only face-to-face encounter with a teacher is at history recitation, where a coordinator runs the tape, gives out assignments, and puts students into groups. Jennifer's teachers inhabit two roles—star lecturer (who is at a remote and inaccessible location) and instructional support (who is servant-like). Because the star lecturers' courses are multimedia productions (not live performances), they have a distinctly cyborgian flavor—it's as if their world-famous essences have been distilled—and vestiges of authority remain, but little active agency. Those inhabiting support roles are always identified as temporary, part time, or nontenure track; the composition teachers are not physically present either as they are telecommuting part timers.

Turoff, in his paired hypothetical stories about a "good" e-learning situation and a "bad" one, positions teachers quite differently in the good and bad stories. Teachers in the good story are retired, tenured professors who are well compensated and are teaching by choice—one wrote that "95% of his time and effort is devoted to instructional activities." The teachers from the bad story are part timers from industry, and there's not much talk about them (or their credentials) as teachers. Notably for us, in the bad story composition instruction is automated. Although obviously, Turoff favors the good story (which moves a university online in fairly traditional ways) that puts authority in the hands of teachers, he also tells the bad story of more a "mass production" virtual university that assigns teachers no important role and renders composition teachers obsolete. This signals readers that Murray expects such a model does/might exist and that it may be attractive to some (so therefore needs to be resisted).

Students/Learners

Students are active learners in these stories, but they also are consumers who are impressed by labels (Jennifer) and not particularly discerning of real credentials (unnamed student in the bad story). Collaboration, which figured prominently in the business stories, is not important to these students. Jennifer's interaction and intellectual stimulation resides primarily in the multimedia she uses, and she seems involved with using it and repurposing it across projects. Turoff's two students, both male, don't speak much about their education processes, talking instead about why they are choosing eU and how they are negotiating an e-University (eU) experiences—perhaps this is to be expected because Turoff's story is told by the students, in first person.

The consumer quality comes through in Jennifer's story as she purchases an e-version of *USA Today*, has high-end software subscriptions, and purchases a psychology course that needs a high-end multimedia computer she owns. Turoff's students display consumer behaviors, too. The student in the good story checks the course evaluations for the schools he's considering and finds "I discovered that eU was rated as highly as the Ivy League school for the quality of its courses. The response of over three million students in the 'Learning Consumer Database' made the results for most of my courses statistically significant to the .05 significance level." The statistically significant metrics seal the deal for him. The student in the bad story is also gathering information as a consumer would, and he focuses on employability: "Most of the instructors for technology courses are from industry and I am told that if you get one from the company you are interested in working for and do a good job you are more likely to get a job offer in the future." This student, who is headed down the wrong path, trusts vague (and human) advice rather than statistics, and we suspect that this makes him an inferior decision maker about college—or at least a poor shopper.

Interestingly, it is in the educators' stories that the cost of education for students is discussed (and not in the business stories where money is mentioned only once and in an entrepreneurial way). Jennifer's wealth is brought up several times in connection with the ways that money affords her extra e-learning options. By contrast, the student in Turoff's bad e-learning story has a more constrained income, and chooses to apply to this eU over Harvard in part because of money problems. Actually, Turoff's students' discussions focus on justifying their decisions to attend these eUs, and it is not clear that either of them has participated in e-learning. So, Jennifer is in control of what she purchases, and the unnamed students are in charge of their decisions to attend eUs. In all three cases, the students have control over their decisions to participate, but they do not project much agency over the content of their educations.

Instructional Spaces

Jennifer is attending school at a traditional campus, and scenes include physical sites (the student union, the learning labs, other computer labs, other computers, and her home computer) and cyberspace sites (online discussion, video feedback on work, satellite video, e-mail, web surfing). There is no traditional classroom in her life, but plenty of computers and computer labs. Turoff's students' stories don't address instruction much, although the student in the good story comments that he eavesdropped on class discussions (which infers that students gather in the online environment) and the student in the bad story complained that students need unique software packages and that grading is automated (which infers drill and practice).

Technologies

Anson focuses attention on multimedia's importance to e-learning, having both courses mentioned be delivered through a complex of CD-ROMs, satellite synchronous video, Web sites, and e-mail. His story also has the composition instructor delivering video feedback about a paper. Although the technology is not totally seamless, as Jennifer has to wander around the campus to use various computers, it is intensive and the center of instruction. Anson has made the (multimedia) technology the agent of instruction.

Turoff's stories, by contrast, do not focus much on technologies. Perhaps because the students are telling the stories and they see the technologies as tools (or part of the environment), not much attention is drawn to them. Both seem to use the Internet to investigate the virtual colleges, and the student in the bad story comments that many courses use tapes or automation, that "major Hollywood studios produce their multimedia software," and he comments that an "intelligent system" designs the exams for the composition course. In fact the student in the bad story complains about automation in more than one place commenting, "some courses use automated graders and I am not clear how that works yet."

Subject Matter

The Anson story mentions three different courses that operate differently for Jennifer—an assumption, perhaps, that different subjects lend themselves to different e-learning procedures. The psychology class resembles a traditional distance education course—a student buys the course materials, reads the book, watches the videos, and takes tests on the material. The history course combines satellite lectures with discussion groups (a traditional approach for continuing education using television) and then as a history-making project. The shape of the composition is not discussed, but it is clear that students are submitting papers electronically and receiving video feedback from their teachers. It is the most labor-intensive subject. The Anson story is also unique in its detailed discussion of Jennifer's work. It unpacks her work on the history project and shows her integrating material she finds in one place into that emerging project. It is only the Anson story that values student work enough to describe it, and actually it is this sort of description that is needed to show that students work differently as they learn different subjects. He provides that best basis for resistance to a universal e-learning software/system/process. Of course, Jennifer does have an untidy day.

Sponsoring Institutions

Turoff's stories focus a good deal of attention on how the good and bad online colleges operate. Because his stories focus on how students are choosing what eU to attend, you might expect them to be student-oriented, and they are. But, although they speak of how the students attempt to choose an institution, that choice recounts how the institutions are organized. The good story sees the eU's faculty as its intellectual capital, and it advertises their credentials, their focus on teaching, and their high course evaluations. The bad story operates more as a factory, touting that its technology was produced in Hollywood, that its teachers are from industry, and that its grading processes are automated. The stories also contrast the institutions' treatment of students: The good one encourages students who have applied to "sit in" on class discussions as a way to confirm their decisions, whereas the bad one requires students to continuously buy new texts, raises its tuition sharply when the local community college closes, and requires students not to disclose their opinions of courses (or else their transcripts may be held hostage). The first resembles an ideal college moved online, whereas the second resembles a business acting as if it is struggling to survive.

E-Learning Economies

Much of this discussion has focused on how authority and agency circulate in these e-learning situations: The stories show authority and agency being shifted slowly (or swiftly) toward technology, with teachers losing control, expertise (and even jobs), and with students playing the roles of participants and consumers. If we consider these stories from the economics within which they work, we find that at least two economies are operating—consumer centric (how students/workers/corporate training departments find, buy, use, and value e-learning products) and institution centric (how a learning organization develops and markets e-learning products that complement, and not undermine, its existing learning products). Not surprisingly, the business stories focus more on consumer-centric economies. But, in the education stories, the focus is split: Anson's story is consumer focused, whereas Turoff's is institutionally focused.

What indicators do we see that consumer-centric economics directs e-learning in the business stories I gathered? First, the students are identified as consumers (and are named as a way to point out that they are special). Second, the delivery mechanisms smooth the path for the student consumers (Babson's electronic campus orients the new student; Rafaela has an edu-agent to guide her; the international collaborators have simultaneous translation to ease communication). Third, the technology is touted as both the agent of innovative learning and a tool for easier living (Rafaela's like is so focused on technology that her baby has an android playmate and the simulation in her course is personalized for easy learning transfer; Babson's e-campus handles the students' class details). Fourth, the learning/knowledge is presented as cutting edge (Jennifer has world-famous cyber professors; the collaborative group solves problems for an automated auto factory). Fifth, and yet the learning is also presented as fitting conveniently into the learner's schedule (students hold absorbing discussions at 10 p.m.; Rafaela's class starts whenever she is ready for it to begin). E-learning is portrayed, then, as attractive to its student-consumers: It's accessible, flexible, customizable, masterable through participation, and loaded with gadget appeal, even when the dark side might be intimated (e.g., there are no professors on Jennifer's campus and the student in Turoff's bad story talks of automated grading),

The stories seem crafted to encourage potential e-learners to feel it is easy to use e-learning. Of course, as in all consumer-centric economies, the stories do not reveal who does the crafting; as it is assumed that the companies marketing the products make the institutional decisions based on economic values that put making profit for stakeholders ahead of other values. In this environment, traditional factors—cost-effectiveness, speed, and product attractiveness to cost ratio—direct decisions. Thus, any agency that teachers might retain over learning will be filtered through the corporation's imperative to successfully market and sell products. Teachers will only retain the agency when they can demonstrate their continued agency in education will improve profits. It is less clear in these stories where the identity of an e-learning institution is/can be lodged. Most of our traditional thinking about higher education presumes that a learning institution has autonomy and exists as a not-for-profit enterprise; but in these consumer-centric narratives e-learning is often linked to profit, so a main assumption about educational institutions is destabilized. What if educational institutions' autonomy is limited in the future sphere of e-learning, in part because of attempts to make them more focused on making them profit generating? How does the institution's subsequent loss of power impact our working lives as teachers? Our efforts to reform education as an institution? Certainly, if the values change from nonprofit to profit-leading values, then reform efforts have to be framed in a very different language: appeals to educating a democratic citizenry may not work as well as appeals to educating a more wealthy wage earner.

Not all of the stories hint that e-learning institutions are/will be structured as profit-making ventures. Turoff, for example, offers two different institution-centric economies in his paired stories: The good one has traditional institutional values and the bad one has embraced a factory model (which I assume must include a profit-making agenda). These stories mention a number of institution-centric criteria: course ratings, logistics of admission, facilities, tuition, course size, faculty credentials, and advising. Turoff suggests that in the "bad" eU the teachers are not faculty but instead are part timers from industry who have not traceable teaching records. This institution, which he sees as a factory, focuses on constantly changing (and by inference up-to-date) software, automated grading, and proximity to future employers. It calls on none of the same credentials that universities use to build their ethos: small classes; interaction with impressive faculty; laboratory and other state-of-the-art facilities; libraries; beautiful campuses; sports; the college experience. Turoff does offer an eU alternative that preserves the university values. Unfortunately, his "good" eU doesn't sound more reasonable than the factory eU sounds. I suspect that we need higher education administrators to write the stories that will include all the institutional considerations that faculty are not so focused on. For that reason, the institution-centric economies are not as robust as the consumer-centric ones in these stories.

IMPLICATIONS FOR TEACHERS AS FUTURE WORKERS

In *Designing World Class E-learning*, a 2001 revised edition of a 1996 book, Roger Schank profiles a *model* distance education program at New York University that is web-driven, describing both an English as a second language (ESL) business writing course and a C + + programming course in ways that suggest no one model of distance learning is universal. In the writing course, trained ESL professionals respond to 14 assignments (and he observes that usually each student revises three times for each assignment); in the programming course segments of programs are submitted as well, but the 90% of the comments are prewritten based on the mistakes typically made on these assignments. If instructors are paid per course, which course would be economically more attractive to the teacher/worker? The answer is obvious. Paper grading remains the main (and perhaps the only) reason why literacy workers are likely to remain employed by e-learning factories. But, these positions also imply that the writing teacher may be severely deskilled because she or he will be positioned only as grader, not as the creative force behind a course, and in collaborative pedagogies not the central figure of the course. To a certain extent this is our fault. We have not distinguished well among types of writing courses or stressed the importance of innovation in teaching writing. So, it is not surprising that outsiders (Schank is a computer scientist and remember that outsiders such as Schank control our e-learning fates) would not expect to need to regularly change syllabi or readings or assignments or approaches; we have not made a case for change. So, promoting a greater understanding of what is taught in writing classes needs to be a top agenda item for those in composition studies who interface with distance education.[10] On the bright side, in this futuristic, academic sweat shop the teacher will no longer have to worry about decentering power and moderating her influence on the class. But, those of us who teach because we enjoy helping students learn, and who adjust our courses on-the-fly to address student needs, find that our potentially marginal contribution to that activity negatively impacts the quality of instruction we can offer. It also chafes at our souls. More importantly, such anemic views of the role teaching plays in e-learning suggest that we need to promote a more robust and far-reaching understanding of writing as a complex skill and writing instruction as skilled labor. Indeed, if we take these stories seriously, such work needs to be a top priority for composition studies.

APPENDIX:
THREE SAMPLE STORIES

IBM Solutions for a Small Planet Ad

We're deep in the heart of the Apennine Mountains in Italy. It's dusk; the sun is setting over a farmhouse tucked away by itself at the end of a road. There we spy the farmer, a retired man in his late 60s, walking with his 25-year-old granddaughter. In this particular corner of the world, it seems like things haven't changed that much in the last 100 years. We move in closer so that we can eavesdrop on their Italian conversation.

    Grandpa: Well I finally finished my doctoral thesis.

    Woman: Way to go, Gramps!

    Grandpa: Did my research at Indiana University.

    Woman: Indiana?

Grandpa: Yup. IBM took the school's library. . . and digitized it. So I could have access to it over the Internet.

Grandpa: You know . . . It's a great time to be alive.

Canton's Story of a Manager Taking a Communications Course

Rafaela Tong, manager of material sciences for BioTechDyne, decides she needs to brush up on communication skills and signs up for a virtual learning course from Ascenta Corp. The course is offered 24 hours a day, 7 days a week online, and can be easily accessed on demand from practically anywhere. Rafaela decides to log on that night after tucking in her child, Mary, and powering down Mary's android playmate.

Rafaela checks on her husband, Frank, who is on the Internet in the den. She goes to the entertainment center couch, dons her virtual reality glasses and dataglove, then energizes the flatwall multimedia system and logs on.

She is immediately transported into a classroom where a session on corporate communication skills is about to begin. There are 10 others in the class, and Rafaela is guided through registration with a rainbow of colored questions to pinpoint her specific goals for the course. She touches the red button and is ready to start the first learning sequence when a holographic blip occurs and she sees her boss and office subordinates having a discussion that interests her. She touches a pastel pause button and is suddenly back in her corporate office overhearing the conversation.

Rafaela is surprised to hear her boss, Monica, tell another employee, Bob, how Tong is invaluable but she doesn't always listen to what is being said. This often results in communication breakdowns and situations that might have otherwise been avoided. Rafaela recalls hearing similar comments from her husband and dictates a note to work on this particular weakness.

In another virtual learning module, Rafaela works on relating to other people in the virtual class who then score her on her ability to retain and communicate accurate information. This is an essential skill for each executive, and she knows it. The interactive setting is a realistic version of her office, and her online edu-agent, Francois, explains in impeccable French how she's scored low in two or three key areas.

Francois then gives Rafaela some ideas on how she might increase her listening power in order to be a more effective manager. Francois also suggests other learning modules to help Rafaela develop better managerial skills. She finds that Francois' coaching is invaluable in helping her navigate through her blocks.

Grateful, Rafaela thanks everyone in the class and decides to log off after 2 hours. Before quitting, she downloads to her e-mail site the details on several other lessons that she can tune in to the next night for additional training.

Turoff's Story of a Negative Future for the Student

I have decided to apply to eU.com rather than Harvard. I really must spend the time learning the family business and my fiancée has told me in no uncertain terms that long separations are not in the cards. Oh well, it is a lot cheaper than Harvard and a lot of those video lectures were prepared by top notch professors at places like Harvard and the University of Chicago. They claim having a professor from Harvard on video is far better than just any old professor in a classroom. Most of the instructors for technology courses are from industry and I am told that if you get one from the company you are interested in working for and do a good job you are more likely to get a job offer in the future. Courses in other areas seem to be mostly those tapes and automation. There was some newspaper article about how the companies holding the most stock in eU.com had the largest number of instructors, buy hey, so what? They require a computer joystick for the educational software packages, so the school cannot be too bad. Major Hollywood studios produce their multimedia software.

It does worry me that their tuition jumped by 20 % in our area as soon as our local community college went out of business. I did not realize their tuition was geographically dependent. Their software costs are quite high since each course uses unique packages, including the ebooks generated by the professors. These materials seem be undergoing constant revision but I suspect that is so the prior year's material cannot be sold in a secondary market among the students. Even though the average course size is one thousand students, eU does have these small discussion sections of 50 to a 100 students run by the course graders. So at least you can get help when you need it. Still, some courses use automated graders and I am not clear how that works yet.

I was told the compositions in the first writing course and the programs in the first computer course are completely graded by the computer without the need for any human to look at them. An intelligent system not only designs the exam so that every exam is unique to every student in the course, but also uses your past performance profile to tailor the exam to your performance level. This allows even C students to get high point scores so they can feel good about themselves and show good results to their parents, who are probably financing their studies. Students are classified as outstanding, above average, or average, and then receive grades within those categories. Everyone has a chance to get a lot of A grades.

They sent me this funny form with their acceptance letter, where I must promise to not divulge any of my experiences in courses to any data collection process not approved by eU.com, or they can deny me any future access to my records and rescind my degree. I don't understand the reason for that one at all. Oh well, I have no real choice, given my situation.

ENDNOTES

1. Storytelling has been used in organizational research since the 1970s, particularly when the goal of the research is to better understand corporate culture. Influenced by ethnographic work in sociology and by folklore research as it interfaced with sociolinguistics, researchers have gathered stories, interpreted them, and also had organizational people interpret them. See Yannis Gabriel for an overview of this work.

2. James Gee, Glynda Hull, and Colin Lankshear refer to the types of books I consulted for this chapter as "fast capitalist texts" that "create on paper a version of the new work order that their authors are trying hard to enact in the world" (24). These texts, they claim, "are important not only in the domains of business and work—their vision and values have deeply informed contemporary calls for reform both in adult education and training in schools across the developed world" (25).

3. The Sloan Consortium reported that 300,000 (14.5 million people were enrolled in college in 1998) took its distance ed courses in 2000–2001, and that the four leading for-profit virtual universities had 27,500 students enrolled in degree programs.

4. Brad Mehlenbacher, for example, recounts how he built a MOO to function as an onlne environment for his program's technical communication classes without ever once mentioning money. In the same volume, Ann Duin and Ray Archee develop an approach to developing distance education via the web by focusing on learners, learning theory, and instructor roles. Again the discussion, this time a theoretical one, does not focus on economic issues.

5. The Food Sciences course studied enrolled more than 400 students and cost more than $40,000 in a traditional setting (nearly half to faculty and ta

salaries) whereas it cost more than $59,000 in an online version (more than $31,000 needed in hardware and programming and more than $12,000 saved in lecture hall rental). In the second offering, however, the online course costs dropped to just over $34,000.

6. The categories are as follows: (a) development costs (stipends for development, hidden costs [supplies consumed, administrative approval time], faculty development [training, software/hardware costs, support personnel in lab, instructional technology support], library support); (b) teaching costs [stipends paid for teachers, hidden costs [office space, university administration, help desk support]); and (c) course server, backup materials and costs, server maintenance/support, communication charges, software costs, evaluation software costs, electronic course administrator salary.

7. In some ways, the economics are not new, as most have already thought about faculty work in terms of student contact hours or student enrollment hours/full-time equivalency. All courses do not cost the same, nor do they yield the same amount of revenue, as the following hypothetical example suggests. A lecture class at a research university with 300 enrolled for 3 hours credit, .25 teacher, and .25 of three graders generates a score of 900 in the student contact hours formula, whereas a 3-hour comp course of 25 students (note that this class size exceeds NCTE guidelines) and .25 of one teacher generates a score of 24. If the tuition is $500 per credit hour, the lecture class generates $450,000, and costs $32,000, whereas the composition course generates $12,000 and costs $3,400 if taught by teacher assistant/lecturer (or $12–15,000 if taught by a professor). It quickly becomes clear that large enrollment classes staffed minimally produce a revenue base that can be used to fund the more costly seminars, lab classes, and so on, whereas the writing class is a very modest producer. This oversimplifies the economics of the costs as it does not include administrative, infrastructure, or facilities costs, or even the cost of tuition remission that most lecture graders and teaching assistants receive as a part of their compensation. But, if corporate (for-profit) distance education companies siphon off the "easy money" courses, and leave the expensive courses to the college, as we discussed earlier, then they manage to reduce a university's funding base. It is clear that colleges have to combat corporate distance education. But, it is not so clear that writing instruction has a place in this fight, as it traditionally has scored a 24 rather than a 900. It is resource-intensive. Of course, if automatic paper-grading programs are perfected, then that need for labor will be substantially reduced and a teacher's load will be eased. But, that automation effort is another discussion.

8. Barnes and Noble Bookstore functioned as the source for this sample of popular business books (many of which would be classified as fast capitalist texts). Each month during 2000, I went to the store in Lafayette, Indiana, and I checked the business section (one of the largest areas of the store) for discussions of training, the use of computers in training (sometimes called e-learning), lifelong learning, distance learning, and writing. I looked at chapter head-

ings and indexes, noting how training, learning, writing, communication, and technology were discussed. Most books that included chapters on technology and learning were built on examples and some included extended stories; few stories referenced working programs. The rationale for these e-learning discussions usually was the search for potential web businesses (remember that the dot-coms had not yet collapsed at that point) or the search for more economical training via technology. The narratives I found, for the most part, would be characterized by Stephen Denning as springboard stories (i.e., stories that "enable a leap of understanding by the audience so as to grasp how an organization or community or complex system may change" (www.stevedenning.com/Main_types_story.html). Denning continues: "A springboard story has an impact not so much through transferring large amounts of information, but through catalyzing understanding. It enables listeners to visualize from a story in one context what is involved in a large-scale transformation in an analogous context."

9. My initial interest in stories about e-learning derived from the story told by Chris Anson in his *College English* article about the dangers of distance education, and, indeed, his story is closer to the business stories than is Turoff's. Anson's story of Jennifer's distance learning classes fascinated me—although I expect the story was intended to demonstrate the horrors of the coming age of technology. I was fascinated by her assertiveness, her consumerism, her facility with technology, and her wealth; I think I was supposed to notice that she took courses that would require many fewer teachers and that her comp teacher was at her beck and call like a tech support phone worker.

10. Some of this work is already underway. Talks by Kathy Yancey and by Darren Cambridge at Computers and Writing 2003, pointed to efforts being made to encourage groups interested in developing e-portfolios for college work to include writing and writing instruction in the design stages. Although e-portfolios were not mentioned in any of the e-learning stories I read, they could easily be adapted to e-learning for writing courses and for writing in other courses.

REFERENCES

Anson, Chris M. "Distant Voices: Teaching and Writing in a Culture of Technology." *College English.* 61, 3 (1999): 63-74. Available online at: http://www.ncte.org/ce/jan99/anson.html.

Brown, John Seely, and Paul Duguid. *The Social Life of Information.* Boston, MA: Harvard Business School Press, 2000.

Bryson, Mary, and DeCastell, Suzanne. "Telling Tales Out of School: Modernist, Critical, and Postmodern 'True Stories' About Educational Computing." *Education/Technology/Power: Educational Computing as a Social Practice.* Eds. Hank Bromley and Michael W. Apple. Albany: State U of NY Press, 1998. 65-84.

Cambridge, Darren. "Virtual Communities of Practice, Global and Local." A talk at Computers and Writing, West Lafayette, IN, 2003.

Canton, James. *Technofutures: How Leading-Edge Technology Will Transform Business in the 21st Century*. Carlsbad, CA: Hay House, 1999.

Denning, Stephen. Springboard stories. Available at: http://www.stevedenning.com /Main_types_story.html (2002).

Duin, Ann Hill, and Ray Archee. "Distance Learning Via the World Wide Web: Information, Engagement, and Community." *Computers and Technical Communication: Pedagogical and Programmatic Perspectives*. Ed. Stuart A. Selber. Greenwich, CT: Ablex, 1997. 149-69.

e-learning success stories. KPMG: Staying in the Know at Internet Speed. http://www.digitalthink.com/els/client/kpmg2.html. Site accessed October 3, 2000.

Gabriel, Yannis. *Storytelling in Organizations: Facts, Fictions and Fantasies*. Oxford: Oxford UP, 2000.

Galagan, Patricia A. "The Cisco Learning Story." *Training and Development*. (2001): 46-56.

Gee, James Paul, Glynda Hull, and Colin Lankshear. *The New Work Order: Behind the Language of New Capitalism*. Boulder, CO: Westview Press, 1996.

Maher M., B. Sommer, C. Acredolo, and H. R. Matthews. *What are the Relevant Costs of Online Eduation?* Report developed for Mellon Foundation, 2002.

Martin, James. *Cybercorp: The New Business Revolution*. New York: American Management Association, 1996.

Mehlenbacher, Brad. "Technologies and Tensions: Designing Online Environments for Teaching Technical Communication." *Computers and Technical Communication: Pedagogical and Programmatic Perspectives*. Ed. Stuart A. Selber. Greenwich, CT: Ablex, 1997. 219-38.

Morgan, Brian. "Is Distance Learning Worth It? Helping to Determine the Costs of Online Courses" http://webpages.marshall.edu/ ~ morgan16/onlinecosts/ (2000).

Pfeffer, Jeffrey and Sutton, Robert I. *The Knowing-Doing Gap: How Smart Companies Turn Knowledge Into Action*. Cambridge, MA: Harvard Business Press, 2000.

Ryan, Steve, Bernard Scott, Howard Freeman, and Daxa Patel. *The Virtual University: The Internet and Resource-Based Learning*. London: Kogan Page, 2000.

Sanger, Ira. "Inside IBM: Internet Business Machines." *BusinessWeek E-Biz*. (1999): 20-38.

Savukinas, Jacqueline L. "E-Learning: The Impact of IT on Education." *Digital Economy 2002* Washington,DC: Department of Commerce, 2002. 59-64.

Schank, Roger C. *Designing World-Class e-Learning: How IBM, Harvard Business School, and Columbia University are Succeeding at e-Learning*. New York: McGraw-Hill, 2002.

Seybold, Patricia B. *Customers.com: How to Create a Profitable Business Strategy for the Internet and Beyond*. New York: Times Business (Random House), 1998.

"School's out" *Business 2.0.* (1999): 30.

Sullivan, Patricia. Uses of Method in Computers and Composition Studies. Computers and Writing Conference, Ann Arbor, May 1993.

Turoff, Murray. Education, Commerce, And Communications: The Era Of Competition http://eies.njit.edu/~turoff/Papers/webnettalk/webnettalk.htm (1998).

Turoff, Murray. An End to Student Segregation: No More Separation Between Distance Learning and Regular Courses. http://eies.njit.edu/~turoff/Papers/canadapresent/segregation.htm (1999).

Webb, Patricia. *Works and Days.*

Yancey, Kathleen. "Re-designing Your Program: Year Three of the Clemson Digital Portfolio Project." A talk at Computers and Writing, West Lafayette, IN, 2003.

PART FOUR

Identifying Sustainable Technological Practices

14

TECHNIQUES, TECHNOLOGIES, AND THE DESKILLING OF RHETORIC AND COMPOSITION

MANAGING THE KNOWLEDGE-INTENSIVE WORK OF WRITING INSTRUCTION

Bill Hart-Davidson
Michigan State University

Tim Peeples
Elon College

Throughout the 1990s two parallel movements combined to change the status of writing programs in U.S. higher education: the professionalization of Writing Program Administrators (WPAs) and the integration of net-worked computer technology into writing curricula. Independently, both movements are regarded as positive developments in our field, and both movements have, no doubt, contributed to an increase over the last 20 years in the number of writing programs, as well as writing specialists who consider themselves disciplinary professionals. Both movements have also come with an implicit promise that they contribute to the growth of rhetoric and composition as a discipline. But do they?

Instead of responding to that question with an unqualified yes, we argue that the answer is both yes and no. Yes, the professionalization of WPAs has been highly valuable, increasing the institutional visibility and security of writing programs, greatly enhancing the quality of teaching done by a cadre of temporary instructors in many places, developing a national presence from which to effect change, and so on. And yes, the integration of computer technologies into writing curricula has helped to promote more engaged pedagogies, increase audience awareness, promote writing as a form of social action beyond the walls of educational institutions, and the like. So yes, both of these movements have greatly enhanced rhetoric and composition.

However, as we continue to carry these movements forward and maintain their positive influences on our field, we should also be careful to attend to possible negative effects these movements may be having or could have on our programs and the discipline. Our profession and, more importantly, each of us as members of the profession need to move forward with a critical reflectiveness that not only examines the possible effects of our techniques and technologies—located in daily practices—but also actively constructs revised practices. We intend this chapter to be part of that critical reflection. As such, it asks critical questions. In general, this chapter questions the roles program administration and networked computer technology can play in the deskilling of writing instructors and, consequently, creating a profession and daily workplace environment that is not knowledge-intensive (KI). The chapter poses, more specifically, these two questions: (a) Can WPAs manage writing programs as knowledge-intensive workplaces if a majority of their programs' labor force lacks a great deal of the knowledge necessary to pursue writing instruction as KI work? and (b) Has the introduction of networked computers into writing curricula exacerbated the already tense labor conditions in writing programs by challenging a teacher's ability to perform KI work? Our tentative answers are no and yes, respectively.

DESKILLING THE KNOWLEDGE-INTENSIVE WORKPLACE

KI workplaces (e.g., consulting agencies) and traditional, product-based organizations (e.g., textile manufacturers) are significantly different types of places. Based on the literature from organizational studies and related fields, as well as his own organizational case studies, Stanley Deetz argues that the key distinction between KI and traditional organizations lies in their primary capital. Traditional organizations rely primarily on financial capital (e.g., profits from product sales and the potential value of material assets), whereas KI organizations rely primarily on three alternative forms of capital, intellectual (specialized expertise), relational (professional networks and trusting relationships with clients). and artifactual (databases, client files, reports, etc.) (155-56). As a result, traditional and KI organizations are characterized by distinctly different organizational features. In traditional organizations, goals and tasks are well defined, products hold primary significance, and work groups are closely and directly managed. Contrastingly, in KI organizations, work goals and tasks are frequently ambiguous and require active communication and negotiation in order to be defined and addressed, the client–service–provider relationship holds primary significance, and work groups have great autonomy and are relatively self-managed (155-57).

Although it may seem obvious, academic work, including the teaching and studying of writing, reflects (or should reflect) the characteristics of KI organizations more than those of traditional ones. Both academic goals and the tasks that can lead to the successful completion of those goals require constant negotiation; the teacher–student relationship is primary; and both faculty and students have high degrees of autonomy and are relatively self-managed.

What is less obvious, however, are some of the ways program administration can, in certain forms, challenge the status of rhetoric and composition as KI work. Deetz points out that "While organizational positions, certifications, and seniority exert constraints" within KI organizations, "employees frequently engage in role creation and negotiation to determine what needs to be done, how to do it, and their personal responsibilities." Consequently, "many traditional management responsibilities" within KI organizations "are shifted to the employee" (157). For instance, in order to support the often self-managed work of KI organizations, workers must have and are typically given access to the construction of organizational ends or goals, as well as means or processes. Supporting KI work also requires that workers have access to what might be called resources for invention (e.g., data, processes, and decision makers). Within traditional workplaces, management typically controls and blocks such access. Administrative "technologies" (understood broadly, also, as social practices) within writing programs, as we examine in depth later, often participate in removing such access, also. As a result, these practices work against constructing the labor and workplace contexts of writing teachers as KI.

The administrative technologies that may participate in removing laborers' access to resources for invention, however, are typically not isolated practices, but part of a larger, dominant organizational rationality that can be found (rarely, however, as total hegemonies) embedded in other organizational technologies. Taylorist management is predicated on this separation of access to inventional resources, and within this managerial paradigm, technology and management cooperate to relocate inventional resources within managerial/administrative sites. Harry Braverman, noted critic of the kind of oppressive management–labor relations technology has enabled in the industrial era, argues this position most emphatically. Braverman's thesis in *Technology and Monopoly Capital* is nicely summarized by Theodore Lewis:

> the basic purpose of introducing technology into workplaces is to foster transference of skill from labor to capital, thereby affording management greater control of the labor process. With the transference of skill comes a loss of worker efficacy. In other words, technology engenders a dialectic between labor and management, mediated by the location of skill, with the stakes being workplace power. (45)

Richard Ohmann echoes Braverman in his 1984 essay "Literacy, Technnology, and Monopoly Capital," suggesting we extend this line of critique to include information technology:

> I am suggesting that, seen from the side of production and work, the computer and its software are an intended and developing technology, carrying forward the deskilling and control of labor that goes back to F.W. Taylor and beyond, and that has been a main project of monopoly capital. Enough. The age of computer technology will bring us some new tools and methods for teaching literacy. I hope we (or rather those of us teachers who are on my side) will manage to shape that technology to democratic forms. (5)

Regardless of whether one agrees with what some might consider their extreme positions toward technology, technology and management can participate in the deskilling of labor by transferring skill and, thus, control, away from laborers, like writing instructors, and toward managers/administrators, like WPAs.

The cases that follow point to some of the ways program administration and networked technologies have challenged rhetoric and composition as KI work by limiting access to the construction of ends and resources for invention. The first case, one concerning teacher assistant (TA) training, focuses on the ways writing program administration can, even with the best of intentions and the highest professional standards of work, limit access to writing instructors' construction of programmatic ends, thus participating in the deskilling of writing instruction and the (re)production of writing programs as non-KI workplaces. The second set of cases focus on how the integration of networked computer technologies can participate in not only limiting access to the construction of ends but also limiting writing instructors' access to the inventional resources necessary to their work, in both instances participating in the deskilling of writing instruction.

MANAGING OURSELVES AS KNOWLEDGE-INTENSIVE WORKERS

The following case examines the challenges WPAs face in terms of managing writing instruction as KI work when the dominant trend in writing programs is to place writing instruction in the hands of writing nonspecialists (e.g., tutors, TAs, [most] adjuncts, and faculty across the curriculum). The question we want to address here is slightly but significantly different from the one that has long been posed in rhetoric and composition, a question that goes something like, "How can we expect people who have limited backgrounds in rhetoric and composition to effectively teach writing?" We believe TA, tutor, adjunct, and faculty development programs have done a pretty good job of responding to this older question through aggressive and innovative in-service training programs. Even so, the labor pool produced by such training programs can be considered at best "skilled," not "expert." These laborers, in general, lack the expertise in writing needed to be considered KI workers. Therefore, we pose an organizational question that impacts the ways we can manage writing programs, and impacts the shape rhetoric and composition is taking and might take. Our question is as follows: Can WPAs manage writing programs as KI workplaces if a majority of a program's labor force lacks a great deal of the knowledge necessary to pursue writing instruction as KI work?

In order to examine this question, we make two assumptions about the organizational characteristics of WPA work. First, we assume that academic labor is most accurately understood as KI. As noted earlier, this distinction may seem obvious, but the distinction is critical, for as numerous organizational and management theorists have noted, different kinds of labor require very different kinds of management (Deetz 155). Consequently, part of what WPAs do is manage KI labor. The second organizational characteristic complicates this conclusion about the nature of the WPA's managerial work, however. Because academics are managed professionals in an

industry that requires greater and greater economic competition, we characteristically see rising corporate emphases to build in structural flexibility
through, among other strategies, the deployment/employment of part-time
and term labor. As a result, academics are becoming more and more stratified (Rhoads 6). Furthermore, a highly stratified organizational structure
tends to exacerbate the divided positions WPAs typically embody, even
more strongly positioning the WPA as a manager of program staff, rather
than a teaching faculty colleague.

Increased stratification, however, is not the complication, per se. All
but the most fluid and ad hoc KI labor still includes stratified structures that
require managerial positions. However, stratified structures in KI workplaces do not also reflect layers of expertise within a knowledge domain.
For instance, a drug development project manager who supervises a team
of medical experts is not expected to know more about biochemistry than
the biochemists, and is not positioned as "manager" because she knows
more about the specialized knowledge domains of those she supervises.
Once labor is stratified in terms of expertise within a knowledge domain
(i.e., when those "above" know more about the labor of those "below" than
those "below" do), then the labor of those below loses its qualities as KI
and they become deskilled. The organizational and managerial complication for WPAs and for rhetoric and composition is that a large proportion
of the part-time and term labor used for writing instruction is stratified in
terms of expertise within the knowledge domain of rhetoric and composition. In other words, the WPA is a manager of KI labor, yet the WPA manages a labor force that can, and often does, lack the knowledge needed to
pursue writing instruction as KI work.

As earlier stated, what we are interested in here is the managerial/organizational issue that arises when we look at the interaction between these
two organizational characteristics of WPA managerial work. The following
case analysis illustrates the issue by examining the kinds of academic organizational spaces enacted by total quality management (TQM) and the WPA
organizational subject positions formulated within them. The case[1] comes
from Christopher C. Burnham and Cheryl Nims' 1995 self-reflective article,
"Closing the Circle: Outcomes Assessment, TQM and the WPA." The article
reflects on Burnham and Nims' decision to turn to TQM practices in order
to improve the TA training program at New Mexico State University (NMSU)
and what they identify as the positive consequences of their project.

We would argue even before the case analysis that TQM has been a
WPA managerial response designed to address a desire to create a more
active and equal community of KI workers in a context where knowledge
equity is actually lacking because of an overwhelming reliance on under-

educated part-time and term laborers. Our analysis concludes, in part, that the organizational context we have outlined has the tendency to hail and reproduce scientific management (SM) practices (practices TQM aims to replace), for the gaps often found between the knowledge workers (WPAs and full-time writing faculty) and "shop-floor" workers (e.g., many of whom are part-time and term writing instructional staff) are (re)produced when writing programs are run by those who are knowledgeable of the field, and who are expected to pass that knowledge onto term laborers, who are then positioned as the workers who create the "product" on the shop floor.

WPAS AND/IN THE ENACTED SPACE OF TQM: A CASE OF TA TRAINING REVISIONS

Burnham and Nims state that NMSU had developed what they felt was a strong TA training program over the years. The program included extensive staff development, with the following features: more than 100 hours of direct training and supervision during the TA's first semester teaching; a week-long orientation; an introductory composition theory and pedagogy course; bi-weekly conferences with the WPA; weekly assistant director-run sessions "providing nuts and bolts information about working through the [program's] syllabus"; informal mentoring from experienced TAs; writing center tutor training; and a 200-plus page program training manual (58-60). Although they viewed their program "as a model, exemplary in assuming administrative responsibility," they "knew it was not working as well as it could." Looking at their program through the lens of TQM, they "discovered that the structure and emphasis of the program maximized administrative control," reducing staff creativity and leading to program resistance and even subversion (58). Although these were critical issues, they decided that the program's key problem lay elsewhere: "Rather than inviting GAs to help establish goals and thereby come to own them, [the program administrators] provided all the values, goals, and practices." The administrators "did not invite GAs to shape or endorse the program" (60).

Having decided that their primary problems were TA alienation and a lack of TA empowerment, Burnham and Nims state that TQM encouraged them to look more closely at their training processes. Guided by TQM process analysis, their aim would be to find places where the training program stifled TA creativity, made them feel alienated, and failed to empower them to shape and own the training program. Their focus became the introductory composition theory and pedagogy course required of their TAs.

With the aim of introducing new TAs to the discipline of rhetoric and offering them membership into this disciplinary community, they had developed a course project that required TAs to focus on a specific issue throughout the course. Over the course of the project, TAs would develop a proposal, write a professional book review, complete a "professional quality essay, targeted at a specific journal," and give a final presentation at a program "Symposia." The point of the symposia was "to share information that [would] allow everyone to teach the course, to do their 'job,' more effectively." The problem with the project, they assessed, was that "the 'job' itself, as detailed on the syllabus and through the course assignments and requirements,[could not] be negotiated" (62). In the words of TQM, the workers had no input into the processes of their work. As in SM, the work processes of TAs were designed and controlled by the program manager(s), the WPA(s). The standard syllabus, assignments, and requirements exerted what Burnham and Nims acknowledge in the language of KI work and TQM was a "normative influence" (62). Under this form of training/management, Burnham and Nims paraphrase the kind of reasoning the organizational space created for the project:

> The program cannot be broken, so the GA must be broken. To begin the assignment, a student must reason: "what am I not doing very well? The program includes it, so it must have value. Obviously, the scholarship will support the program and offer a solution to the problem. I will review the scholarship, find the solution, and offer it to all the future incompetents who, like me, may have problems in the same area." The message is not a healthy one. (62)

Although the project itself may be a very good way to introduce students to the discipline of rhetoric and composition and also invite them into the disciplinary community, it cannot be considered outside of the managerial/organizational context in which it is enacted. Within the SM managerial context, Burnham and Nims characterize, the project failed to achieve its (stated) aims. The project entered an administrative space that caused TAs' creativity to be stifled and made them feel disempowered. Burnham and Nims had clearly identified this as part of the program's problem, and TQM was valuable in giving them the tools to see into the effects of their own managerial practices. However, the following analysis illustrates that TQM fails to produce any significant changes in the managerial context.

The changes they make to the project are for the sake of quality and ownership. Rather than contextualizing the project within the symposia as a report addressed to the other TAs on something they found lacking in their own practice and suggested ways to improve it, the project revision contextualized the final presentation as a program critique directed to TAs, administrators, and faculty. As Burnham and Nims describe it, their goals are "to provide a sense of ownership for every instructor" and "to encourage new GAs to place themselves in relation to current program structure but to develop an innovation." These innovations can be "something not included within the program or an approach different from current recommended practice" (62-63). For example, "a new GA with a creative writing concentration," they point out, "might design ways to incorporate imaginative writing exercises in her course." Then, in the revised symposia, TAs explain their innovations, discuss their successes, and lead discussions about whether their innovations should be "incorporated into the program, offered as an alternative activity for use by individuals so inclined, reconceived and retested, or abandoned" (63).

Not so obvious in this revision is the fact that TAs are invited to improve quality in and become stakeholders of a standardized program with predetermined ends. They are invited, that is, to suggest innovations or revisions as the means by which already determined ends are reached. The creative writing TA exemplified above is invited—no, required to!—create, test, and present ways to improve the processes by which the Curriculum (with a capital C) can be produced. The curriculum itself is beyond revision by the TA, for this is the domain of the WPA. Here, the WPA's disciplinary subjectivity collaborates with managerial subjectivity to (re)produce the controlling SM managerial position that is trying to be revised. The desire to increase ownership challenges the control, both disciplinary and managerial, of the WPA. At one point in their article, Burnham and Nims state directly that WPAs' curricula and training programs "reflect [their] best sense of how students learn to write," and "[w]e hold this [disciplinary] value to such a degree that we disregard how individual teachers might best teach writing" (60). Consequently, they as WPAs approach the construction of curricula as reflections of their own expert understandings of writing and the teaching of writing, and resist letting nonexperts question programmatic ends. Such is also the case in SM. Scientific managers see themselves as the experts and, thus, resist letting workers question or participate in determining product ends. SM positions the manager as the technocratic boss. A disciplinary perspective that sees WPAs as the experts who are responsible for constructing curricula positions WPAs in the same sort of way.

The TQM-based revision proposed by Burnham and Nims at the end of their article reflects Janice Klein's description of TQM as but a dynamic SM: it emphasizes continuous (micro)improvements of an already standardized program; engages TAs, faculty, and administrators in collaborative exploration of better means to reach predetermined ends; and focuses on managing through commitment without replacing technocratic control (187). Even though Burnham and Nims realize that their tightly sequenced managerial practices have led to their problems, TQM (re)produces a managerial space very similar to that of SM and, consequently, (re)produces technocratic, controlling subject positions for the WPAs. KI workplaces make it easier to give up this technocratic control because managers of KI work assume that individual employees know their work better than the managers do. The employees are experts. But what happens when one's "employees" are also one's "students"? That is, what if one is managing KI work being performed by experts-in-training? Even tougher, what if one is managing writing instructors who have no or very limited intentions of pursuing expertise in rhetoric and composition? Such is the case of WPAs working with TAs, many (if not most) adjuncts, peer tutors, and faculty across the curriculum who teach writing-intensive courses. In this context, the WPA-as-manager is positioned by upper-administrators as one who must oversee and take responsibility for the production of a coherent, quality product; the WPA-as-disciplinary-expert is positioned by faculty and the discipline of rhetoric and composition as one who must develop and secure curricula based on our best understandings of writing and the teaching of writing. In this way, WPAs' positions as both academic managers and disciplinary experts resist creating the kind of space where their instructional staff are able to truly negotiate their jobs in the sense that they are involved in negotiating ends as well as means.

Rather than effecting hierarchical remediation-oriented assessment, Burnham and Nims' employment of TQM leads them to enact an organizational space that is but a more dynamic SM one. Their project revision develops (micro)improvements for a standardized curriculum, builds collaborations that explore revised means without questioning ends, and increases TA commitment as a means of greater managerial control. As such, it maintains the technocratic position of the WPA. Without question, such revisions reduce the tensions Burnham and Nims feel as a result of simultaneously enacting administrative and faculty positions. Their revisions most likely also make TAs feel like they have more control of their work. And in these ways, we might say that the professionalization of program administration improves the work-lives of writing teachers. However, Burnham and Nims are ineffective in actually changing organizational space and WPA subject positions; they are ineffective in re-constructing writing instructional work as KI. So in this sense, the professionalization of program administration participates in re-constructing a disempowering organizational context for the work and workers of writing instruction.

A dominant issue related to managing writing instruction as KI is raised in this case: in order to pursue writing instruction as KI, teachers of writing must have access to the negotiation/construction of organizational ends or goals, as well as means or processes of production. The following case analyses highlight a second dominant issue related to managing writing instruction as KI: writing instruction as KI requires that teachers of writing have access to what we have called resources for invention, and it requires that they have a credible voice in the design of the technologies that support the practice/teaching/learning of the discipline.

CONSTRUCTING A KNOWLEDGE-INTENSIVE NETWORK

In the case analyses that follow, we present evidence that network environments can threaten teacher's expertise in two ways:

1. by making alternate pedagogies, usually discredited or misinformed ones from the teachers' point of view, not only available but in some cases more high-profile, more readily accessed, or more appealing than the teachers' own pedagogy (if you have ever assigned a memo or a resume and gotten back a stack of documents, all of which adhere alarmingly to the templates provided in Microsoft Word, you have a sense of what we are suggesting here); and
2. by magnifying cultural assumptions about technology and the types of people who are authorized to control, use, and teach others to use it (in particular, the networked classroom provides students in technical fields space to challenge instructors who are perceived as somehow "different" from the White, male image of technological authority).

Both of these issues impact the role of the writing instructor as a KI worker by introducing competing factors into the very structure of the institutional space meant to support teaching and learning: the classroom. To illustrate what we mean by this, we offer a shorter example that involves a teacher who we call Felix before turning to the more complex situation addressed in the case of another teacher, Hector.[2] Despite their relative expertise in rhetoric and composition as well as their previous experiences teaching writing in networked environments, the networked classroom posed significant challenges to each of these teachers and, we might add, to the other six participants in the study.

Felix's candid statements during the study put these challenges into perspective. In an interview, Felix explained that his apprehension about teaching technical writing in a networked environment boiled down to "worrying more about knowing the technology than about knowing the rhetorical stuff." In addition, when asked about the kinds of preparation he might have had in order to feel more adequately prepared for his experience teaching in the networked classroom, he suggested that mentoring or training sessions focus more on the real-time actions a teacher has to perform in the computer environment. It was in these moments, Felix felt, that his expertise in writing and rhetoric, and therefore his efficacy as an instructor, was most challenged by the technological environment. An example, taken from Felix's classroom, will help demonstrate how networks can harbor other pedagogies that alter the intellective skills needed to succeed in the computer classroom. Felix was using Microsoft Excel (Office '97), a spreadsheet program that, among other things, generates visual displays of data through a semi-automated interface known as the "chart wizard." Such a lesson required a great deal of technical skill with the chart wizard, the spreadsheet, and with the overhead display that allowed him to make changes to a visual on the fly as he demonstrated the various ways students might "argue" with visuals. The lesson also required enough savvy to recognize and critique the assumptions about writing, visual rhetoric, and end-users that are built into the software by its designers.

The chart wizard generates a visual by using data that has been selected on a spreadsheet. Many impressive formats are available and can be selected by the user with a simple click on a picture of the type of chart desired. The chart formats range from simple, black and white line graphs and bar charts to complicated color, three-dimensional (3-D), area graphs. Once the initial chart has been generated using the selected data, the user can change formats, manipulate color, 3-D perspective, category and chart titles, and other variables. Many of these changes, however, are not obvious steps in the chart wizard interface because it is designed to make the production of visuals as simple as possible. Quite often, students stick with the default settings of the chart wizard interface, which can actually make their visual work against their rhetorical purpose. A common problem in the instructional labs in which Felix and others in the program taught, for example, was the use of *colors* in the default formats that were too dark or too light to appear as different shades of gray on the black and white laser printer. Another common problem arises when the 3-D perspective of a pie chart distorts the appearance of the section in the front of the pie because the viewer sees not only the area, but the volume of that particular slice, making it appear larger than those slices whose volume is hidden because they are in the back of the pie. Felix's lesson sought to sensitize students to these and other rhetorical problems that could arise when they allowed the default settings of the chart wizard to do too much of the decision making in creating a visual. What this meant, however, was that most of Felix's moves with the software during his presentation were under close scrutiny and, because they deviated from or downplayed the importance of some of the default and most compelling features of the software (such as "cool" colors and 3-D perspective), his ideas were challenged.

When Felix described the ways he felt underprepared for the computer environment, he was expressing concerns about the types of KI demands the networked classroom regularly makes of teachers new to those spaces. He was also noting the student resistance to his teaching, a resistance that had its basis in the ability of the technology to present a coherent, and quite rational view of the very same writing tasks that he had asked his students to perform, but a view opposed to his own. In other words, Felix found the network of writing technologies in which he taught to be already full of writing pedagogies—specialized knowledge that we usually think of the teacher as the mediator of—and these pedagogies explicitly challenged his own.

How should we characterize the kind of knowledge, the kind of expertise required to deal adequately with situations like the one described here? Such descriptions of KI work are frequently difficult to formulate without diminishing the sophistication of the tasks performed or the strategies pursued by practitioners. We know, for example, that what teachers of writing bring to classrooms and to students via our pedagogy is not accurately described by the word "skill." And, therefore, all that we bring cannot simply be captured in Tayloresque time–motion studies and transferred by mechanical means to a machine that stands in for the teacher. To be fair, even the most sophisticated writing software, then, does not aim to replace writing instructors so much as it aims to support the goals of writers in the midst of their writing task, whatever it might be. Therefore, we need a more appropriate view of "skill" suited to KI work and to the design and functionality of information technologies so that we might better assess the risk of deskilling writing specialists as KI workers.

For this view of information-age skill, we turn to Shoshana Zuboff, who faced a similar analytic problem in her study of the effects of information technologies on the work of both middle management and front-line laborers in paper mills. Zuboff suggests a new term—"intellective skill"—which, for her, described work that "came to depend more upon thinking about and responding to an electronically present symbolic medium than upon acting out know-how derived from sentient [in this case, bodily] experience." Zuboff further describes intellective skill this way:

> . . . it encompasses a shift away from physical cues, toward sense-making based more exclusively upon abstract rules . . . it uses the symbolic medium to ascertain the condition of "reality" in ways that cannot be reduced to correspondence with physical objects (for example, the ability to discern states, trends, underlying causes, relations, dynamics, predictions, sources of suboptimization, opportunities for improvement, etc.). (95-96)

Zuboff's definition of intellective skill suggests that we might more appropriately focus our attention on the ways, in any networked classroom, a writing teacher's expertise is either supported or compromised by the technology—either because the technology intervenes and supplants the teacher's normal role by attempting to automate their role, essentially taking over the "intellective skills," or because the technology challenges the authority of the teacher's expertise in some other way. As we have argued elsewhere, the view of expertise most compatible with the rhetorical ability writing teachers command and seek to foster in students involves a complex interaction between persistent, cross-contextual knowledge and local, contingent, and contextual strategies. This view of expertise locates "expert knowledge" in the network of relations that constitutes any given situation where expertise might be measured and includes the individual as well as the various other people, resources, and objects that comprise that network (Peeples and Hart-Davidson, 1997). "Network expertise" does not deny the powerful cognitive component of expert knowledge. Rather, it seeks to acknowledge both the cognitive and social factors contributing to expertise and the moment(s) in which any person might be judged to be an expert.

In the foregoing example, we saw a glimpse of the way the networked environment challenged Felix's expertise by introducing new objects and relations which, when put into motion in the real-time practice of teaching, can complicate the teacher's ability to, in Zuboff's terms, "discern states, trends, underlying causes, relations, dynamics, predictions, sources of suboptimization, opportunities for improvement" (78) related not merely to technology skills, but to rhetoric and writing as well. We might restate Zuboff's claim, more simply, to say that the networked environment introduces enough unfamiliar objects and relationships that new teachers find it very difficult to focus on anything but the means of teaching. The focus, as Felix indicated, is on surviving in this new landscape where your tried and true methods are no longer valid or sufficient. Feeling sufficiently comfortable to experiment with new methods of doing familiar tasks, let alone feeling empowered to challenge the ends as well as means of a writing program's curriculum, can be slow in coming.

Can programs make networked spaces that provide more or easier access to the resources for invention needed to question the ends as well as the means of writing instruction? In our next case example, we consider this challenge a bit more and learn from a teacher whose efforts in the networked classroom help to demonstrate how fundamental the ability to question the ends of writing instruction are to the day-to-day teaching of rhetoric and writing.

POWER AND THE NETWORK: A CASE OF VISIBLE ETHNICITY AND (IN)VISIBLE EXPERTISE

The teacher who we call Hector in this case is, himself, a dedicated researcher of technology and literacy and was, to say the least, a proficient user of computers in general as well as the networked environment in which he taught. He is also visibly ethnic, although not necessarily Hispanic as his self-chosen pseudonym might cause one to believe. This choice of pseudonym, like many others Hector makes, was at least partially motivated by his commitment to disrupting entrenched assumptions about race and power, particularly in technological settings—a notable characteristic of his teaching practice. But this choice was also motivated by his sense of humor, and his admiration for a particular writer who shared the name. These characteristics—humor, and an appreciation for the interconnectedness of the textual worlds we ask students to participate in—also happen to be notable aspects of Hector's teaching practice.

Even before the opportunity to visit Hector's classroom arose, he had talked in an interview about facing frequent challenges to his ability to use the technology in the classroom, challenges motivated by assumptions his students made based on his ethnicity. These were, he felt, not subtle doubts but rather overt assumptions and expectations that technology difficulties that arose in class were due to his being "unprepared" or unknowl-edgable about the technology.

Despite and in some cases because of these kinds of exchanges with students, Hector often chose to present material *inductively* in class, posing problems rather than organizing lectures in a deductive way. This tech-nique, beginning with uncertainty and the raising of questions rather than stating facts and working towards a coherent solution to problems, is a well-established pedagogy for the writing classroom, and particularly a "decentered" one. In business and technical writing pedagogy, this tech-nique is often taken a step further with the use of workplace cases. Teachers pose challenging rhetorical problems to students to help them learn how to apply rhetorical strategies and techniques covered in class. And usually students are content to play along. But, Hector discovered, they are not always so willing when the teacher is "different."

Hector described several situations where technology-related problems that arose were implicitly or explicitly attributed to his lack of expertise in such environments, despite any evidence to the contrary. Even more alarming, however, were incidents in which he felt students attempted to explicitly challenge his authority by taking advantage of a technology-relat-ed issue they assumed he was not equipped to handle. He suspected, for example, that students might have tampered with files stored on the class's shared server space, altering due dates or other important data on sched-ules and/or assignment descriptions. It was not until the day of the actual visit to Hector's class, however, that the dynamics of these sorts of situa-tions became clear to the researcher.

Upon visiting Hector's class, one of the authors was able to witness pre-cisely what Hector was talking about. Because it was a common practice for undergraduate and graduate students as well as faculty to work quietly and inconspicuously in the instructional labs while other classes were going on, the presence of an observer did not seem out of the ordinary to the students in Hector' class. Even though, in this particular case, Hector pointed out the researcher and announced that there would be an observ-er in class that day collecting data about the interactions among the teacher, the students, and the technologies in the room, the students con-sistently made candidly challenging remarks about the teacher's level of experience and expertise that were explicitly connected to his ethnic iden-tity. They could be heard openly "scheming," in fact, to take advantage of what they thought was a weakness of this particular teacher to extend a deadline on an upcoming assignment.

The day of observation in question was a Friday and, with weekend plans in full swing, the students were confronting a due date for a major project in the course the following Monday. The project was a response to a case scenario which called for a response constituted of several documents, including a policy document meant to circulate among audiences external to the fictional organization the student teams supposedly worked for and a memo meant for the eyes of their supervisor. Other supporting documents were also possible for a complete and effective response, including a summary of resources consulted in formulating the policy document, and so on, all with the aim of documenting and/or justifying the positions laid forth in the policy document and the memo.

As one can infer from the range of possible responses to the case scenario, the project was a challenging one. It was not an assignment that could be easily tackled in a single meeting or by one person. A quality response in the allotted time—approximately 2 weeks with drafts of the primary deliverables due after the first week and final versions delivered the following week—required the teams to plan carefully and distribute the research and drafting workload across the team. All of this was by design, of course, as the project sought to introduce students to the collaborative and complex dynamic of workplace writing. Moreover, Hector was careful to spend time during class introducing these specific challenges as key factors in the success of the teams. He also offered the teams strategies for using the computer network's ability to facilitate document storage and retrieval among a distributed team to address the challenges posed in the case scenario. But as the Monday deadline loomed, some students in the class joked about exploiting the network's features for an alternative purpose: extending the deadline until the Wednesday class meeting.

Because one of the goals of the study in which this observation occurred was to invent a more effective means by which to prepare teachers for the networked classroom, and for situations like the one Hector faced, he agreed to turn the incident that followed that day into a scenario to be used in a teacher-preparation session. This and other scenarios would be presented to instructors preparing to teach in the networked environment for the first time as well as those in their first semester of doing so. The scenario, as co-constructed by Hector and the researcher, looked like this:

Scenario: It's Due Wednesday!

Your class is wrapping up work on assignment 1, the Insurance Company Case. In the assignment document for the case project, you have specified a due date for the initial drafts of the deliverables of 10/2. The final versions will be due 10/9—both dates are Mondays.

10/2 comes around and all the teams turn in a draft, some obviously pounded one out before class, and one you think was actually composed *during* class. But all the teams are making some progress at the halfway point.

When 10/9 rolls around, one team shows up with their file of documents ready. In fact, you note, it had been posted to the server Sunday evening. But the other teams haven't updated their folders. When you ask why they haven't turned in the assignment on the appointed day, they point to a conflict in the due date specified in the assignment description and the one on the course schedule which resides on the web-based syllabus for your section. The one on the assignment sheet, located in the public area of the server, says 10/11, Wednesday, while the schedule posted on the web says 10/9, Monday.

This scenario accurately recounts the situation Hector faced on the Monday following the Friday of the observation. What the scenario does not explicitly include, but rather leaves the new teachers to ponder, is the possibility that the students in the class altered the due date on the assignment sheet document—a file they had read/write access to as a practically unalterable feature of the file-sharing preferences on the course server. This would explain a conflict arising between the date on the server and the date on the World Wide Web-published course schedule, a file to which only the instructor had write access. During the observation, the researcher had heard such a plan being discussed in what could hardly be characterized as whispered tones. Although there was a definite humorous undertone to these plans to clear the way for a weekend free of the work required to meet a Monday deadline, the possibility that at least a few of the students took the plan seriously was definitely there.

A closer look at some of the decisions Hector made both before and after this situation, helps to reveal the way the networked environment can be seen to threaten the expertise of writing instructors and may, in fact, pose a more serious threat of "deskilling" by attempting to automate some of the intellective skill-driven activity of teachers in the networked classroom. Hector's response, however, reveals what can happen when the network space is seen as a location for storing and sharing the kinds of "resources for invention" that we have talked about above. The decisions Hector makes question the ends of the assignment as well as the means by which it is accomplished.

First, the decision to use the class server as a place where students could openly share files with full read/write access makes for both the exciting possibility of a genuine collaborative assignment and the potential danger of a due-date sabotage. Hector had decided early on in planning his pedagogical approach to the course that this was a risk worth taking. He might have made the network space a read-only environment for students, ensuring his authority and limiting students' ability to tamper with important shared resources. This would also have limited the students ability to set up team folders to share files, however, and would have made the scenario which drove the case being discussed, as well as other projects, more like "school" and less like "work," in the eyes of Hector and, in all likelihood, his students.

A second decision Hector made was a bit broader in scope than the decision to make the class server a public space. This decision, to pursue a decentered classroom in which the authority of the teacher was not based on his ability, in this instance, to confer knowledge but rather to encourage its growth among a community of learners, was a pretty risky one for Hector. His ethnicity prompted some students to quite explicitly wonder whether his strategy of posing problems and foregrounding uncertainties in teaching the strategies of rhetoric and writing might not be due to his own lack of expertise in these areas? Or perhaps his lack of expertise in the technology environment?

Hector might have chosen to go the other way, using the resources of the networked classroom to create a more coherent and less easily challenged position of authority for himself as "The Teacher." But he did not do this. Indeed, in resolving the problem that arose with the conflicting due dates, Hector might simply have checked to see when the file had last been changed, which might have revealed a clue to the mystery of how the conflict in due dates arose. Had the file been changed recently, foul play might be more likely. A more full-scale investigation might then have ensued, using the network's ability to monitor logins and file transfers to determine the likely network node or workstation on which a recent edit to the document occurred. But Hector chose to deal with the situation within the boundaries of the case scenario itself, in effect extending the rhetorical and ethical complexity of the case scenario that framed the assignment. Acting within his role as the team leader in the context of the case scenario, Hector simply reasserted the need for the deliverables to be completed by the end-of-business on Monday. Rather than simply pass off this responsibility onto the students, he devoted the rest of the class period to the kind of "war-room" planning session that might occur in any workplace where a similar pressing deadline was in effect. Hector's approach once again asked the students to consider how they could best use the technological resources the networked environment made available to solve the problem at hand: completing the project by the end of the day. In this way, Hector asked his students to engage in a reevaluation of the ends of the assignment as well, refocusing the rhetorical task on managing the available resources, including the remaining time and the technologies available for producing documents in response to the problem at hand, to complete the task successfully.

Hector's story in this case has, in some respects, a happy ending. But the more serious implications of the case are certainly not to be glossed over. Not every teacher is sufficiently comfortable or knowledgeable about the electronic environments in which they teach to pursue the tactics that Hector did. This example shows how the networked classroom introduces new objects, new processes, and new relationships among the various players in an educational setting which, given the cultural conditions necessary, can severely challenge the expertise of the writing teacher on grounds that are biased in terms of race, gender, or other cultural factors.

We clearly see in this case, as well as Felix's, how the introduction of networked computers into writing curricula can exacerbate the already tense labor conditions in writing programs by challenging a teacher's ability to perform KI work. And in the NMSU TA training case, we see quite clearly how the part-time, term labor conditions that currently dominate writing instruction, especially at the introductory course level, can thwart even the best attempts to construct KI writing instructional workplaces. What we learn from such research requires us, if we adopt the critically reflective stance for which we argue at the beginning of this piece, to ask some tough questions about our work.

CONCLUSION: QUESTIONING INSTITUTIONAL SPACES, VIRTUAL AND MATERIAL

As Ohmann, Selfe, and others have urged, the field must deliberate carefully regarding the impact of introducing information technology into our work, our lives as professionals, and into our students' lives as well. For Braverman the underlying purpose for introducing any new technology into a workplace environment is control. If we consider, just for a moment, our own workplaces (e.g., the classrooms, departments, and schools in which we all do our teaching and research), we may wonder, "Could it be that the spread of information technology has been about control in these spaces too?"

Rather than pick apart Braverman's unfashionably orthodox Marxist position here, we will simply acknowledge that his rhetoric is indeed dramatic in suggesting an overwhelming agency, even a plan, on the part of the owners of "the factory" (Deans? Trustees? Athletic programs?) to capture worker skill and further tip the balance of workplace power. As we have argued, simple divisions between management and labor are not entirely accurate when we talk about academic workplaces as KI. Still, we'd like to take Bravermann's question seriously for just a moment in order to test Ohmann's more carefully framed cautionary argument that the introduction of the computer software and—although he didn't foresee network technology in 1984, we will extend his gaze a bit to 1994—networks might be a further attempt at control. Do we have the disciplinary wherewithal to, as Ohmann suggests, "shape technology to democratic forms"?

We believe that answering this question first requires that the field address another basic and more chilling one: Is there a threat of deskilling created by information technology in the networked writing classroom? A threat that the value teachers of writing bring to the classroom—their rhetorical expertise—is being transferred, via network technologies, to the institution? The cases presented here don't settle this question, but they do suggest that the issue deserves more careful study. Anecdotally, we might say that such a threat exists. Consider, for example, that despite valiant struggles by computers and writing specialists who had to argue for networked facilities (especially prior to 1994 and the emergence of the World Wide Web), schools have, since 1994, invested enormous amounts of money in technology that supports literacy and literacy instruction. There is, still, tremendous momentum for adding new technologies in writing instruction and across the curriculum: building wireless networks, expanding distance education programs, and upgrading network facilities, much of this in the interest of more efficiently providing "basic" instruction like writing. But has there been equal enthusiasm and support for staffing these new facilities, building these new curricula?

Cynthia Selfe, in her book *Technology and Literacy in the Twenty-First Century* documents inequities in funding for technology vs. teacher preparation in the context of the Clinton Administration's Technology Literacy efforts. She notes that "[t]he 1999 budget President Clinton sent to congress for the Department of Education, for example, requested $721 million of direct federal funding for educational technology . . . less than one-tenth of that amount, $67 million, for Teacher Recruitment and Participation" (16). Comparing this figure with other statistics Selfe mentions, helps to demonstrate that the discrepancy is one of priority and not merely due to scarce resources. The State of California, Selfe explains, spent $279 million in 1 year for "information technology and deferred maintenance." One district, in Union City California, spent $27 million on technology for 11 schools! (16). Such large-scale investment in technology by educational institutions continues to make news. In May 2001, for example, a school district in Henrico County, Virginia, purchased 23,000 laptop computers, a move that constituted the largest sale of portable computers in education in history, according to Apple Computer (http://www.apple.com/pr/library/2001/may/ 1henrico.html).

These kinds of funding inequities that favor hardware over training may not be particularly surprising to many writing faculty who have seen similar kinds of moves on their own campuses. But we think they should cause us to consider, quite a bit more carefully, whether or not these conditions are part of a larger pattern. If it is not an administrative agenda, then perhaps it might be an administrative "dream" that an infusion of information technology will make the struggles of basic instruction go away? In other words, even if we are not seeing deliberate "de jure" deskilling, then how about de facto deskilling of writing instructors? Wherein administrations spend more and more on high-tech instructional environments in which teachers of writing are perceived to be less and less a factor . . . eventually (hopefully?) to be supplanted altogether. Is this what is happening?

As alarmist as this question sounds when it is based on a few budget statistics and anecdotal summaries of campus trends, we believe that this question and others like it must be given careful consideration going forward. Here, for example, is a list that readers of this article might consider asking themselves regarding the networked spaces they build, inhabit and/or maintain:

- Are you preparing teachers for the new intellective skills demanded by the networked classroom?
- Do you exert design control over the networked spaces—both physical and virtual—that your teachers work in, or is this largely in the hands of campus computing? Do teachers participate in design activity?
- Are issues of difference, discrimination, and prejudice part of the discussions about classroom technologies on your campus?
- How are network technologies and the refiguring of rhetorical expertise represented, curricularly, in your program? New courses? Projects? New faculty positions?
- Is there support and space for teachers—grad students, part-time and full-time faculty—to engage in critical and inventional work in information technologies?

In addition to the tough questions we need to ask about the relationships between networked technologies and the potential deskilling of writing instructors, we face equally tough questions about the possible roles WPAs play in (re)producing writing programs as something other than KI workplaces. Even though Burnham and Nims' desire to draw the TAs and themselves into a community of KI workers co-inquiring into the means-ends relationships of the writing program, our analysis illustrates that their organizational context positions them in such a way that they cannot achieve this organization or form of management. What this kind of analysis also shows us is that designing the future shape of rhetoric and composition requires us to carefully construct and enact administrative plans of action.

Based on the NMSU case, how would we respond to our opening question, Can WPAs manage writing programs as knowledge-intensive workplaces if a majority of their programs' labor force lacks a great deal of the knowledge necessary to pursue writing instruction as KI work? We would have to say "probably not," *if* we assume the following: (a) if writing instruction is KI labor, (b) if a department is the appropriate home for a discipline, (c) if the ubiquitous required first-year composition course, which creates an ongoing need for flexible part-time and term labor, is housed within those departments housing rhetoric and composition, and (d) if the composition of our labor force remains stratified in structural and knowledge-based terms.

However, each of these assumptions points us toward possible avenues of action that could change our organizational context and, thus, the possibilities for re-creating rhetoric and composition as a full-time discipline. Our first assumption requires us to consider writing instruction KI work. We could argue that not all writing instruction is knowledge-intensive, consequently avoiding the whole concern over managing such work as KI. We have seen these moves already made in our field, where some have said, for instance, that teaching first-year composition does not require a degree—or even coursework—in rhetoric and composition (we have seen such arguments only in less "official" but still professionally public sites like the listserv for writing program administrators, WPA-L). We would not want to make this argument, and we would not want us to go down that road.

The second assumption leading us to conclude we cannot manage writing programs as KI within current labor conditions is the assumption that disciplines must be housed within departments. We could argue that rhetoric and composition is a discipline of a different breed that requires a different kind of "home" than other disciplines. This would require that we simultaneously redefine "discipline" and create institutional spaces where our new breed of discipline can reside. In our new homes, we could also create new kinds of "disciplinary memberships" that are not based on traditional academic criteria. We believe an article by Joe Harris (*CCC*, 2000) shows how we might possibly move in this direction.

Assuming that first-year writing continues to be required, thus (re)producing the demand for so many rhet/comp experts, also leads us to conclude that we cannot manage writing programs as KI workplaces within our current economic context. We could abolish the requirement attached to the first-year composition course, the organizational feature that is probably most responsible for re-creating stratifications in disciplinary domain knowledge. This would require us to plan the best ways to manage ourselves "out" of the requirement, so we create the least amount of harm to all involved. Many have certainly raised this possibility as both an entire strategy (e.g., Crowley) and as part of a larger strategy (e.g., Harris).

Finally, if we assume that the current stratification characterizing the profession of writing instruction continues, we will continue to be unable to manage writing programs as KI. We could, however, effect the structural and/or knowledge-based tiers dividing rhetoric and composition laborers. Some have begun changing structures by hiring a much larger full-time writing instructional staff. There are several other ways we could effect the knowledge-based tiers. For instance, we could build more undergraduate requirements and majors in rhetoric and composition, or writing studies in general, thus improving the numbers of TAs entering graduate programs who have some disciplinary background. Faculty in departments/programs responsible for delivering writing instruction could share, in the long run, a more in-depth, disciplined background in rhetoric and writing. In other words, we may be able to assume that undergraduate English majors, for instance, are as familiar with rhetoric and composition as they are with literature. More short-term strategies (although still administratively challenging) can also be developed: maintaining deadline dates after which no more sections of a required writing course can be added because staff will not be able to complete summer development programs; or, institutionalizing longer "training" programs for new staff during which they are probationary employees learning but not teaching.

These issues certainly need to be deliberated over across our profession, but as is often noted in writing program administration scholarship, much of the deliberation and action concerning how we re-construct institutional space in order to create contexts in which writing instruction can be pursued as KI work will have to be done in local settings. The questions we have posed and suggestions we have made are not limited to large-scale movements nor isolated to conversations held in the pages, lists, and offices of our profession. We can, and should, ask these questions and consider ways to enact these suggestions on scales both large and small. We construct our discipline and workplaces as much or more through our local, daily practices as we do our large-scale, occasional ones.

ENDNOTES

1. Two notes about the "case." First, we want to emphasize that we have chosen it, in part, because what Burnham and Nims describe reflects some of our field's best work in addressing the issue at hand. Second, we refer to Burnham and Nim's published self-report as a "case" in a casuistic way, rather than an empirical way. That is, we are using it as a publicly shared, fairly typified example through which we can reason and reflect.
2. Both the example and the case data were gathered by one of the authors in the fall of 1998 as part of a study of teachers facing the challenge of teaching an upper division business or technical writing course in a networked computer classroom for the first time. Both Hector and Felix had taught introductory writing courses in both traditional as well as computer-based environments prior to teaching a professional writing course in such a classroom, and Felix had taught professional writing courses in traditional classrooms previously as well. In neither case, therefore, were the two teachers you will read about "raw novices."

REFERENCES

Braverman, Harry. *Labor & Monopoly Capital: The Degradation of Work in the Twentieth Century*. New York: Monthly Review Press, 1975.

Burnham, Christopher C. and Cheryl Nims "Closing the Circle: Outcomes Assessment, TQM and the WPA." *Writing Program Administration*. (1995): 50-65.

Crowley, Sharon. *Composition in the University: Historical and Polemical Essays*. Pittsburgh: U of Pittsburgh P, 1998.

Deetz, Stanley. "Discursive Formations, Strategized Subordination and Self-surveillance." *Foucault, Management and Organization Theory*. Eds. Alan McKinlay and Ken Starkey. Thousand Oaks: Sage, 1998. 151-72.

Harris, Joseph. "Meet the New Boss, Same as the Old Boss: Class Consciousness in Composition." *College Composition and Communication. 52* (2000): 43-68.

Klein, Janice A. "The Paradox of Quality Management: Commitment, Ownership, and Control." *The Post-Bureaucratic Organization. New Perspectives on*

Organizational Change. Eds. Charles Heckscher and Anne Donnellon. Thousand Oaks: Sage, 1994. 178-94.

Lewis, Theodore. "Studying the Impact of Technology on Work and Jobs." *Journal of Industrial Teacher Education*. *33* (1996): 44-65.

Ohmann, Richard. "Literacy, Technology, and Monopoly Capital." *College Composition and Communication*. *47* (1985): 675-89.

Peeples, Tim and Bill Hart-Davidson. "Grading the 'Subject': Questions of Expertise and Evaluation." *Grading in the Post-Process Classroom: Theory to Practice*. Eds. Libby Allison, Lizbeth Bryant, & Maureen Hanigan. New York: Boynton Cook, 1997. 99-113.

Selfe, Cynthia. *Technology and Literacy in the Twenty-First Century: The Importance of Paying Attention*. Carbondale: Southern Illinois UP, 1999.

Zuboff, Shoshanna. *In the Age of the Smart Machine: The Future of Work and Power*. New York: Basic Books, 1988.

15

WRITING ASSESSMENT AND THE LABOR OF "REFORM" IN THE ACADEMY

Margaret K. Willard-Traub

Oakland University

In this chapter I examine a specific variety of academic labor—the labor of writing assessment—and explore the ways in which still-evolving assessment practices nationwide both shape and are shaped by broader political realities impinging on the field of composition. First this chapter responds to the work of Richard E. Miller, who posits assessment as the central "bureaucratic" activity of the academy. Miller argues that, at a time when the institution is being reformed by "economic powers over which no single individual or corporate entity exercises control," denying the "symbiotic relationship" (216) that exists between intellectual and bureaucratic work may mean sacrificing the gains either could accomplish in the best interests of students. Second, this chapter responds to the notion held by scholars such as Peter Elbow and Pat Belanoff that "one of the inherent potentialities of portfolio assessment is to invite change. For the portfolio brings more of the writing process and the teaching process . . . right into the center of the assessment process" (32).

Elbow's and Belanoff's focus on change is a productive starting point for a discussion of the links between writing assessment and institutional reform. Although the use of writing portfolios in classrooms and large-scale assessments has comprised an "explosion" in the view of many,[1] discussions of portfolios most often are framed by an examination of changes in classroom practice, or by a retheorization of the role validity and/or reliability should play in large-scale assessment, for example. In these discussions, the labor of portfolio assessment also may be contextualized by the drive for educational "reform," but reform defined in ways that stress (changes in) ostensible problems such as grade inflation.[2]

The labor of writing assessment also is linked frequently to a notion of reform that uses some kind of improvement in student performance (or even increase in student autonomy) as its primary measure, but that pays scant attention to the potential of formal assessment procedures for supporting the professional development of teachers. Although much has been written of the uses of teaching portfolios for professional development,[3] here I would like to suggest that meaningful assessments *of students* designed to support the *professional development of teachers* are important not only because they help to improve the learning of students, but also because they can help to improve the widely varying working conditions under which teachers—full-time faculty, part-time faculty, and graduate students—labor. And for faculty who do not teach writing on a regular basis, or who may not view the teaching of writing as worthy of their labor, meaningful assessments involving collaboration and dialogue among colleagues offer the kinds of opportunities for seeing "the work that compositionists have done in rethinking the teaching of writing" that Joseph Harris argues is necessary if tenure-stream faculty in composition and English are to be persuaded to help improve the working conditions of all teachers of writing by themselves more often teaching first-year writing (64). Through the labor of assessment the work of writing instruction, in other words, is not "limited to the efforts of individuals, but . . . instead (is) made into a collective project, a means of bringing several faculty together to work at a new location in the curriculum" (Harris 64).

Nevertheless, assessment's "reform" function generally is equated with its ability to promote not collaboration but "accountability." "Accountability" as a buzz-word is currently pervasive not only within the academy, but also in the U.S. media in the context of discussion and debates about the aims and philosophies of public education; it is, perhaps, a word which in the current political climate signifies an accusation as much as it does an invitation to change.

The language of assessment and "reform" circulating within and outside the academy thus is bound up with calls for accountability on the part of educators, but this accountability most often is measured (often simplistically) in terms of the performance of students: high school graduation rates, standardized test scores, and the like. In order to focus on how assessment can improve the conditions under which students learn by improving the conditions under which college and university writing teachers labor, I would like to frame assessment and "reform" differently, however, using the professional development of faculty over time as a measure of accountability. Like Harris, I would argue that "improving working conditions (of all writing teachers) needs to be posed not simply as a labor issue but also as a means of improving the quality of undergraduate education" (61). Along with fair salaries, benefits, and job security, so, too, is formal, institutional support for the intellectual development of teachers necessary to improving the conditions under which we all labor, students and teachers alike.

Formal institutional support for their own intellectual development in turn can lead teachers, who have been given both the room and the encouragement to reflect on their classroom philosophies and methods, to give students greater room in their writing to maneuver around or beyond received ideologies. The case I discuss later illustrates how the opportunity to engage in sustained conversation about student writing can make possible for a teacher new insights about her pedagogy, leading her to consider unexamined assumptions underlying her reading and evaluation practices.

ASSESSING PORTFOLIOS: DEVELOPING PROFESSIONALS

At the University of Michigan (where I labored as a graduate student teacher and researcher), the move in the early 1990s to portfolios as a placement "technology" was occasioned first by the desire to offer entering students greater latitude in choosing how to represent themselves as writers: Aiming for a more "learner-centered" (Courts and McInerney 25), and context-specific, assessment than the timed impromptu essay had provided, we hoped to "include students in the conversation (about assessment), to better examine what it is they are learning, how they believe they learn, and what components of the educational system assist or prevent them in coming to know" (Courts and McInerney 27). Second, Michigan's move to portfolios was occasioned by the desire on the part of the writing teachers in the English Composition Board (ECB) who oversaw the entrance assessment, to acknowledge and encourage the intellectual work of teaching. The large-scale, portfolio entrance assessment, therefore, was developed to encourage dialogue between and among high school and university teachers about attributes of student writing and how those attributes were related to instruction, for example. (Re)conceptualizing assessment in this way was consistent with a view that holds that assessment and accountability should "honor (both) the purposes and lived experiences of students and the professional, collaborative judgments of teachers" (Moss, "Validity" 10). Robert Broad's description of the (exit) portfolio assessment at "City University" ("Crises") likewise outlines a desire to construct what Moss termed a "hermeneutic approach to assessment . . . that privilege(s) readers who are most knowledgeable about the context in which the assessment occurs, and that ground(s) those interpretations . . . in a rational debate among the community of interpreters" (7).

With this increased dialogue among teachers at Michigan, however, came the need for a common language that teachers could use when discussing attributes of student writing, and their relationship to assessment. In 1994, such a common language took the form of a scoring scheme that clustered attributes of student writing within four broad categories. On the basis of written feedback from portfolio readers in 1995, we developed a more complex analytical scoring matrix, but we ultimately were still dissatisfied with our heuristic, in particular because of the adverse impact we (and administrators) felt it had on the rate of agreement between readers in their placement decisions, and because the scores it yielded were not easily translatable into feedback that we could give to students. As a consequence of these concerns, we reconceived our criteria and the reading process for the 1996 portfolio assessment, trying to balance our desire to increase reliability of placement decisions, however, with a concern not to compromise the professionalism and integrity of our teacher-readers, nor to compromise a complex consideration of students' writing.

Over the winter of 1996, we held a series of research meetings with a group of 12 portfolio readers (all of whom taught different courses fulfilling the composition requirement or the precomposition "Practicum" course). We used these meetings to read and discuss a wide variety of both entrance portfolios and exit portfolios (or major essays) completed in the courses group members had taught, in order to develop lists of characteristics that should describe entrance portfolios at each placement level (Practicum, Composition, or Exempt). In this we followed as much as we could Broad's call for a shift from ranking students for purposes of placement, to assessing students' writing on the basis of the question, "with which . . . instructor will this writer grow and learn best?" ("Portfolio Scoring" 273), a question also underlying the placement process at the University of Pittsburgh.[4]

As we conducted these research and development meetings, we devoted substantial group time to the discussion of curricular and pedagogical concerns, enacting what Brian Huot described as "an epistemological basis (for the research) that honors local standards, includes a specific context for both the composing and reading of student writing, and allows for the communal interpretation of written communication" (561). (For a fuller discussion of the development of the entrance portfolio assessment at Michigan, see Willard-Traub et al. 1999.) At the conclusion of this series of meetings I conducted (and audiotaped) exit interviews with the members of the research group, asking them to reconsider in more depth a sample of student writing which the group previously had considered. An essay that played a central role in one of our winter research group discussions, and that also formed part of the basis for discussion during our exit interviews the following spring, was the "reflective piece" or cover letter for the portfolio of a student named "Kerry."[5]

This reflective piece contains in some ways an unremarkable description of the rest of the contents of the portfolio, yet it contributed to a split placement decision when the portfolio was first assessed by readers in 1995 and prompted a highly charged discussion again in the 1996 research group meeting:[6]

> My research paper called, "A Christian view of Homosexuality and the Gay Rights Movement," was written for my Bible class called Understanding the Times. We were told to write a research paper on a current social issue complete with endnotes and bibliography. A big requirement of the paper was to properly give credit to every source or quote we used so as to avoid any possibility of plagarism. This is my most recent paper. . . . I enjoyed writing this piece because, although it was a lot of work, It felt good to sit down and really know the subject. I spent many hours at the library researching the material and reading different books about the topic. I learned a lot more about the whole issue than I thought I would. I wrote the paper to Christians in an effort to inform them about the facts involved in the Gay Rights Movement. I also wanted them to know the biblical view concerning homosexuality. It is not really a paper for just anyone to read and be able to completely understand where I'm coming from. This paper was the most involved research paper I've written and also only the third I've written since eigth grade.

I would suggest that in this reflective piece, Kerry, who attended the Christian high school identified on the cover sheet of her portfolio, makes all the "right" moves for impressing portfolio readers with her seriousness as a writer: She gestures toward the time and effort she has invested in the paper, saying that regardless of the work she enjoyed the process; she portrays that process as one in which she vigilantly guarded against plagiarism, and one in which she learned more than she thought she would; she even goes so far as to identify explicitly her audience for the portfolio, a relatively rare move in the portfolios submitted by most entering students at Michigan.

But, despite these characteristics, as well as despite what I would suggest is the preponderance of evidence in the rest of the portfolio that would situate her writing clearly in terms of a straightforward Composition placement, Kerry's portfolio drew urgent responses from many of its (experienced) readers. One of the first two readers in 1995, the reader who placed the portfolio in Composition, nevertheless attached a flag to her decision, writing: "Student writes from Christian school, in a way not likely to be well received at UM. A comp class will address this harshly. Do we communicate anything? ww?" This reader's notation "ww?" suggests that, as part of her placement into the Composition course, the student also might be required to attend a faculty-taught "writing workshop" for extra guidance about her writing. The second reader in 1995, who placed the portfolio in Practicum, also attached a flag to her decision (an infrequently used signal, here used twice by two independent readers) and expressed offense more than alarm: "The 'Christian View of Homosexuality and the Gay Rights Movement' is one of the more offensive pieces I've read—repetitive and relies solely on a literal interpretation of Bible as evidence."

(RE)FORMING INTELLECTUAL-BUREAUCRATIC WORK: LEARNING TO READ "BETWEEN THE LINES"

After being placed (by a third 1995 reader) into Composition, we selected Kerry's portfolio to be read again by members of the 1996 research group. During this meeting, which involved extensive conversation about a few different portfolios, the collective assessment that readers made of Kerry's writing seemed even more conflicted than had the two (separate) assessments made in 1995.[7] Two readers in 1996, for example, raised the possibility that certain examples of student writing, including Kerry's, were more likely to invite ideological readings (or a different kind of ideological reading) on the part of assessors than would others; a third reader dismissed the notion that ideology—either a student's or a reader's—plays any role in the assessment of student writing.

One of the respects in which Kerry's reflective piece and portfolio are unusual compared to those of many entering undergraduates at Michigan at the time, and what I would suggest is significant for explaining the various and conflicted assessments surrounding them, is the inscription of a complex array of audiences—both the audience of assessment readers and an audience of Christians whom the writer wishes to inform "about the facts involved in the Gay Rights Movement" and about "the biblical view concerning homosexuality." Such a complex inscription of various and distinct audiences—and so of various and distinct relationships between the writer and those audiences—problematizes the notions of voice and subjectivity in her portfolio, shattering the illusion of a coherent, writerly "self" and complicating the practice of assessment for readers who, as Lester Faigley contends, at best oscillate between valuing a modern and postmodern view of the writing subject. The fact that one of the audiences that Kerry inscribes is composed of Christians whose ideology may differ dramatically from that of her other audience (the audience of portfolio readers) further complicates the assessment. Kerry herself writes that her essay on gay rights is "not really a paper for just anyone to read," suggesting her own awareness of the complexity and conflict involved in such an endeavor to write in the contact zone.

Tellingly, in an interview marking the conclusion of our work together devising the criteria we called "Descriptive Placements" (see Table 15.1, page 302), at the end of our series of research group meetings, one of the group members, a graduate student with substantial experience teaching writing, acknowledges the same complexity and also reveals how her own participation as a reader and researcher in the portfolio assessment helped her to develop a new ethics and a new practice for reading student texts. The quality of this teacher's reflection and of what she says about the evolution of her own approach to reading not only lends insights into how the subjectivities of what Miller would call the "intellectual" and "bureaucrat" circulate within various institutional sites; they testify as well to the power of a "bureaucratic" activity such as assessment for inviting change in teachers, as well as in students.

Miller argues that, as much as academics might like to believe otherwise, our individual scholarship and teaching are always being shaped by bureaucratic constraints, and will always be imperfectly realized because of this. Not acknowledging such a reality, Miller contends, inevitably leads academics to resist "even the most well-intentioned efforts to reform academic practice" and to experience ceaselessly feelings of frustration and "powerlessness" (205-06). In particular, Miller points to the "business" of assessment as the bureaucratic activity that most provokes a "felt sense of betrayal . . . (in) a workforce that has been lured by the promise of academic freedom and the unbounded pleasures of the life of the mind" (210):

> The important point to recognize is that *all* teaching positions in accredited programs require a terminal assessment of student work. . . . The central activity of reading and assessing the labor of others remains the same, whether the labor is that of a first-year student, an advanced graduate student, a metaphysical poet, or a postmodern theorist. Thus, the absolutely predictable anxiety that emerges around the business of grading papers . . . *must* be read as an expression of distress at discovering the essentially bureaucratic nature of teaching in the academy. . . . And even for those teachers who enjoy this evaluative work quite a bit, the business of separating the wheat from the chaff inevitably appears as a distraction from the more important work of delivering a good lecture, producing a solid piece of research, serving on an important panel at a national conference. (209-10)

Miller concludes that it is in recognizing that "*constraining* conditions are not *paralyzing* conditions" (211) that our best hope for reforming educational practice lies; and that fostering the development of a "hybrid persona—the intellectual-bureaucrat"—will produce an academic environment that rewards, for example, teaching as well as research, and "thinking creatively about administrative matters" (212), ultimately improving the working and learning conditions of students and teachers alike.

I would like to posit portfolio assessment—especially the dialogue that is part of teachers' collaboratively focusing their attention on rich examples of student writing—as an activity that can foster the development of an "intellectual-bureaucrat" who thinks creatively and humanely about her academic work. "Alicia,"[8] a PhD student in literature who was a member of the ECB's 1996 research group and who had several years of experience teaching courses fulfilling the introductory composition requirement, demonstrates the development of just this kind of thinking in the exit interview that concluded our work together.

In this interview, Alicia sets the agenda for our discussion by focusing on how rereading Kerry's piece had reminded her of a recent *PMLA* Forum on the role of interdisciplinarity in literary studies:

> As I'm rereading [Kerry's portfolio], actually I'm thinking about this morning when I was eating breakfast I was reading this piece in the

March *PMLA* by Valerie Traub and someone else, about interdisciplinary work. And one of the points of the piece was that in different disciplinary paradigms different kinds of things count as, or constitute evidence. . . .

She . . . is using the Bible as evidence. And, I mean, the writer does it really skillfully, I think. . . .

Again, it's not spectacularly framed, but just this idea that, you know how this (gay rights) movement started, what does it entail, and what does the Bible have to say? And that's *exactly* what she addresses, pretty systematically, and with a great degree of thoroughness. So it is a kind of social science piece, right? . . .

I mean she's looking at the purported intents of the movement, which aren't necessarily accurately portrayed in the paper, but to the best of her ability in reading them through and against the Biblical injunction against homosexuality, which is . . . a fairly complicated task, right.

Prompted by her reading of *PMLA* earlier that day, Alicia goes on to explain her new understanding of interdisciplinarity as a self-consciousness about what constitutes proof or evidence. And Alicia connects this new understanding of interdisciplinarity to what happens—and doesn't happen—in Kerry's essay, positing that if Kerry were to *acknowledge* explicitly that the Bible is not accepted as evidence in all contexts, but that nonetheless its validity would be accepted by her here; and that if Kerry were *reflective* about her reasons for including the Bible as valid evidence, then her essay (if not also her entire portfolio) would comprise an example of interdisciplinary work that Alicia would view as both "sophisticated" and unusual at the undergraduate level.

Having made these insights, Alicia goes on to reflect on how her own experience of reading portfolios and participating in the research group might have affected her ways of reading student writing:

I find myself, I'm not sure what I mean by this, but I feel like this time when I'm reading . . . portfolios, I'm looking at . . . the interstices of . . . things. . . . I guess reading between the lines would be another way (to say it), but actually it's not really reading between the lines. . . .

Like . . . I'm not as swayed or interested or engaged . . . one way or another in the social science paradigm or the close literary reading paradigm. . . .

I'm looking at sort of what, within that structure, like what's going on. Where I feel like earlier on in my reading, like years past . . . I was just looking at how well those forms were executed. Do you see what I'm saying?

And . . . this has to do with letting the student *establish* the authority of their text. And I think that has to do with . . . a sense of interdisciplinary reading too, because it's like, OK in this essay the woman [Kerry] is saying . . . OK she's not as reflective about it, but the implication is that "I'm using . . . the Bible, and I think this constitutes evidence for my paradigm." So I'm like, OK, I'll go with that. I don't believe it, but I'll go with it.

It's saying to this student . . . OK . . . I'm letting you set up the paradigm, you're legitimating it, you're working with it, and then I'll evaluate how effective it is on the basis of what you're giving me. And I guess that's what I meant by reading the interstices, or reading between the lines, or . . . allowing students in my mind more room to maneuver, maybe.

Although at the beginning of our interview Alicia leans toward wanting (still) to "disciplinize" Kerry's essay, identifying it as a "social science piece," by the end of the interview she no longer seems as invested in wanting to make such a judgment. Instead, she seems more *involved* with the ideas being expressed, and interested in engaging in what Peter Elbow called the "believing game": Thus, Alicia reads Kerry's essay sympathetically even though she may not agree with all (or even many) of its propositions.[9] At the end of the interview, Alicia also observes that she has become "much more flexible" in her teaching. Alicia sees some connections between this "flexibility" and her new practice of reading student texts but says she is unsure whether this new practice has emerged because of her experience as a portfolio reader or just because that is where she's "at" in her teaching at this point in time.

My sense then and now is that both of these reasons are true: such formal opportunities for reflection like Michigan's portfolio assessment, and the subsequent work of the research group, not only helped to improve the quality of teaching and of learning at the university; they provided occasions for graduate-student teachers like Alicia, along with the full-time teachers who were her colleagues, to exercise the kind of reflexivity which Pierre Bourdieu argues for in support of the pursuit of disciplinary knowledge. Bourdieu insists that such reflexivity helps us to scrutinize the "collective . . . unconscious embedded in (the) theories, problems, and . . . categories of scholarly judgment" (40) that shape our intellectual work. I argue such reflexivity also helps those of us in English studies to examine "the epistemological unconscious" (Bourdieu 41) of our own learning and professionalization—the assumptions we bring to our teaching and scholar-ship about how to define "good writing," for example—helping us to labor more intently in the spaces *between* disciplines.

Learning to see the interstitial spaces—what Mary Louise Pratt might term the *contact zones*—that exist between one discipline and another as fertile ground for reconsidering our beliefs and practices in turn ultimately encourages us to see as a productive work-space the ground that exists between the academy and the larger society. Thus learning to read (as Alicia would say) "between the lines," we have an opportunity for *reform-ing* not only our notions about the relationship between our "intellectual" and our "bureaucratic" work, but also about what it means to labor as "intellectual-bureaucrats" (Miller 212) within our fields of specialization and increasingly beyond them, in the complicated borderlands that constitute much of the terrain in higher education.

ASSESSING (ACADEMIC) LABOR

Interestingly, at a time when performance-based and highly contextualized assessment technologies such as portfolios have gained much intellectual and political ground because of the assumptions held by composition teachers and even by some administrators about their potential for serving as catalysts for institutional reform, new approaches to assessment may signify a backing away from teacher involvement in assessment. For exam-ple, "directed self-placement" (DSP) is described by Dan Royer and Roger Gilles as a procedure in place at their institution that they say upset "the prevailing student/teacher power relations by presenting students with an authentic educative choice" (54) about which of two introductory composi-tion courses they should take as they begin their college careers. This choice, "directed self-placement," shifts responsibility for the placement decision to students; students are encouraged to ask for help in making their decisions, but as Royer and Gilles describe it, "the placement respon-sibility lies with the student" (67) alone. Because students are responsible ultimately for thinking about how their writing might make appropriate a particular placement, Royer and Gilles claim that the "risk" of DSP (I under-stand this new "technology" now has an acronym, a sure sign of its wide acceptance) is virtually nonexistent: "it can't really fail" (70), they say, because teachers have not been primary participants in the placement decision.

I would agree with Royer and Gilles that, in fact, teachers cannot fail at a particular kind of work in which they have not much been involved. But in fact, I would say that in many instances of DSP it is very likely that we *do* fail. In the context of such an "assessment" process we risk failing our students, who do not have the experience of knowing that their teachers are *involved* in reading and understanding their writing, or as interested as they might be in becoming familiar with students' varied histories as learners.[10] And we risk failing ourselves (and by extension our students) by not using the opportunity presented by large-scale assessment for engaging in the kind of bureaucratic-intellectual work that can expand the boundaries of our professional training, reforming educational practice by fostering "an academic environment that rewards versatility as well as specialization, teaching as well as research, public service as well as investment in the self" (Miller 212).

I argue that bureaucratic assessment processes like DSP are just that, bureaucratic, with little potential for the kind of intellectual work that Alicia was able to accomplish as a portfolio reader and member of an assessment research group (saying nothing of the intellectual work Kerry might have accomplished in putting together the portfolio, or her high school teachers might have accomplished in designing their pedagogies in order to help her do this). Assessment procedures like the one at Michigan, which incorporated frequent opportunities for dialogue about student writing, and which involved teachers of diverse rank, experience, and disciplinary training, are most able to promote change in both the working conditions of teachers and the learning "outcomes" of students. Portfolio assessments like those at Miami of Ohio, Cincinnati and Pittsburgh, for example, although differing in substantial ways, also all incorporate significant opportunities for dialogue and so the potential for promoting change.

For example, at the time this chapter was written Cincinnati's exit process emphasized frequent dialogue within the context of "trio meetings" in which teachers of composition engaged in "lively and at times intense discussion of critical issues in writing evaluation" (Durst 288) throughout a given quarter. An entrance assessment like Michigan's might follow Cincinnati's lead in this regard, increasing the opportunities for readers to express the "evaluative differences" (Broad, "Crises" 248) undergirding a hermeneutic approach to assessment, by allowing for regular inter-rater dialogue. At the same time, it could be argued that Michigan's attitude toward "standardizing" strategies such as norming sessions and the use of a rubric evolved in such a way as to be consistent with the value that a hermeneutic approach attaches to diversity: Over the course of several years the norming sessions at Michigan changed substantially, finally encouraging readers "not to think of (the) criteria (appearing in the "Descriptive Placements" rubric) simply as a 'tool' that always could be applied in the same way by all readers to very complex sets of writing, but rather as a heuristic each reader could use as he or she made judgments about placement. We came to see, finally, that these criteria could help readers . . . be(come) aware of their own biases as they used these, or any other, criteria in making their judgments" (Willard-Traub, Decker, Reed, and Johnston 80-1).

The assessment experiences of Kerry and Alicia perhaps underscore this notion of change within a context that values diversity. Indeed, based on my experiences at Michigan and at my present institution, I continue to believe that the first rule of designing any assessment process should be to consider how it might promote positive change in individual students and teachers, as well as in larger structures inside and outside of the institution. At the same time, assessment processes must be designed in ways that make them flexible and able to respond to multiple, contending forces in continually changing curricular, institutional, and political contexts. The kinds of forces shaping any assessment process may include disciplinary-specific epistemological shifts, changes in institutional economies of value that privilege certain kinds of writing over others, and varying material conditions (like adequate release time) that make it possible (or impossible) for faculty to accomplish the necessary intellectual work of reflecting on and revising their bureaucratic practices. It may not be too ambitious to think about how an assessment process, for example, could provide both teachers and students with the opportunity "to rethink the assumed opposition between the academy and the business world, the intellectual and the bureaucrat . . . (and) to promote (in them) the development of . . . a state of mind . . . (characterized by) tolerance for ambiguity, an appreciation for structured contradictions . . . and a recognition of the inherently political character of all matters emerging from the power/knowledge nexus" (Miller 212-13).

I come to such a conclusion primarily because of the example of Kerry and Alicia, and other individuals like them—a student and teacher who never actually met but who would have lost a lot in the absence of the assessment that brought them into "contact": Alicia giving testimony to the sovereignty (if not the absolute "correctness") of Kerry's words; and Kerry, challenging Alicia and the other portfolio readers to conceive of their labor in the assessment process differently—and to reflect upon the ways in which they might construct for themselves "and for the academic community at large some inhabitable version of the intellectual-bureaucrat" (Miller

216). Although Kerry perhaps was finally correct in assuming that hers was "not really a paper for just anyone to read," it was one of the papers from which *everyone* involved in our portfolio assessment process learned the most, Alicia and myself included.

TABLE 15.1   1996/1997 Descriptive Placements

Exemptable attributes in student writing:
   1. Writing successfully isolates a task or frames a question for a specific audience
   2. Integrated evidence of mission/vision/larger purpose; writing effectively addresses the "so what" question
   3. Outstanding conceptual clarity even though concepts are often quite complex
   4. Sustained exploration or response which productively addresses the task or question
   5. Intellectual progress (development) and/or thoroughness appropriate for discipline and/or task
   6. Strong ability to choose, arrange and evaluate resources appropriate for a specific audience and purpose
   7. Structural organization that fosters a sustained exploration of a question or thorough response to a task
   8. Transitions serve a reader-friendly purpose
   9. Fluency with language

Comp attributes in student writing:
   1. Clearly articulates a position or assertion
   2. Provides some context for task, either in individual pieces or reflective piece
   3. Writing is more reader-based than writer-based
   4. Development of ideas relevant to topic or position
   5. Much of the evidence and/or support for ideas is directed and/or discerning
   6. Demonstrates global (overall) organization appropriate for task
   7. Demonstrates sentence-to-sentence (local) organization
   8. Variation in sentence structure and word choice demonstrates overall competence
   9. Relatively standard use of grammar and mechanics
   10. Maintains appropriate tone or register for task

Practicum attributes in student writing: (practicum portfolios always reflect some strengths, and the writing in them almost always makes sense; typically though, in more formal terms, they also reflect some or all of the following.)

1. Representation of intellectual tasks tends to be very simple or reductive
2. While papers have subjects, the focus tends to be unstated, unstable, or unclear
3. Writing is more writer-based than reader-based
4. Ideas lack development or development is uneven
5. Use of terms is simplistic or key terms remain undefined
6. Other perspectives may overwhelm student's voice
7. Much of the evidence is indiscriminate, inadequate, or ineffective given the task at hand
8. Local and/or global organization (including paragraphing) may be confusing or inadequate for the task
9. Sentence structure and/or word choice may be limited
10. May exhibit noticeable grammatical or mechanical errors
11. Inconsistent or inappropriate tone or register for the task at hand

ENDNOTES

1. Gail Stygall, Laurel Black, Donald A. Daiker, and Jeffrey Sommers describe the roots and implications of the profession's "tenacious belief" in portfolios, in their introduction to *New Directions in Portfolio Assessment: Reflective Practice, Critical Theory, and Large-Scale Scoring*.

2. In *Assessment of Writing: Politics, Policies, Practices*, contributor Richard Larson discusses the impact of increasingly common calls for "accountability" on assessment procedures, as well as the perception among teachers that "advocates of accountability . . . prefer instruments such as tests holistically scored by teams of trained readers, tests that can be judged according to precisely formulated criteria that are widely accepted and understood among those with experience in testing" (279) as opposed to the relatively "messy" instrument of portfolio assessment.

3. See, for example, essays by Chris Anson, Kathleen Blake Yancey, and Irwin Weiser in *New Directions in Portfolio Assessment: Reflective Practice, Critical Theory, and Large-Scale Scoring*. See also essays by Yancey, Weiser, and Robert P. Yagelski in *Situating Portfolios: Four Perspectives*.

4. Given that by 1996 the ECB was assessing close to 5,000 portfolios a year, and dealing with an instructional staff in excess of 150, neither were we able to make exactly the shift Broad calls for, nor were we able to follow exactly the process employed at Pittsburg where portfolio raters are asked to use a scale that is "based on the curriculum, the assumptions about composition, and the purposes of each course" (Smith 149). We were, however, able to change to a placement process that asked readers to describe a portfolio by choosing among three sets of characteristics (see Table 1), with each set linked to a particular placement. Because we had found that there was considerable variance, especially among instructors of Composition with regard to expectations for that course, we concluded that reforming our process in this way made the most sense. Until the time when we hoped portfolios would lead to consensus on expectations for Composition, we felt we could not ask readers to make judgments based either on a particular match between student and instructor or even between student and curriculum: Rather, we concluded that we needed to be asking readers to make decisions based on a normative construction of the various placement levels.

5. "Kerry" is the pseudonym I have chosen to identify this student throughout the remainder of the chapter.

6. Excerpts from Kerry's text are reproduced here exactly as they appeared to placement readers and to members of the 1996 research group, including any errors in spelling, etc. made by the student.

7. During the 1995 reading for placement, portfolios were read independently by two teachers who did not converse with each other, and who were not aware of each other's decision. "Split" decisions were decided by a third reader, who was aware of the previous split, but who usually did not engage in dialogue with either of the first two readers.

8. "Alicia" is a pseudonym.

9. Elbow describes two interdependent modes for seeking "truth": the "doubting game" and the "believing game." Whereas the doubting game "seeks truth . . . by seeking error" (148), the believing game arrives at understanding by refraining from doubt: "it helps to think of (the believing game) as trying to get inside the head of someone who saw things this way. Perhaps even constructing such a person for yourself. Try to have the experience of someone who made this assertion. To do this you must make, not an act of self-extrication, but an act of self-insertion, self-involvement—an act of projection" (149).

10. In the spring of 1999 the portfolio assessment at Michigan was discontinued by administrators who pointed to the financial cost of the program and to the fact that "placement into introductory writing courses can be achieved by less costly and less time-intensive methods" (Willard-Traub, Decker, Reed, and Johnston 82). In its stead was instituted a DSP process. Perhaps not surprisingly, this decision received a lot of attention not only from faculty but also from students. At the time this decision went into effect, I was teaching in the College of Engineering's technical communications program. One of my first-

year engineering students, after reading an article in the *Michigan Daily* about the portfolio assessment's demise, commented to me that he thought the administration's decision wrong-headed because "students need to know that teachers here care about their writing." The student writer of the *Michigan Daily* article took a somewhat different tack, arguing that the decision was unfair because entering students no longer would have a way to be exempted from the first-year writing requirement (about 5% of entering students each year were exempted on the strength of the writing in their portfolios). This writer also suggested that at the very least it was reasonable to expect the university to rebate to students any savings realized by discontinuing the portfolio assessment.

REFERENCES

Anson, Chris M. "Portfolios for Teachers: Writing Our Way to Reflective Practice." *New Directions in Portfolio Assessment: Reflective Practice, Critical Theory, and Large-Scale Scoring.* Eds. Laurel Black, Donald A. Daiker, Jeffrey Sommers, and Gail Stygall. Portsmouth: Boynton/Cook, 1994. 185-200.

Bourdieu, Pierre, and Loic J.D. Wacquant. *An Invitation to Reflexive Sociology.* Chicago: The University of Chicago Press, 1992.

Broad, Robert. "'Portfolio Scoring': A Contradiction in Terms." *New Directions in Portfolio Assessment: Reflective Practice, Critical Theory, and Large-Scale Scoring.* Eds. Laurel Black, Donald A. Daiker, Jeffrey Sommers, and Gail Stygall. Portsmouth: Boynton/Cook, 1994. 263-276.

_____. "Pulling Your Hair Out: Crises of Standardization in Communal Writing Assessment." *Research in the Teaching of English.* 35.2 (2000): 213-260.

Courts, Patrick, and Kathleen McInerney. *Assessment in Higher Education: Politics, Pedagogy, and Portfolios.* Westport: Praeger, 1993.

Durst, Russel K., Marjorie Roemer, and Lucille M. Schultz. "Portfolio Negotiations: Acts in Speech." *New Directions in Portfolio Assessment: Reflective Practice, Critical Theory, and Large-Scale Scoring.* Eds. Laurel Black, Donald A. Daiker, Jeffrey Sommers, and Gail Stygall. Portsmouth: Boynton/Cook, 1994. 286-300.

Elbow, Peter. *Writing Without Teachers.* London: Oxford, 1973.

Elbow, Peter and Pat Belanoff. "Reflections on an Explosion: Portfolios in the '90s and Beyond." *Situating Portfolios: Four Perspectives.* Eds. Kathleen Blake Yancey and Irwin Weiser. Logan: Utah State University Press, 1997.

Faigley, Lester. *Fragments of Rationality: Postmodernity and the Subject of Composition.* Pittsburgh: University of Pittsburgh Press, 1993.

Harris, Joseph. "Meet the New Boss, Same as the Old Boss: Class Consciousness in Composition." *CCC.* 52 (2000): 43-68.

Huot, Brian. "Toward a New Theory of Writing Assessment." *CCC.* 47 (1996): 549-566.

Larson, Richard. "Portfolios in the Assessment of Writing: A Political Perspective." *Assessment of Writing: Politics, Policies, Practices*. Eds. Edward M. White, William D. Lutz, and Sandra Kamusikiri. New York: MLA, 1996. 271-283.

Miller, Richard E. *As if Learning Mattered: Reforming Higher Education*. Ithaca, NY: Cornell University Press, 1998.

Moss, Pamela. "Can There Be Validity Without Reliability?" *Educational Researcher*. 23.2 (1994): 5-12.

Pratt, Mary Louise. "Arts of the Contact Zone." *Profession*. 91 (1991): 33-40.

Royer, Daniel J. and Roger Gilles. "Directed Self-Placement: An Attitude of Orientation." *CCC*. 50 (1998): 54-70.

Smith, William L. "Assessing the Reliability and Adequacy of Using Holistic Scoring of Essays as a College Composition Placement Technique." *Validating Holistic Scoring for Writing Assessment: Theoretical and Empirical Foundations*. Eds. Michael M. Williamson and Brian A. Huot. Cresskill, NJ: Hampton Press, 1993. 142-205.

Stygall, Gail, Laurel Black, Donald A. Daiker, and Jeffrey Sommers. Introduction. *New Directions in Portfolio Assessment: Reflective Practice, Critical Theory, and Large-Scale Scoring*. Eds. Laurel Black, Donald A. Daiker, Jeffrey Sommers, and Gail Stygall. Portsmouth: Boynton/Cook, 1994. 1-9.

Traub, Valerie and Mark Schoenfield. Letter. *PMLA*. 111 (1996): 280-282.

Weiser, Irwin. "Portfolios and the New Teacher of Writing." *New Directions in Portfolio Assessment: Reflective Practice, Critical Theory, and Large-Scale Scoring*. Eds. Laurel Black, Donald A. Daiker, Jeffrey Sommers, and Gail Stygall. Portsmouth: Boynton/Cook, 1994. 219-229.

_____. "Revising Our Practices: How Portfolios Help Teachers Learn." *Situating Portfolios: Four Perspectives*. Eds. Kathleen Blake Yancey and Irwin Weiser. Logan: Utah State University Press, 1997. 293-301.

Willard-Traub, Emily Decker, Rebecca Reed, and Jerome Johnston. "The Development of Large-Scale Portfolio Placement Assessment at the University of Michigan: 1992-1998." *Assessing Writing*. 6.1 (1999). 41-84.

Yagelski, Robert P. "Portfolios as a Way to Encourage Reflective Practice Among Preservice English Teachers." *Situating Portfolios: Four Perspectives*. Eds. Kathleen Blake Yancey and Irwin Weiser. Logan: Utah State University Press, 1997. 225-243.

Yancey, Kathleen Blake. "Make Haste Slowly: Graduate Teaching Assistants and Portfolios." *New Directions in Portfolio Assessment: Reflective Practice, Critical Theory, and Large-Scale Scoring*. Eds. Laurel Black, Donald A. Daiker, Jeffrey Sommers, and Gail Stygall. Portsmouth: Boynton/Cook, 1994. 210-218.

_____. Teacher Portfolios: Lessons in Resistance, Readiness, and Reflection." *Situating Portfolios: Four Perspectives*. Ed. Kathleen Blake Yancey and Irwin Weiser. Logan: Utah State University Press, 1997. 244-262.

16

BETWEEN ETHNOGRAPHIC AND VIRTUAL WORLDS

TOWARD A PEDAGOGY OF MEDIATION

David Seitz
Wright State Univeristy

Julie Lindquist
Michigan State University

THE VIRTUES OF PROXIMITY

By now, just about everyone believes we can improve any recipe for instruction if we add computers and stir. As part of a renovation of the liberal arts building, Wright State University devoted great sums of money to eight new computer classrooms intended mainly for first-year writing classes. Several years back, the English Department agreed to this conversion in exchange for a reasonable teaching load for full-time instructors. The Writing Program Administrator (WPA) knows the department's teaching assistants (TAs) and adjuncts will need time to learn how to integrate Internet and web-based technology into their teaching philosophy and methods. Yet it's tough to make space in the workday for such reflection as the building is being gutted and rewired, and the College of Liberal Arts has been scattered across campus for a 2-year diaspora.

These specific technological changes, and similar ones in many universities, will radically affect our future labor as composition teachers in multiple ways, such as increased online responding to student papers. As Cynthia Selfe has shown, these labor issues for literacy workers coincide with changes in students' literacies as the dominant culture, supported by corporations and government, educational institutions, and many parents' expectations, encourages further online engagement. As teachers of ethnographic research writing, we are beginning to sense an institutional pressure to focus on the computers in the classrooms, not on the physical world outside the university and the screen.

Following Selfe, and many others, we see this institutional and technological juncture as the moment when we must design a pro-active approach to shape our future teaching practices and analyze their possible social implications. We agree with Selfe that "Citizens are also responsible for understanding the social and cultural contexts for online discourse and communication . . ." (148). As ethnographers, we see the place for students analyzing these social and cultural contexts through the complex relation of physical and virtual environments.

When David complained to a colleague in sociology about the displacement of the liberal arts college faculty during the redesigning of their building, suggesting that they would *really* have to rely on e-mail now, his colleague agreed, adding "It's not the same as bumping into bodies." We begin this chapter by making a case for the heuristic and ideological benefits of "bumping into bodies" and its generative power for fostering the critical technological literacy Selfe and others have called for. Traditional ethnography—the practice of bumping into bodies—seeks to interpret meaning as it emerges from points of contact between material predicaments and discursive products. Technocritic Kevin Robins shares this concern for material conditions in his analysis of the "technological imaginary" that all too often fuels technological change without critical considerations of social needs. Robins contends the "technological imaginary is driven by the fantasy of rational mastery of humans over nature and their own nature" (137). Although we understand that there are as many possible uses of technology as there are users of it, we fear that when administrators and legislators act on technological faith, they implicitly view computer-mediated communication (CMC) as a technological mastery over material issues of our lived experiences. Ethnographic research—a form of inquiry that is beholden to local, physical spaces—can function as a valuable counter-practice to this over-determination of technology in teaching writing.

For this reason, we suggest that students' ethnographic research involving physical sites can lay important conceptual ground for students to more critically understand ethnographic research involving virtual sites.

Students' analysis of off-line material worlds from ethnographic perspectives can foster an awareness of mediation in their virtual worlds and digital technology when they later encounter cultural formations online. This awareness of cultural and technological mediation is a prerequisite for the rhetorical sensibility that leads to critical technological literacy. We first address the importance of continuing physically based ethnographic projects with students (even as our writing classes adapt to more CMC). We then suggest the possibilities and liabilities of a dialectic approach for a class that would explore ethnographic research in the physical world and the life on the screen.

In encouraging this dialectic, we offer one possibility for reconciling some of the tensions between two pedagogical approaches prevalent in professional debates over teaching college writing: computer-mediated composition and critical cultural pedagogies. Although these approaches to writing instruction appear to represent divergent or competing trends, the problem of *mediation*—between student and world, phenomenological and interpretive domains—is fundamental to both. Those who teach writing with computers wonder about the practical and epistemic implications of introducing a mediating technology into rhetorical situations. Those who teach students to critique cultural texts worry about how to make persuasive connections between the local and the systemic, between the experiential and the interpretive. We see our emphasis on the dialectic between what is embodied, material, and situated and what is symbolic, displaced, and seemingly virtual—that is, between realms or forms of mediation—as a way to attend to problems of learning and persuasion inherent in both computer-based and critical cultural pedagogies.

At this point, however, two disclaimers are in order. First, to design the theories and practices of this future teaching, we draw on our teaching of ethnographic research in physical field-sites. But because we have not yet taught online ethnographic research, we also draw on the research practices of ethnographers of online cultures and the practices of writing teachers who have created assignments for computer-mediated ethnographic work similar to our pedagogical goals. Nevertheless, teaching writing in an age of ever-changing computer-mediated technology is always about projecting future teaching practices. With this view in mind, we offer here our projected pedagogy of critically informed meditation as a necessary way to pay attention to the technologies that continually reshape our labor and our students' literacies.

Second, we offer an argument for a methodological dialectic—a shuttling of ethnographic research between physical and virtual worlds. In the spirit of that dialectic, each section of our chapter moves between the two kinds of teaching ethnographic research writing to show how students would examine these issues of cultural and technological mediation as a dialectical process. But before we set out this dialectic approach, we want to establish the value for continuing the teaching of writing and rhetoric through students' ethnographic research in physical field sites as a counter-practice to university administrations' push to use computer technology as an end in itself.

ETHNOGRAPHY AND EMBODIED KNOWLEDGE

Like other proponents of critical and cultural pedagogy, we believe that undergraduate writing instruction should, in James Berlin's often quoted words, teach students to "become better readers and writers as citizens, workers, and critics of their cultures" (145). Yet, although we see this as an important function of first-year writing courses, we share some of the concerns of recent critics of critical pedagogies such as Jeff Smith, Frank Farmer, Richard Miller, Kurt Spellmeyer, and Thomas Newkirk. Approaching this issue from different angles, these critics worry that the emphasis of cultural studies on what Cary Nelson calls describes as "the politics of signification" too often translates into equipping students with a one-size-fits-all debunking apparatus to apply to supposedly suspicious cultural phenomena. Our experiences with students' resistance to the claims and practices of critical pedagogy have convinced us that while students, like any of us, may not be fully aware of the ideologies that structure their lives, it is nonetheless important to approach conflicts between our own teacherly goals and students' worldviews with humility. For us, ethnography is a "kinder and gentler"—and ultimately a more persuasive—way to achieve the political and rhetorical goals of critical and cultural-studies writing classes. As Seth Kahn explains, many cultural and critical pedagogies make the mistake of viewing students as *potential* citizen-rhetors, rather than treating them as active practitioners of cultural work ("Grassroots"). As fieldworkers in familiar cultural scenes, students work not as critics who identify examples of unequal power relations in cultural texts but as participant-observers who enter and inhabit these texts to build structures of meaning "from the ground up." By becoming participant-observers of the everyday, in other words, students can witness cultural groups in the act of rhetorical invention, of establishing and performing commonplaces. As Sharon Crowley and Debra Hawhee make clear, commonplaces are patterns of ideology, "bodies of beliefs, doctrines, familiar ways of thinking that are characteristic of a group or culture" (76). In encouraging students to participate in these scenes of rhetorical invention, we aim to teach from a place where neither discourse nor "pure experience" is privileged. From this approach, we can honor "the relation between experience and discourse," a relation that "is not polar and hierarchical but dialectical" (Lu and Horner 38).

Beyond its uses as a way to practice and teach good rhetoric, we see local field research as a particularly appropriate method for nontraditional students, and not only because these students may not arrive in first-year English with language-inquiry resources that comport with academic styles and rituals of inquiry. For students from well-defined working-class and ethnic communities, ethnographic research offers opportunities for social affirmation that also enable self-motivated cultural critique. For those students whose class and cultural identities may be undermined by the forms of inquiry demanded by cultural studies pedagogies, doing field research offers them a chance to build their own critical theories from the inside out.

The ethnographic research writing of Rebekah Graves, one of David's students, illustrates how this kind of critique can emerge from students' observations, interviews, and cultural analysis.[1] For her project, Rebekah set out to learn about her mother's bowling league team. In her first observations of the team, Rebekah was surprised to see her mother's teammates' raucous and sometimes rude behavior toward the teams of older, retired women. As one woman put it to her team, "Guess what, ladies? We are bowling against those old bitches tonight. Remember to be as obnoxious as you can be to piss them off." Unlike the older women who treated the game seriously like a job, the middle-aged women implicitly viewed their bowling as an opportunity to escape the conventional social roles of mothers in the home and workers in the factories and in other working-class jobs. Preferring to act like girls Rebekah's age, they would challenge each other to sneak jello-shots past the snooty older ladies. Rebekah initially saw the middle-aged women's social meanings as only play, especially because they didn't particularly care how well they bowled. But through further observation and group interviews, Rebekah came to interpret her mother's friends' behaviors as responses to larger issues of power and control in the work and domestic domains of their lives—domains in which they most often had to answer to men. For Rebekah, the experience of field research invited social critique in a way that was ultimately more persuasive than the claims of critical theory delivered as course "content."

Teaching students rhetoric through their experiences in particular field sites fosters a pedagogy sensitive to students' class differences, as well. In teaching working-class students, we have continually seen the importance

of place in their ways of reading the world. If there is one cultural commonplace ethnographers studying working-class communities in America have
identified, it is that working-class people define their values and interests
in terms of a common place (see, e.g., Eckert, Foley, Fox, Heath, Lindquist,
Philipsen, Stack). People who inhabit these communities are not only less
geographically mobile than their middle-class counterparts, but their habits
of inquiry and critical understanding are also frequently tied to local experiences and interests. For example, Leah Brown, another of David's students, researched the "deli girls" at her job in a small independently owned
market in a medium-sized rural town. Among other conclusions, Leah
found how important the culture and atmosphere of this 40-year-old store
were for these women who worked there full time. The women compared
their interactions with each other and their regular customers to the com-
mercialized impersonality of the supermarket chains that have taken away
most of the local store's business.

As many critical teachers have learned, working-class students who are
required to try on the discourses of academic inquiry are sometimes suspicious of the motives of middle-class teachers who try to get them to "leave
home" in the interests of becoming more experientially and intellectually
mobile. For these students, the process of using a familiar location as the
place where research inquiry begins helps them understand what is at
stake for them in making such rhetorical moves. When students begin by
researching the narratives that organize experience in their home communities, they necessarily engage forms of situated, local knowledge that
might otherwise be left untapped as a learning resource.

We see, then, an orientation to the physical geography of the local
scene and to the materials of culture as an approach to rhetoric that helps
students to recognize the meaning and potential of their own embodied
knowledge. The idea that knowledge develops across conceptual and physical domains is a commonplace in the study of social cognition of learning
and activity theory. The implications of this view haven't been fully developed in composition studies, where (to borrow David Fleming's term) "big
rhetoric"—the idea that all social processes are semiotic and hermeneutic—dominates ("Rhetoric"). Yet Mike Rose's latest research on the social
cognition of various workplace activities demonstrates how embodied
knowledge encompasses specific spatial location, body languages, and
affects. Rose wants to dismantle the dichotomy between "mental activity
defined as abstract, theoretical, or conceptual and physical activity that we
define as material, concrete and applied" ("Our Hands" 152), so that educators can better understand the limits of the rhetorical in processes of
knowledge-making.

In "The Working Life of a Waitress," Rose takes his mother, a career waitress, as ethnographic subject to discover the social and cognitive constitution of the knowledge necessary for her job. What kind of knowledge, Rose wondered, did Emily Rose draw on to negotiate the simultaneous and overlapping systems of activity in which she had to participate from moment to moment? How could she remember orders, deliver food, effect an ongoing demeanor of sociability, and gauge customers' moods and reactions, all the while smoothly and efficiently managing her physical environment? He concludes that "the answer lies in the dynamic coherence of the automatic response and the quick thought; of a keen memory, but a memory keen in the physical moment; of the way routine contains within it multiple instantaneous decisions. . . . The key concepts here [are] related to coherence and rhythm, synchronicity, integration" (24).

Clearly, if we want to help students understand how everyday intelligences can serve them in their educational lives, if we want to establish connections between everyday activity outside the university and the work of writing and inquiry, then students should begin inquiry in the fields where these "other" intelligences operate. This is especially important for students who experience "knowing" as a process that confounds academic boundaries between knowing and doing, working and thinking. As Jennifer Beech recently showed in her exploration of working-class perceptions of the relation of academic work to forms of labor and class mobility, working-class students' doubts about the value of writing-as-inquiry arise not only from their views about what counts as "real" work but also from their experience of knowledge as embodied and organic. Our emphasis on the situational and embodied is not meant to devalue academic inquiry and the academic emphasis on distance, critique, and dialectic— only to make this academic inquiry more available to students who might otherwise find its terms alienating or inaccessible.

Nor do we mean to suggest that ethnography gives unproblematic access to experience. Postmodern anthropologists and critics (e.g., Rosaldo, Clifford, Clifford and Marcus) have for decades acknowledged that ethnography is not a pure or authentic form of experience or discourse. As Bella Dicks and Bruce Mason remind us, ethnography is from field to page "a form of mediation, which inevitably translates one form of knowledge (that of the research 'subjects') into another (that of the author/readers)" ("Hypermedia" 2.4). In that sense, Paul Atkinson concludes that "there is no textual format that pictures the social world as a perfect simulacrum" (p. 22, qtd. in Dicks and Mason, 2.4). We are all too aware that nobody can ever wholly inhabit another's embodied knowledge of lived experience— or be able to represent this experience unproblematically in text. But given that ethnography is itself a process of mediation, we believe that when our students have experienced first hand the difficulties of mediating cultural interpretations of material situations in their field sites, they have been better positioned to understand issues of power when representing cultures.

We often find students themselves raise ethical and political issues of cultural mediation when they move from fieldsite to analysis to representation. When Rebekah Graves sought out secondary research for her study of the women bowlers, she was surprised at the scarcity of academic research on white working-class women, particularly on their leisure choices. As a result of this frustration, she came to see herself as a spokesperson for these women's lives. Whereas Rebekah came to question the academic researchers, Ari Jennings, another student of David's, found herself questioning her initial ethnographic portrayal of the full-time workers at the local GM plant where she worked part time. Ari's father had worked his way up from line worker to labor management in the corporation, so Ari was both familiar with and wary of working on the line. Yet it was only when Ari compared her social position to the full-time workers that she saw their ambivalent responses to her as a "college hire." When Ari reflected carefully on these ambivalences, she refocused her study on issues of labor and education in the insider and outsider perspectives of the GM workers. It is this immediate engagement with the vexations of accounting for lived experience that can help students to witness imbrications of rhetoric in social and material lifeworlds.

One might object that the whole point of university education, and particularly education in writing, is precisely to teach students how to participate in processes of mediation, that we are in the mediation business, that our job is to share our expertise as mediators. One might, we recognize, begin to suspect that we are simply advocating the kind of education that happens outside the university "naturally," that we are merely promoting (as students themselves might say) "street smarts" over "book learning." But it is more accurate to say that we are beginning with *what is experienced as* the real, the most immediate, to understand processes of social construction rather than disengenuously stripping away layers of ideology to arrive at an institutionally sanctioned critical reading. What we presume to do, in other words, is to structure a way for students to understand practices of mediation by experiencing them, by putting themselves, bodily and experientially, in the way of interpretation. Students participate in mediations, observe their effects, and find themselves wrestling with the ethics of how to interpret these experiences for different purposes and audiences as Rebekah and Ari did. This approach is more effective because it does not begin by forcing students to mediate the experiences they have interests in preserving the immediacy of. Nor do the processes of ethnographic research erect a wall of theory separating students from their experiences.

As we argue throughout this chapter, ethnographers of online communications are also researching situated and local knowledge, but the study of an online social group's embodied knowledge is far more complicated, particularly for first-year college students new to ethnographic methods. Much of this embodied knowledge is unavailable within the mediation of computer technology; specifically, the proxemics and the kinesthetics of the field are gone. Yet as our discussion of embodied knowledge has suggested, we cannot critically understand virtual worlds and communications unless we have a grounded understanding of how we are always embedded in physical, material conditions. The economic and cultural overdetermination of computer technology requires that we address this problem for our teaching of writing from an ethnographic perspective; that is, these problems of physical and virtual lived experiences forced by the technological changes must become an integral part of our pedagogy.

We believe the embodied experience of mediation promoted by ethnography could be a precondition for greater critical awareness of technological mediation in computer environments. In the remainder of this chapter, we will address how three key features of CMC and virtual communites can act as catalysts for this critical awareness. First, students' comparative ethnographic research of local and online groups invites students to discover how much of culture is material. Second, online research can help our students determine larger social contexts for the local situations they research. And third, the mediation of hypertext can help us rethink the ways students represent their ethnographic research.

VIRTUAL ENVIRONMENTS, MEDIATION, AND LEARNING

Recent scholars of CMC have demonstrated that electronic spaces are not inherently virtual but enmeshed in specific material cultures (Hine, Hawisher and Selfe). Daniel Miller and Don Slater stress the importance of disaggregating the "pre-given entity called the 'Internet'" (15-16). When we research people's Internet use from this perspective, we begin with the assumption that users are not only consumers of mass technologies, but producers of cultural meanings embedded in local and material situations. In other words, people create *their* Internet. As researchers, we need to

examine how people select the specific technological practices and components that they endow with local cultural meanings from among the many
available possibilities of the Internet. Nevertheless, Miller and Slater argue,
the commercial discourse of "*the* Internet" often leads people to view the
Internet as a monolithic structure. This commercial discourse also makes it
harder for our students to analyze particular social meanings of space in an
electronic field site or indeed across several related sites.

If students first experience cultural mediation through their ethnographic research in physical spaces, these experiences will likely heighten
their rhetorical awareness of group members' implicit design and meanings of electronic spaces. When our students examine the interactions of
communication, identity, and location in ethnographic research of field
sites, they draw maps of the physical space. On these maps, they sketch in
how people negotiate their movements within it, claim ownership of it, and
mark it with cultural meanings understood by other members of the group.
For instance, one of David's students recognized how people of different
social classes congregated in particular sections of a suburban bar. Another
examined the workers' use of spaces in a local Wendy's restaurant, noting
how they would frequently retreat to the space next to the drive-thru window to hide from a particular manager's gaze.

In our projected course, after students experience the complexity of
cultural mediation in a physical field site, they would do ethnographic
research of an online community or group to learn how much of social
meaning is contingent on the interaction of physical bodies, physical space,
and material environments. We would have them explore what kinds of
power relations are manifested in this particular computer-mediated environment. How do these shifting social structures develop from online
behaviors and talk? How do these power relations evolve from the ways
various group members use, interpret, and possibly design these virtual
spaces? All these questions would interrogate the technological mediation
of sociocultural groups.

Two recent academic studies of specific online groups suggest possible
approaches for student field research in an online environment. Whereas
Nessim Watson's analysis of phish-net offers an example of negotiating
meanings of space within the realm of popular culture, Anandra Mitra's
research of conflicts within an Indian use net group shows how community members' constructions of online space are embedded in nationalist
discourses.

Watson's study of phish.net, an online fan community dedicated to the
alternative rock band Phish, examines the mediation of online space, symbolic actions, and power relations among textual bodies. At the time of

Watson's study, phish.net had 50,000 subscribers and was one of the largest online fan communities. As the subscribership grew, factions of the larger group attempted to create alternative online spaces, using separate listservs cross listed on the larger usenet subscriber list, to carry out specifically designated Phish fan transactions, mainly exchanges of tapes and concert information. Other subscribers began to call for listservs with restricted memberships, smaller rooms to preserve the sense of intimacy fans felt the online space was losing. In response to these actions, others sought to design enclaves of what they valued as pure fan behaviors by offering personally filtered digests of the daily postings. Some veteran members, however, rejected these efforts to redesign the space, claiming they violated violate the social democratic values of the Phish fan collective identity, a set of values meant to counter the commercialism of entertainment industry conglomerates (115-17).

Anandra Mitra's study of the usenet group "soc.culture.indian" also points to violations of culturally determined virtual boundaries but more on the scale of nationalist discourse. Mitra examines how the organizers of the larger "soc.culture" newsgroup tacitly shape the space like ethnic ghettos in a large city where outsiders are unwelcome. Yet, unlike city neighborhoods with physical boundaries of culturally defined spaces, usenet groups can all cross-post to several lists, which "makes it much easier to violate the conventions of 'neighborhoods'" (62). Mitra claims that most of the posters on this Indian usenet group are immigrants now residing in America or Europe who debate online the cultural and nationalist meanings of their previous home. Posters raise controversies over the place of Hinduism in India and India's conflicts with Pakistan. "The struggle that is commonplace in India now becomes a struggle over meaning in the space of the internet," sometimes in low-level harangues, suggestive of the physical violence in India itself (71). In the midst of these debates over India's social contradictions, immigrant representatives of other subcontinent groups (particularly Pakistanis, according to Mitra) cross-post anti-Indian nationalist rhetoric into the Indian net group, throwing verbal firebombs over the virtual walls. Mitra speculates that some posters on the Indian group also practice this same tactic on other subcontinent groups. Mitra's examples clearly indicate the re-creation of physical and nationalist borders within seemingly borderless virtual space.

These two field studies suggest how the cultural meanings of online space shape, and are shaped by, users' online personas. We believe that once students have analyzed embodied meanings of physical spaces, they will be more likely to understand and critically assess the intersecting constructions of identity and cultural meanings of place in online spaces. For instance, Corrine Calice at Wayne State University in Detroit encourages her students to test the borders of computer mediation and embodied identity in electronic chatrooms. In a sequence of assignments, Calice has her students electronically masquerade as the opposite gender in several chat rooms to investigate and reflect on how much they can escape their physical bodies in virtual spaces.

Calice's version of the participant-observer role requires a methodology appropriate to the material circumstances and values of many online cultures, such as those in MOOs and MUDs. If an ethnographer in virtual spaces means to participate in, and so personally experience, the behaviors of its inhabitants, then she must take on alternative fluid identities in the field site as a precondition for the fieldwork itself. When Sherry Turkle, noted psychologist-ethnographer of cyberscapes, researched the values and behaviors of participants in MUDs and MOOs, she took on multiple identities in these environments. Ironically, she even found in one MOO a character named Dr. Sherry who wanted to interview everyone about their online experiences. The character of Dr. Sherry turned out to be two psychology graduate students conducting their own research.

Even though Calice's assignment does not require the students to disclose their research to others in the chatroom, we identify this activity as beginning a kind of participant-observation unique to online environments—the ethnographer's equivalent of the necessary "hanging out" on the street corner "playing the dozens." If so, what about the ethical standard that the ethnographer make her presence and general purposes known to the community she means to learn from? In virtual spaces, group members are not continually made aware of the ethnographer's presence. Similarly, there is no infallible way to know how others' behaviors may change because of the presence of the ethnographer's body, and all of its cultural baggage, in the common space. So does the ethnographer lose this primary means of critically reflecting on her subject positions in relation to various members of the social group? These are valuable questions students would explore through specific local situations they encounter.

LOCAL SCENES, LARGER CONTEXTS

The greater opportunities for online research occasioned by growing computer technology in our classrooms can also help our students see larger social contexts for the local situations they explore physically and online.

Because the material situations our students research are so local, they can have difficulty identifying larger social contexts for the issues they discover within their field sites. When we taught in Chicago with multicultural students, Julie would joke about her students complaining that they could not, for example, find journal articles on the verbal performances of Lithuanian-American carpet installers. On the one hand, this perennial quandary can be a richly generative problem. In more traditional, text-based research writing courses, students often start with a publicly recognized issue (such as violence in public schools) and can practically pluck their sources prepackaged. In contrast, students doing ethnographic research must conceptualize their study more fully. The student researching the language games of Lithuanian-American carpet installers at work would need to brainstorm various domains of inquiry: In order to find other sources that situate the project in larger conversations and public concerns, he would have to develop keyword searches on issues or disciplinary terms such as labor, working-class culture, verbal performance, the nature of ritual, community and ethnic history, and local demographics. This process helps students practice important moves in more general research. They learn how to recognize what counts as a good question, to package their research as an original response to a customary problem, and to imbricate their findings into "gaps" in larger structures of inquiry.

In addition to these advantages of traditional ethnographic research projects, working online offers students yet another way to locate issues that emerge from their field research in larger contexts of inquiry. Students can situate their local ethnographic observations in wider domains by interrogating the discourse of Web sites or newsgroups related to their field sites. This approach could work several ways. Students might, for example, conduct cross-cultural research by finding on the Internet other branches of the same group or organization they are learning about. Similarly, teachers might set up correspondences between students researching similar cultures or cultural phenomena in different physical locations. When Julie taught ethnography in the deep south, she found that students' deep commitments to local cultural institutions left them with few global points of reference against which to read cultural processes. After being directed to brainstorm cultural memberships and possible sites of field research, they collectively generated a list of area churches, almost all of them Southern Baptist. Students like these, who live in isolated areas and whose repertoire of social experiences extends only as far as the outskirts of their rural communities, could clearly benefit from online access to other groups, other places, other scenes. In a future incorporating more computer-mediated technology, Julie's students could gain access to other perspectives about what it means to be southern and Christian through e-mail partnerships with David's students researching religious communities in Ohio.

Students might also analyze larger representative Web sites or newsgroups of their local field sites, comparing the officially sanctioned values and purposes of the larger group to locally situated behaviors and assumptions from the field. A student in Julie's class researching the culture of her local Baptist church could set her analysis of her church's "organic" culture against the corporate culture, or official discourse, of the Southern Baptist convention. Many sociocultural groups in the United States and the world may not have access to, or interest in, representing themselves on the web or Internet (see Hawisher and Selfe). So this approach would likely work best for students doing field research on local branches of larger organizations or workplaces connected to large companies. It could also work for some informal groups, like fan groups, who are more likely to inhabit the net.

It is also important to differentiate what kinds of viewpoints students would likely find in newsgroups and Web sites. Whereas the conversation of newsgroups would offer multiple perspectives that would enrich the students' view of the local situation, official Web sites of organizations and companies will likelier illustrate authoritative discourse. Studying this language can show the researcher how the larger communicative economy circulates symbolic actions, images, and beliefs in which the local group participates. Clearly, we would not expect our students to render comprehensive analyses of such communicative economies or conduct ethnographic research comparing an organization's online public face to that used in its upper echelons. Yet if students paid some attention to these various levels of social structure—to how particular forms of communication, beliefs, and expected behaviors circulate between local situation and larger social context—they might be in a better position to recognize the larger implications of power relations they observe in their field sites. To return to the previous example, a student doing fieldwork in churches in the deep South could interrogate differences between what she sees happening in her own church and at various Baptist newsgroups and Web sites.

ETHNOGRAPHIC MEDIATION AND HYPERTEXT FORM

Finally, working with hypertext and multimedia technology can help us rethink how students represent cultures in their ethnographic research. Postmodern theories have demonstrated that linear text cannot adequately represent the embedded, overlapping, and conflicting worlds circulating within a cultural group. Moreover, the ethnographer often has to translate the visual rhetorics within a cultural experience into a written form that removes the social meanings further from the group he or she is trying to represent to others. Elizabeth Chiseri-Strater and Bonnie Sunstein well understood these constraints of linear narrative and cultural analysis when they built ethnographic portfolios into their writing pedagogy. As the authors describe it, the ethnographic portfolio includes not only texts that emerge from students' experiences in the field (observation and interview notes, interview questions, etc.) but also collected items and artifacts. Sunset and Chiseri-Strater also suggest including "maps, transcripts, sketches or photographs" as possibilities (37) to illustrate the material density of cultural experience.

In just this way, we envision hypertext ethnographic portfolios that will help students render their cultural interpretations in more textured ways, allowing them to present the complexity of multiple voices and group members' different interpretations. In hypertext, student ethnographers could also juxtapose the visual worlds of the field site with the verbal performances of its group members. Additionally, the necessity of choosing between writing ethnography in linear or hypertext form makes the students' decisions of interpreting and representing culture all the more visible and concrete. Here again, we have opportunities to be critically reflective with our students about the mediation of the technology—what it can and cannot offer, and how its limitations may tacitly promote some forms of cultural representation over others. The physical act of designing hypertext arrangements may make student writers consider more thoroughly how social life is layered, textured, imbricated in other contexts. This work could also lead to productive discussions about the rhetorical effects of these choices, about ethnography as persuasion—and indeed, about the rhetorical nature, and critical potential, of all processes of information selection, documentation, and narration.

Moreover, when students publish hypertext ethnographies on the web where their research participants may read it, they become more aware of the ethnographer's ethical responsibility toward a dual audience. As Clifford Geertz articulated this responsibility, the ethnographer's credibility lies in demonstrating to an audience of outsiders, most often academics, the experience of "being there" while maintaining the integrity of insiders' perspectives of "being here." When Eileen Williamson created her Web site on the Boomtown Babes, a locally celebrated girls' drill team in Burkburnett, Texas (a town known for its oil boom in the early 1900s), her concern to treat the group in "a responsible and tasteful manner" shaped every aspect of the site design. Eileen organized the pages by cultural themes from collective stories—such as the girls; rites of passage of on the team, team traditions, try-outs (including mandatory weigh-ins), and uniforms—told by former Boomtown Babes ranging from the team's foundation in 1979 to the present. As a former resident of Burkburnett and a cheerleader who did not make the Babes team when she was in high school, Eileen had a skeptical and more distanced view of the team. Over the course of her interviews, however, Eileen learned about the strength these women drew from each other and how their experiences inspired their confidence later in life. As her respect for former Babes grew, Eileen tried to avoid calling attention to the negative aspects on the site, such as the frustrations some team members endured for the team's official image of physical beauty. Yet, when some of the women did reveal difficult experiences, she knew she "couldn't just leave it out"—that she "had the responsibility to be their reporter"(personal interview with Williamson). In the end, she developed two separate links from the subpage "Life After Babes," one entitled "read about their stories" and another, "learn about their issues." Thus, Eileen recognized that her ethical concerns were an issue of web design as well as writing. Although not many of the women did bring up painful memories, once Eileen published her site, several women who read the site wrote stories to her that "contained more negative sides." Eileen believes her careful representation of the Boomtown Babe culture helped inspire these other women's trust.

Eileen's project grew out of Nancy Mack's folklore class at Wright State University in southwestern Ohio. Having to interview people over the Internet who were located in Texas and all over America made her more conscious of her responsibilities to this broad audience that were also her group participants. Consequently, technological issues of access in both interviewing group members and distributing her interpretations to the group across space further alerted her to how she could better serve the group as folklorist by offering a website. From her interviews with nearly 30 people, she "knew they would want to read it." Having looked at other Web sites related to drill teams, she also saw that none of them told the women's stories. She also needed a way to collect all the interviews, photos, and artifacts in one space convenient to all without having to make "possibly 300 copies if you consider every drill team member over the years."

In this spirit, Eileen's site also offers a space for women to write in their Babe stories. But technological and ethnographic issues of access and representation aren't always about large gaps in space and time; some situations might call for websites to surmount other kinds of accessibility issues. At Wayne State University, Marshall Kitchens (English 3010), co-teaching with Ruth Ray, had students work collaboratively with local senior citizens to write ethnographic memoirs embedded in historical research of Detroit. The students posted these individual and collective ethnographic projects to a website now accessible to the seniors in the nearby community centers as well as a university audience.

When we add this technological complexity to the students' writing tasks, we need to pay attention to issues of their computer access, time constraints, and technical abilities. As Cynthia and Richard Selfe remind us, when teachers pursue the cutting edge of technology, students are often the ones who get sliced, particularly working class students. But we can also take their advice and work with the trailing edge, using not video clips and sound waves but simple visual juxtapositions of image and text. Marshall Kitchens' (American Studies 2010) recent teaching with the Wayne State students in Detroit offers a good model. In his cultural studies course, Kitchens' students created web collages of texts and images by excerpting and analyzing critical writings they read on city living and juxtaposing these writings with images of Detroit. Each students' Web page highlights a local cultural theme tied to issues of urbanization and postmodern experience using icons, landmarks, or locations that show Detroit's complex meanings. For instance, one student contrasted pictures of storefront churches in Detroit to the opulence of the surrounding suburb's churches. With these images she interweaves critical text about the urban and suburban fortification of churches and the resulting tension between welcoming newcomers and keeping out perceived dangers. Another student used issues of consumerism and architectural space to look at historical and current photos of a specific downtown shopping area and its deterioration over the past century. To demonstrate the severe effects of local advertising campaigns, another student juxtaposed images from liquor advertising billboards and their environment in specific Detroit neighborhoods. These students' projects echo Bakhtin's theories of the centering and de-centering forces of language and their rhetorical effects on power and authority in these urban landscapes. Yet the students did all this using their class time and what they learned in two lessons on Netscape composer, a simple hypertext editor.

CONCLUSION AND CAVEAT

Moving between local and online sites impels students to experience tensions between place and placelessness, between levels or spheres of mediation. Although technologically mediated field research does not guarantee successful critical thinking, we continue to insist that the potential for technology in teaching will be more fully realized when it follows from the experience of fieldwork in material cultures. Robins reminds us that "through the development of new technologies, we are, indeed, more open to experiences of de-realization and de-localization. But we continue to have physical and localized existences. We must consider our state of suspension between these conditions" (153). As the technological situation in our classrooms continues to change the ways we teach writing, and what counts as writing, we both find ourselves experiencing that uneasy suspension between our material conditions and the "de-realized" domains of computer-mediated environments. We think a dialectic pedagogy of online and material ethnographic research will promote our students' crucial analysis of this "state of suspension."

ENDNOTE

1. Our students have given permission to use their real names when we refer to their written work. In this way, we mean to show our admiration for their research and their critical insights. In cases where we have referred to other teachers' students' writings, we have omitted all the names.

REFERENCES

Beech, Jennifer. "Writing As/Or Work: Locating the Materials of a Working-Class Pedagogy." Diss. U of Southern Mississippi, 2001.
Berlin, James. *Rhetorics, Poetics, Cultures*. Urbana, IL: NCTE, 1996.
Brown, Leah. "A Little Deeper into the Deli." Unpublished essay, 1999
Calice, Corrine. Embodied Identity and the Internet. http://www.english.wayne.edu/~calice/index.html. Retrieved on June 13, 2001.
Chiseri-Strater, Elizabeth, and Bonnie Stone Sunstein. *FieldWorking*. Bedford, MA: St. Martin's, 2000.
Clifford, James. *The Predicament of Culture*. Cambridge, MA: Harvard UP, 1988.
Clifford, James, and George E. Marcus. *Writing Culture: The Poetics and Politics of Ethnography*. Berkeley: University of California Press, 1996.
Crowley, Sharon, and Debra Hawhee. *Ancient Rhetorics for Contemporary Students*, 2nd ed. Boston, MA: Allyn and Bacon, 1999.

Dicks, Bella, and Bruce Mason. "Hypermedia and Ethnography: Reflections on the Construction of a Research Approach." *Sociological Research Online.* 3.3 (1998).

Eckert, Penelope. *Jocks and Burnouts: Social Categories and Identity in the High School.* New York: Teachers College Press, 1989.

Fleming, David. "Rhetoric as a Course of Study." *College English.* 61:2 (1998): 169-91.

Foley, Douglas. *Learning Capitalist Culture: Deep in the Heart of Texas.* Philadelphia, PA: University of Pennsylvania Press, 1990.

Fox, Aaron A. "Split-Subjectivity in Country Music and Honky-Tonk Discourse." *All That Glitters: Country Music in America.* Ed. George H. Lewis. Bowling Green, OH: Bowling Green State University Popular Press, 1993. 131-140.

Geertz, Clifford. *Works and Lives: The Anthropologist as Author.* Stanford, CA: Stanford UP, 1988.

Graves, Rebekah. "Power and Control Within a Women's Bowling League." Unpublished essay, 1999.

Hawisher, Gail E. and Cynthia L. Selfe. *Global Literacies and the World-Wide Web.* New York: Routledge, 2000.

Heath, Shirley. *Ways With Words: Language, Life, and Work in Communities and Classrooms.* Cambridge: Cambridge Univeristy Press, 1983.

Hine, Christine. *Virtual Ethnography.* London: Sage Publications, 2000

Jennings, Ari. "Work Ethnography at General Motors." Ethnographic Paper for English 101, Wright State University, 2001.

Kahn, Seth. "Grassroots Democracy in Process: Ethnographic Writing as a Site of Democratic Action." Diss. Syracuse University, 2002.

Kitchens, Marshall. American Studies 2010: Introduction to American Culture, 1998. Retrieved on June 13, 2001. http://www.english.wayne.edu/kitchens/Am Studies.html

_____. English 3010: Ethnography and Detroit History, 1999. http://www.english.wayne.edu/students/index.html. Retrieved on June 13, 2001.

Lindquist, Julie. *A Place to Stand: Politics and Persuasion in the Working Class Bar.* New York: Oxford UP, 2002.

Lu, Min-Zhan and Bruce Horner. "The Problematic of Experience." *College English.* 60 (1998): 257-77.

Miller, Daniel and Don Slater. *The Internet: An Ethnographic Approach.* Oxford: Berg, 2000.

Mitra, Anandra. "Virtual Commonality: Looking for India on the Internet." *Virtual Culture: Identity and Communication in Cyberspace.* Ed. Stephen Jones. London, Sage, 1997. 55-79.

Nelson, Cary. "Always Already Cultural Studies." *The Journal of the Midwestern Modern Langauge Association.* 24.1 (1991): 24-38.

Philipsen, Gerry. *Speaking Culturally: Explorations in Social Communication.* Albany: SUNY Press, 1992.

Robins, Kevin. "Cyberspace and the World We Live In." *Cyberspace, Cyberbodies, Cyberpunk: Cultures of Technological Embodiment.* Eds. Michael Featherstone and Roger Burrows. London: Sage, 1995.

Rosaldo, Renato. *Culture and Truth: The Remaking of Social Analysis.* Boston, MA: Beacon, 1993.

Rose, Mike. "Our Hands Will Know": The Development of Tactile Diagnostic Skill—Teaching, Learning, and Situated Cognition in a Physical Therapy Program." *Anthropology and Education Quarterly.* 30.2 (1999): 133-61.

_____. "The Working Life of a Waitress." *Mind, Culture, and Activity.* 8.1 (2001): 3-27.

Selfe, Cynthia L. *Technology and Literacy in the Twenty-First Century: The Importance of Paying Attention.* Carbondale: Southern Illinois University Press, 1999.

Stack, Carol. *All Our Kin: Strategies for Survival in a Black Community.* New York: Harper and Row, 1974.

Turkle, Sherry. *Life on the Screen: Identity in the Age of the Internet.* New York: Simon and Schuster, 1995.

Watson, Nessim. "Why We Argue About Virtual Community: A Case Study of the Phish.Net Fan Community." *Virtual Culture: Identity and Communication in Cyberspace.* Ed. Stephen Jones. London, Sage, 1997. 102-32.

Williamson, Eileen. The Burkburnett High School Boomtown Babes. Retrieved on June 13, 2001. http://members.nbci.com/burkhs89/babes

17

SUSTAINING COMMUNITY-BASED WORK

COMMUNITY-BASED RESEARCH
AND COMMUNITY BUILDING

Jeffrey T. Grabill

Michigan State University

There has been much written of late regarding "the community" as a site to relocate our work. This comes in the form of books and articles on community literacy and service learning, and within technical and professional communication, in the form of interests in public policy, risk communication, and the civic functions of writers (e.g., Peck, Flower and Higgins on community literacy, on service learning, Adler-Kassner, Crooks and Watters, Flower, Bacon, Huckin). For the most part, community-based work has been praised for injecting more "realism" into writing assignments (Huckin), for advancing "the conventional goals of writing instruction" (Bacon 39), and for generally making the communicative functions of the composition classroom "matter" (Adler-Kassner et al. 2).

However, my fear is that we have launched ourselves into the community without much understanding of communities or of how our work affects the communities we enter. Although I support most community service learning and composition's interest in community-based work, my opening paragraph, as selective as it may be, illustrates some commonplaces of community work in composition: the way in which we often rearticulate community work in terms of traditional university classroom needs; the emphasis on teaching and/or service; and the almost nonexistent interrogation of the concept of "community" or of the affect we have on communities through our work.

Linda Flower articulates some of these very same concerns (concerns I'm sure many others share). She writes that "town and gown" relationships have always been strained, have always been marked by asymmetries of power that current compositionists would be well served to remember. She also notes that the current enthusiasm for community-based work is at least to some degree a function of cyclical interests, and that this enthusiasm will wane unless community-based work is "rooted in the intellectual agenda of the university" (96). Flower calls for community-based work that is animated by a spirit of inquiry, and although this has a precise meaning for Flower, I want to pick up on the general spirit of her argument and on her insistence that community-based work be rooted in the intellectual work of the academy. Rooted, in other words, in research.

My focus on research is not based solely on institutional value systems, although at most colleges and universities, research is more highly valued than teaching and service. My argument is that community-based work *requires* research. Any serious interrogation of "community" requires inquiries into the nature and meaning of communities themselves. And any serious, sustained community-based work that avoids the cyclical attentions of academic fashion requires the sustained and sustainable activities that community-based research can provide. In this chapter, then, I argue that writing researchers can indeed be useful to the communities we work with, but that in order to be useful, compositionists and the discipline at large must find a way to sustain community-based work. I make this argument by focusing largely on the *practices* of research, the often invisible activities of a researcher than can and often do affect research participants and the research itself. I focus on these practices as activities that must change us and the way we approach communities and community-based work if they are to be of any use for community development and change.

UNDERSTANDING COMMUNITIES

I don't think we, as writing teachers and researchers, understand communities very well. Outside of important and relevant work on community as an audience construct and interests in civic rhetoric (e.g., Ervin, Herzberg, Miller, Cooper and Julier), we haven't thought critically about the dynamics of "real" communities. As I argue, this is a problem. We can understand communities by seeing community-based work as activities that require inquiry, and in many cases, full-blown research. An inquiry-focused approach to community work will first help us understand more fully the communities with which we are working, and second, an inquiry focus will change the nature of our work with communities because the methodologies used, problems raised to be solved, and the practices required of us will be significantly different than our current discourse (at least) about working with communities. I begin with a framework for understanding communities that assumes their complexity and the need for inquiry on our part.

What I take from readings of recent attempts in political and social theory to define community is that it is relatively easy to name small, homogenous communities, like tight cultural or family groups, particularly when they are situated within a shared space. The task becomes more difficult when confronted with a contemporary heterogeneous society or distributions of people across time and space. In such a context, sociologists like Anthony Cohen argue that community is constructed symbolically as a system of values, norms, and moral codes that provide boundaries and identity (9). For Cohen, the term "community" is relational. One locates community by recognizing boundary construction (see Sibley as well). Although some boundaries may certainly be material or biological, most are symbolic—constructed through the communication of shared symbols and meanings. Boundaries are, in other words, rhetorical. Any discussion of community, therefore, must deal with the diversity and fluidity of communities, with the inherent difficulty of understanding communities, and with the issue of how they are constructed.

Communities are constructed and can be conceived in terms of any number of issues: race, ethnicity, spatiality, ideas, or other affinities. Citizens, activists, and others help construct communities in many ways. I have worked with organizations, both large and small, that have helped construct community around issues such as crime and community safety (see Grabill, chapter 5). I have also seen community constructed around housing issues, political issues, health issues (think of the history of HIV/AIDS activism), and institution building (e.g., civic associations and advocacy groups). What most of these examples have in common is the necessity of constructing community—or more properly—of participating in the always ongoing processes of community construction.

A community, then, is a highly variable and situated construct, and it is fair to say that even within a given geographic area, various "communities" can coalesce around different issues and institutions, making the determination of exactly which community writing teachers and researchers are working with an open inquiry question. Given all that we

don't know and understand about the relationships between writing programs, teachers, researchers, and communities, there is a real need to
frame the complicated processes of work with communities as a research
problem that deserves the attention of faculty. "Research," in this sense,
means at least two things: First, community involvement of any kind—
service learning, outreach, and explicit research—should begin with the
assumption that communities are not found places but moving targets.
And so we might ask questions like "who is the community with whom we
are working?" and "in whose interests are we teaching/serving/research-
ing?" Basic, fundamental questions about who, exactly, are these people
with whom we are working, how this community formed (its history, passions, issues and interests), and what assets they have and needs that they
possess that will impact our interactions with them. Understanding a community in these ways seems a necessary precondition to ethical, sustainable work outside the academy.

There is another, more engaged sense of community-based research
that is recognizable as such. This type of community-based work involves
researchers working with communities to solve problems or develop a
community in ways articulated by community members. My sense of community-based research comes from experiences and publications associated with the Loka Institute, although there is a considerable body of relevant
literature on the subject of community-based research and related
approaches such as participatory and other action research methodologies
(e.g., Sclove, Scammell and Holland; Greenwood and Levin). Loka is a nonprofit organization founded in 1987 that is dedicated to making science
and technology more responsive to citizens, communities, and larger democratic processes. The Institute sponsors publications, networks of
researchers and activists, and a conference.

I went to the Loka conference during the summer of 2000 looking for
definitions of community and community-based research and was pleased
not to find many. I was also pleased that people were uncomfortable about
the lack of definitional consensus because it made for a productive meeting. Community-based research is generally thought of as research that
involves citizens working with professionally trained researchers in a com-
munity-driven process to answer local questions or solve local problems.
Much like discussions of the role of participants in writing research, community-based researchers are focused on developing the relationships necessary to engage community members in the practices of research, analysis, and writing. Community-based research is also action driven, and so
community outreach activities like education, political and social change,
and policy making are often explicit project goals.

Community-based research is not without its conceptual and practical problems. Those involved spend considerable energy defining what "counts" as community-based research, usually on the basis of the nature of community participation: Is research done on community members or with them? Are community members supplying questions and initiating research projects or not? Are community members primary participants or merely consultants? And so on. To do "true" community based research is extremely difficult: Communities must be well organized; researchers must be open and flexible to working in new ways (ways that funding cycles aren't sensitive to); and meaningful participation is difficult to achieve.

I don't want to get trapped in the definitional squabbles and problems of community-based research because they distract from the two key issues that I, at least, take away from this approach to community-based work. The first is the persuasive argument that locating research in communities—particularly communities of need—should fundamentally change how research is conceived, practiced, and used. Community-based researchers share with participatory action researchers a concern—supported by considerable evidence—that traditional research simply relocated to the community can be useless and even violent.[1] There is an implied conversion narrative here: Community activists are saying "change your ways" to universities, and I wonder if we in writing studies have heard that call. The second issue has to do with community-building, another implied message. One of the burdens of community-based research is the necessity of building meaningful relationships with specific communities. In other words, the key research practice may be community and institution building, and this, I suggest, is a radical departure from our current understanding of what research is and what researchers do.

COMMUNITY AND INSTITUTION BUILDING

When most of us think about research, we consider issues that motivate inquiry (questions, problems, activist commitments) and issues of method (e.g., data sources, collection, analysis). We don't often think about the practices of research and how they impact both our studies and the people with whom we are working (see Sullivan and Porter). It is precisely the practices of community-based research that interest me, particularly the need, as I have argued, to participate in community and institution building in order to help produce useful knowledge and community change. I want to explore these practices of community building largely through a narrative of my own involvement with one community.

In claiming that community-based research involves community-building, I am building on my argument that communities must be built. The primary means by which communities are constructed are rhetorical, through the symbols that represent the values, morals, codes—the ideologies—of a given community. In other places, my colleagues and I have argued that institutions are similarly constructed (Porter, Sullivan, Grabill, Blythe, and Miles). Therefore, the issue is how to construct communities and their related institutions such that they reinforce each other. As community-organizer Harold DeRienzo, writing about the dynamics of community building notes, "If a community is a collection of people united around common goals, then institutions are those vehicles created by the community to achieve shared purposes" (11).

The most concrete approach to community building that I am aware of is called asset-based community development (Kretzmann and McKnight). Asset-based community development is an approach to community development that positions itself in stark contrast to current social service practice. The "traditional path" to community development, what Kretzmann and McKnight call a deficit model, is an approach that focuses exclusively on needs. Kretzmann and McKnight—who are collectively communications researchers, sociologists, community organizers, and planners—argue that such a focus on needs and problems fails to lead to community building and ultimately fails to solve problems. They describe the deficit approach in the following way:

> Public, private and non-profit human service systems, often supported by university research and foundation funding, translate the programs [deficiency oriented programs] into local activities that teach people the nature and extent of their problems, and the value of services as the answer to their problems. As a result, many lower income urban neighborhoods are now environments of service where behaviors are affected because residents come to believe that their well-being depends upon being a client. They begin to see themselves as people with special needs that can only be met by outsiders. They become consumers of services, with no incentive to be producers. Consumers of services focus vast amounts of creativity and intelligence on the survival-motivated challenge of outwitting the "system," or on finding ways—in the informal or even illegal economy—to bypass the system entirely. (2)

Kretzmann and McKnight's work is a devastating critique of most contemporary social service and community-located research models. In the deficit models as they describe them, people cannot construct communities, design institutions, or participate in research because as "clients," they are given no agency and credit for the expertise that arises from their lived experiences.

They term the alternative to deficit models "capacity-focused development" or asset-based development. For my purposes here, there are two necessary elements to this model: (a) a focus on community assets, and (b) a focus on the necessity of building long-term relationships and networks within communities. Kretzmann and McKnight argue that community building and change only happens when local people invest themselves and their resources in the effort. A focus on assets does not deny problems; rather, an emphasis on assets refocuses local efforts on developing a participating community, a necessary precondition for sustainable solutions.

Kretzmann and McKnight use a community asset map to develop a picture of a given community's assets. (See Fig 17.1). This map has significant heuristic potential as a model for how a community can be constructed. According to this map, a community is composed of three elements: individuals, associations, and institutions. The focus on individuals in the construction of community allows community-builders to examine individual strengths in a community. The move to consider associations allows community-builders to look for loose institutional associations that may be deeply rooted in a given community and therefore open to local concerns and action. Finally, this model of community emphasizes the role of institutions in a community, like a community-based literacy program or a university-based writing program with significant community relationships (service learning, writing projects, research, internships). Faced with the prospect of community-building, a map such as this is a heuristic for conceptualizing community and then going about the processes of constructing it. To build a community, then, people must map and mobilize assets, build relationships, and leverage assets and relationships to solve problems. In other words, community-building names strengths, names problems, builds a collectivity, and acts collectively.

The concept of community-building actually glosses a wide range of research practices that depend on the kinds of community understanding and engagement that I have been arguing for throughout this chapter. At this point, let me focus on some specific research practices I have used in my attempt to understand and work with members of one community in Atlanta. For about 3 years, I worked in a neighborhood and community called Mechanicsville. During those years, my work varied. Initially, I

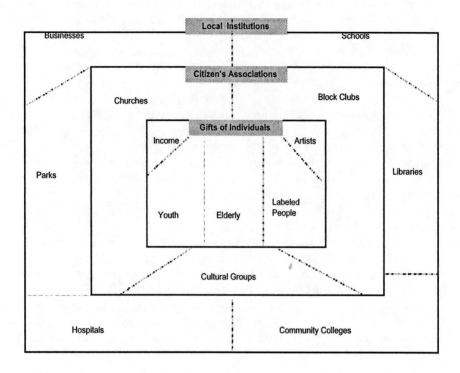

FIGURE 5.2.   Community assets map.

worked on service-learning projects located in Mechanicsville. Over time, and as my relationships with people and organizations developed, I became connected to a larger community development and planning project, also located in Mechanicsville. I began working with colleagues to develop Mechanicsville's capacity to participate in planning and other civic processes through the development of web-based tools—a neighborhood Web site that contains local information, data, and communicative functions.

Mechanicsville is an interesting and important community. The neighborhood is one of Atlanta's oldest, built, like many early neighborhoods, on level land adjacent to the railroads tracks that were central to the city's early growth and identity. Although once a stable and diverse community, urban renewal efforts, highway construction projects, and the social upheaval of the Civil Rights Movement turned Mechanicsville into a homo-

geneous and uprooted place by the 1980s. Planning, community development, and social change have literally left their mark on the community,
and so to this day, these issues are very important in Mechanicsville. I
worked with members in this community to develop a neighborhood
Web.site that could be used to support community development efforts.

I began this project with the belief that in order for a community Web
site to become a productive part of the Mechanicsville community, it needed to be designed with the community. The design process focused on the
following goals: (a) to create with Mechanicsville residents a usable web-
based tool that met their civic and community needs, and (b) to build the
capacity of community residents to use advanced information technologies
and write with computers, particularly so that they could remain productive with the Web site. These goals gave rise to the following questions:

- What is the current state of computer access in the community (both individually and institutionally)?
- What are the features and functions of a usable Web site that
  meets community needs?
- In what ways can the Web site facilitate civic and planning-
  related action and increase community capacity to use information technologies?

Based on the goals and questions as just outlined, the process of development and design looked roughly like this:

- Relationship building and community networking
- Needs assessments through focus groups and key informant
  interviews
- Community mapping, information-technology profiles, and
  resource research (done in part with a technical writing class)
- Construction of first design (with technical writing class)
- Usability (with technical writing class)
- Construction of the second design (and a continuation of the
  development process)

The development process is the place where the research practices that
concern me are most visible. There were certain community assets already
in place that conceptualized the project and made its completion possible.
Members of the civic association—both citizens who were politically active
in the city and those more interested in their local community—wanted a
community Web site and ensured that it was included in a Housing and

Urban Development grant written with a number of partnering organizations.[2] But more to the point, some citizens in this community were sophisticated collaborators on research and community development projects,
and others were sophisticated users of information technologies and
understood their potential use. There were significant assets, in other
words, that were important for me to recognize, to listen to, and to work
with during the initial stages of my work on the web project.

Hand in hand with recognizing and utilizing Mechanicsville's assets is
the need for relationship-building. In many ways, building relationships is
the most fundamental community-building activity associated with any
community-based project, but I'm not sure many would see it as a *research*
activity. Relationship-building is a critical research activity in at least three
senses. First, for my work in Mechanicsville, I had a need to understand
this community—indeed to try and figure out just who, exactly, this community was.[3] Relationship-building practices such as attending group meetings, scheduling face-to-face meetings with individuals, and showing up for
community functions allow community-based researchers to understand
community dynamics, identify key individuals, understand important
issues and concerns, and get a handle on who constitutes the active portion of a community. Second, these same "relationship" practices changed
the very nature of my inquiry. I heard hidden narratives, saw potential and
real stumbling blocks, and got a more realistic sense of the possibilities for
the project not possible in early grant-writing sessions. Absent the information-rich relationship-building practices, my work in Mechanicsville would
have been more poorly conceived and at risk than it proved to be. Third,
and perhaps most obviously, long-term relationship-building made the
project possible. Some measure of community building was necessary for
the project to have any chance of success.

Of course, sustainability is a problem beyond this specific research
project (see Cushman). The ability of research to enhance community
development activity stems from its ability to act as a lever for capacity
building. With respect to the Mechanicsville web project, I became interested in how we might use the development process not just as a way to collect information and design a Web site but also as a way to enhance the
capacity of individuals, associations, and organizations within the community to be better able to use advanced information technologies for productive activity.

I built into this research project, then, some modest first steps toward
capacity building. Research practices, in other words, that don't just generate information but also sustain a project's life. I worked with individuals to
tutor them on web writing, and I encouraged the civic association to train

and pay community members to maintain the Web site once it moved to their server space. There are other possibilities connected to the opening of a community technology center in that neighborhood.[4] Regardless of the specifics, one principle is important for both community-based research and the creation of productive communities—research must be used to leverage activities that increase the capacity of a community to be productive. Research practices are an often hidden yet powerful mechanism for doing so.

COMMUNITY-BASED WORK SHOULD CHANGE US

At the Watson conference, my talk was driven largely by my fear that the increase in community-based work driven by service learning and an interest in literate practices outside schools would be a squandered opportunity to expand and positively alter the work of composition. Since the conference, I have also become interested in sustaining my own community-based work. My fear and interests are related. If all compositionists do is rearticulate community-based work as more "content" for the first-year writing classroom, and if all compositionists do is approach community-based work on our terms, frame inquiries in terms of our disciplinary concerns, and work in communities utilizing unaltered methodologies from other domains, then we have indeed squandered a significant opportunity to play a meaningful role in the lives of the communities near our universities.

Community-based researchers argue forcefully that they must first change how they do their work before they can help communities do theirs. And here lies the source of my greatest fear—that we will be unable to change how we research, teach, and serve in and with communities—for that change is critical to sustained and sustainable community-based work. In this chapter I have focused on research practices themselves, and in choosing research practices, my intent is to foreground research as the necessary site of activity for compositionists. My focus on research practices is also intended to highlight the most mundane and often invisible part of a researcher's work. It is here, I think, in the practices of research, that it is possible to see both how community-based research is different from other types of research and that these differences must be meaningful and productive for community-based work to continue. It is my hope that composition can develop disciplinary practices both large and small that value sustained community involvement; it is my hope that we are capable of the methodological vigilance and flexibility necessary to understand the communities around us and the ways we can participate in their community development projects.

ENDNOTES

1. Steven Epstein, in his book *Impure Science*, writes about the complex interactions that led to "knowledge" about HIV and AIDS. With respect to the issue of pharmaceuticals, Epstein writes that by the mid-1980s, patients, activists, and their doctors were tired of waiting for clinical drug trials conducted at academic centers according to "cumbersome" protocols and so decided to design and conduct their own trials. He then details a long story, which I will gloss here, that gets to the heart of what I am trying to say about useful knowledge.

    These frustrated doctors and patients conducted research within the contexts of everyday medical practice, a form of community-based research. Two models of community-based research developed; both were highly participatory. Despite the participatory nature of these models, researchers had to confront some significant problems. Established researchers doubted the ability of practicing doctors and patients to conduct good trials. Community-based research also suffered from the lack of infrastructure necessary for sophisticated lab work. As a partial solution to the problem of infrastructure, drug companies, annoyed with the slow process of drug approval, began supporting some community-based research.

    Community-based drug trials had one significant advantage over traditional research, however. Patients, especially when given some decision making access and power, were more likely to support such studies and enhance compliance (a problem with traditional AIDS drug trials).

    While the scientific community doubted the credibility of community trials, community-based drug research proved successful. Epstein writes that "public demonstration of the credibility and viability of community-based AIDS research came with the testing of aerosolized pentamidine, a form of prevention against deadly pneumocystis pneumonia. It was therapy that community-based research at the CCC and CRI effectively rescued after NIAID bungled its own efforts to test it" (218). With this important instance of success and with other subsequent achievements, community programs began to be seen as compatible with the interests of more traditionally institutionalized research efforts and with the larger mission of AIDS research and prevention.

    Epstein writes that "AIDS activists have emphasized the *local* and *contextual* character of usable scientific knowledge," and that examples of community-based AIDS research show that people are "willing to surrender claims to universal validity in exchange for knowledge that bears some local and circum-scribed utility" (342).

2. The grant was not initially funded before we completed the project (it was funded 3 years later). The grant project became the formal mechanism for my involvement in the development of a Web site as a research project. During the grant-writing process, I promised to complete the project with interested par-ties in Mechanicsville regardless of funding.

3. My technical writing students, in fact, were more sophisticated than I was about the issue of community. They kept pushing me to help them find the "real" community in Mechanicsville. They doubted that the institutional repre-sentatives and active citizens with whom we interacted were the "real" com-munity and often observed that in their neighborhoods, people who fit the "type" that we interacted with were disliked and thought of as "busybodies." We searched in vain for the "real" community.

4. The city of Atlanta has an ambitious program to eliminate the digital divide in center city neighborhoods. The City's program is an $8.1 million effort to pro-mote access to new media and tele-computing, an effort funded in part by the city's cable franchising fee. The goals for the project are to promote communi-ty, opportunity, and equality and "to create awareness, ownership, and empowerment among Atlanta residents who have not been exposed, or insuf-ficiently exposed, to computer technology or the need to acquire, at a mini-mum, basic computer literacy skills" (Strategic Plan 29). There are a number of practical components to this program, but for Mechanicsville, the most important is the location of a community technology center in the neighbor-hood center. These technology centers are high-tech facilities with about 35 computers connected via T1 lines to the Internet. The computers also have a robust software package consisting of mostly Microsoft products. The centers are the location for computer classes as well as time for open access use.

REFERENCES

Adler-Kassner, Linda, Robert Crooks, and Ann Watters. (Eds.). *Writing the Community: Concepts and Models for Service Learning in Composition.* Urbana, IL: National Council of Teachers of English, 1997.

Bacon, Nora. "Community Service Writing: Problems, Challenges, Questions." *Writing the Community: Concepts and Models for Service Learning in Composition.* Eds. Linda Adler-Kassner, Robert Crooks, and Ann Watters. Urbana, IL: National Council of Teachers of English, 1997. 39-55.

City of Altanta. "Strategic Plan for Atlanta Community Technology Initiative." Executvie Summary Available online: < http://www.atlantacommunitytech.com/strategic_plan_summary.htm > 1999

Cohen, Anthony Paul. *The Symbolic Construction of Community.* London: Tavistock, 1985.

Cooper, David D. and Laura Julier. "Democratic Conversations: Civic Literacy and Service-Learning in the American Grains." *Writing the Community: Concepts and Models for Service Learning in Composition.* Eds., Linda Adler-Kassner, Robert Crooks, and Ann Watters. Urbana, IL: National Council of Teachers of English, 1997. 79-94.

Cushman, Ellen. "Sustainable Service Learning Programs." *College Composition and Communication.* 64 (2002): 40-65.

DeRienzo, Harold. "Beyond the Melting Pot: Preserving Culture, Building Community. *National Civic Review.* 84.1 (1995): 5-15.

Epstein, Steven. *Impure Science: AIDS, Activism, and the Politics of Knowledge.* Berkeley: University of California Press, 1996.

Ervin, Elizabeth. "Learning to Write with a Civic Tongue." *Blundering for Change: Errors and Expectations in Critical Pedagogy.* Eds. John Paul Tassoni and William H. Thelin. Portsmouth, NH: Boynton/Cook, 2000.

Flower, Linda. "Partners in Inquiry: A Logic for Community Outreach." *Writing the Community: Concepts and Models for Service Learning in Composition.* Eds. Linda Adler-Kassner, Robert Crooks, and Ann Watters. Urbana, IL: National Council of Teachers of English, 1997. 95-117.

Grabill, Jeffrey T. *Community Literacy Programs and the Politics of Change.* Albany: SUNY Press, 2001.

Greenwood, Davyyd, J., & Morten Levin. *Introduction to Action Research: Social Research for Social Change.* Thousand Oaks, CA: Sage, 1998.

Herzberg, Bruce. "Civic Literacy and Service Learning." *Coming of Age: The Advanced Writing Curriculum.* Eds., Linda K. Shamoon, Sandra Jamieson, and Robert A. Schwegler. Portsmouth, NH: Boynton/Cook, 2000.

Huckin, Thomas N. "Technical Writing and Community Service." *Journal of Business and Technical Communication.* 11 (1997): 49-59.

Kretzmann, John P., & McKnight, John L. *Building Communities from the Inside Out: A Path Toward Finding and Mobilizing a Community's Assets.* Chicago, IL: ACTA Publications, 1993.

Miller, Thomas P. "Rhetoric Within and Without Composition: Reimagining the Civic." *Coming of Age: The Advanced Writing Curriculum.* Eds., Linda K. Shamoon, Sandra Jamieson, and Robert A. Schwegler. Portsmouth, NH: Boynton/Cook, 2000.

Peck, Wayne. C., Linda Flower, and Lorraine Higgins. "Community Literacy." *College Composition and Communication.* 46 (1995): 199-222.

Porter, James E., Patricia Sullivan, Stuart Blythe, Jeffrey T. Grabill, and Libby Miles. "Institutional Critique: A Rhetorical Methodology for Change." *College Composition and Communication.* 51 (2000): 610-42.

Sclove Richard E., Madeleine L. Scammell, and Breena Holland. *Community-Based Research in the US: An Introductory Reconnaissance, Including Twelve Organizational Case Studies and Comparison with the Dutch Science Shops and the Mainstream American Research System.* Amherst, MA: Loka, 1998.

Sibley, David. *Geographies of Exclusion: Society and Difference in the West.* London: Routledge, 1995

Sullivan, Patricia, and James E. Porter. *Opening Spaces: Writing Technologies and Critical Research Practices.* Norwood, NJ: Ablex and Computers and Composition, 1997.

AUTHOR INDEX

SUBJECT INDEX

A

access, 8, 10, 13, 15, 31, 32, 89, 101–103, 154–155, 158–160, 162, 194–195, 198–199, 263–265

agency, 14, 112, 167–186, 187, 191, 230, 234, 247–248

assessment, 72, 75–93, 287–303,
computer-assisted, 79
directed self placement, 297–299
of student work, 59, 104, 105, 291–297
professional, 59
written examinations, 80–83, 85
see also Tenure and Promotion

C

CCCC Promotion and Tenure
Guidelines, 62

class, 138, 141, 309–311, 321

collaborative work, 34, 65, 68, 71, 103–108, 200, 213, 214–216, 225, 238–243, 243–250, 270, 288, 295

college entrance examinations, 82–87

community, 23–24, 112–114, 118, 148–149, 154–155, 192–194, 197–199, 200–201, 325–336
virtual, 24, 193, 197

cultural studies, 306–307, 321

cyberhumans, 154

cyborg, 97–98, 108, 116, 238–239, 243

D

data collection, 98–99, 100

Digital Divide, 159, 188, 337

digital media, 23–24, 63

distance education, 7, 209–210, 230–233, 233–235

E

email, 135–136

empirical research and methodologies, 40, 46, 47, 59, 62, 83–85, 285
assessment as, 75
community-based, 326, 328, 331–335
ethnographies, 40, 50, 253, 305–324

Printed in the United States
67101LVS00002BC/13